# THE LIVING LIGHT DIALOGUE

*Volume 12*

# THE LIVING LIGHT DIALOGUE

*Volume 12*

*Through the mediumship of*
Richard P. Goodwin

Living Light Books

The Living Light Dialogue Volume 12
Copyright © 2019 Serenity Association

Through the mediumship of Richard P. Goodwin.

All rights reserved. Printed in the United States of America. No portion of this book may be reproduced—electronically, mechanically, or via internet transmission—without advance, express written permission of the publisher except in the case of brief quotations embodied in critical articles and reviews. No derivative work—games supplemental material, video—may be created without advance, express written permission of the publisher. For information address Living Light Books, P.O. Box 4187, San Rafael, CA 94913-4187.

Cover design copyright © 2019 by Serenity Association
Cover photograph by Serenity Association, 2019; copyright © 2019 by Serenity Association.

www.livinglight.org

Library of Congress Control Number  2007929762

FIRST EDITION

This volume of teachings is dedicated to the spirit friends who brought to Earth the Living Light Philosophy. With eternal gratitude, we pray that we may demonstrate these principles and continue to bring to publication these teachings.

## CONTENTS

Acknowledgement ................................. ix
Preface ......................................... xiii
Introduction .................................... xv
A/V Special Seminar .............................. 3
A/V Seminar 1 ................................... 39
A/V Seminar 2 ................................... 81
A/V Seminar 3 ................................... 107
A/V Seminar 4 ................................... 127
A/V Seminar 5 ................................... 157
A/V Seminar 6 ................................... 187
A/V Seminar 7 ................................... 219
A/V Seminar 8 ................................... 239
A/V Seminar 9 ................................... 263
A/V Seminar 10 .................................. 283
A/V Seminar 11 .................................. 301
A/V Seminar 12 .................................. 333
A/V Seminar 13 .................................. 365
A/V Seminar 14 .................................. 381
A/V Seminar 15 .................................. 407
A/V Seminar 16 .................................. 433
A/V Seminar 17 .................................. 453
A/V Seminar 18 .................................. 479
Appendix ........................................ 501

# ACKNOWLEDGMENT

Grateful acknowledgement is made to the many friends and associates for invaluable aid in compiling this book, for their helpful suggestions, for their loyal interest and encouragement.

Special acknowledgement is due to those who painstakingly and selflessly transcribed and proofread the text.

# PREFACE

It was through the mediumship of the Serenity Association founder, Mr. Richard P. Goodwin, that a philosophy known as the Living Light was given in more than 700 classes over a twenty-five-year period.

To be specific, the philosophy was imparted through Mr. Goodwin by a magistrate who had lived on Earth some 8,000 years ago. The former magistrate is known to Living Light students as "the Wise One," and he narrated the journey of his soul on the other side of life, the experiences—especially the difficulties—he encountered in having to face himself, as well as the teachings he earned to help himself through the realms in which he traveled. It was his decision to share the teachings with souls on both sides of "the curtain."

Prior to the advent of the Wise One, Mr. Goodwin had prayed for a teacher from the realms of light. Mr. Goodwin, since age fourteen, had been the instrument through which spirit was able to communicate with those seeking help. But he saw that his mediumship brought only temporary solace, because the people he was trying to help soon became fascinated with the phenomena and ignored the help that spirit was imparting. He prayed for someone who would bring forth teachings that would benefit any soul seeking a path to a greater awareness of himself and of God.

His prayers were answered in 1964 when the Wise One came through for the first time. Mr. Goodwin, at first apprehensive about what this new teacher would impart, was taken into deep trance and not able to control what was being revealed through him. Upon hearing the recorded classes afterward, however, he became convinced of the goodness of the teacher and of the value of the simple, beautiful teachings. This, then, was the beginning of the Living Light Philosophy given to Earth through the mediumship of Richard P. Goodwin.

In carrying out the request of the Wise One and Mr. Goodwin, students of the Serenity Association transcribed from audiotape the classes that had been brought through. Because most are in the form of teacher-student interaction, the classes became known as The Living Light Dialogue; and the students were instructed to publish the classes as a multi-volume set of the Living Light Philosophy. Volume 1 was published in the autumn of 2007.

The present book, Volume 12, begins with the A/V Seminars series of classes, which were generally delivered by Mr. Goodwin on the third Thursday of the month at the Serenity Association temple. These classes were recorded on videotape and made available to students both as audio and video recordings. A/V Special Seminar was held on Saturday, August 4, 1984, and was not part of a series of classes. The use of the word special in a class title may indicate that the class is not part of a series of classes, was held on an atypical day, or it may refer to the subject matter discussed. A/V Seminar 1 and 2, which were held on Sunday, June 3, 1984 and Sunday, June 2, 1985, respectively, were, again, not part of a series of classes. Once a year the American Legion used the log cabin where Serenity Spiritualist Church held services. Initially, on those Sundays, church services were moved from the morning to the evening. But later, services were held at the temple. So A/V Seminar 1 and 2 are the classes that were given when the log cabin was unavailable. A/V Seminar 3 is the first of the Thursday evening classes that were held intermittently, but often once a month, from June 13, 1985, until February 16, 1989, just before Mr. Goodwin passed on. Volume 12 concludes with A/V Seminar 18, which was held on Thursday, November 13, 1986.

The foundation of the classes—the foundation of the Living Light Philosophy itself—is the Law of Personal Responsibility which states, in part, that we are responsible for all our experiences, and that our experiences are the return of the laws that we have established with our thoughts, acts, and deeds. Through greater awareness of our thoughts and by exercising our divine right of choice, we may choose to establish laws of greater harmony and goodness.

The Living Light Dialogue teaches that we have come to Earth to learn the lessons that are necessary to free us from the dictates and limits of our own thoughts and judgments, which are the mental patterns that we follow through our own lack of awareness and are so very potent, forceful, and limiting. These teachings guide us in making the necessary changes in our thinking in order to free ourselves from those patterns and to express our soul consciousness.

The choice of guiding the direction of our life, as stated by the Wise One when he speaks of being with a person, place, or thing, is, in essence, of being in this world and not a part of this world. He further explains that no matter what experiences we encounter, no matter what we do or do not do, we—our spirit—may view the experience in objectivity from a soul level of consciousness where peace reigns supreme.

The teachings of this volume help us to restore harmony or balance in our life by flooding the consciousness with spiritual affirmations and prayers, a few of which can be found in the appendix. When reason is restored, by balancing our sense functions with our soul faculties, we will consciously experience peace. Without annihilating our ego or our sense functions, we will find a pathway of expression for our soul. Where there was once disturbance, now there is acceptance. Where there was disease, now there is poise. And where there was hopelessness and despair, now there is reason, divine neutrality; and peace shows the way.

If you make the effort to apply these laws, such as, "If man is a law unto himself, what are you doing with the law that you are?", and demonstrate the wisdom of patience, the truth of this philosophy will be your living demonstration.

As the teacher states in CC 130, "My journey of many centuries and much experience has brought me here to Earth to share with you these simple teachings that have come as the effect of a long, long, long journey. Let not your journey be so long in the realms of illusion. For it is not necessary for you. For in your evolution, you have earned an awakening. But it is up to you to do something that is constructive and worthwhile."

# INTRODUCTION

[This introduction was written by Mr. Goodwin and originally appeared in *The Living Light*, which were the first teachings of the Living Light Philosophy published in book form. The entire text of *The Living Light* was republished in *The Living Light Dialogue*, Volume 1.]

"Think, children. Think more often and think more deeply."

The teachings in this book were given as a progressive series of lessons to a group of four students who were sitting for spiritual unfoldment with me beginning in January of 1964. The communications were regular until October of that year when nearly a seven-year silence ensued and resumed in 1971 to the present. They were received in three ways by me as a channel. The main text was taped from a direct control of my voice in deep trance at special sittings of our group during which I had no experience of the voice or what was being transmitted. A few scattered verses were given independently when I was privileged to see and hear our teacher clairvoyantly. I have also been a channel for this communicant when speaking from the podium at church and in answering difficult questions at our public seminars.

Nearly all we know about our teacher is contained in the lectures. He reports that he had tried for sixteen years to break through an interference barrier that the channel had to deep trance. When our conditions were in resonance with his patient wisdom, he came through ready to teach his understanding. I have seen him as an old man dressed in white with long flowing white hair. He has blue eyes, slightly smiling and deeply compassionate. I have always called him the Old Man. The students liked to call him the Wise One. He is surely one of those often called a Teacher of Light. I do not know his country, although he indicated at one time that he was from 6000 B.C. and a form of a judge in his time.

The text is often difficult but it is complete, having been transcribed word for word from the original tapes recording the trance voice. It is presented with a minimum of punctuation to be freer for the individual interpretation of each reader. The lessons given before the long silence are phrased with many allegories often paradoxical. There are repetitions and renewals of theme, but it is explained that if an understanding is not perceived, compassion dictates that it be said again. Some of the topics have but a simple mention with little development but all are revealed, we are told, according to merit.

The Old Man is a fine teacher. He has in a hundred ways intertwined his allegory, progressive explanations, unfolding exercises and timely references to reach a multitude of levels of individual understanding. A notable change is his more direct style of presentation beginning in 1971.

There is an endearing intimacy of person that can be felt through his lectures, a meaningful and loving encounter with a wise friend. Like an old man, he makes a mistake and conscientiously corrects himself a few paragraphs later. He listens often and carefully to our earnest discussions of his words. He consults with a group of experts on evolution and cites their learning in his lesson. His use of the direct address "children" or "my children" is not patronizing but infinitely loving and supportive.

A word must be said about the teachings. The Old Man makes clear that his lessons are not dogma, a creed or a narrow way, but simply his own understanding offered to us as a form of instruction to aid us in our own individual progression. When he speaks of Laws, he does not refer to man-made rules or moral traditions but to the cosmic and atomic way-things-are, the natural world of what-is, the universal laws of life, part of the original creative design and through which creation is fulfilled. These laws are beyond the possibility of being changed, suspended, transcended, or destroyed but they are ever a tool of mankind, not his master. First, through our awareness of the universal laws and then slowly through our developed understanding, the powers of creation are accessible to us. Not power over men's minds or circumstances, but power over whatever is selfish and imperfect in ourselves is the way up the eternal ladder of progression. When the Old Man cautions us concerning the Law of Responsibility or gives us a thinking exercise to explore the Law of Identity in a dynamic manner, he prepares us to take another step. And all move in accordance with the Law of What Can Be Borne.

Our teacher shows us how the two worlds are drawn together. In his realm, he describes, there is a great diversity of thought, many schools of understanding; but the Light is always known by the Light. Because of the interdependence of the two realms, listening to our discussions helped to clarify his teaching to others on his side of the curtain. His love and gratitude he humbly equates with ours.

The lessons to be perceived are not new, they are very old, but they are new to certain levels of our being. I would personally advise the reader, after reading this volume of discourses in full, to make a daily habit (or when there is a feeling or need) to sit quietly with the book. Open it at random and be guided to the Light by the passage that is there for the day. This technique is still used by the original students who were given the lessons and by many students after them who have studied in unfolding classes with me through these teachings.

Go beyond the words into feeling, into the immediate meanings for you. Touch into the inspiration that flows into the form of this book. It is from the Divine.

RICHARD P. GOODWIN
*San Geronimo, California*
*June, 1972*

# A/V SEMINARS

## A/V Special Seminar

The discussion today, for this seminar, is the descent and the ascent of man. Now man is divided in consciousness between his mind, which is dependent upon what he has already experienced, and what is called his soul, which has been in the process, and continues to be in the process, of evolution. And so it is the nature of the human mind to divide in order to conquer. Now the mind's division and conquering is an effect of the mind's need. For when the mind looks out at the world, it judges what it has and what it has not, for the mind is dependent upon what it senses, what it hears, and what it sees. That, of course, is known as knowledge. And so man having this experience called need, through the Law of Comparison, establishes his own destiny to divide and to conquer.

The necessary ingredient that keeps the mental substance forming the various thoughts and the judgments that it entertains is known as belief. So we find that man, throughout eons of time, believes many things and is in a constant process of changing his own beliefs. In comparison to the eternal being which he is, which is faith and unity, the mind offers to us belief and division. So at any moment man has available to him the choice between belief [and] division [or] faith and unity.

Now that that is united is strengthened by the process of uniting itself. That which divides destroys itself, for division weakens the original of anything.

The human mind is the reflection of what we are. The human mind or mental substance never was and never can be what we are for it only reflects what we are, and it reflects what we are in keeping with what we believe at any given moment.

And so when we find our self in this contradiction within our own consciousness, the only way to free our self from the disturbance, from the concern, from the worry of what's to be—for man's mind worries and is concerned over the next moment, the next day, the next week, and the next year. The reason that man worries over what is to be is because man believes what he thinks is what he is. But what man thinks he is, is far lesser than what he truly is. And so we find that man, believing the many thoughts that are in his mind, believing that he is those thoughts at any given moment and because the human mind offers to us contradictions in thought, man worries and is concerned over what is yet to be.

Now that is a lack of awareness on the part of man. The lack of awareness followed, of course, by the lack of acceptance for we do not accept whatever we are not aware of. Consequently, the first step to make is to gain control over the thought that insists on playing in your mind at any given moment.

We've stated so often that truth needs no defense. Of course, it needs no defense for truth does not exist in the realm of consciousness that experiences need. Only falsehood exists in a realm of consciousness that experiences need. The human mind experiences need because the human mind denies the existence of what *is* and relies upon and is dependent upon what has been. So we find in our work and in our activities that when we think about what is going to happen, we are controlled by the contradictions in our life and in our mind of what has already been. So we go through the process of comparison. We compare what we think is, in any given moment, to all of the things that are related to it through the Law of Association. And so the human mind comparing its present situation, at any moment, with all of the past experiences, with all of the contradictions within the consciousness, experiences worry, concern, and frustration.

It is the nature of the human mind to control anything and everything that enters it. That is because need exists in the human mind. Need does not exist in truth. It exists only in the human mind where denial is prevalent. When we move, through our own effort, from these mental thoughts, when we slowly, but surely, begin to accept that we are not the thought, that we are the power that moves the thought—we are the power that is indispensable to the forming and the moving of any thought, of anything within our consciousness—when we slowly, but surely, evolve in our lives to the acceptance that we are the mover and not the moved, we will no longer suffer the seeming uncontrollable circumstances and conditions that we seem to experience.

Many philosophies have revealed, in so many different ways, the descent of man. And so it is that you have in some religions and philosophies, you have the discussion of Satan, you have the discussion of the fallen angel, you have the discussion of Lucifer. And what are these stories telling us that are truthful, that can easily be applicable to our present situations and our evolution at this time? As I stated, we are much more than what we think. But we will have to make the effort to stop believing we are the thought of any moment.

When we in our experiences of need, which is the direct effect of denial—for no one can experience need of anything until they first deny, with their own mind, that they have it. When we pause to look inside where everything good truly is, deep inside our own consciousness, when we begin to make that effort, we will stop denying. And by our effort to stop denying, we will no longer experience the need of anything. And when the effort is made daily, when the declaration of truth is not only what floods our consciousness but the declaration of truth is what is expressed with our mouth—for the spoken word is life-giving energy. Unfortunately, the spoken word, being life-giving energy, is not recognized by the speaker when it returns as an experience.

Now when you speak of anything and you think the opposite of what you speak, you establish, for you, and guarantee the failure of what you are speaking. That is because you are, through your own energy flowing through you, creating direct opposite forms in consciousness. And so the experience from that is absolute failure in anything. So first man establishes within his consciousness what it is that he wants to do. He accepts the possibility beyond the shadow of any doubt and is not deceived by the seeming appearances of experiences that are necessary before his own success.

We quit before the victory for we do not understand the many forms that are in front of the very thing that we desire. And so we look at the forms that precede our desire. We do not relate directly, inside of our self, that they are the doubts, the fears, the past experiences of yesterday, of yesteryear. We look around and we see others who have failed; then we see a few who have succeeded. And rather than face personal responsibility, which reveals clearly to us that what is possible for one, in keeping with the law established, is possible for all, we deny personal responsibility, and we justify that they have succeeded because of certain circumstances and conditions. This is unfortunate not for those who have succeeded, but this is, indeed, unfortunate for us for it denies our own right to attain whatever we seek in life to attain. We are the ones, and we alone, who close the doors of opportunity after taking a quick and brief look at what is possible.

No matter what your endeavor in life may be, it is your endeavor and your right to direct eternal, intelligent, infinite Energy to it and to reap the harvest of your actions. But the things that we insist on standing in our way are the beliefs which cause us to be dependent upon things outside. The moment we permit our self to rely and to be dependent upon anything beyond our own conscious choice for direction, that is the moment that we are in the bondage of belief, instead of in the freedom of faith.

Faith is not limited to any religious concept. Faith is this intelligent, infinite Power that is flowing through all form at all time. It is available to us moment by moment by moment. When we direct this intelligent Energy, this Power of the universes, to our limited mind, that is when we establish, for us, the Law of Bondage, known to man as his own belief. Now sometimes a person will direct this great Power to a belief [in a way] that its experiences are most successful to the unawakened. But remember, whatever in life we seek to control, we, in time, find that we are controlled by it. For the law is very just. The law is totally impartial. When we permit our self to experience a temporary thrill of controlling anything or anyone, we establish the Law of Bondage, and we live to see the day that that which we seem to gain satisfaction from controlling is now controlling us.

How do we experience that? Why, it's quite simple. In the energy we direct to controlling anything, we establish within our consciousness a form. That form is dependent upon us for its own survival, for it has and is created from mental substance. It is known as a thought form. It does not live, it does not survive without the continuous direction of intelligent energy to it from its creator. And so we create many forms.

And we serve, consciously or not consciously, we serve those forms until we awaken and make the final decision that a thought is a vehicle; that we alone have created the form of the vehicle; that it is destined to serve the purpose for which we alone have created it. The intelligent decision is to place in the forming of the thought its duration of existence. For this day, we still find that thoughts, emotions, which are the effects of thought patterns and thoughts, still limit and still control our lives. We react emotionally in ways that we reacted when we were much, much younger than we are today. Those thought forms, created in those days, served their purpose. But they didn't know that they had served their purpose for we did not create them intelligently and give them the limited time of expression to serve us. And so we find today they insist and demand on their own continuity, although they do not serve us as well as they did twenty or thirty years ago.

All of our experiences, all of our successes, all of our failures are revelations of where we are in consciousness at any given moment. We can turn the tide when we intelligently choose being in mental substance, being over-identified with the thought of I. We believe, we believe all that we want to believe. We believe that we don't believe, and still, that's belief.

And so it's up to us to decide, and to decide every day, many times a day, number one: what is it that we truly want from life. For whatever it is that we want from life, we must, in keeping with the law that like attracts like and becomes the Law of Attachment, we must therefore be willing to give to life. So look at your records. View them. Make intelligent decisions of what it is you want from life. Weigh it out, then, on what you're willing to give to life. And after you have come to your own conclusion, the law, for you, will be well established.

Now we're going to take a few moments here for questions on the matters already discussed, and then continue on. So if you will raise your hand with any questions that you may have at this moment. Yes, please.

*How does one tell the thought form at the onset how long it can stay?*

In reference to the question in telling a thought, which is a creation in mental substance, a form, how long that it can stay, that depends upon your own light of reason: how long that you believe it will take that particular thought form or vehicle of energy to accomplish what you want it to accomplish. So, of course, you, being the creator, have the right, in the creating of any form, to make the intelligent decision of how long that form shall take to serve the purpose for which you have created it. Does that help with your question?

You see, say a person—I think I can see here what you are speaking about. You see, for example, say that a person, they want to have a promotion in their job; they want to have an expansion of their business. All right, let's take an expansion of one's business, for example, more success and different things. Now the first thing that happens within the mind when a person says, "I want my business to be more successful and I want my business to expand," the mind doesn't stop at that point. Rising up into the consciousness are all of these conditions: "Well, now let me see. In order to expand my business, it's going to take this. It's going to take that. It's going to take that, that, that." And the next thing you know, we got thirty or forty different forms being created. They're all dictating the circumstances. They're all dictating the conditions. That, of course, then, is the law that you are establishing. And so each of those circumstances and conditions must be fulfilled before you can get what you want, for you alone, being the creator, have established all of those different forms, and they must go out and do all those different things. That reveals to you that you are dependent upon, through your own belief, upon other people in order to accomplish what you choose to accomplish. That's the bondage of belief.

You have, however, a choice. You can choose, intelligently, faith, instead of belief. Then you have it all within your own consciousness to work with. It is not dependent on the marketplace. It is not dependent on a friend. It is not dependent on a banker. It certainly isn't dependent on good luck: a loser's excuse for a winner's position. It's certainly not dependent upon that.

And so, you see, you have the left path of bondage and belief, and you have the right path of faith and freedom. Now when a person is faced with dependence on another person for accomplishing what they alone choose to accomplish, then they must accept the demonstrable truth that they are in bondage to their belief that their fulfillment, their success is dependent upon something and someone that they have no control over. A person who permits themselves to believe that their success in life, a person who permits themselves to believe that their abundant good, to believe that their happiness is dependent on something beyond their control, is a person who shall remain in the bondage of circumstances and conditions until they awaken and make an intelligent choice that faith is the power and belief is the force. Does that help with your question?

Yes. The lady there, please.

*This question might sound confused, because I'm confused about it. In dealing with people who are difficult and come from a long line of difficult people who are difficult in the same way or in dealing with my own life, when I find myself reacting to things the way my, certain members of my family have always reacted, have we made choices before we were born as to what kind of personality we, we want to have? Or are we able to—is a person who becomes angry and abusive and cruel routinely, is that person able to change that if that is the genetic gift they were given?*

Thank you very much. Now in reference to your question in dealing with difficult people and in reference to your question, do we have certain traits and characteristics prior to our birth here on earth, we most certainly do for we are in a process of evolutionary incarnation. And in reference to a person who seemingly is angry most of the time, can they change? Anyone can change anything at any moment they choose to change it, for, you see, we are never left without the divine right of choice.

Now the human body and its genetics is susceptible to the truth that we are. Therefore, the chemistry of the human body is under the direct control of the consciousness. Now that does not mean to imply that in our present state of evolution that medical science does not give some benefit to the human race, because it certainly does, ever in keeping with man's belief. You see, if man believes that a rabbit's foot will bring him good luck, ever in keeping with his belief, so it shall be, for that is the law of the bondage of the human mind.

Now in dealing or communicating with difficult people, it is not difficult people out there. It is difficult people in our own consciousness for we are controlled by our belief in the judgment that has been established with experiences that have passed. Therefore, that places us as a victim of circumstances and conditions, for we, in our consciousness upon meeting the individual again, through the Law of Association within our own mind, the form, the judgment, rises up, says, "This person is a difficult person. I've had many experiences with them. They're not going to change for I have already judged they're not going to change." Therefore, what we are truly doing, we are serving our own belief in reference to the person that we have judged is difficult.

Now a person who makes the effort to control their own mind is in a position, as an effect of that effort, and in keeping with the law that like attracts like and becomes the Law of Attachment, to attract from a difficult person a very pleasant experience. Now that does not mean that you, as an individual, control the other person, for the other person exists within your own consciousness. It is within that we have the power. It is within the control exists. The freedom from circumstances exists within us. And so we first must become aware.

We see a person, instantaneously our mind starts working through these laws of association. All past experiences rise up and gain control of our consciousness. But that is the moment that we can make the change. We can take control of all those forms of past experiences, and we can place our self in a position in consciousness where we shall act in our communicating with the individual instead of react. Does that help with your question? You won't change—

*In a practical sense, yes. If, if one is working with a difficult person, it is best to bring out the best in them or to not see them as difficult.*

That is true. You see, seeing a person as difficult is totally dependent upon us. We may see the world any way we choose to see the world. But the thing that causes us to see the world not as beautiful as we would like the world to be is because we are seeing the world through judgments of the past. We are not seeing the world as the world is. We are seeing the world as we make it in our consciousness. Our efforts here are to help you in showing you a way to see the world the way you consciously choose to see the world and not to see the world through a subconscious addiction. For we see things ever in keeping with our own addiction to what has been. Therefore, everything we see, everything we hear, everything we sense, everything we feel, everything we touch is censored by what has been. Therefore, our world begins to shrink. Our purpose is to help to broaden the horizons by showing the various processes of the human mind that cause the world to shrink in our consciousness.

Pause for a moment and look at the leaf of the tree. It is as beautiful, it is as intelligent as we, in our consciousness, make the effort to clear away all past experiences in reference to the leaf of the tree. We can only experience the goodness of life through an uncensored, *uncensored* viewing of the world. That takes a little effort, known as self-control, the effect of which is freedom. Did that help with your question?

*Then the victims of cruelty are wrongheaded.*

I didn't say they're wrong- or right-headed. The victims of cruelty, if you accept an infinite, intelligent Energy, known to man as God, if you accept personal responsibility, if you accept that whatever happens in eternity to us is caused by us, in keeping with the very foundation of this philosophy, known as personal responsibility, then you must accept it impartially for all people by first accepting it impartially for oneself.

Now there are no accidents in the universe. Seeming accidents are nothing more and they are nothing less than a lack of understanding the Law of Cause. We are at a certain place at a certain time in keeping with the law that we alone establish. And if we permit our self to believe that we are at a certain place at a certain time because someone else wanted us there, then we have not gone deep enough within our consciousness to see that someone else wanted us there in keeping with what we alone have established. Only through personal responsibility can we ever experience freedom and the abundant good and joy of life. It is available to us at any given moment that we choose to take control of our mind and clear away the shadows of yesterday that censor our view. Did that help with your question?

*Thank you.*

Yes, you're welcome. Are there any other questions during this time? Yes, the lady there, please.

*In regards to controlling other people—*

Yes.

*In a parent's situation, what if we're not controlling our child, as a responsibility to ourselves and society until they're old enough to do their thing, what is our task, then?*

Thank you. In reference to your question, if one is not controlling their child in keeping with responsibility as a parent and in keeping with responsibility to society, well, first of all, I would like to share with you our understanding of control in comparison, speaking in this mental world, in comparison to guidance. Our understanding of anything, whether it be a baby, a child, a human, an animal, a dog, or a cat, that the light of reason, which will transfigure anything that it shines upon, reveals clearly that we guide a child, we guide an animal. That's a vast difference between controlling a child or controlling an animal.

You see, control of anything guarantees the victimization of what we've made the effort to control. Therefore, a wise person does not make effort to control a child or they live to see the day when, by the child, they are controlled. So, you see, control offers to us attachment to the fruits of action. Guidance offers us freedom from attachment to the fruits of action. Guidance, under the light of reason, for that's where guidance exists, clearly reveals personal responsibility. "I have been loaned the responsibility of guiding this animal. I have been loaned the responsibility of guiding this child." It clearly reveals that you guide the child until the child is capable of guiding themselves. But you never make the effort to control them because it places you in bondage to them, the victim of them, sooner to some parents than to others. Does that help with your question?

*Yes.*

You see, if we look at nature, we see the wonderful demonstration of the mother bear. So she has her little babies. And she cares for them and looks after them. And it's not long before she sees it's time; it's time that what she has taught them, they must now be given the opportunity to apply. And so she drives them out! Oh, they try to come back, because, you know, in all form is what you call a lazy streak. [They] would much rather, the little cubs, not bother to have to forage for the food and the berries themselves, as long as the mother will go do it for them. And so she makes great effort, and she makes sure that they are driven out away from her because she knows, as all intelligent beings know, if she does not do that, she has given birth to the world a cripple, not capable of feeding and caring for itself; that she has taught the little cubs, but the cubs are too lazy. And therefore, it would be a titanic ego of a mother bear not to drive her cubs away that they may apply what she has made the effort to teach them. Does that help you with your question?

*[Thank you.]*

You're welcome. Are there any other questions now? *[After a pause, the teacher continues.]* Silence is the best of all. For in silence there is a wonderful experience available, of course, to all of us. Just a moment of perfect silence. *[The teacher continues after a short pause.]* And so we've had our moment of perfect silence.

And so we'll just go on now here to the lady's question over there which opened up, I think, for all of us, a most interesting door. And it's the evolution of coming to this planet in the first place and all of the different experiences, all of the work and the emotions that we put our self through, ever trying to gather and to gain, only in the final analysis to leave it all behind. A wise person uses it as they go along, never knowing when it's going to be left behind. For that's something that man in his present evolution and through lack of effort, he's not aware of the number of days he's to stay on that planet Earth. He's not aware of the exact moment when he is to go. Because if he would make that effort to be honest with himself, that awareness is available to all people. It's not hidden and denied by some partial god that says, "I'm going to put you on planet Earth and leave you blind, deaf, and dumb for 20 years, 30 years, 50 years, 70 years, 90 years, or etc." Oh, yes, indeed, that which we are, called by man truth, it knows. It knows why we're here, why we've come to Earth, how long we're going to be here, when our day, exact, and our moment, that we have done what we have to do and we move on.

Now we come to the Earth planet like we go to any planet. The Living Light Philosophy teaches evolutionary incarnation. We didn't come from nothing, and therefore we won't return to nothing. And so we come to this planet, blond hair, brown hair, black hair, gray hair, blue eyes, brown eyes, gray eyes, green eyes. We all come in a little house called a human body. And it has its strengths and it has its weaknesses. Now each part of that house represents a sense function and a soul faculty. And it reveals to the initiated what they've been doing with their sense functions and their corresponding soul faculties throughout their own evolution.

And so as man pauses and he takes a look and he puts his attention on some of his strengths; he uses those strengths wisely. He puts some of his attention on some of his weaknesses, and as energy follows attention, by placing the attention there, in the right frame of mind, he strengthens his own weaknesses and brings about a balance in his own life.

Now we have been a long, long time in this evolving process, and we've come here, this day, to share with you our understanding of not only your day-to-day problems and solutions but your eternal evolution.

We see the world, moment by moment, the way that any particular form in our mind chooses to distort it. Man looks at the grass, but he sees it with his own distortion. And he looks at the sky, and he sees it the same way. But you don't have to look at things. You can view things. The difference between viewing something and looking at something is the difference between clearly seeing—clearly, without any forms, without any colorization, without any distortion, that's when you view something.

And so when you meet a person, make the effort to view them. Because in making the effort to view the person, you will be able to clearly communicate with them. I have found that people who have difficulty in communicating are people who talk with people. They don't communicate with people; they talk with them. And [in] talking with a person, you're limited by all your prejudices. Because the truth reveals that we all prejudge what we see, hear, feel, and taste. We prejudge it. Because we see it, we hear it, we taste it, censored by our past experiences, the shadows that we are looking at it through. And because of that, it clearly reveals that, in our present state of evolution, we are very prejudiced for we are constantly prejudging. We're prejudging when we awake in the morning.

We listen to the picture box and we hear that it's going to be a hot day tomorrow. Instantaneously, seemingly automatically, we enter the realm of prejudice; we prejudge. And our next day, which we have already established the law for us, is already colored by and every experience contained in that day by the prejudice that we're serving. And think, that one little experience is based upon what you heard on a television weather report. Think of what, through a lack of effort, life for us has become. The telephone rings and it's so-and-so. Before the person can speak, the prejudgments become firmly established. And so what they have to say is already to our ear being censored by the shadows of past experiences with that person. That's prejudice. That is, indeed, unfortunate. That's when we hear, but we do not listen. And so the effort to be made is to listen, the effort to be made is to view, the effort to be made is to feel, free from mountains of prejudice.

When you demonstrate for yourself this law, that like attracts like and becomes the Law of Attachment, and in your efforts to communicate and work with people, and when, during your effort, you find things not going the way that you would like them to go, pause and be still. Declare the truth: "Like attracts like and becomes the Law of Attachment. What I am experiencing I do not like. Now I must accept personal responsibility in order to be free from this experience within my consciousness. Therefore, I accept personal responsibility, that through that person I am experiencing something I dislike." You make the change within your own consciousness for you now have within your consciousness that law, like attracts like. "Something within me is attracting that to me, and I don't like it." You make the change in your own consciousness, for you will find it through the light of honesty. You make the change within your consciousness and suddenly they seem—*they* seemingly are transformed.

What you have done—you see, reason is this great power that transfigures us—what you have done is permitted yourself the moment to pause to permit the light of reason to shine in your consciousness for where light is, no shadow can exist. And all past experiences are shadows. So when you permit the light of reason to enter your consciousness, the shadows disappear. You are no longer controlled by them. Therefore, you are able to listen, instead of hear; therefore, you are able to view, instead of see; therefore, you are free in those moments to experience the joy of living. And all of that takes place in such a very simple way, and it takes, in truth, so little effort and utilizes such a small amount of energy.

And so it behooves man—man wants many things, for man has denied many things. And therefore, man experiences need for many things. Yet these many things already exist for you. It's only your prejudice that keeps you from experiencing them. It's only prejudgment that denies you that goodness that waits for you moment by moment in the intelligent atmosphere in which you are moving.

We'll take a moment to pause for any questions. *[After a short pause, the teacher continues.]* I always like to pause for a few questions because that gives you an opportunity to put something in. And you know the law is so clear that we get out of anything what we put into it and not one iota more. Yes, the lady there, please.

*Some people are pit bulls. Some people are cocker spaniels. Now for those of us who are lucky enough to have the temperament of a cocker spaniel, do we have a responsibility to go around healing pit bulls?*

Well, in reference to the, ah, analogy there, I guess, of some people being pit bulls, is that it? I thought you said pet bulls. But pit bulls. And some people being cocker spaniels. Is it the responsibility of the cocker spaniels to turn the pit bulls into cocker spaniels? Well, no, no, no, no, no, no, no. That's—unsolicited help is ever to no avail. And I find that everyone is little lambs ever in keeping with the effort that we make to communicate without prejudice with them. You see, to God or goodness all things are possible. Nothing is greater than goodness, which, of course, is God. Therefore, this power of greatness, of goodness, of God is ours at any moment of our choice. There is nothing that can withstand the power of the infinite, intelligent Energy, which is available to all of us at any moment.

Now we alone make the choice to choose between faith and belief. Now if we choose belief, then we do believe that someone is greater than this great goodness called God, that is. That's when we descend. You see, that's the descent of man. That's the direct opposite of the ascent of man. The ascent and descent is not something that just happened over a period of, of eons of time. It is something that's happening moment by moment. At any moment we choose to ascend and be free. At any moment we choose to descend and be bound. So as we, through our own experiences, through our own prejudgments, which are called by man prejudices, as we choose the path of bondage, as we look and we see pet bulls, I mean, pit bulls and cocker spaniels, we alone, you see, we must understand that we alone make those judgments. You see, a person says, "Based upon my experiences with this individual, they're a pit bull. Based upon my experiences with this individual, they are a cocker spaniel." Now we must accept and we must understand in order that we may accept that the pit bull and the cocker spaniel are dependent upon the prejudges of the individual who is attempting to communicate with the pit bull and the cocker spaniel. The question is, Are they pit bulls? Are they cocker spaniels? If they are, is that reality or is that truth?

Now there's a vast difference between reality and truth. Reality is a conscious realization of passing events. That's not truth, but that's reality. So we can—when we *see*, we experience reality. When we *view*, we awaken; the truth within is joined with the truth without, you see. That takes unity. And that takes faith. So our reality and our world, we clearly see, is ever dependent upon shadows of the past in reference to what we see and in reference to what we hear.

But there is a better way. There is the path of Light, the path of freedom, the path of truth.

Just because a past experience tells a person that that individual is a pit bull, that is totally dependent upon the judgments made by the individual who is looking at the person. Now someone else may come up to that person and say, "They're a darling cocker spaniel." Is that not true? *[After a short pause, the teacher restates his question.]* Is that not possible?

*It's possible.*

Fine. That which is possible is clear. It is possible. It is possible for anyone to change. Would you not agree?

*I don't know.*

Ah! Well, do you accept that to the divine, infinite, intelligent Energy, known by man as God, that all things are possible?

*Yes.*

If you accept that to God—*[At this point there is an interruption in the audio recording and twenty seconds of the recording are missing.]*—which all things are possible, exists within our own consciousness, then there is no question whatsoever that change is possible for any and every [one].

*Thank you.*

Nature reveals to us that change is the law through which evolution is made possible. You see, first of all, repetition is the law through which change is made possible, and change is the law through which evolution is possible. And because our forms are an inseparable part of nature and because our forms are an inseparable part of the process of evolution, everyone everywhere at all times is changing.

You see, the changes take place in our lives, and ofttimes we are not aware of the changes while they're in the process, [but] we're aware of the frustration. You see, man experiences frustration from, from many varying avenues. Man experiences frustrations for there are changes chemically, physiologically, psychologically taking place. It's happening all the time. And once in a while, man becomes aware: "Something's happening inside of me!" [It's] probably been going on for years. Obviously, it has to be. It's the Law of Evolution. And then we get all frustrated.

We must realize that we become frustrated over things that our mind can't control. A man becomes frustrated over what his wife does [or] a wife becomes frustrated over what her husband does simply because they feel they cannot control them. And when we make great effort to control someone and they do not react in keeping with the effort that we believe that we have made to control them, suddenly we begin to experience—I know what that means. *[The teacher is addressing the recording technician.]*—suddenly we begin to experience, don't you see, that, oh, we're frustrated. Would you not agree?

*Yes.*

Yes. So how does a person free themselves from frustration? Stop this stupidity of denial; don't experience what you call need. Then you won't have the desire to control someone else, and you won't be frustrated. Now isn't that a much better way to live?

*If you're—unless you're a mother.*

A mother?

*I'm talking about the difficulties in getting a, a child to behave like a cocker spaniel when it's obviously a pit bull.*

Oh! But now we have to pause in just a moment. I still have two minutes. *[The teacher refers to the time remaining on the recording tape.]*

*No, it's over.* [The recording technician announces.] *The tape is*—we've run out of tape.

Well, why didn't you give me a 5-minute [warning]?

*[This class was recorded simultaneously on both videotape and on a microcassette audio recorder. Although the microcassette recorder ran out of tape before the video recorder, the video recording faintly captured much, but not all, of what the microcassette recorder missed, which allowed a more complete transcription. The video recorder was paused while a new audio cassette was put into the microcassette recorder.]*

We're going to get right down to mothers. Now, now let's stop and think about mothers. Now what are we talking about, about mothers? About the mother's child is not doing what she wants it to do. It's turned out to be one of those pit bulls down there, which is really a pet bull if we look at it in a different view, if we view it instead of look at it. And we're talking about little cocker spaniels over there. Well, I know some very spiteful, nippy little cocker spaniels, I'll tell you. *[Many of the students laugh.]*

But anyway, we're talking about the fruit of the womb. Now this is very important. Because the fruit of the womb is known as the child. There's the fruit of someone's womb. It happens to be the fruit of this lady's womb right there. *[The teacher refers to a student in the class and her child, who is also a student.]* So what does that represent to the human mind? Well, it's quite simple. It represents what it is: the fruit of the mother's womb. Now in keeping with the mother's mental attachment to that particular part of her anatomy does she have problems with the fruit of her womb. Now if we will face that honestly, we won't have any problem at all, you see.

You see, now if, if we choose to be attached to the toe, instead of to that part of the anatomy, there won't be as many problems with the fruit of the womb, which is known as the little child, you see. Then we will be able to guide the child, to respect the child's right of its evolution to go its particular way, to respect the right of the child, after the effort has been made to properly guide them, proper, of course, in our own thinking, then we will respect their divine right as an individual to do what they choose to do, as long, of course, as they don't infringe upon our rights. Now if they infringe upon our rights—and we all should know our own rights—then we have to face personal responsibility and to awaken to what avenue we have open that tempts them to impose upon us. Did that help with the question? We must learn to be good mother bears. Hmm?

*Yes, indeed. But the nature that we do not want will be there no matter what we do, OK? In other words, it's easy to walk away.*

No, no, no, no, no. I'm not talking about walking away at all. I'm talking about personal responsibility to free our self from the need to control, and how we free our self from the need to control is to stop denying. And when we stop denying, we'll stop being destined to that bondage and start accepting the divine right of all, facing personal responsibility. And whether they change or do not change is no longer a factor in our consciousness for we are free. We have, we have accepted their divine right, like the mother bear does. She accepts she has guided the little cubs. The time has come for them to demonstrate and for them to apply what she has trained them and educated them to. And whether they fly or they fall is their responsibility. Mother bear goes right about her business and has the next fruit of her womb at the proper season.

*Thank you very much.*

Does that help with your question? Then, you see, we're free. Isn't it better to be free than to be bound by denial, experience need, and be frustrated in our efforts to control that which is not controllable?

*Yes, I was just checking—*

Yes. You see, individualized soul carries with it the Divinity to do its thing. Now we may want it to do something else. Well, we soon find out, sooner or later, that's just too bad. Because we do not want someone to dictate to us what we're to do at any moment, and because we don't want that, we experience great frustration when we want to do it to someone else. You see, we must desire to have done to us what we, in moments of an error of ignorance, do unto others.

So we stop and place our self—you know, it's like people who don't consider the other creatures here that have their divine right to be on the planet. And so they go along and they step on them and they squash them and they throw them around and mistreat them. Well, I always recall my experiences so very long ago in a realm of consciousness where some people, who had a terrible resentment to certain types of animals, denying them their right to existence on the planet Earth. And, of course, in keeping with the law they have established, they got to live for a long, long time with their own adversities. You see, our adversities are our attachments. That's just the way that it is.

So a wise man chooses not to be adverse to anything, for in being adverse, you direct intelligent, infinite Energy to the form of your own adversity. And because you are the creator of it, the son shall ever return to the father. And so all our chickens, they come home to roost. So let's, from this moment, perhaps, let us, if we must create anything, let's create a few lambs. We've had enough of the chickens and certainly plenty of the roosters. And how we do that is to free our self from all this prejudice, this terrible, terrible prejudice. You can't have prejudice without denial, for you cannot have judgment without denial. And you cannot have comparison without denial. And so it is that man destines himself through his own denials when man can free himself, through the will of God that he truly is, by total acceptance.

You see, it doesn't mean that you must experience everything that old creation has to offer to be in total acceptance. It means that you look at the tree and you accept its divine right to be a tree, to express itself in the way of its own individuality. You accept the divine right of the little ant to have its home on the Earth and on the planet. You accept the divine right of all people, of all nature to express itself, though its expression is not in keeping with your own prejudgment. For, you see, your freedom, your goodness is ever in keeping with your acceptance of the divine right of life.

We are an inseparable part of this great stream of consciousness known as life. We are not greater than it. As the drop of water from the great oceans of time are not greater than the ocean itself, but they do contain all the constituents of the ocean, but they are not greater than the ocean. So we must learn to respect the infinite, divine Intelligence no matter what form it expresses through. We must learn to accept its right to express, because by denying its right to express in our consciousness we become greater than God, and we pay the price of experiencing the opposite of abundant goodness. Does that help with your question?

*Thank you.*

You're welcome. You're welcome. Any other questions at this time? Yes.

*All that you say is true. It has a lot of validity to it. How does one change his methods of existing within those prejudices that exist in the world?*

Yes. By first accepting your divine right to your world. How one exists and frees themselves in a world of creation, in a world of bondage: first of all, we must accept that we see it as a world of bondage, of a world of differences, of a world of contradiction. That's how we, we see it. Is that not correct? Now *we* can change everything in here. *[With his right hand, the teacher points to his head.]* And by changing everything in here we become instruments through which changes gradually, slowly, but surely, happen out there. For as a person makes changes within their consciousness and in keeping with the law that like attracts like and becomes the Law of Attachment, they will start attracting into their life people and experiences in keeping with their own change. Do you follow me so far? Now, each person has a great responsibility to the world. They can do everything that they choose to do with their personal world. That is their divine right.

Now as we make the effort to see the world different than we have seen it, as we make that effort within our consciousness, we will begin to attract to us people of like kind. They will start to enter into our atmosphere and into our zone of action. Slowly but surely, in keeping with our effort, we will soon begin to realize, "These people are different. They're not like the masses out there." They are more harmonious with your type of thinking that is changing, you see. Now as that happens, a wise person associates—and attracts and associates with people who are in a little different understanding, you see, because that way they support each other. Do you understand? And God (goodness) helps those who help themselves by helping others. So that's how God helps us, is as we help our self in helping others. Because physician first must heal thyself to be the instrument of this transformation and changeover.

So we make the effort to make these changes about the world. We no, we no longer see the world. We begin to view the world. And when we begin to view the world, these forms that have clouded our vision (and we cannot see clearly), they begin to disappear. And we see the world clearly, the way it truly is, not the way we have prejudged it. We are no longer, then, controlled by those shadows of yesteryear. And as we do that, our circle of associates and the things that we attract into our life, they are ever in keeping with our stage of evolution. It goes back to one of your sayings in your world of long ago: man is known by the company he keeps, and birds of a feather, they flock together. See? And so it's beneficial, you see. Even the little, lower creatures, the animals and the birds and things, they know; for their own protection, they flock together for their own strength. You see, they demonstrate this great power of faith for they demonstrate the unity for the common good.

And so a wise man in his efforts to free himself from bondage, he looks around and he begins to choose wisely because, you see, like attracts like. The people will be pulled into your, your zone of action. They'll be pulled into your aura. But you alone must look at all of these associates to see which ones—to view them and to see these changes. Because they will happen. Whether it's in personal life, business—it'll be in all parts of one's life. Absolutely. That's something that *we* can do, and we can do it each and every moment. It's not dependent on anything or anyone. That's something that's available to us.

And, you see, if man makes a little effort, he'll have a little experience. But that little experience will be encouraging. And, as the law says, whoever is grateful for the crumb of life establishes the Law of Gratitude through which they are destined to have the loaf. That's the way it is. All of nature reveals that great truth. Did that help with your question?

*Yes. [Thank you.]*

You're welcome. Any other questions at this time?

And if you're in the sun and it's getting warm, you'll move to the shade. I'm sure there's shade around here somewhere. Perhaps we can move that little crib down there so that someone will sit in the shade because he's not using it. Or if you want to get up a little closer you can. There's more shade up here. *[This class was given outdoors in the garden at the temple. As time passed, students who were in the shade were now in the direct sun, and some may have become uncomfortable.]* I think I'll move over because we still have a while to go. Oops! [I] knocked that over. *[The teacher knocked over the microcassette recorder that was recording the class.]* Well, anyway. There. Why don't you move up so you can get a little more shade? I don't like to see anyone uncomfortable because, you see, I know—perhaps

I'm a bit selfish—I know if you're uncomfortable, that I'm not getting your full attention. And if I'm not getting your full attention, in keeping with the law that energy follows attention, I'm using all of my own, and I'll be exhausted. And I don't intend to be exhausted. And I consider that practical, not selfish. Yes. So, please, don't be uncomfortable. Now, hopefully by next seminar they'll have all of these mats and some cushions and it'll be a little more comfortable. All right. Now are there any other questions? *[The teacher continues after a short pause.]* No questions? Then—Yes.

*I have another question dealing with knowledge.*

Knowledge, yes.

*Lack of knowledge in coping with, you know, people in certain spheres—*

Yes.

*—of the different levels of knowledge.*

Yes.

*And communicating within that, you know, sphere.*

I understand.

*From lack of that ability of knowledge, the knowledge itself, how do you deal with that?*

Well, you see, if, for example, in reference to that question and in having the knowledge in order to communicate and work with certain people—is that basically the question?

*[Yes.]*

There is something greater than knowledge. Now how do we first establish the law within our self for the value for something that is greater than knowledge, and by establishing that value, without speaking a word, to emanate that value so that like attracts like and the person coming to us will have the same experience? Well, first of all, we have within our consciousness— first, I want to establish knowledge. Knowledge knows much; wisdom knows better. Let's go beyond that point and see what knowledge is dependent upon. Knowledge is dependent upon past experience. Is that not correct? And knowledge is certainly useful, and it's absolutely and totally limiting, for man's knowledge is dependent upon his efforts. And man's efforts, in any given realm of consciousness, is limited by his desires. So what we know with our mind today proves, as time passes, no longer to be what we thought it was. Would you not agree?

*Yes.*

In many, many things. All right. Because you're constantly in a process of change.

And so, first of all, man must say to himself, "Now just a moment. I know this, that, that, that, that, that and on down the list. I've got to communicate with a person over there. Now they know things that I don't know. Shall I judge that I cannot communicate with them, I cannot reach them until I learn what they know and I learn it better?" Now, you see, this is where prejudice comes in. This is where prejudgment comes in. But we alone, we have the control of that, for we can also accept the possibility, we can accept the possibility that we have something of value for which we are very grateful. All right? Now we have that. Everyone has something of value that someone wants, needs, and desires. Would you not agree? Now to different people, that person may not want what that person has to offer that they have valuable, but everyone has something. Everyone has something.

Now, so you're going to communicate with a person, and you're not knowledgeable in the particular areas in which they are knowledgeable. We must first, within our own consciousness, broaden our horizon and accept the possibility, within our consciousness, that they have things in life that interest them that are not dependent, not dependent upon knowledge, not dependent upon judgment. We can always reach a person if we first reach our self. If we reach our self first, then we are qualified to reach whatever person we choose to reach, for in the moment, in the moment it shall be granted unto us in keeping with the law of our faith.

You see, there's the benefit. You see, here, with belief, you have knowledge, and you have all of the bondage that it—and judgment and comparison; you have all that creation has to offer. Here with faith, you have unity; you have wisdom; you have the guidance of the Infinite Intelligence. And so one transfers from belief to faith and is not a bit concerned and has control of their mind and is not a bit concerned over the result. Does that help with your question?

For in keeping with your own value and your own effort for goodness, only goodness can return. But we cannot dictate and control how it shall return for we do not dictate and control how it's going out. Only belief would do that. You see, only belief, mental substance, the human mind, that's the only thing that manipulates because it's the only thing that has need. You see, whatever experiences need destines itself to manipulation, because it has to control to fill its need. People who are free, people who are enjoying life to its fullest are people who have faith. They have no need. Where they have faith, there is no need. They have total acceptance and they have all of these things that we know in this philosophy as the soul faculties. And all over here is all these needs, manipulations, controls, and all the worries, the concerns, and the fears. When on this path over here, all of that is, and we don't have to be a bit concerned.

Now that doesn't mean that a person just sits down and does nothing. Oh, no, no, no, no. One does what they know is right for them to do, and they care less what the world does with it because they're not attached to it. You see, it is in the doing of anything that you have the joy of the thing. That's where the joy is. It's in the actual doing. It's not [in] what the critics say later; that only feeds the bondage. It's in the actual process. For example, if you're filming on the camera or something, it's in the process that you get the joy. That's where the goodness is. It's not in what's developed later; that feeds the belief; that feeds prejudice. The joy is in the actual doing. That's the only place it exists. Anyone who desires to remain free, anyone who desires the abundant good of life, must accept the demonstrable truth: in the doing is the joy; in the getting is the sadness. You see?

So whatever it is you have to do, do it. It doesn't matter what the world does with it, for you're not doing it for that out there. Try to remember that. You're doing it for the goodness inside of yourself. It is not only your personal responsibility, it is not only your divine right, it is the Law of Joy, the Law of Life itself. You see, because in the doing is when you're giving. And the Law of Giving is the Law of Living. That's when man really lives, is when he's giving. So many people think giving means to take something and give it to someone. No, no, no, no, no. You're doing something. You're giving your energy, your attention, your consciousness to the job you have at hand. That's where the joy is. All of the other is sadness and grief; guaranteed. A temporary thrill for a long-time grief. It's not worth it. Did that help with your question?

*It did.*

No, it's not worth it at all. That's not what life is about. Hmm?

*You were going to explain wisdom.*

Ah, wisdom. Well, now, you see, we have knowledge. And that knows much. It is totally dependent upon the shadows of past experiences. Man studies a book, and now he knows something, right? He knows what the book has to offer. He goes and has experiences on a job; and now, in keeping with his own prejudgments, he knows about that particular work. All right? But he's still very limited because it's dependent upon his own personal shadows or judgments.

Now wisdom, you see, it's like the dawn of life. Wisdom is that which is our true being. It is that which is not clouded by mental substance. Wisdom is that that contains the joy of total acceptance; nothing is limited; nothing is denied. Wisdom is that intelligent energy flowing through our being unobstructed by the thought of man. And so man is inspired. Those are moments of the expression of wisdom. And so inspiration, of course, then, being the expression of wisdom, is an instrument through which great good and upliftment comes to mankind. So man looks at a painting, and he is inspired by the painting. He is inspired by the painting because, you see, he becomes receptive to the inspiration of the channel through which it flowed from the light of wisdom. And we can clearly see when man is concerned about the job that he is doing, there's not much flow of any wisdom, but there may be a great torrent of knowledge.

But you can only go—as life reveals itself through demonstration, so man, doing a job, sets all his necessary mental activities. He gets everything set just so. And then, just before he pushes the button, he gives it to God. He gives it to the goodness within him. He's not a bit concerned. He's done his part there. And he's got it all set up. Now his next part, his real part is to get out of the way. That's the real job. That's the hardest job for so many people. They want to walk around and say, "[Is this] just so? Is this just right? Have I got this just right?" And if they would just get their setup done and get out of the way, the greatest good could flow because it flows through an unobstructed channel. Then, when it's time to shut it off, shut it off. And let the chips fall where they may. As long as we've done the best that we can, only the best can come out of it, no matter what people say.

You see, we lose the joy of life when we permit our self the need, through our own denials, we permit our self the need for critics. That's when we do our self in. You see, we do a job and do the best that we can, and we loan it to the world. You see, people who have need, they loan their effort to the world. You see, it's like taking a picture. So you get everything all done.

You've gone all through your mental substance, done the best that you can. You step out of the way. The little camera keeps whirling away. Time comes, you shut it down and then you take a look at it. If you are attached to what has taken place, then you will experience need for someone to, to see it and to tell you it's terrible or tell you that it's good. You see, you're bound by belief. You've lost the beautiful faith. You've lost the great joy in the doing, and now you're bound by what some idiot has to say about it, just because they may have some certificate of authenticity about their position, you see. This is ridiculous. All goodness comes from the one Source. And it's available to us whenever we want, but when we sell out and enter the realm of belief, then we got to have the critics tell us how great it is. And you never know what they're going to tell you because they're prejudiced. Just like all minds. They're in their process of prejudgment. So it depends on the moment that you expose it to them, where they are in space, whether they hate it ("It's horrible!") or something else.

And your history clearly reveals what ofttimes in life they said was a terrible actress or terrible film, turns out 30, 40 years later to be one of the great classics. Well, what happened? Prejudice. That's what it is. So what does that have to do with truth? What does that have to do with experiencing the goodness of life? Look at some of the greatest paintings of all time. Why, the artist starved to death. And 50, a 100 years later, they're the most valuable things on your planet, these great art, [the] paintings and things.

But, you see, that's the way that realm really is. That's why there's nothing but bondage to belief. There's nothing but bondage when you need to have someone tell you how great you are. You can't tell yourself how good you feel; you got to have somebody else tell you how good you feel. That's a horrible way to live. That's like, you know, as I say, give what you have to give to the world, care less what the world does with it for the world is controlled by creation and they're very fickle. You never know what moment they're going to stab you in the back or lift you up to their heavenly heights, the heavenly heights of their consciousness, you understand. It depends on what *their* need is.

So, you see, another person is great to another person and the work they have to do depending upon the people that want something out of it. You see, if you have a little film or something, and you show it to a group of people, they're going to tell you how great or how terrible that is depending on what need they have at the moment (what they want out of you). Now, you see, if they really want something out of you, they're going to tell you according to what their judgments tell them they can get from you. Do you understand that? And it's just the way that it is.

But what does that have to do with being a good film producer? What does that have to do with giving to the world something that is good and worthwhile? Maybe it takes a hundred years for them to wake up how great and good it really is, but it's still there. Like a painting, it's still available. What does it matter? You didn't do it for their fickle minds anyway. What does it matter if they suddenly lay all the credit on you after you're long gone into realms that are totally free from this insanity down here? Hmm? It doesn't matter at all. Because all the joy of life is in the doing. Because it's in the doing that you're giving. So that's where you should be experiencing all this wonderful goodness. Did that help with the question?

*Yes.*

All right. Fine. Ah, yes, I see the time is marching on. We still have a little time. Would you like to tell me how many minutes or would you like me to tell you? You tell me. *[The teacher addresses the technician recording the class.]*

*Thirty.*

Yes. Thirty. [We] have a little time. All right. Are there any other questions here? Because I know that everybody's hungry and they want to get to the barbeque. Yes.

*When you cast the light of reason on something, is it then that you release resistance?*

One cannot resist what one does not fear. And one cannot fear what one first does not judge will be detrimental to them in some way.

So as I said some time ago, the path of peace is passive. Now where is this passiveness taking place? I do not teach nor have I ever taught lay down and let them stomp you again. I don't teach that foolishness. I do not teach: they slugged you on one side; turn the other one, let them slug that. No, that is not the teaching of this philosophy at all. That's totally contrary to personal responsibility. But you can pause in your consciousness, and you can accept the truth: that it's all taking place within your consciousness. And someone slugs you on one cheek, you can pause. Accept personal responsibility for attracting it in the first place, prepare yourself, and slug them on both cheeks. Now that's intelligent. *[Many students laugh.]* But not denying personal responsibility.

You see, you live in a world of creation. You are living in an animal world. You must learn to be in it and stop being a part of it. Now there is a difference. You be in it and stop being a part of it, you see. Does that help with your question?

*Yes. Thank you.*

Hmm. Yes, the lady here, please.

*You were talking about the fruit of the mother's womb. How does that—*

The fruit of any womb. A womb's a womb, and the fruit is the fruit. Yes, thank you. Go ahead.

*OK. Well, that, that applies to the father, too, then?*

Well, I think that's quite an interesting question, and that's certainly worth more than a half-hour discussion. However, we'll try to put it in a little capsule. It'll have to be a small capsule. Now, in reference to the fruit of the womb or the seed or this or that or whatever we're talking about. That's fine. Now we have had a little bit of discussion on the over-identification with that part of the anatomy and the problems that it causes with the fruit of the womb as the fruit is beginning to ripen as the child grows up, you understand. Now you have asked—and it's a most interesting question. And I don't want to be known as prejudiced in this day of women's rights; so we'll carry on with the question that you have. Does that apply to men and their attachment to a particular part of their anatomy? Well, of course, it applies to those who make it apply for them.

Now if a person believes, in speaking of men, that their manhood is dependent on their big toe, then they're going to make sure their big toe is in good working order, wouldn't you say? So that's an individual choice of each person. If they choose to believe that the only way they can be a man and the only way they can stay a man, as some women choose to believe the only way they can have fulfillment as a woman is to give birth to a child, that's totally dependent on your choice of what you want to believe. Did it help with your question?

*I think I was directing it more to the, being controlled by the child.*

Well, haven't you noticed that men are nowheres near as controlled as women by their babies. Hmm? But, then, where did the fruit pass through? Does that help you with your question? Who carried the weight for nine months?

*Right.*

Pardon?

*Yes.*

You see, when you take a person carrying in their belly that weight, you know, for nine long months, twenty-four hours a day, you know, and when you consider all of that, there is continuous opportunity for the mind to become attached to what's weighting it down. Now if you had to carry a 20-pound sack on your belly for several months, wouldn't you slowly, but surely, become over-identified with it? Pardon?

*Yes.*

Does that help with your question?

*Yes.*

And, after all, considering the chemical changes, as a mother carrying the child, considering the physiological changes taking place and the psychological changes and the embryo living off the mother like, like a parasite, you see, well, then you have to understand that great work must be done.

You see, in your Earth planet, the soul, in its entering, of course, is subject to the forms created at the moment of conception. Now if you can visualize a pure, perfect sphere of light entering into your universe here on the Earth planet and a mass of clouds of mist, which is the closest I can get in your terms to the mental forms and emotional forms, prior to that very moment of conception, this perfect sphere must pass through this mist [and] enter—you understand—as the negative and positive poles come together. That's when the soul enters at that instant. In the passing through anything, that which passes through a thing is contaminated by the thing through which it passes. As water passes through a pipe, it carries with it the contamination of what the pipe consists of. And so as the soul, entering the earth realm, must pass through the forms of desires, of fears, of upset, etc., and etc. at the very moment of conception, it, as it passes through, it is contaminated by or covered by this mass of forms and enters, finally, nine months later, in a little form with certain tendencies, you see. That's where they're being impinged or imprinted into the consciousness.

Now, for nine long months the emotions, especially the emotions, for the emotions, you see—a person's emotions release more energy than just a thought. You see, they release energy. And it is the release of this energy that imprints into mental substance. And consequently, as the mother carrying the child is imprinting these forms into the consciousness of the embryo, it is critically important that the mother, especially—the father, in keeping with the mother's reaction to the father, for the embryo is the parasite on the mother's body, you understand, and mind and emotions. And so for that nine-month period, all the emotions, especially, and the attitudes and the feelings and the thoughts and the experiences that the mother has continues to imprint upon the consciousness of the embryo. And so the child, nine months later, comes out with certain very strong tendencies. Does that help with your question?

And it looks like our time is up. And this is—one more question, if there's anyone [who] has it? Yes, that boy there. Go ahead.

*Could—how can we grow in acceptance? How can we grow more in acceptance?*

How can we grow in acceptance? By stop being concerned about it and just doing it. You see, it's like eating. When you want to eat, you don't keep thinking about, "Oh, I want to eat. I want to eat." And you're looking at the food and you say, "Well, I want to eat. And I want to eat," and get all concerned about it. You move your hand (action) and you lift up the hamburger or the whatever it is, and you put it in your mouth and you eat, you see? You see, that's the step we're moving to. It's just to do it, you see?

There's no, there's no miracle. There's no magic about acceptance. Accept whatever you want. You accept the right of the blade of grass to grow. You accept the right of the weed. You can say, accept whatever you choose to accept. And when you enter total acceptance, you will experience the abundant good of life. For, you see, that which disturbs us controls us. And so when we, with all these denials—and everyone else has a right to live and everything else and they pass by our universe along our path and they disturb us. And what are they doing? They're controlling us. Because *we* chose to deny their right of expression. I hope that's helped with your question.

Thank you very much.

AUGUST 4, 1984

## A/V Seminar 1

Good morning, everyone.

Now this special seminar, which you are all attending, is a seminar on the evolution and the true purpose of being.

From something we have come. Therefore, to something we are returning. Our purpose of being is the awareness of the evolutionary path that we are on, for, simply stated, we cannot control what we are not aware of. We are—ofttimes we believe we are the victim of circumstances and conditions that are beyond our control. The reason that we believe that circumstances and conditions, therefore, experiences, are beyond our control is from our lack of awareness of the cause of experience, which in truth, demonstrably, is an effect of laws that we alone have established and continue to establish.

The lack of awareness of the cause of experiences or effects establishes within the consciousness a denial of the truth. And the law reveals to us whatever we deny we are destined to experience. For example, a person goes through life on their evolutionary path and they have a repetition of certain experiences that they do not appreciate. And as they establish within their consciousness the adversity to those distasteful experiences, they establish and guarantee the continuity of them for the Law of Adversity is the Law of Attachment in keeping with our choice of directing intelligent, neutral, infinite energy to the form that we find distasteful.

So often in life we look and we see that we are in a condition, a circumstance, and an experience, and our mind tells us—and it justifies—the reason that we are in those experiences is because what someone else has done, what someone else is doing. When we permit our self to believe that way, we are in truth accepting that it is not possible for us to change the experience for the cause of the experience is something beyond our control. When we permit the type of thinking that states anything that we experience in our life is beyond our control, then what we do is deny the ability to respond intelligently to the experience and to bring about the change within our consciousness that will attract, by the law that like attracts like and becomes the Law of Attachment, to bring about in our life a new experience, an experience that we feel would be more beneficial, more harmonious to what we choose to do in life.

And so we entered this earth realm, this Earth planet, in keeping with those laws we established. We attracted, by laws we set into motion, the particular parents that we have. We attracted into our lives the location of where we would be born on the Earth planet and everything that we are experiencing. Now some of us may feel that that is predestination; therefore, we are helpless to make changes in our life. That is not true.

There are three factors that control our life. Those factors are the hereditary influences in keeping with our law of evolution; [there] are the environmental influences in keeping with our own choices, conscious, usually subconscious; and there is also the law of awakening to accept the ability to personally respond and, through that acceptance, to bring about the necessary changes in our life.

The statement that man is a law unto himself; and therefore, what, man, are you doing with the law that you are? is clearly the path of personal responsibility, is clearly the path of the control of our own life.

Now we find great difficulty, it seems, at times, in bringing about the changes that we desire. We find, it seems, great difficulty in having the goodness of life, which is not something that some partial god in some dimension somewhere has handed to some and deprived others of. No, the goodness of life is the Law of Life. The discord and the opposite of goodness is an interference with the natural Law of Divine Flow. It is, in truth, our divine right. It is, in fact, our divine responsibility to enjoy the goodness of life. That is a part of our purpose of being. We do not often experience this goodness of life for in our errors we go against the law, the divine Law of Harmony.

We identify with the panorama of creation, and in that identification, through our limited view of the true purpose of life, we establish the Law of Prejudice. We find, when we are honest with our self, that we are extremely prejudiced. We prejudge what someone is going to say. We prejudge how someone is going to act. We prejudge what tomorrow will be like. We prejudge how we're going to feel in certain circumstances and conditions. This prejudice reveals to us that we are relying and dependent upon what past experiences are offering to us in our consciousness. For example, we meet a person early in our life. We have what we consider a real bad experience with that person. That is recorded in our consciousness. Years pass by. We meet someone that looks or acts similar to that person we had the seeming bad experience with in past times. Through the Law of Association in our consciousness, if we permit our self to be over-identified with our self, then we establish that Law of Prejudice or prejudgment, and we have a similar experience with that person.

Now many of us are aware of those things happening in our lives through various marriages, divorces, relationships, and associations that we have already had. So often I hear a man or a woman say, "Just like the wife before. Does the same identical thing." Well, if we would pause in that kind of thinking, we would be aware that within our consciousness we are not living in the present moment, but we are experiencing our own prejudice or prejudgment. A shadow of a past experience is in control of our present experience. In fact and in truth, it is the shadow of the past experience that established the Law of Attraction, through adversity, that brought us another wife like the one we had before, that is, the one we worked to get rid of. And, of course, vice versa.

Now that, of course, is not limited in any way or respect to relationships, husbands, and wives. It happens with our work.

It happens with our employment. The purpose of being is the awakening of how this takes place within our consciousness, how we can gain control over our mind and not be the victim of shadows or experiences that have already passed. We all realize, I am sure, that what has passed exists only as what we call a memory in our consciousness. It affects our present moment when we, through lack of effort, permit our mind to over-identify with our self. Because we do not spend much of our time pausing in consciousness and asking our self, honestly, who are we? Where are we? And what are we doing?

We *think* we know where we are by the presence of our physical body. We do not know where we are simply by the presence, the awareness of where our physical body is, for we already know we have met people, including our self, that say, "Where was I? I did not hear that. I did not see that. Where was I?" We are ofttimes directing energy to the shadows, to the twilight zone where the shadows or past experiences live in our consciousness.

Now, for example, you have an experience with a person. You first judge the experience is a pleasant or a pleasurable one. Time passes. Same person. Different experience. It is not pleasurable. It does not meet the expectations of the experience before. Now the question, in those situations, must be asked by the individual, "Is this something taking place within my consciousness?" We rarely ask that question, for we immediately judge that that person that we had such a pleasant experience with a week before, or a month or a day, they're doing something different. Something's changed. But, in truth, has something changed? And, if so, where is the change? The last place we want to look is inside of our self.

Now here is the law, so clear, that like attracts like. So we say we have a pleasant experience with a person, and a week later we have a terrible experience with the same person. That judgment of whether it is pleasant or distasteful is taking place within our consciousness. It's not taking place anywhere else.

Now the freedom is where the truth is. The truth is that the experience is taking place within our consciousness. That's the truth, the demonstrable truth. It's our mind and it is our thought. Now if we start with the truth, we will be free. Then we take a look at our mind, our own mind, and we see that there was something a little different. And it wasn't in keeping with our prejudice or our prejudgment; therefore, it is distasteful. We alone have made the judgment, based upon judgments that have preceded the judgment, which are known as prejudices: that this is not a pleasant experience. So we go to work, in our error of ignorance, to make the other person change. Completely and wholly and totally denying the law. Number one: it is taking place within our consciousness. It is based upon our own prejudices and prejudgments, and we have attracted it into our life in keeping with the demonstrable law that like attracts like.

Now when we start with that type of thinking and we work on that every day, year after year after year, we will very soon find that life is as beautiful, as good, as abundant, and as beneficial to us as we at any moment choose to make it.

Now we all want the constant experience of the true purpose of life. We all want to declare our divine right to goodness. Now stop and think. If God was a form, then God or goodness would be limited. Therefore, God or goodness, demonstrably, is not limited. God cannot be form and be the goodness everywhere in everything, for there is one God, one Infinite Intelligence, one Divine Power that sustains all form or all creation. God is not creation. God is the Divine Love and goodness that sustains creation.

So the goodness—the flower expresses its goodness in the beauty that it shares with all who view it. And so the tree. And so the human. For, you see, love, goodness, is a reflection in another of the goodness in oneself. One may experience that reflection from the sunset or the sunrise, from the flower or the blade of grass or from the weed. And when we awaken that that is what love is—the reflection in another of the goodness in oneself—therefore, love is not limited nor restricted to any particular human being, any particular blade of grass, flower, or tree, cloud, sunrise, or sunset. For love or goodness is ever present when we choose at any moment to take control of our own mind and permit our being to reflect what is in it, what we truly are.

Now we come to the left path and to the right path in our evolution. Here we have, through over-identification with self, that is, with mental substance, we rely upon what we know as the human mind, which is limited to the experiences of a short earth life. So in our over-identification with, our dependence and reliance upon the human mind, we believe, based upon experiences and past events. So we believe in many things. We believe it's a beautiful day or we believe it's a terrible day. We believe we had sufficient sleep the night before or we believe we did not. We believe that our employer is going to give us a raise in a few months or we believe he is not. All of those experiences in our consciousness are based upon what has been. They are based upon the shadows or the twilight zone of creation.

Then we have the right path. Here, on the right path, we see clearly this passing panorama. We see that creation, it comes and it goes. We also see that all form is designed to serve its purpose. Even the form of a thought is designed to serve the purpose of its design. And so the flower grows and serves the purpose of its design. Within the seed of the flower is the complete plant. It is already existing microscopic within the seed itself. And so it is with the seed of the human being: the angel within us is already there. For it is the angel that has come from the source of Light and, therefore, coming from it, is designed and is in the process of returning to it. The return to the true being, which we are, is not dependent on anything that is beyond our control. It is not dependent upon a God that we can pray to, to bring us back home sooner, immediately, because we don't like the experience we are having. That God is present to us. The only obstruction to what we are and what we *think* we are is our dependence upon our own prejudices, our own experiences, and prejudgments of past events. There are no other obstructions.

So whether it's an ant or an angel, God is there, ever present and never absent or away. It is we, in our consciousness, that are absent and away. We don't have to be. But that change comes only when we're ready.

And so here we have faith. Faith is not based upon the forms of creation. Faith is not dependent upon what we think and what we believe. Faith goes far beyond that. Faith is greater than knowledge, far greater than knowledge, for knowledge knows much, for the human mind knows much. Wisdom knows better than knowing much, and therefore, of course, it is wisdom. That's where faith is. Faith is the path of wisdom. It is the awakening within our consciousness that we have entered this earth realm of creation to serve a purpose.

And what is that purpose?

The Bible teaches you that God, goodness, has given you charge over all creation. Now stop and think. Here, the prophets have revealed the demonstrable truth. God, Intelligent Goodness, has given you charge over all creation. Now all creation is exactly what it says. Man creates a thought in his consciousness. That is creation. He forms mental substance and he calls it a thought. You feel that you're having a good day; that is based upon and dependent, if you are trapped on the path of belief, on what your mind, in its comparison to other days, judges. And so that form of judgment can be good or the opposite. There is something far greater than that. And that something, that something is what we truly are.

Now in our purpose of being, in our awakening—our awareness and our awakening on this path of evolution, we have a responsibility to that which we are in charge of. We have a responsibility to any and every thing that is within our domain of responsibility. Some of us have a very narrow sphere of responsibility, very small. Some have a very large. It is ever dependent upon your awakening in consciousness. For you have been given charge over all creation, and creation begins at home within our own mind.

When you permit your mind to tell you that the experience you are having you do not appreciate, that's the time to pause. That's the time to say, "Just a minute," before your mind gets a chance to enter the realms of prejudice and tell you it's because what someone else did. You see, if you don't grab ahold of your mind the instant it tells you that you don't like what's happening, if you don't pause at that moment and declare the truth, "It's my mind. I have the ability to personally respond to it," stop at that point. Take control of your mind, and in controlling your mind you have the opportunity to experience the joy of living. Your true purpose of being *is* the joy of living.

This philosophy does not teach nor does it demonstrate some God of great wrath. God is not a judge, for goodness cannot judge. For goodness to judge, it would have to establish the Law of Comparison. And for goodness to compare, then goodness is no longer goodness, for it is now opposites. Therefore, God, the goodness of life that sustains the weed as well as the rose, cannot judge for it cannot compare and still be what we think it is. Therefore, when man permits himself to be greater than that which sustains him, when man permits his mind to judge, he establishes the law, the falsehood of believing that he is greater than God. Therefore, the effect of that error of ignorance of believing that he is greater than God by judging what is right and what is wrong, by judging who shall eat and who shan't eat, by judging who shall live and who shall not live, when man permits himself that great luxury of error, then man suffers the effects of that error. God, goodness, does not suffer, for God, goodness, did not establish that. Man, creation, through his over-identification with his own past experiences, man establishes that law and pays the price thereof. That is not the way to enjoy life. That is not the way to experience the abundant goodness.

So often we have, seemingly, these problems. These problems—a lack of supply. We're always thinking about how we can get more money. We're always thinking about how we can get more of this and how we can get more of that. And then we awaken one day and we find that life is a phenomenal weight of responsibility. We have permitted into our life so many things, they weigh us down. We have temporarily forgotten that the so-called weight of responsibility must never ever exceed our love of God. For, you see, the love of God is the experiencing of the goodness of life. That is what the love of God is.

And so here we are at this moment. And let us pause to think. And in our thinking, let us go more deeply within our consciousness. We are not the thought. We are the creator of the thought. And in that awakening [that] we are not the thought, we can then begin to establish the Law of Disassociation. We are responsible for what we create. The Bible prophets have told us that, and it has been demonstrated repeatedly. We are responsible for all creation. So we are responsible for the thought that we create, but we are not the thought that we create. That's like telling our self that we are the shovel that we are using in the garden. That's like telling our self that we are the automobile that we are driving.

Unfortunately, many of us do believe that we are the automobile that we are driving. Well, how do we believe that? How is that law demonstrated? Well, just have somebody put a scratch on it or, or smash the fender and we'll see how quickly we believe that we are the car that we are driving. Think of that now. Our emotional upset reveals clearly to us how much we believe we are the vehicle that we are driving.

Now when we begin to disassociate, we see that there's an automobile. It was designed and made to serve a purpose. It has entered our law—entered our life through laws that we alone have established. We use it, and if we're smart, we don't abuse it, and it serves us well. If someone dents or puts a scratch upon it, it is in keeping with a law that *we* have established. We have established a law that has placed us into a situation through which someone would damage it. Now accepting that personal responsibility, we are immediately disassociated from the terrible trap that believes we are the vehicle we are driving.

Now if we start doing that, and that's our automobile, the next step is to do it with our shoes and our clothes. And once we gain a little headway on doing it with our shoes and our clothes, the next step is to do it with our toothbrush. And [when] we get it done with our toothbrush and our hairbrush and our comb, and then we're on our way. We can look at our foot and we say, "Yes, you serve to move my true being around the universe, but you are not me! I have a responsibility to take care of my foot and my toe, [to] take care of my hands. That is my responsibility. Like it is my responsibility to take care of the automobile that, by law I have established, has come into my life. My body, my hair, my hands, my feet, and my eyes, my physical being and my mental being is creation. I have a responsibility to take charge over all my creation."

And so you take charge of your automobile. You take charge of your body. You take charge of your mind. And your little soul, the angel inside of you, the goodness that you truly are, will guide you for that is the Light of eternal truth. It will not fail you.

And the only thing that will ever fail you is the temporary ignorance, the error of believing that you are your hands, believing that you are your physical body. For if you do not make the effort to free yourself from believing that you are your physical body, in the natural process of evolution, as your physical body slowly, but surely, changes—for it's constantly in a process of changing—if you permit yourself to believe that you are your physical body, you will suffer the inevitable changes that are the Law of Creation. So as your body goes through its changes and you permit yourself to believe that you are your body, you will suffer the consequences of that falsehood. Then, when the day comes for your eternal being, the angel inside of you, the eternal soul, to leave the vehicle, it will not be so easy because of the attachment to it.

Now it does not mean that you should not consider your vehicle, your body, for you have a responsibility to it, just like your car. You have a responsibility to it. But make the effort to stop the falsehood of believing you are the physical body. Then you will not have to stand at the graveyard watching the decaying process of an old shoe that has served its purpose and is returning to the source from whence it came.

Now it has been said long ago by a wise man, "Dust thou art, to dust returnest / Was not spoken of the soul" *[from "A Psalm of Life" by Henry Wadsworth Longfellow]*. Think, my friends. If the effort is not made today to stop believing you are your physical body, then how can the effort be made to stop believing that you are the thoughts that at different moments of your day enter your consciousness. It is only our belief that we are the thought, instead of the creator of the thought, that is our problem.

The path of faith is the path of true awakening. It is not dependent upon form. It is not dependent upon churches or synagogues. Faith is not dependent on anything outside of you. Faith is something that you are! You cannot tell it what to do. You cannot order it what to do. It is. Faith is that great power inside of you that is intelligent, that is waiting to guide your life when you make the slightest effort to gain control of your mind, to stop believing that you are the thought, and to use mental substance intelligently to create the forms that will serve you well that your life may be the true divinity and the experience of the joy of living. It's in your hands. No one can take it from you. No one can give it to you. You had it when you came to earth. It is with you, and you are never without it. It will be with you throughout all eternity because it *is* what you are. It's not what you believe you are. It's not what you think you are. It is what you are. It is not dependent on what someone else thinks you are or doesn't think you are.

So much of our life we permit to be dependent on what a person's going to do with what we say or don't say. There is no freedom in dependence on anything that is beyond our control. The instant that we permit our minds to depend on anything that's beyond our control we place our self right into the slavery and the bondage of what someone else does or doesn't do at any given moment. No one can ever say that that is goodness, let alone God.

Creation comes and creation goes. Nature reveals that to us moment by moment. There is no way that you can find reliability or stability in depending on that which is form. And thought is form. Belief is a dependence upon form. There's no freedom there for there's no truth there. There's no goodness there for it is governed by the Law of Opposites. It is governed by the Law of Duality. Only to rise, shall we fall, when we depend and are reliant upon the forms of our mind, the forms which are creation.

In leaving this physical world, we experience all the shadows we've permitted our self to identify with. We don't have to be affected by it, for there is the path of light where they cannot enter. But that path of light is within our consciousness, and we have the awareness of it when we take control over the thoughts of our mind.

For when we leave this physical body, we no longer have physical substance that acts as a buffer. Now, we experience a thought within our mind, but we do not see the form of the thought. Now, we have a feeling. We experience an emotion, but we do not see nor do we hear the forms that they are. We have the effect of them. Sometimes we feel very upset and very angry. Sometimes we feel very excited and very thrilled. And we do experience the effects of those forms, but we don't see them. Usually we don't see them. Some people see them, but usually, most of us, we do not see them.

When this physical substance (the body) begins its return to the source from whence it came—for all things are returning to the source from whence they came. The angel within us is on its way home, and the physical body, coming from the earth, is in the process of returning to it. We leave the physical body and the first experience that we—most of us—will have is an awareness of looking at it. It doesn't move. It's like stone. We don't like that. Many people who have the experience don't like it. Untold millions don't like the experience. They don't like it because of the identification that it is them! They can't move it. They move the hand; they move the body they're now in, which is known as their astral body, which we all have, and it just goes through it. It is a distressing experience for untold millions, in keeping with the Law of Over-Identification of Physical Substance.

And so after a time of trying to make it move and trying to make it talk, [we] next experience various forms and people, usually talking or chattering, dependent [upon] and in keeping with where we are in consciousness. If we were terribly upset just before the Isle of Hist separated when we left the physical body, then, of course, we then experience, through the laws of attraction, forms in the astral world, which we're now expressing through, that are upset and like kind. They tell us all kinds of things. And we go either with them into their realm with our astral body or we stand still and take control over our mind and we wait.

Many, many philosophies have taught—and continue to teach, in the Far East, especially—how to find your way through the various realms of consciousness in order that you may stay on the path and enter the realm of consciousness that is in keeping with your evolution through control of your mind.

Now one is not wise to wait until that final day comes, for to do so they are not prepared nor qualified to have the necessary control to get them home, where they truly belong. And so I have taught over these years, some of my students, how to, slowly but surely, gain control so that you don't have to go off into those realms.

Now some teachers, I am aware, teach, "Well, just cast that white light of God around you and you [will] just be fine." Well, if that was true, how come we don't just simply, when we're terribly upset and in the forces of emotion, how come we just don't say, "I cast the white light of God around me and therefore, I'm fine"? How come we don't do that and it works? Well, it doesn't work. I ask any of you, and you know very well that's a bunch of foolishness.

You see, you're not qualified. We're not qualified without making the effort. A person doesn't learn to paint a picture just by sitting down and moving a brush and some paint. You must make the effort and qualify yourself in anything and especially qualify yourself in the joy of living.

And so I teach my students to learn to flood their consciousness before they go to sleep; for when we go to sleep that is when the astral and mental bodies are their most active. For the faculty of reason, through which light flows, that soul faculty, is awake in the conscious mind, not the subconscious. The subconscious is a reactor, and it is in a process of constantly reacting to what is fed into it.

You see, change we find to be difficult for us because when we go to make a change in our life and a change in our thinking, we have a battle with all of the patterns of mind, with all of the forms that we have directed so much energy to over a lifetime. If you take a person that, for example, is used to getting up at a certain time every morning, is used to having a toothbrush to brush their teeth, and you put them over on an island and they have to wake up at a different time every morning and they don't get to brush their teeth every morning, you get to have a reaction, you see. The person doesn't feel right and they get upset, in anything. What is it that's upset? *They're* not upset. Their identification, through belief, that they are the form—all of those patterns, all those forms they have created, that's who is upset, and you are experiencing that. That's all. That's the only thing that's upset.

And so when you go off to sleep at night, whenever you go to sleep, take control of your mind. Make an intelligent, conscious choice of where you want your energy to go while you're unaware, consciously unaware, of what's happening. You choose intelligently where you want to be. Intelligently. And by so doing, you guarantee the law, and the day, that you will experience that which you consciously choose to experience. If that effort is not made, when the day comes that you leave the old physical body, you will go in keeping with whatever your greatest weakness may be.

You see, the prayer says, "Lord, lead us not into temptation." What is temptation? What does the prayer say? It says "Lord." What is the "Lord"? The Lord is the law of your universe. That's the law. So it says, Law, lead me not into temptation. Law, free me from my own weakness, for what is temptation, but our own weakness. We're tempted to overeat, and then we're unhappy after we have overeaten that we don't feel too good. Is that reason? Is that strength? Is that control of our mind? No, that is not strength. No, that is not control of our mind. But it is a beautiful living demonstration of our weakness.

As a child is weak until, through discipline, the child becomes strong. If discipline isn't made, which is the light of reason guiding the form—that's what discipline is. I'm not talking about this so-called discipline that people think is discipline that they take and half beat a child to death after he does not demonstrate what they tell him to do when they've made no effort with the light of reason to guide the form intelligently.

And so through the lack of self-discipline we are tempted. Through the lack of self-discipline, we are weak in certain areas. And so we leave the physical body and these forms in the mental and astral realms of consciousness, hungry, waiting to be fed—and they're fed by the divine Energy flowing through the form, like our own form. They tempt us. They appeal to our weakness. Now think about how important that is. We all can relate.

What happens with a person's weakness? What does weakness truly serve? What does weakness serve? Politicians, I think, are a wonderful demonstration. They look at the weakness of the masses. They feed the weakness and they get the vote. And so what is it the politician is truly after? Not all politicians, God forbid, but some politicians are [a] lovely demonstration and example. They look and see, "Ah, yes. They are weak in that area. I therefore may control them through that weakness that I see." And so the politician gains control by getting votes, and the weak masses, they follow the politician and he becomes their god, representing the goodness in their life. That's the purpose that weakness serves to those who have the need, of selfishness and greed, to control others.

Now try to understand [that] a person who makes the effort to control another is denying, *denying* their own divinity, which reveals the need to control themselves. And so the laws are so clear, so clean, and so just. For those who make the effort to control another shall be controlled by those who they are controlling. For the person, the politician or anyone else, who makes the effort to control, through the weakness of others, soon finds, someday, they are dependent upon those weak souls that they are controlling. For without those weak souls, they do not long remain in the position that they have gained through the weakness of others. And so the law returns, so just and so beautiful.

Now ofttimes, to relate more, perhaps, easily, we take a husband and a wife and the years pass on. And we see all of the effort. One studies the other. One sees, "Ah, that's their weakness there." The other one looks and says, "Ah! I see there's a weakness there." And so they start feeding each other's weakness. And then the day comes that a person gets a little stronger, starts to strengthen their weakness, and they take another look and they don't appreciate [it]. They start to see, "Why, she's controlling me! She's telling me what to do, when to do it, how to do it, and etc. And I don't like that." And the next thing you know, the divorce courts are filled, for there's an awakening that takes place. You see, we have a certain repulsive feeling to being controlled by anything or anyone. Something inside of us revolts to that because something inside of us knows that we are, in truth, free.

And so you have all of these problems with relationships and marriages and things as the motive for the association is not clear in our view. You see, an intelligent person says, "Let me see. I have a desire for this, that, that, [and] that in my life. I look and I see, yes, this person I now believe"—because that's what creation offers—"this person has the potential of filling these desires in my life." Now, intelligently, living in that realm of consciousness, the other person would say, "Now let me see, what do you have to offer?" And so they come to some harmonious accord.

Now if that is all covered up through this so-called emotion [of] conjugal love and all that foolishness, the day is simply guaranteed the battle shall rise and, "So long," I think it says, "It's been good to know you," shall take place. That's not intelligent. That isn't even reasonable. That's far from honesty.

A person can say, "Yes,"—now you remember, a person always says, "I believe I love you." Oh, yes, they start off [with]

"I believe," you see. Because they're telling the truth. First, they *believe* that they love this or that, then the next step is "I do," depending, of course, in keeping with the filling of their own desires.

It's a very simple thing. It's a very practical thing, if you look at it the way it is and not the way you want to believe that it is, but just the way that it is. That fine philosopher Emerson once said ofttimes we make an acquaintance which is useful. Now it's happening quite, quite often. Ofttimes there are marriages; moment by moment there are marriages; moment by moment there are involvements and relationships. So Emerson is absolutely correct. Ofttimes we make an acquaintance which is useful.

Now if we're honest and we say to the person, "Yes, I feel that an acquaintance with you would be useful to me. How do you feel?" That's honesty. Take away all of that smoke screen. Just be honest. Because, you see, honesty will lead you through anything, and it will lead you through everything, for honesty is the lamp of the light of reason—honesty with oneself. In a world that has spent so much of its time and energy in cover-up, so much of its time and energy interested and concerned with its image, honesty seems to be, at times, a rare commodity in our life. But honesty with who? And honesty with what? No, no, no. Don't start with honesty with someone else. Whatever you do, don't fall into that pit of hypocrisy, for the law reveals you cannot grant to another what we have not first granted unto our self. So let us not be hypocritical. Let us first start with being honest with our self.

Now to be honest with oneself, of course, being the lamp of the light of reason, is an instrument to free us. So we become aware of this phenomenal censorship. We want to tell someone exactly what we think about them, and this prejudice rises up, this censorship [and says,] "No! [I] can't say that!" Why? Because something else in our consciousness wants something out of them, you see? Ofttimes we make an acquaintance which is useful. So if we're honest, we [will] take a look and we'll see why we're constantly selling out. And then we're upset (after we sold out) that we didn't tell them exactly what we thought. But that's what's at stake.

We're censored. We don't tell them what we thought. We don't tell them how we feel. We're not honest about it because we've got something else at stake, and we are not ready to go on our way and do our thing. Yet if we were honest, we could tell the person, "This is the way I feel. This is the way I am. I have no intention of changing."

What happens with people, so often, [they say,] "Oh, yes, yes. Well, I'll do this and that." And they work very diligently to do what the other person wants and they suppress their own desires. And the most detrimental thing in our life—one of the most detrimental things is the suppression of desire, for it is guaranteed to rise again. I have always said, for many, many, many years, may God ever save me from the reformers, for the reformers do not educate their desire. They suppress their desire and that suppressed desire diligently goes to work to change everyone else. Because if it didn't do that, the person could not live with their own suppression. So the suppressed desire gets an opportunity to express itself by enforcing the change on everyone else. And may God forever save us from the reformers, be they religion or anything else.

However, through honesty we wouldn't have to go through this emotional upset and all of this disturbance and discord in our marriages and in our relationship[s], in our jobs that we work on, and etc. But that takes what I think most of you would call a little bit of guts. You see, to be honest, to be freed from the censorship of mental substance, one must free themselves from the dependence of mental substance. Therefore, one must make the effort to stop the belief that the thought that's in their mind is them, because that's not them. It's no more them than their automobile. But, as I say, some people really do believe that the automobile is them; it's just like their right foot. Something happens to it, [and because] it's just like their right foot, something has damaged their foot. Because of the over-identification with mental substance.

Now the mind, mental substance, is not a bad thing. It's not a good thing. It's just a thing. Let's face that. The mind is something that is designed to be used to serve the goodness that we are. When we forget what it is, it starts to believe that it is what we are, and it starts to tell our little soul what to do, when to do it, how to do it, and if we don't do it, it tells us "or else" and it lets us have it.

Now, for example, you have a desire. You've got to have it fulfilled. You go through that experience and you get all frustrated and it's not fulfilled yet. What happens within your consciousness? This form, this desire based upon past experiences, runs you all over the universe to fill it. And if you still don't get it filled, it tells you in your mind, "You either do that or else!" And the next step you have is a compulsion to do it. Then, after the compulsion, the very next step is an absolute possession. Either you fill that desire or you become a total nervous wreck.

Now tell me something, is that you? Why, of course, that's not you! No intelligent person would tell themselves, after the desire is filled, that that was them. In fact, they would say the experience never met the expectation at all. How could it possibly? There's no way you could put that much energy, which has been directed to frustration and running all over the universe to fill the desire, into one short moment. There's no way possible. It'd be like the nuclear bomb. You'd blow yourself up. No, no, no.

So let us think about these things for what they really are, not what we believe they are. Number one: they are not us. But they are things that we have created. We're responsible to them. We have the intelligence to say, "No, no. I choose not to do that.

If you bother me again, I'll let *you* have it. Don't tell me who's having what!"

You see, it's just like smoking or any habit. For years and years I've tried to teach my students and to demonstrate when you want something really bad, when it's just about causing you to have an epileptic attack, say, "No. Five minutes. And if you bother me in that five minutes, I'll give you another five minutes." That's when you start to gain control.

The Living Light Philosophy does not teach nor does it demonstrate that you must do without the goodness of life. If you in your evolution have decided, based upon your experience, that you enjoy a cup of coffee or that you enjoy a cigarette or that you enjoy these various things of creation, there's nothing wrong with that if you are awake, aware, and alert. Because you must face the truth that, "This feeling of goodness that I am experiencing, that's God. I have, however, limited this goodness or God to doing this particular thing." Now if you have the intelligent awakening of that truth, you'll have no problem. You decide. "All right. I wish to experience this goodness, this feeling, through this avenue of expression. However, my God, *my God* is not such a small God that that's the only way that he may enter my universe. Oh, no! I can do that if I choose or I don't have to because I will still experience the goodness, the God, that is my divine right, that is within me." Now if you look at all of these things that way, intelligently, then you're not going to be trapped, frustrated, dependent upon, and the victim of these forms of creation. Because, you see, then you may experience God in that way or that way or that way, but you will never be left without experiencing the goodness of life, the joy of living. For, you see, creation is everywhere. It is not limited—God is not limited to any particular avenue for you to experience the goodness of life.

It is when you permit your mind to tell you, "This is what I must have because this is how I feel good or know God"—because that's what you're really telling yourself. It's a sad thing because it's dependent upon another person. I haven't found any person that reliable yet. Perhaps when you need God the greatest, they tell you no. Then what do you do? No, that's, that's a sad, I think, that's a very sad way. That certainly isn't the joy of living, you see.

Now if you would sit down and you say, "I wish to experience God in this way. How about you?" She or he says, "No!" [Then you] say, "Well, fine. I am not so stupid or so childish that this goodness and this wonderful God, that is my divine right, relies upon your ego and what you want to do and what you don't what to do." That [reliance upon another] cannot be freedom for it is not truth. It is *not* truth. It is the direct opposite. It is a limiting of one's consciousness because of their dependence, through belief, that they are their form.

Now, each part of our vehicle, the toe, the nose, the ear, all parts of it, reveal to us our evolutionary journey. We have brown hair or blonde hair. We have blue eyes or brown eyes not by some accident, not by some choice. They tell us, moment by moment, through our own reflection, "These are the lessons that I have to learn," for they are mapped out representing the soul faculties and the sense functions. For we are balanced in this world of creation through our efforts of directing intelligent, infinite Energy to forty sense functions and forty soul faculties. That which we are, that Oneness, the Life Eternal, is what we call the eighty-first [level].

And so we stand in consciousness on the left hand of creation and the right hand of the Light. And as we, in our function, make effort to direct intelligent Energy to the corresponding soul faculty, we no longer experience dependence upon the forms of life. We use them. We benefit from them. We are in charge and control of them. They never again rise to tell us what to do. We, consciously, moment by moment tell them what to do. It's like the hand. Should the hand be permitted to tell us to scratch our head when we don't want to? Should it? Or is the hand designed as part of the vehicle to tell the hand [to] move to the right, move to the left? This is what's happening in our life. We are not telling this mental substance what to do, when to do it, and how to do it. Now when we move in our awakening to that step, which is our next step in our evolution, then we will tell the mental substance, "This is the form I choose to create. This is the day I choose to experience." For man, you, being a law unto yourself, that is your divine right to do.

And so you go out into creation. It does not matter who comes or goes. It does not matter what they say or they do not say, for you know, beyond a shadow of any doubt, the law: you have attracted that person to smile or you have attracted that person to frown, for the law does not fail us. And those who enter into our realm of consciousness can only enter in keeping with the law that we alone establish. And so in our life if there is someone that we find that is not in keeping with what we feel is beneficial to us, there is no problem. It is not necessary—it is contrary to the law—to tell them to go. For you change the law within your consciousness and it guarantees they shall go or they shall grow. That's what happens with all creation. In keeping with your effort to make the changes, your experiences, they evolve and grow or they go right out of your life. That's just the way that it truly is.

So the benefit of making the conscious effort to personally respond, that wonderful benefit of personal responsibility, is exactly the avenue through which you experience the truth that you are and the freedom and the joy of living that is your divinity. Everything else, the struggles, the upsets, are the effects of denials within your consciousness. And those are denials as an effect, an effect of your dependence. You see, when you depend on something that's limited—a thought, a person, or a form—when you depend on it, you limit, you limit. And by limiting, you are not free. And if you are not free, you are not in the fullness of truth. So as you depend on anything, you deny everything else. So it is through your dependence that you establish the Law of Denial, which in truth is the path of destiny. All of that is in our hands, to do with what we consciously, at any moment, choose to do.

Become aware of your dependence[s] for they reveal to you the limits of your life. For they are the denials of truth and, being the denials, become the destiny. Now a wise man—if you feel you must believe, at least choose something that won't limit your life. Believe in the sky, if you must, and watch the birds freely fly. But don't believe in something that will so narrow and limit your life that life no longer, for you, is worth living.

The next step of evolution beyond belief, of course, is the inevitable step when you no longer believe. You experience the great power of faith that you are. Then these weaknesses, they come and they go. You recognize them for what they are. You consciously choose to go down there. You tell yourself how long you're going to stay. You tell yourself when you're coming back. So you go down, and you serve the limit of these forms of your desire. You know exactly what you're doing. You have intelligently, consciously chosen to go down there. You have also consciously chosen to come back up. You can take a look and say, "Fine. Now I've done that. I feel good. Nothing guilty about that at all. I'm free from that until the next time. *I* will choose consciously when the next time shall be. I shall not have something in my consciousness, some prejudice that I have directed energy to and created in times past in the twilight zone, order me when to go down there." Now that's growing up.

The child knows that Christmas comes in December. But if he permits his little mind to so over-identify and attach to the presents of Christmas, the child will soon demand Christmas every week. If the child is not guided by the light of reason, known as discipline, Christmas soon shall become a weekly affair. With some children it would be a daily affair. For without guidance of the light of reason, known as discipline, you have the bondage of license. And license—the effect of license to the human mind is known as suffering.

And so when you have a desire and you cannot get it filled because your mind tells you due to circumstances beyond your control—what it's really telling you, the filling of the desire is dependent upon another person; you're no longer able to control them. Therefore, you must wait 'til they're ready, if they're ever ready. My goodness, friends, surely that is not the way to live. That is not freedom for it is not truth.

That does not mean, of course, that you should not be without desire. It does mean desire is the divine expression. Desire is the Divinity. It's what man does with it. Desire is formless and free. Man is receptive to this Divinity, the divine expression called God. But then what does man do with it? Man says it may be filled in this way by that person or that or that or that and he creates all of these obstructions and then becomes frustrated because of his own creations. That's a total denial of the Law of Personal Responsibility. Desire *is* the divine expression. What we do with it ofttimes is far from the Divinity. So far I don't feel that it's recognizable sometimes.

But that doesn't mean that we should not be without the goodness of life. For a person without desire is a person who is not moving in the stream of consciousness.

We do not teach the denial of desire, for to teach the denial of desire is to go contrary to the very law, to the Divinity, to the Law of Life. You see, when there is no desire, there is no suffering—the desire of limit, not the Divinity, the dictate of the human mind. We are receptive, moment by moment, to what is called the divine expression, known to us in our consciousness as desire. We, based upon our own prejudice, *we* limit God's expression! God does not limit it. We limit God's expression! We tell the Divinity, the divine expression, based upon our own experiences, our own limits, we tell that Divinity, "I will permit myself to experience the fullness of this Divinity, this divine expression, through this avenue, that avenue, that avenue, that avenue in that way, that way, that way, and that way. And no other way."

Now, in your world there is so much literature on these so-called sex problems and sex therapy. One time a person says they feel so good from experiencing the divine expression known as desire. The next time, it was terrible. And, of course, it's always someone else's fault. Our egos couldn't permit for us to tell us, "Something's wrong with me." Something has to be wrong with her or with him. Absolutely. And so we create all these problems.

But what is wrong? That's the question. Here we have this form, these prejudices that we've established in our consciousness, and the person fits into the prejudice rather nicely and we say, "Oh, that's a wonderful experience." Go back at another time. Not having control of our mind, we really don't know where we're at, you see. We really don't know. We think we know; we believe we know, but we don't know. The demonstration is the revelation. You go back again [and then say], "That was terrible! Where were you? That was just awful." Where were *we*? Because we don't know, we have no right to ask another person where they were because we really don't know where we were, you see?

What does that have to do with the joy of living? If you decide that you will experience the goodness of life through certain limits, through certain forms of creation, then it is only intelligent, intelligent that you say, "All right, I will experience it in this way." And you take control of those forms of your consciousness so they don't interfere with your effort, you see. But if you aren't aware of those forms, if the effort isn't made—first, you've got to be aware in order to control them. And so first the effort must be made to be aware of them and to be awake and to be alert. And then to tell them exactly, in your consciousness, what to do, you see.

You see, those forms control the movement of our hand. They control the movement and the flow of energy through our being when *we* are not controlling it. When we say, "Oh, I feel so sleepy," did you consciously decide that you would feel sleepy? No, you did not consciously decide that you would now feel sleepy. If you sit down and you say, "Now, I will feel sleepy," and you start to feel sleepy and you go to sleep and you make a decision, that's control of this vehicle, like your automobile. You get in your car. You tell the car. "I turn the key. I do this. I do that. It takes me where I want to go." Think of what you are doing with your body. What are you doing with your mind? Do you say, "I shall sit down now. I shall go to sleep for five minutes. Then I will completely rest and I will awaken feeling fully rejuvenated"? No, no, no. That takes control of your mind. That is what is the design of your being: that you take charge of all creation. You must first start with the creation that you are now inside of, you see. And when you start with that, you will truly experience the joy of living.

So when you go to eat, do you stop and say, "Now let me see, I will have that and that and that and that and that, and I will take this length of time to enjoy all of that"? No, we don't do that. Something else comes up and says [something else]. And we go through the whole table [and] we heap it up as much as possible. But what is in control? Do you see?

You see, if you are not in control of experiencing the divine expression, if you are not consciously in control—whenever you are not consciously in control of your mind, you must be guaranteed, for the law reveals itself, something else is doing it for you. Something else is controlling your mind when you are not consciously in control of it. What is that something else? Wouldn't you like to see it? Wouldn't you like to become aware of it? Because if you don't become aware of it, you can't do a thing about it. It orders you around. It tells you what to do. It tells you when to go to sleep. It tells you when to wake up. It tells you whether you got rest or you didn't get rest.

Now you go to bed at night and you wake up in the morning and you feel wonderful. You go to bed another night and you wake up in the morning and you just feel terrible. And you want to know why. And so all these forms of justification tell you why you feel terrible, see? Now those, those armies of justification, they're the defense, the first line of defense of your judgments, your prejudices. That's what they are. So they tell you any lie that they, having access to your mind, being mental entities, that they believe you will accept. So their job, this first line of the defenses, their job is to protect the judgments back here so you don't see them. Because if you see them, you'd make some changes. All right.

So you wake up and you say, "I feel terrible. Just awful." And the first line of defense comes up and talks in your mind and says because of such and such, such and such. And be rest assured it's always something outside. There's no personal responsibility: because of what something else, you know, and etc., and it's all out there. That's the first line of defense.

[The] second line—[it] starts to back off a little [and says], "So, well, you know, you did that and you really shouldn't have done that." That's the second line of defense. You get through that and then you face the judgments.

All right. You go to sleep, and because you don't control your mind, those forms, prejudices, judgments, they come up for their feeding. Now you have all kinds of judgments and they're not in harmony or accord with each other. It's like having 10,000 people at a feast, and they all rush to the table at the same time. They are not harmonious. They are not disciplined. They are not in accord. The only thing: they all want to eat. Now these mental forms created, rising up while you're sleeping—they do it in the daytime, too, but people aren't aware of it—but especially while you're sleeping, they rise up, shadows, skinny, hungry, starving to death, because you have not directed energy, through identification, to them for some time. So they're rushing to the table—you're the person, you're the table with all the food on it—to have all that they can get.

Now try to understand that a thought form, a judgment of the mind, is created to serve a purpose that you have chosen to serve at any particular moment. Now the problem with that is, they've been created since we entered the earth realm, you see. So you have these judgments of ten years ago. They've served their purpose, but they don't know that, for you never took conscious control of them. So they're back there in the shadowland, the twilight zone, the door opens up to the feast—for your conscious mind is now at rest—the door opens up to the feast—and the door opens up to the feast whenever you over-identify with self—and they all rush in to have their feeding.

Now some nights, while you're supposedly resting—sleep? I do not accept; it is not necessary. Rest is the path of wisdom. Man requires rest, not sleep. Sleep is a loss of control of the Light. Sleep is very dangerous. Rest is the wisdom of the ages. When a person learns the process of resting, they will not lose conscious awareness nor the Light. And they will not spend their nights feeding forms that are not beneficial, that don't even serve them anymore.

However, so they come in during your sleep and because they have—thousands of them—eaten so much—now look at it this way, you have a vital body. It represents the vitality of your body. That vital body is dependent upon the flow of an infinite, intelligent Energy, for you to be receptive to that, to enter your vital body. When these forms rush in to the feast—they were not created to be interested in your vitality. They have no interest or concern. Their only interest and their only concern is their purpose of design. *You* formed and created them to serve a purpose years ago, but they still are there for you have not cast the light of reason upon them. Therefore, they continue to feed. You do not consciously choose to rest. You find your eyes closing and off you go. But you did not make that conscious choice. Something else is making those choices for you.

Ofttimes a person will go off to sleep and then they suddenly awaken, and they're very embarrassed. They did not consciously choose to go to sleep. Something else chose to do that. And when they wake up and they're embarrassed why they went to sleep, the first line of defense of justification says, "This is why you went to sleep: it was too warm. It was too boring. It was this. I didn't rest last night." That's all justification. That's all falsehood. That's the very opposite of truth.

Now remember, friends, the one thing about truth: truth at our convenience is not truth. For when we decide that truth shall be at our convenience, we are saying, "Truth," for us, "is dependent upon what the forms of my mind tell me when they shall receive it." And so those forms of our mind put us to sleep. They wake us up. We feel exhausted some mornings because the forms rushed in and they gobbled up all the feast, all the energy available and then they still weren't satisfied and they went and took energy required by our vital body for our good health. They even took that! And we woke up feeling terrible, exhausted, and tired. That's what happens.

Now whoever makes the effort to take control and charge of all creation in keeping with the law of this planet, and in keeping with the law of all planets and all universes, shall experience their true home at any moment of their choice.

I'm going to give to you, before our little seminar here closes today, a little saying that was brought through. And if you will relate it to your space in consciousness, it will certainly—you can benefit by it. Pause, for a moment, and tell yourself that wonderful truth:

> You are in a controlled spiritual environment of
> truth and freedom
> Where peace and harmony reign supreme.
> Be awake, be aware, be alert.
> Your purpose of being is freedom from what has been.
> Thoughts of self are foreign to this environment.
> Take control of your mind and experience the joy
> of living.

When you declare that demonstrable truth, when you flood your consciousness with that light, the shadows cannot control you. You see, try to understand a shadow is the effect of an obstruction to the Light. Without an obstruction to the Light, a shadow does not exist.

And so these shadows, which are the effects of created forms, known as judgment, which are now prejudgments or prejudices from past experiences, they are obstructions to your light. They dare to tempt you to feed that which has no interest in the fullness and the wholeness of your life.

And so the prophets have taught us "Judge not, that ye be not judged," for each time you permit yourself to direct intelligent Energy to the twilight zone, where the shadows live in consciousness, each time a judgment rises, you are judged by it. "Judge not, that ye be not judged" is something that is taking place within our consciousness. The moment we judge, that which we judge judges us and feeds off of us.

The shadow world is self-consuming. It steals like a thief in the night, because it is a thief in the night. We enter the night when we do not consciously—are not consciously aware. When we are not consciously aware, we are in the night. We are in the darkness and that's when they come to steal our goodness and our light.

You see, all things are the effect of energy, whether it's a glass or the flower, the human or the plant. The ant or the angel is an effect of intelligent, infinite Energy. Only an effect. The form is an effect. For we *are* formless and free, the goodness of life. Everything else is an effect. Now we have, flowing through us, an abundance of this infinite, intelligent Energy in keeping with what obstructions are in the way. You see, [when] we pause and we're still in our consciousness, then we are receptive to the fullness of this infinite, intelligent Energy. [When] we permit activity of our mind, an obstruction moves between us and this infinite, intelligent Energy that we are making the effort to be receptive to. And so man has his money problems; he has his sex problems; he has his ego problems because all of these obstructions, you see, he's permitting to get in the way. And that's where all the problem is.

A person says, "I'm short. I don't have enough money." We know that's a judgment. That judgment is based upon experience, as all judgments are based upon experiences. Now he has a choice to make. He may continue to direct intelligent Energy to the obstruction, so the shadowland can feed off of his, off this energy, or he can say to the obstruction, "Get thee behind me." Because the obstruction only exists in belief. That's the cohesion of the form: belief.

Now man, standing, looking at the Light, these obstructions [are] in the way—and money, like everything else, being an effect of directed energy, that energy coming to him, he wants to put God in it, and God can't get in it because he's in it, all those shadows. He's got to take control of his mind. Set those shadows over there and know, beyond a shadow of any doubt, *beyond* doubt, he steps on the path of faith: God, the goodness of life, never fails. Now he may or may not experience instantaneously that goodness because he may or may not be able, in his evolution, to move *all* the obstructions out of the way, to move *all* the judgments out of the way.

Our teaching is, and has always been, put God in it or forget it, for we get out of a thing in life whatever we put into the thing. So if you don't want to put good or God in it, don't even get involved. Now if you get involved and you say, "Oh, this is so good," you're putting good in; so you get good out. The instant you no longer get any good back out, you must understand and accept the Law of Personal Responsibility: somehow you stopped putting any good in. And [when] you stop putting any good in, you're putting in something else: the opposite of it.

So whatever your days are, whatever your experiences are, remember, the good you put in is the good you get back. And if something else is what you're getting back, pause and take control of your mind because something else that you don't like, you see, has been putting something else in there. You do that, you're going to have an entirely different life, in keeping with your right to the experiencing of the goodness of life.

You see, so many people, you know, they do so many things. And then they feel, they feel guilty. They feel guilty about this. It's a terrible disease of the soul, for it is based upon an educated conscience—has absolutely nothing to do with the spiritual conscience, but it has a lot to do with an educated conscience. So a person walks around filled with the weight and the baggage of guilt complexes, they call them. You feel guilty about this, guilty about that. All these rejected desires. You walk away from a person and you feel a little guilty that you didn't say what you really wanted to say. You are experiencing the rejection of your own desire. When you reject desire, try to understand, you are denying the right of the Divinity to its expression. This philosophy doesn't teach the blatant license of desire; that's the pure insanity of mental substance. When you reject desire, you deny the Divinity its right of expression.

The problem is we have risen greater than God. *We* have decided how God shall express in whatever limited ways that the errors of our mental substance may dictate at any given moment. So our teaching is you do not reject or suppress desire, for you're going against God, you're going against the goodness of life, you're going against the very Divinity itself. You broaden your horizon. You don't permit your limited mind to order you that this is and that is the only way you, your mind—which isn't even you—will allow you to experience the goodness of life. Now there's a vast difference between that intelligent way and blatant license that has its own very high cost.

I want to speak on a few other things that are so important, especially on what is known to man as divine grace. We hear a lot about divine grace. We hear a lot about our prayers to God, to his ministering angels, to the saints, and all of these things to pray for divine grace. Now it would, of course, seem to many of us that anyone in any dimension that can intercede on our behalf, how could we then accept an impartial, divine, neutral God? if that was what was really happening.

But then again, if we look at it a little bit more intelligently, we see that in keeping with a person's faith do they have various results and effects of their prayers to those that they believe are in a position to intercede with the Divinity for the greater goodness in their life. Now let us go a little step further. Man believes many things. Some men believe in the goodness or good luck of a rabbit's foot, and they would swear on a stack of Bibles what goodness came into their life. There is no question or the possibility that goodness came into their life ever in keeping with their own belief. For the belief is the cohesion of the judgments of which they are identified [with] and, therefore, depend upon. Well, [we'll] go beyond all that foolishness.

And let's get to this divine grace. How does that law work? We are the instruments through which intelligent Energy, known as God, is directed to a world of creation. We are those instruments. That is why we are in charge and, therefore, in control of all creation. That is the Law of Evolution and what we have merited and earned.

Now we go to work and we believe that we're working for God, trying to do what is right. Therefore, surely God has some reward for us. Well, I have always felt, and I continue to feel, that working so hard to do what is right and hoping for that reward of goodness—it takes too long. That's not in keeping with any law that I've ever been able to perceive. The goodness of life is an effect of what we do and is not dependent upon twenty centuries from now from some partial God that will finally hand it out to us. Of course, in keeping with our various beliefs shall that be and, certainly, is in many realms of consciousness.

When we take control of our mind, energy flowing through that mental being, being under control of the light of reason, is uncontaminated. It is not siphoned off or censored by mental substance. It goes out into the universe. That's when you put God in it. You don't have to say "Oh, God, God, God." God is in it, for you are out of it. This limit is out. The mental substance is out. You become an unobstructed vehicle through which this divine, intelligent Energy flows out into the universe. Being that unobstructed vehicle through which it flows, it goes out into the universe. And, like the great circle, all things return unto their source. And so it returns unto you. Now how does this work? Say that only 20 percent of mental substance was out of the way. Only 20 percent was out of the way. The other 80 percent went to mental substance. Well, 20 percent of that energy flowing through you, as you are working, now goes into what you understand, later, the effect of, as divine grace.

You've got yourself in a real problem [and] you need some help from somewhere. So you have to draw that back into your universe. Well, you can relate best to the banks that you have in your world. You go to the bank and you make a deposit. And you go, frequently, and you make your little deposits. And someday there's a little amount there for you to draw on in your time of need. Through the transgressions of natural law, we always experience something called need.

Now you go to that bank and you need to withdraw $20,000, but you find out you've only got $3,000. So you're $17,000 short. But the disaster that you have stepped into is going to cost you $20,000. You [have] got to get $17,000 from somewhere. Now stop and think. Every moment of every day energy flowing through you is going into a mental bank account or a spiritual bank account. Now if it's going into a spiritual bank account, in your times of mental disasters you can draw from that spiritual bank account and experience what is known as divine grace.

Now some people, they pray to the saints and the various angels for divine grace. And they take a look in that bank account and they say, "They need $20,000. There's only $3,000 there. They're $17,000 short." And so a person, their faith strengthens or it weakens in keeping with what they believe that the saints have brought them through that particular situation. Well, you can't blame the saints. You can't blame the angels. They go to the bank, the spiritual bank, and see how much deposit you have. Well, are they supposed to take it out of their pockets? No, they're not even in a realm like that. That's what we're down here for.

Now what happens is simple. So a person prays to God and the angels and the saints. Nothing happens in this terrible disaster they're in or not enough happens. So they go to their mother or father [and] to their friends for them to pray, too. And it's very wise. Very wise, if they're sincere, because now, maybe, they have fifteen or twenty people praying over their situation. So then, in keeping with the law, they go to fifteen or twenty bank accounts in these spiritual realms of consciousness, you know. They're not up there or down there. They're just right there. And they all withdraw. Now they have $20,000 to bail the poor soul out from his transgression of natural law, and he doesn't have this disastrous experience.

So, you see, so much of this, you know, that some people think is superstition, there's truth there. There are those who know about those things. And that's what happens when you put God in it or forget it. You are making deposits in bank accounts [and] in your time of need—for no one is perfect in an old mental world of creation—that can be withdrawn to help you through that.

Now if you have a friend and you go to them for help, because the truth of the matter is you don't have enough on deposit, and if they're willing to help you, what really takes place [is] they start withdrawing from their bank account to add to what you have withdrawn. And if there's enough, you say "My God, I had divine grace. Here I had this horrible accident and I didn't get killed." Yes, you had divine grace; you had enough on deposit.

Now the thing is, you don't have to go to a church, you don't have to be religious, to make deposits in the divine bank and experience its return [as] divine grace. All you have to do is to be a good person and not be thinking of yourself when you're working all the time. I mean, after all, you could be out selling newspapers and making spiritual deposits in the bank account that you may have when you have a time of need and divine grace. Many people are doing it. They never even heard of a church, let alone a religion. It's not dependent upon those things. It is the goodness within you [that] is not obstructed by over self-identification; so in your great time of need, there's something there and there's enough on deposit. And a wise man makes sure he has enough on deposit by doing something about it every day, at least once a day, because you never know when you're going to need to be bailed out.

You see, we get our self busted so many times by going against these laws here in creation, you see, and we do that because we're not controlling our mind. We find our self sleeping, [but] we don't want to be sleeping and then we open our eyes and we think we've been hypnotized. But who hypnotized us? Nothing outside hypnotized us. Certainly not the birds. Not the trees or the flowers or this beautiful day. What is it that is controlling our mind? Who is it that's controlling our mind? That's the question that we must ask our self, "Just who is in charge of me? I don't appreciate my experience. I've got to wake up and find out who is in charge of me."

Now we have just about nine minutes left here, if anyone has any question on today's seminar. You just raise your hands and I'll get to as many as I possibly can. Yes, certainly.

*How does the grace of Jesus Christ apply to the law of grace you were talking about?*

Yes. Well, in keeping with—now you understand, you're speaking in reference to Jesus?

*Right.*

Yes. Jesus of Nazareth. Well, now in reference to that, you see, you have millions of people who believe—think of this now—who believe that he wiped away the sins of mankind, including their own. All right?

*Yes.*

Now what does that do to a person's mind? If they believe in that, then they feel clean and free from sin, because, through their belief in what he did, they are now free from sin. You understand? Sin is nothing more [than] error; transgression of natural law, that's what sin is. All right. Now if a person in their belief that Jesus of Nazareth cleansed the sins of man—took them on his own shoulders—and they go around and do their thing and transgress the law and sin that much more, be rest assured, their price is very great.

Now all souls come into your Earth realm planet in keeping with laws established in the great evolution through the many planets of the universes. The teachings of the Nazarene clearly demonstrate that he taught if man would follow his example, he would be cleansed of the error and the transgression of natural law. The interpretation of those simple and beautiful teachings is ever in keeping with man's own greed and selfishness. For anyone to deny personal responsibility—that someone else is paying the price of all of their transgressions—is certainly contrary to demonstrable, natural law, would you not say?

*Yes.*

Absolutely contrary! Now, as I explained in reference to divine grace, if you have a friend that has a bank account and you don't have enough and they're willing to make a withdrawal, then you can get through some of those transgressions, you see? But we must never forget that whatever happens to us in life is created by us and that we are freed in any moment that we truly choose to be free.

We do not have a living hell or purgatory to look forward to, unless that is the law that we have established. If that's the law that we have established, heaven is the moment in which we are aware. For example, heaven is not a place we're going to. It is a state of consciousness that we are growing to in this very instant. So by control of your mind, you may experience the goodness of life, that heaven that is yours. It is ever available to you because you are the angel and you are not what you believe you are. Because in truth you are the angel, heaven, your home, waits for you at the moment of your choice. It's not dependent on anything outside of you. Never was and never can be for it's totally contrary to the natural law. Does that help with your question?

*Thank you.*

You're welcome. *[After a short pause, the teacher continues.]* Six minutes left for the sleepy heads. Yes, the lady here, please.

*What about—I understand that the Bible says Jesus had the only perfect blood of, of God or Christ and that's what Christians tend to use as a—not taking responsibility.*

Well, if—

*What's the truth of that?*

Well, if I believed that I was a part of anything that had the only perfect blood of goodness, it would, I would say, certainly be instrumental in puffivating my mind 'til I believed that I was God himself. You see, this is all dependent upon belief. If you want to believe that, of course, that is your right. But what does the law reveal? Are we to deny, through our prejudice, all the rights of the Buddhists and their wonderful work in life? Are we to deny the rights and the goodness and the love and the salvation, if you want to think of salvation, of all the Muslims in the world? Are we to deny all of their goodness? You see, that's totally contrary, my dear, to intelligent, reasonable thinking.

When we permit the Christians their space in the universe and we permit the Buddhists their space and we permit the Zoroastrians their space and we permit the Muslims their space, when we permit all of these people their space in the universe to find goodness in their way, then, truly, goodness shall be and heaven shall enter earth. Does that help with your question?

*Thank you.*

You're welcome.

*Could you explain the purpose of the crucifixion in relation to all this?*

Yes, certainly. Absolutely. Man believes in the weight of his own responsibility. Man is often times sitting, contemplating the great weight of his responsibility. The cross is representative of the struggle or weight of responsibility. And it is sad when we permit the weight of responsibility to exceed our love of God, for then we no longer see the goodness of life for we are blinded by the obstructions. The cross is representative of suffering and pain.

Now on the positive side of that, through suffering and pain man finally makes intelligent choices. Ofttimes man puts him[self] through a great torture and a great suffering and great pain, and he finally makes an intelligent choice in his consciousness [to] no longer to identify [with] that which was the instrument—which was the vehicle instrumental, rather, in his suffering. For example, if you are associated with a person and the only experiences you finally get to have are suffering and pain, don't you finally make an intelligent choice? You're going or they're going? Is that not true?

*Aye.*

And so it is with the cross, the weight of responsibility. And so what it is revealing to us is that through this great weight of responsibility, through our over-identification of it, do we suffer and do we struggle. We don't have to. We don't have to. We do not have to enter the goodness of life through the pain of hell. That is, we enter that way—that's the only way our minds permit us to enter heaven.

You see, we have to give in order to receive. Our cup overfloweth. Now, for example, you want to experience the heavenly state of consciousness which is your divine right, that means you must control the hissing hounds of hell. All those shadows, all those past experiences, all those things you believe you are, they all have to go. You give them all up and you'll enter heaven. You see, when you give up everything, everything good is added unto you. But first you must give it up. Some people give up 5 percent or 10 percent; and so they get 5 percent or 10 percent of the goodness. But if you give up 100 percent, you will have 100 percent of goodness flood into your consciousness. That's the law. It does not fail.

But when man identifies with mental substance, mental substance, those forms, those shadows of the past, no, no, no, they won't let go. Because, you see, for them to let go means their annihilation. There's no energy directed to them anymore. So when you go to make a change, when you go to give up anything of your mind, you must pay the price. That's the cross to bear. That's the suffering. Your identification with them is the cross you carry to Calvary's heights.

Thank you. Our time is up. Thank you very much.

JUNE 3, 1984

## A/V Seminar 2

Welcome to this special seminar on Sunday morning, June 2, 1985, a seminar of the Living Light Philosophy on our inevitable journey.

As we face the inevitable, ofttimes we find ourselves depressed. *[At this point, there is a dropout of several seconds on the master recording and some of the teachings are lost.]* . . . for their day the way that they had hoped that they would. Ofttimes they think that something they desire would have worked out had it not been for some obstruction caused by so-called circumstances or conditions, specifically because of what someone else did or did not do in response to their efforts. And so we, in those experiences, have an indicator of what our life—how we have made it and what it is for us.

And how does this experience, that we encounter nightly, affect what life is going to be for us when we leave this physical world? Many philosophies and many people over the centuries have expressed a light that is experienced by those who pass from this physical world. And that is true. All people, regardless of religious backgrounds or convictions, including the agnostic and the atheist, experience a living Light as they leave their physical body at the moment of transition. This living, glowing Light is not dependent upon the substance of the mind. It is not dependent upon belief or conviction. It is the experience that one registers within their consciousness when the actual spirit, that which we are, leaves the physical substance. Therefore, all people who have reported the so-called experience of death and returned, all agree in their explanation of experiencing a living Light.

However, that experience is of very short duration. The light that one must learn to follow is the light of their soul, which, when leaving this physical body and in keeping with the divine laws of nature, all souls have attracted unto them, in keeping with their own evolution, so-called angels, guides, or teachers who meet us at the moment of our leaving this physical world. The great difficulty in the passing is not the efforts of God's angels, who have [been] given charge (to them) over our passing. That is not the difficulty. The difficulty is the battle between the gentle guidance of the angels that we follow the Light to the Halls of Repose, to the schools of awakening in the so-called spirit world: that gentle whisper from the angels must be faced by the individual and the loud cries and calls of the worlds of temptation.

For example, here in this physical world when we, in our efforts to awaken and to grow, we find that we are ofttimes distracted from our efforts and endeavors. We are distracted by thoughts that we believe are ours to do something other than what we have decided to do. We make a choice in our life to attain a certain goal. And time passes, and we find that we have yet to attain that goal. And in our awakening that we have yet to attain the goal that we decided to attain, we begin to become discouraged. We begin to lose faith in the fulfillment of our goal. And in that mental attitude of discouragement we begin to experience what is known to our mind as hopelessness. We begin to judge that it is not going to happen for us, and then we support the judgment that we make that because of others, something beyond our control, we are not going to attain our goal. What happens to us in those times is that we, instead of remaining the captain of our ship, to guide it to the destination we have chosen, we give control of our ship, of our life, to someone else. When we do that, someone else we are serving. We are no longer serving the goal, the purpose that we originally have chosen.

And so we find in passing from this world, because of habit patterns of judging that our lives are ever dependent upon what someone else is doing and what someone else is not doing, we enter the next world with that firm, established pattern of our mind. And so at that time of passing, as the angels that have been sent to guide us to the Halls of Repose, to the schools of awakening, we are tempted by the voices that we have created, by the distractions. And in that temptation if we have established a pattern of mind that is dependent upon voices outside of our own, upon people who we depend upon, then we go with those forms to the realms where we believe we can get what we desire for little or no effort.

And so in some religions it's known as the realms of purgatory, and in other religions it's known as the realms of hell itself. At that time of passing, if we will consciously make the effort to remember that heaven and all the things that we desire are not dependent upon anything outside of our self, that they are not dependent on someone's promise, they are not dependent on anything that we do not have, by divine right, the power to control within our self, then we shall follow the light of the angels into the Halls of Repose. We shall then be awakened. We shall then move on to the schools of learning, and there, ever in keeping with our own efforts, ever in keeping with our own evolution, we shall face the tests, the lessons we have to face.

This philosophy has always taught God, or goodness, is not a judge. That's not where judgment is. Judgment exists only in a mental world and can only govern a mental body, which, in turn, a physical body is the victim thereof. And so we have this mental body here and now. We do not lose this mental body when we leave the physical body. The physical body loses its sustenance. The physical body loses the mental body.

Now should we, intelligently, make the effort to follow the guidance of the angels who have charge over us and not be distracted by the temptations of a mental world, then we enter these Halls of Repose and we awaken. And there in the schools of learning we face all of the judgments that we have made in our life on earth. There the list is presented to us, not by a God who judges us that we've been good or bad. No, that is not what judges us. The mental educated conscience is our judge.

He exists inside of us. He knows why we have done whatever we have done. Those are the lessons that we face. And there we live. We leave this spiritual school, and we're sent out to the mental worlds to pay the debt that our educated conscience, which is king of a mental world, dictates we must pay. For each judgment that we make is a denial of the right of a part of the whole. For there is one God. There is one good. And whatever denies its right of existence must pay the price of its own denial. For whoever rises to judge the rights of another has in truth denied the rights of themselves.

And so that is the opportunity that we have as we enter those schools of learning: to be sent from the school, for a time, that we may face step by step, judgment by judgment, our denials of the Principle of Good, known as God. That is the path of wisdom: to enter the schools of learning; to be still in consciousness that you may hear the soft voice of the guardian angels that no one, no matter who they are, is ever without.

Should we not choose the path of wisdom, should we not make that effort, whatever patterns of mind, whatever temptations that we believe that we are, whatever judgments, the effects of which are needs, for they are denials, whatever needs we believe we have, then we shall go with those mental realms in an astral body to an earth-bound world, known as the earth-bound spirits. We will not have a school to which we may return after we have made the effort to pass certain tests or judgments in our life. No. We will go into that astral-mental, earth-bound realm known to many as purgatory, to others as hell, there to serve out for whatever length of time, whatever duration that we demand by our own belief that we are the needs, by our own belief that we are the judgments, there, without the guidance of the angels—for angels, which are the expression of [the] Principle of Abundant Good, are not permitted to enter the domain that is ruled by the king of creation.

This so-called devil, this so-called henchman, known as Lucifer, denied the Principle of Good, for he experienced, sitting at the right hand of the Principle of Good, called God, he experienced in his consciousness, from his own weakness, a judgment. And he looked at God and judged that God had more power than him. He looked at the Principle of Good and judged that he was dependent upon it, and he wanted to control what he judged he was dependent upon. And from that judgment he experienced ever-increasing need, for he denied what he was and believed what he was not. He denied what he was for he sat at the right hand of good or God. And being at the right hand of good or God, he was a part of good or God. This fallen angel, known as Lucifer, denied what he was and, by that denial, experienced need to be. And from the ever-increasing need for what he had denied, in truth, he tempted himself to be something he could not be. For he tempted himself to be God after denying his own godhood. So whoever denies the Principle of Good that they truly are by believing that which they are not must pay the price of that denial, and it is a great price for anyone to pay.

Here in this physical world we rarely consider the cost, for we are overly tempted. And being overly tempted, we are filled with burning desire for the things, the goodness in life, that we have denied ourselves. And because we fill our consciousness with burning desire, we enter the realms controlled by the fallen angel, known as Lucifer. And those realms are the realms of lust. They can never be filled. One cannot fill a cup that overfloweth. And so the realms of lust are the exclusive domain of the king of creation, and in our world down here we often say there's never enough. There's never enough of what we desire. For we do not say it, we frequently demonstrate it. And the reason that there is never enough is because our cup overfloweth with abundant good. Our denial of what is, is the experience of the lust of what is not.

And so a wise man prepares himself not tomorrow, [but] today. A wise man knows that eternity is the moment of his own awareness. And so we prepare our self in the moment, each and every moment. And then we will not have to continue to experience this great search for what we believe we need, the effect of denying what we have.

We look in our lives by comparison, and because we look at our lives through the view of comparison, there's never enough for someone always has more. When we stop looking at our life through the eyes of comparison, which are in truth the effect of judgment, which is in truth the effect of denial, when we stop looking at our lives through denial, we will begin to experience that we have all of the good that is necessary for us. But when we look through the eyes of denial and experience judgment, which guarantees comparison by looking outside instead of in, then we will never have enough. There will always be, to judgment, something better. And there will always be someone else who has it in order to support within our consciousness that which we know as need.

That is the exclusive domain of the prince of darkness. That is his domain. He earned that domain by his own choice eons and eons ago. And so whoever chooses, through error of ignorance, to serve the realms that are the justful, right, and domain of the prince of darkness must pay the price that he extracts. And the price is far greater than whatever you get in return. It has to be in order to support the original judgment, the effects, the final effects of which are known as need.

In preparing for the eternal, inevitable journey, preparation does not wait within our consciousness to the day that we judge it's going to happen, for that is the day when it is truly late. For in those days we are filled with what we know as fear. We are fearful of what we are not convinced about. We are fearful of that which we are not sure about. We do not fear what we know, and through knowing, judge that we control. We only fear what we judge we cannot control. And so in those latter days in our time of passing from this world we fear all the things we judge we cannot control. And so in our own ignorance, in our own understanding we judge we cannot control God. Therefore, in those times we fear God. We judge we cannot control that which is not known to us. Therefore, we fear what we judge is death. And fear, we know, in the Living Light Philosophy, is the absolute and total control of the mind over the soul, the spirit that you are.

And it is fear that tempts us. Fear tempts us as we pass from this world as surely as it tempts us in our daily experiences in this physical world. We are tempted to our weaknesses for we fear being without them. We fear what life could possibly be like if we change and do not serve our weaknesses called our temptations. We fear it because it is unknown what our life will be like, and because it is unknown we judge we cannot control it. Therefore, we make it difficult to evolve. We make it difficult to change. We find security in that with which we are familiar. We only find emotional security in what we are familiar [with] because we judge that with which we are familiar we can and do control.

My good friends, whatever in life you believe you control be rest assured, in truth, you are controlled by it. How many experiences must we all have to understand that whatever we believe we are controlling is in truth controlling us? Now stop and think how that applies in your daily life. We teach "Control your mind." It is a vehicle of your soul. How do you control it when in truth it controls you? No one will disagree with the demonstrable truth that we, as beings on an Earth planet, follow the orders and the dictates of the thoughts of our mind dutifully and religiously. It is rare when a thought and a desire in our mind demands its fulfillment that we do not serve it and usually serve it very well. We do that only because we believe that we are that thought. We believe we are that desire.

And because we truly believe it, an effect of denying God, the goodness that we are, because we believe the desire and the thought, because it offers to us fulfillment, we *think*, because we believe it. The demonstration in our lives is it does just the opposite. It is a temptation because there's never enough of it. That which is a temptation and that which is in truth fulfillment—fulfillment is exactly what it says: it fills. And that which fills does not tempt for that which is filled is freed from desire. The only thing, if you may call it a thing, that is capable of fulfilling our lives is that which we truly are, never that which we seek to be. For seeking is looking out for something that we judge we lack. And we have our days filled with the judgments of what we lack and rarely filled with the gratitude for what is filled. So this reveals to us that in our efforts to control our mind, the just, divine vehicle of our soul and our spirit, we are controlled by it. And then, from the lack of any effort to control our mind, we are totally, completely controlled by it.

So what does man do, when, as someone once said, it's indeed hell if you do and it's also hell if you don't? What do you do with the world of creation that you are not and will never be? What do you do when, in your efforts in life, it all seems to turn, in the final analysis, to the opposite of what you had hoped it would be? That, my friends, is the experience we all encounter when we insist on depending on the judgment that tells us we are the form, and being it, it is king. For that is the price that we must pay.

Now when you awaken in the morning, you experience the effects, the effects of a nighttime of suppressed desires. Some people awaken in the morning, they feel very good. Some people do not desire to awaken at all, and when finally forced by their own judgments to awaken they do not feel well at all. What takes place during your sleep is revealing what will take place in your passing from this world, for it is revealing the patterns of mind that you believe that you are.

The Living Light clearly teaches educate all desires in your life, for the principle of desire is the expression of the Divine. The divine expression is known as desire. The divine will or the will of God, the Principle of Good, is known as the totality of acceptance. So for man to be tempted to suppress desire, man is bucking the very principle of the expression of God. Therefore, a wise man does not suppress desire. A wise man fulfills his desires or educates them.

Now we all know people in the world who have yet to learn to educate their desires, and we see where they finally end up in an earth realm. So we have no problem in accepting the wisdom of educating the desires that you, by your own law, cannot fulfill. For the alternative, known as suppression of the divine expression of God, is destruction of what is known as the self.

And so we find people awaken in the morning and we find their efforts continuing on as they are awakening to suppress the desires that have risen from the depths of the deep of their own subconscious mind. For whoever suppresses a desire directs energy to the desire and locks it in a cellblock in the depths of one's own consciousness. It does not remain there forever, for it is a child that we alone have created. The child shall escape and demand, beyond a shadow of any doubt it shall demand its right to be fed. That's known as expression of it. And yet we continue to suppress the desires.

We do not make the effort to speak to them for we are the mothers and fathers of them. We do not talk to them as entities that we alone have created, for any thought in our mind that is, has ever been, or yet to be is a form created by mental substance of which we are the fathers and mothers of. And because we are the creators of those forms we are responsible for those forms. We are their father and their mother. They know who is their creator. To them, we are god. They are dependent upon us for their sustenance as we, as beings, are dependent on a greater God.

We are gods of creation. Infinite Intelligence is God of all. We create. God, Truth, does not create. For what is there for Truth to create when Truth is? Truth, being Truth, does not desire to limit itself, to contain itself. No. Only limit desires to create, to contain. Therefore, we are gods of creation. We are creating each moment and our families are indeed very, very, very large.

The time has come for those of you who have come by the laws of evolution into this school to receive, yea, even more Light and truth. What you do with that is your choice and your right. Whoever by the laws of evolution has earned a greater awakening of Light in their consciousness bears a greater responsibility unto themselves. The bearing of that responsibility is a cross and a burden ever in keeping with your efforts to turn to the Principle of Good within your own consciousness.

And so we do not, our minds, know the moment that we shall—what our minds say—die. For, you see, we die each moment. We die to one thought only to give birth to another. And it is this process of birth or death in creation that we believe that we are that is the true and only cause of our suffering and our struggle. We believe we are the children we have created. We no longer separate truth from creation.

The child was born, an unfulfilled desire, when we were ten. We made no effort to fulfill—to feed the child properly, to care for them. We made no effort to educate him. And so we have these mountains of children that we carry with us each moment of our day and our night.

Now these children, mental creations, exist in a mental world. We experience the effects of their needs and their hunger and their thirst, whenever we, through lack of effort, enter a mental world. We enter a mental world through the denial of God by believing in the thought of I. We separate, then, ourselves from what we are and start on the path of believing what we are not. That's known as the thought of self, separation from truth, the total separation, the denial of God, service to the prince of darkness. And in keeping with that error of ignorance we enter those mental realms and there experience the frustrations, the hunger, the starvation of the children that we have created, which are the forms, the limits of a suppressed desire in our lives. They're ours and they know us very well. They have, in their forms, all of the intelligence that's available to our form. We are their father.

And so each time we enter thoughts of self, we enter that realm and they all wait for us. And some of them we haven't fed for a long time. And they cry and they scream and they battle and they fight. Demanding our attention, for that's how they're fed energy. The law reveals that energy follows attention. And as those hungry, starving children we have created scream and do their various little games, they receive our attention or energy. And when they have received enough to fill themselves, they leave our little realm for a time and go do their thing.

So we find in our lives what we call frustration. We experience frustration, unfulfilled desire. We look out and we insist that someone has done it to us. Now that is partially true. Someone has done it to us. Indeed, indeed they have. They're known as our children. We have entered the thought of self, the thought of I, we have entered the mental realm of our own consciousness and there we face all of those forms that we have created. Yes, indeed, they are doing it to us. They are doing it to us in keeping with a just law.

We have created them. How, then, shall we be freed from them? That is the purgatory. That is the realm of purification. For it inspires us, sooner or later, to leave that realm, to have no need nor desire for anything it has to offer us. That's when we pause in consciousness. That's when we stop playing the game of thinking of what we call self. That's when we stop believing that we are separate; and in being separate, we are special; and in being special, we therefore are perfect. When that moment of saturation of our consciousness arrives, we hear ourselves saying, "I have had enough." That's when we choose to go to a better world, a fine world, a world where peace and harmony reign supreme. For that is when we awaken to the truth that dissension is a disease, the true and only cause of disaster. That's when we no longer experience need, want, and desire for we have entered the realms of the divine expression. We cannot desire, for we already are the fulfillment of it. One cannot desire what they already are and are awakened to. One cannot search for goodness when they finally awaken that that's what they are. One cannot hope for something better when they no longer experience denial of God, judgment and, therefore, comparison. When the eye is single, the soul is in heaven. And so when you are able to see one and are no longer distracted by two, you will know you indeed have arrived.

You see, it is belief that is dual. It is belief that's two-sided. It is belief that experiences want. It is belief that experiences need, for it takes two eyes to look at a world of creation. It takes two eyes to experience delusion, deception, and illusion. And when your eye is single, you no longer feel greater than God. For when your eye is single, there's nothing in life to compare.

And so upon this awakening each morning and we feel so-called good or so-called bad. We feel frustrated. We feel irritated. We want to awaken or we don't want to awaken. That is ever dependent on what we have done with our family while we thought we were sleeping. Did we discipline our children that have come to demand their rightful meal? Did we make that effort? If we did not, they're going to have their meal even if they must steal it from us, for they correctly judge, being creatures of judgments of our own mind, they correctly judge that we owe it to them. And because in truth we do, they are going to receive it. If they don't get their way from their pleading and their cry, they will get their way from whatever device their little minds can and do create.

And so we have and bear a great responsibility when we leave this world, as we do each time we lose conscious awareness. For the faculty of reason, the light which transforms us, exists only in a conscious world, not in a subconscious world. Therefore, we have this responsibility to ourselves, to all we have created, to guide them, our creations. We have that responsibility when they come during our sleep. So we must do our part to take charge before we lose conscious awareness. For when we lose conscious awareness, we no longer have at our disposal the faculty of reason. So we must use the faculty of reason just prior to losing control, just prior to losing conscious awareness that we may establish the law unto ourselves of what we're going to do and what we will do as we've lost conscious awareness and gone into the so-called sleep of satisfaction.

Why is sleep known as a realm of satisfaction? For that so-called sleep, where the faculty of reason does not exist, is where the forms fill themselves, and when they fill themselves, that's known as being satisfied. And so when you sleep at night, you are the source of energy through which your children may receive their filling, their breakfast, their lunch, and their dinner, and, unfortunately, far too many snacks. And so you awaken ofttimes exhausted. Totally depleted. Like you haven't had a moment's rest. And the truth is you have not had a moment's rest for all of your energy has been used to feed the large family of your own creations of a lifetime.

And so the wise policy, of course, is to rest, not to sleep. For whoever rests has within their hand the faculty of reason to use at any moment of its guidance. So a wise man is still mentally and, therefore, of course, physically, and he rests five minutes, ten minutes, even twenty minutes. That's rest. You are consciously aware of your surroundings. You are consciously aware of any of the thieves trying to come in the night and steal the goodness that you are. You are aware. You are on guard duty at the very door of your conscience, and therefore, you do not have to let them in.

No one would ever think of allowing strangers into their home without first making an intelligent decision based upon the faculty of reason. And yet we find we allow many strangers into the temple of God. That vehicle is our responsibility. It is the temple of the Principle of Goodness. And yet we let in many strangers. Strangers in the sense that we are not consciously aware of them. Yet we pay the price and experience the effect of their robbing the temple of God. Those are the thieves in the night. Thieves enter the temple only when the light is out, only when there is no light of the faculty of reason. This is why it is the thieves in the night, for there are none in the day for they cannot survive the light. Therefore, all thieves do their robbing in the night. They rob us when we permit our minds to judge we're satisfied. They rob us when we permit our minds to lose the faculty of reason at so-called sleep.

For many, many, many centuries in the earth world, for many centuries man did not experience what you call and know as sleep. He only experienced very short moments of rest. Rest rejuvenates. Sleep destroys. The more you sleep, the more you need to sleep. The more you rest, the less you need to sleep. For sleep is one of the great opiates of the masses. Its short experience, known to our minds as satisfaction, cannot pay for the cost to our vital body, to our energy, to our health, to our abundant good. And we find, as we go on in life, times in our life when we say to ourselves we require more sleep. We require eight hours, ten hours, twelve hours. And in a way we're speaking a partial truth. That those children that we believe we are, are telling us they require more food, more energy, more sustenance. And because we believe we are creation, they use us and abuse us. For any child without the kindness of guidance known as discipline will not only use what it finds, it will abuse it, for it knows no better.

And so the unfulfilled desires of our minds, the children that we have created, they use us and, from our lack of effort and guidance and discipline, indeed abuse us. And the final result is a weakening of our health, the health of our body, the temple of God, the health of our supply, the goodness of life, the health of our mind, the peace that passeth all understanding. Of course, the Divine design did not design it that way. But in the Divine design of the Principle of Good is ever the opportunity of choice. For without choice there could not be a world of creation. Without choice, which exists in the principle of division, there could not be unity. And so in order to experience duality, we have to have the principle of choice in order that we, as beings of the Light and, therefore, designed servants of the Light, in order that we may enter a world of limit, the principle of division, duality, had to be established. And so our responsibility, as servants of the eternal Light, that which we are, is to awaken the limit that it may know, in time, beyond a shadow of any doubt, that expansion and contraction is the law governing all limit in all worlds at all times.

And so knowing the Law of Expansion and Contraction, it would indeed take a foolish person to be attached and, therefore, believe that they are in truth limit. For they are only choosing the path of self-suffering, of self-destruction. For self, in order to be self, establishes its boundaries, known as limit. So man chooses to follow the path of division and, without the light of reason, to believe that he is the division and, in so doing, to serve the prince of darkness. Or man chooses to follow the path of unity, that he is in truth a piece of the One. And being a piece of the One, contains all of the ingredients of the One, and in so doing, carries his lamp of honesty and the light of reason into the domain and realm of the prince of darkness but never forgets that is what he is seeing; that is not what he is. For if man was in truth what he thinks, then man in truth would be a frustrated being of no value or use to either the world of creation or to the world of truth.

This planet, Earth, symbolizing faith, the fifth planet in the system. All forms upon it, in order to be free, free from the delusion that they are the division, that they are the self, freed from the darkness they are tempted by in the twilight zone, they all have, the planet and the forms upon it, the one thing necessary to free them: it's known as faith. This is the planet of faith. Faith has no dependence. Faith is the power.

Because it does not contain within it dependence, man cannot control faith. Man can and does control belief. He cannot, by the very nature of faith, control it. Therefore, man does not consciously serve it, yet on very rare occasions. He confuses belief with the power that's known as faith. He believes that through his faith such and such will happen. That is not faith; that is, however, belief. It is not faith.

Faith is service to the Principle of Good that one is, beyond a shadow of any doubt in consciousness and, therefore, no temptation nor distraction to their service. One has no question when one is in service to the principle known as faith. One is peaceful. One knows beyond a shadow of any doubt only good shall prevail. One knows that for they have been a servant of the principle of faith before. And therefore, there is nothing to question; there is nothing to be concerned about; there is nothing to hope for; there is nothing to wait for. That is faith. That is our true purpose. That is what brings us through a world of creation.

For not to serve our purpose of being on Earth only establishes the law to return to it. That's not reincarnation, unless you choose to call earth-bound spirits reincarnated upon the planet. Whoever does not fulfill the purpose of their journey on the planet Earth, by the law of not fulfilling and doing their just job that they have earned in evolution, must remain upon the planet until the job is done.

We all know what our job is. We have no need to question nor to ask. For we all have a spiritual conscience: it knows; it doesn't have to be told by mental substance. It is of spiritual substance. It knows why we're here. It knows the job we have to do. And it knows when we do not do our job or we do it not well at all.

Now when we leave this world and we—be it in Divine order—enter the Halls of Repose and the schools of awakening and we face the list—and some lists are very, very long. They contain each and every judgment, which in truth contains each and every dependence, for no judgment exists within our consciousness that is not dependent on what someone else has done, or hasn't done, including nature, the weather. We awaken and we are not happy; that only reveals our prejudice. We have prejudged the day should be such and such. And because we are prejudiced, we awaken and are not happy with what the nature spirits, known as weather, have offered to us. And so that, along with the many lists of other prejudgments, we must pay for, for our conscience in a mental world is responsible and takes care of that.

Our purpose here, in this school, is to be the instruments of the Light through which you may make intelligent choices in your life. You have that divine right to make an intelligent choice. To choose the path of peace and harmony and abundant good, for that is your path. That is the path of all mankind. And to make that little effort each day, every day, so that you may remain on the path of peace and harmony and abundant good. The only time that you ever experience the lack of peace and harmony, the only time that we ever experience the lack of abundant good is when we depend on something beyond our right to control. That is the only time that we experience the opposite of abundant good. And we can only be tempted to depend on that which we cannot control by a judgment of our own mind. Because it's our mind and because we make the judgment, we have the right to change it; we have the right to educate it. And experiences in life reveal to us constantly: change your judgment, walk the path of peace and abundant good, or that which you depend upon shall be an instrument to change it for you.

You see, when you depend on another for your goodness, which means you have denied the true God and your God now can only enter your life through their prejudices, that is, the person you're depending on, then you must pay the price for denying your God, the true God. And you must experience, now, your God through the censorship and through the prejudice, the prejudgments of another human mind. We do that first by depending on our mind and how God can get in. For we can only offer to another, of course, what we have first offered to our self. And by depending on our thoughts, our little children, our creations—some of them are quite adult and quite old, the children we've created, of course—by letting God into our consciousness through the censorship of our own prejudice, we only guarantee to be the victim of God getting in through the prejudice and the censorship of another person. That is slavery. That is the slavery of the soul. That is the bondage. Those are the chains that are shackled to our ankles and to our wrists. That is the true slavery. It is emancipation from soul slavery that is, in truth, the purpose of the Living Light Philosophy. For there are untold millions of souls this day and this moment in slavery, and it is that emancipation that God's angels diligently work for. For they are in the slavery and the bondage of the dependence upon what they know as self, upon their own mind, and by offering that to their soul, they guarantee to be the victims of another mind, of another person or persons and their prejudice and their censorship.

There is no emancipation from the slavery by leaving a physical world. For cut off your hand if it does not serve you well, but your hand still exists, for you have a mental hand that is not dependent. Pluck out your eye if it does not serve you well; cut off your foot if it does not serve the Principle of Good;

you still have a mental form, a mental foot. You have a mental eye. So when you leave the physical world, you are not emancipated from the slavery and bondage of your eternal soul for you still are in a mental body. And it is the mental body and the ruler of the mental world where the slavery and the bondage exist. That's the emancipation. That's where it takes place for that's where the prince of darkness keeps the souls.

Not just here, while yet in earthly form, but the mental world is his domain for that is the world of division; that is the world of contradiction; that is the world of dissension; that is the world of destruction; that is the world of violence; that is the world of battle; that is the world of war. That, my friends, is where it is. And so we are in that world now. We are only buffeted by a physical body in which the mental body is expressing, but we're in that world. Let us emancipate our self for we know the way. The thought of I, the belief in self, is entrance. That is the trap. That is the trapdoor we step into, and that is where suffering is. That *is* purgatory; that *is* hell; that is where Satan sits supreme on his throne. That is where it is. You, or I, or anyone, do not, by the laws of goodness, go there. We go there from our ignorance.

We enter and we leave and we enter. My friends, we are fortunate to be in physical form. For we can enter and come out, and enter and come back out. When we lose physical substance, there is no visiting and coming out, for at that choice when you leave the physical body should you permit the weakness of your mind to distract you into the realms of satisfaction, then you serve the centuries until the job is done. Should you by a practice of the control of your mind in the here and now and, therefore, prepare yourself for the inevitable, then [when] you leave the physical body and you are still and hear the whisper of God's guardian angels and you are taken into the Halls of Repose, you are awakened and go through the centuries of schooling where you're able to go down to those realms and pay your just debt and to come back. It is, indeed, in one's own best interest to make the conscious choice each day and every day.

It does not mean that one should not fulfill their desires, for suppression is a guarantee of service to the prince of darkness. It means that one should cast the light of reason upon all thoughts and all desires; that one should act in life and not react, for whoever reacts is the victim of another by first being the victim of that which they are not. So a person who does not react is a person who is free and, being free, consciously chooses when, and if, they will service a desire of their mind.

You see, the divine expression, known as desire, is available to all forms at all times. Our mind experiences desire, for it is the expression of God. We, our minds, based upon our own experiences in life, we form the desire; *we limit God.* We make that choice. We decide with this experience of divine goodness called desire, the divine expression, we decide that we will permit God, this Goodness, to be experienced by our mind in this particular way at this particular time. And go down the list of restrictions that our mind creates based upon what we believe that we are from what the past experiences in our lives have offered to us. And so whoever limits or tempts to limit the Limitless must pay the price for their own temptation.

If you wanted a glass of water, is it the glass or the water that you desire? Does the water taste better from the glass of your choice or from the glass of the choice of another? That is the question to ask your mind. Is the water still water because another has chosen the vessel in which it shall be poured? That is the question intelligent people must ask their mind. If there is a difference in the water because another has chosen the vessel in which it is poured, then be rest assured the difference in the taste of the water is your experience of the forms of your own judgments who demand not the water for your thirst, but the vessel for your glory.

And so the servants and children we have created ever seek to be glory. And they look at you as their god and judge that you are glory; and therefore, they must have the power that they judge that you have. And so the children of the unawakened mind are the children of the prince of darkness, for that's what Lucifer did at the right hand of God.

So each desire that you have, each time that you limit the divine expression and form a form, a child, he sits at your right hand, for you are his god; you have created him. And he looks at you and he does what all children do: judge that you have what they want. And because they judge, like Lucifer, that you have what they want, they're going to get it. That is an undisciplined child who will not listen to the light of reason. And so as fathers and mothers of these many children that have been and continue to be created, you have a great responsibility to guide them. For if you do not guide and control them, then you must be willing, graciously, to pay the price. And every time they tell your mind that you don't have what you should have, then you must pay the price of believing that that is you.

And we look at this physical world and we see many parents who believe that their physical children are them; that they are simply some type of a rubber band extension of their own being and treat them accordingly. For we offer to our children only what we offer our self, for the law is very clear: we cannot grant unto another what we have not first granted unto our self. And so if we grant unto our children license to do what they want when they want, then that's the only thing we're granting to our self. Outward manifestations in life are nothing more nor less than the revelation of inner attitudes of mind.

We are known by what we do. And in a world, if we do not leave it a little better than we found it, then, indeed, are we takers, certainly not givers. Our responsibility is to leave the atmosphere better than we entered it, and if we do not do that, we shall remain on the planet until the job is done. The earth world is filled with its graveyards where the earth-bound spirits hover. It's filled with many places. And an earth-bound spirit, not having a physical body anymore through which registration and so-called sensation can register in the consciousness, uses the physical bodies who have those tendencies and weaknesses to experience this, what you call, satisfaction of the senses. And so we find masses possessed, they say, by demons. But what is a demon? A demon, too, is a form. And from where is the word derived? And is not *demon* a word for spirit? For, indeed, it is.

Let us test the spirit, our own, and let us test the spirit, our experiences. Are they of good, therefore, of God, or do they tempt us to dependence and, by so doing, are instruments not of God? For they offer us dependence on that which is not true, that which is not dependable nor reliable. They offer us dependence on that which is temporal, that comes and goes. Test the spirit of your temptations. If they are of God, they shall endure, and if they are not, they shall not.

And so whoever is possessed by the thirsty demons or earth-bound spirits of the planet has little chance of going on from this world to the Halls of Repose, to the schools of awakening. And so, but, of course, it is in our best interests to make some effort. It does not mean to be without the goodness life. It means to experience the goodness of life. It does mean freedom from dependence on that which is beyond our domain, the rights of another person to experience goodness. It does mean personal responsibility. It does mean accepting demonstrable truth that whatever the experience, we and we alone set it into motion. Someone else didn't cause it, unless we are in service to the prince of darkness. When we are in service to the prince of darkness, the cause of our joy, the cause of our satisfaction, the cause of our upset, the cause of our suffering is ever and always another, for that's what Lucifer offers. That's his dictate: someone else did him in. And that someone else to Lucifer is God Himself.

Lucifer cannot be God. He was the right hand of God. Lucifer was the angel, you must understand in your studies of religions, for the story is very, very, very old. It is not new. All religions speak the truth: an angel sat at the right hand of God. That angel was God's action. That angel, in its acting for God, the Principle of Good, having control over that which was division, called creation, [was] tempted by his own judgment and tried to be God. That was his fall. He was no longer grateful in being the servant of God, for he grew in the darkness of an uneducated ego.

And so because Lucifer desired that which was beyond Lucifer's right to desire, he was granted, by the very Principle of Goodness, a realm exclusively his own. And that realm is a realm whose very principles demand and dictate that the cause of our experience is outside. And so we know, in honesty, when we lose control, we know, in honesty, when things don't go right and we look outside to blame another, we know in that moment, though we may not like it, that we are in service to the prince of darkness who denied the goodness of life.

And so whoever dictates someone and something outside is where good and God is, is tempting themselves to the service of denial and is destined to the experience that it has to offer.

To our mind, as I sit here in this class, to some minds I see the temptation of discouragement, but when you understand what that temptation is, when you understand that is not you, but that is one of the many children who do not want you to make the effort to awaken, for they fear that in your awakening you will not feed them all that you have been feeding them in your life. They are not happy. And because they are composed of the substance of your own mind and intelligence, they don't want you to be encouraged. God forbid! For they would lose you as their slave.

Let us, as I say once again, emancipate our self. Let us have in this world a true emancipation. Let us not think of slavery and bondage of something that happened physically centuries ago. Let us face the slavery and bondage of the day, for the slavery and bondage of the human mind is something that we can do something about. We can do something about it and truly enjoy life. And it is through the enjoyment of life that we fulfill the purpose of our journey here on this planet. For when we are in the soul faculty of joy, we are the servants of the true God, that which we are an inseparable part of. We must first free our self from the deception of our mind that something outside is necessary for our experiencing God and goodness. That is the first step to make, and once you make that step, all the joy of life is waiting for you, inside of you.

You don't have to go anyplace physically, for you have the ability and the right to go everyplace mentally and spiritually. And so because you have not only that divine right, because you have that ability, you may go to any realm at any time. But go to the realms of your choice. Make the conscious choice when you go off in these realms. Choose the realms of happiness and joy. Choose the realms of emancipation from bondage, and that emancipation is the absolute absence of dependence on anything. For you have everything.

The only reason at any time that you ever permit yourself to believe that you don't have everything for the goodness in your life is when, through ignorance, you enter the bondage and serve the prince of darkness. There is no place you need to go to experience good. There is no thing that you need that isn't already available to you. There's only one step: enter the realms of joy through the arc of personal responsibility where the angels of reason wait to guide your footsteps into the true fulfillment of life. There, in that step, you will not only enter the schools of awakening but there will be nothing to tempt you to fear.

The inevitable of so-called death or transition, which, to some of you, is not so far off, which, to others, the years shall pass, but you, in making that effort today and each and every day will serve as lamps in the world that is in great need from the ignorance of believing they are the servants of denial, need, and disaster.

Remember, you have that ability. If you do not use it, the law clearly reveals that you are abusing it. For that which is yours and you do not use, from the lack of use, you are abusing. For all things are designed by God to serve a just and beautiful purpose. If they are not serving and you are responsible for them, then you are denying the rights of their design and must pay the price thereof.

Thank you and good day.

JUNE 2, 1985

## A/V Seminar 3

Good evening, students, and welcome to this seminar this evening.

We are going to discuss the expanding consciousness. The expanding consciousness or evolutionary incarnation is directly contrary to the popular theory, based upon fact and based upon partial truth, the theory of return or reincarnation, which is a contraction of the consciousness. For example, as we may be likened unto a dewdrop, we differ not than the dew itself, except in quantity.

Now we see difference only from an effect of denial. For in order to deny we must first judge. And so God, the Principle of Good, the will of God, total acceptance has no denial [and], therefore, has no judgments.

And so here, in a world of creation we see with our eyes; we see with two eyes. And in a world of creation we speak, as wise men have often stated, with forked tongues. We see with dual sight. We do not view singly. We do not speak singly. Difference therefore [is] the effect of judgment, the effect of denial. Therefore, we believe; we believe because we judge. And we believe because, from that path of judgment and denial, we experience what you call the duality of life. We are one in truth. We are many in falsehood. And so our gods, those gods of belief, are ever changing.

We experience in our consciousness so many things, the effect of denial of truth. We experience so much want. We experience so much need. And we believe that we are those experiences, the effects of our judgments, the effects of our denials. We believe all those things for we have, from our denial, accepted what we aren't. And because we have accepted what we are not, we live in a shadow of falsehood.

One God is one Light. One Light is one Truth. And life, in truth, is Light. Where there is no light, there is no life. Where there is no life, you experience what you call its opposite. In a world of creation, seeing with a duality and speaking with a forked tongue, you see life and you see death. There is no death, only to the I that is divided. And only in division can you experience need, for division is the effect, the effect of denial. Division is the discord in consciousness. It offers to your minds a difference, and yet there is no difference. Because you cannot have difference and truth, for truth is; difference is not. And so experiencing that which is not and believing that which is not, we fill our lives with want, we fill our lives with need, we fill our lives with frustration, the division in consciousness experienced by the emotional body.

All of life is what we are. Separate and so-called different is what we are not. The expanding consciousness moves through uncountable numbers of experiences of difference. In that expansion, it slowly, surely, gradually awakens. I am. I be. That I is not the dewdrop. That is the I of eternity. That is the I of truth. That is what we are. *[Please consider the possibility that the teacher could be saying "the eye of eternity."]*

Because we, ofttimes in our errors of ignorance, we hold tenaciously to believing our needs, we hold tenaciously to our experiences of denial. We insist on proving our individuality, when that which is individualized, being only separate in consciousness, yet a part of the whole. We suffer in separation, and we experience joy in unity. Where there is unity, there is happiness for where there is unity all things are harmoniously in motion. So let there be unity in your thoughts. Let there be unity in your acts. Let there be unity in your deeds, and you will not have to experience the unending race to find something that you know you are missing, to find that something that you know is your right. You won't have to continue the race and the search. You will accept that you are. You are all good that is. That is what you are. It is sad to permit the mind, the vehicle that you are temporarily using, to convince you, from your lack of efforts, to convince you to bind you, by belief, that you are what you are not.

How can we experience the joy of living when we deny its just and rightful expression? Oh, indeed, it takes, one might call, great strength. One, however, must consider that it takes great strength to bind oneself to falsehood. It takes great strength for anyone to convince themselves that they are special, different, perfect, or unique. It takes great strength for any individual to believe that.

And so, my friends, let us not hasten to judgment. Let us not be so anxious to find outside something that will bring to us the goodness that is inside.

Some time ago I spoke to my channel, perhaps fourteen or more years ago, and I said to him at that time, "O suffer senses not in vain for freedom of your soul is gain." Freedom of your soul. That which you are, not that that fills your mind with need, want, frustration, grief, sorrow, and suffering. And so throughout these years of my channel's service, he has benefited, as anyone who serves God is destined by that Law of Goodness to benefit. He has had the wonderful opportunities of experiencing the suffering of senses. And let us see the good it has to offer: the good is even a greater turning in the consciousness to God, to that which we are.

When creation, limits, and forms offer to the human mind, to say the least, distasteful experiences, then the human mind rises in determination to its dedication to whatever it is dedicated to. And so, my friends, let us not forget, let us ever remember, we all dedicate ourselves to something. What have we dedicated our self to? Have we dedicated our self to division, to discord, and to distraction? Are we united in consciousness for the greater good? For you must understand you are not the form. Understand it, and you will not only, of course, survive—that which is you—but in your times of greatest need, remember who controls need, remember the king of judgment.

And so when your judgments offer unto you the temptation, the temptation to sacrifice what you are dedicated to in life, then remember what you choose, should you sacrifice your dedication, is not a moment or two moments; it is not a day or a month [or] a year. You are speaking of centuries yet to be. Centuries. Let us not dedicate ourselves to distraction. Let us not dedicate ourselves to discord and division. Let us not dedicate ourselves to judgment and continue the experiences of need. Let us dedicate ourselves to the only thing that is life, to the only thing—for minds, you must realize, only register and only accept things. Because minds only accept things, minds reveal unto the universes who controls them. For things are separate from what is. Things are forms. They are limits of truth. And so a partial truth is more dangerous than no truth for a partial truth contains the indispensable ingredient of tempting the human mind. Let us dedicate our self to what is. And the only thing that is, is what we are. And what we are is truth. What we are is peace. What we are is good. What we are not are all these things of our mind.

In this expanding consciousness, we believe so many things, for, my friends, only in the belief of a thing is the thing enabled to live for a time. A thought, which is form, created by mental substance, cannot move without light, energy, that which you are. It only moves as long as you move it, for you formed it. And when you no longer believe you are that which you have created, it will no longer have you as its servant. And when that which controls the realm of things, things of mental substance—for that's the only realm that thing can control. Things control things. Truth frees what is.

And so do not permit your minds the discord, the disease of denial. When your minds tell you you've turned to God and still experience need, tell your mind, "Yes, the God I turn to, and still need, reveals to me the god I'm serving." For when you permit the thing to convince you that you need, remember, that's not you, and not being you, you are not disturbed by it. For that which disturbs us controls us. And until the moment that we control that which we have created, what we have created shall continue to control us.

Here, in this Living Light, you have the opportunity to apply truth and to experience what something greater than your thought can and does do. But like anything in your world of creation, you must learn to give without thought of gain. You must learn to give is to free. To give the thought of your mind for you have taken the substance that is under the domain of the king of creation. From his substance you have formed a thought. He has loaned you that substance for the purpose that you in, ofttimes, in errors of ignorance, ofttimes by conscious choice, he has loaned you the substance to form your thought.

And so many years ago I shared with some of my students present the practice of the control of thoughts. The practice, through proper breath, not to permit the tempter to register within your consciousness judgment, denial, and need, and, in so doing, not to borrow from the king of creation the substance from which you form these children in his realm. The mind borrows the substance, for the vehicle of the mind and that king is a very selfish taskmaster. For every bit of substance that you borrow from Lucifer, the king of creation, for every bit of substance, you shall pay back many fold. The debt mounts up, not daily, [but] moment by moment. "When of thy mind thou seekest to know the truth, / On the wheel of delusion thou shalt traverse." So many of your earth years ago I shared that with you; perhaps today you may understand. *[That teaching was given in Discourse 1 on January 6, 1964.]* It can be nothing but a wheel of delusion for it is ever a spinning, moving debt.

Now let us pause that we may personally relate. Peace is the power of God beyond a mental realm. The gift of the heart is the gift of truth. The heart is the expression of the soul, which is the expression of God, the Principle of Good.

And so, my friends, when you're tempted to think and you do not make the effort to think more deeply to find out who owns the substance, whose domain is it, who is the king of it—long ago I asked my students present at that time to think and think and think more deeply. I did not ask them to think and think and think higher. Is there any height to Lucifer's realm? My friends, in your need to intellectualize, in your needs to control, which is mental need, of course—you may take of my good student and bring him to class, please. *[The teacher instructs a student to bring into the room Serenity's dog, Reddy, who had been barking.]*

*Thank you.*

In that need from denial I shared with you, "Follow your need. Follow it all the way." It's very deep down there, before you can find him. And so I asked you to think and to think and to think more deeply. I didn't ask you to think and to think and to think higher. For high and low, to the king below, is ever dependent upon your need. If you need to believe that your thoughts are high and heavenly, oh, he will offer you that. He will offer whatever you need, and the payment will be very great. Therefore, need not. Want not. Let God in. Let the peace that passeth all understanding flood your consciousness.

All of the ways necessary for you to be freed, from anytime that you permit yourself to increase the debt to creation, you have the way. The only thing waiting patiently is application. Application.

One is discouraged only by mental substance. Knowing who controls mental substance, a wise man makes a choice to encourage himself or herself as quickly as possible. We must not permit ourselves to forget what we are and what we are not. And in that separation of truth from creation you no longer have two eyes; you only have one in keeping with one Light, one God, one Truth.

Religions have divided in keeping with the ever-increasing control of religions by the human mind. And so the more we exercise the human mind to satisfy the insatiable thirst of mental substance—try to understand how thirsty mental substance is. When you receive a class, you have a mind that it must pass through, and it's like going through a sieve. However, if you make the effort to control your mind, then the Light that is ever present will strengthen your heart. You will be encouraged. You will be determined. You will know beyond a shadow of any doubt what you are, who you are, and what you are not.

Indeed, it's time, my students, to truly awaken just a bit more. Awaken a bit more and enjoy life. Creation is limited form, and understand: God is in it, not controlling it. God doesn't control. God serves. God serves the flower. Without God, the flower has no life. Without God, the seed cannot sprout, grow, and express its beauty. So God, goodness, is everywhere. It is only when *we* believe that we experience goodness when certain children are satisfied in our consciousness. Those children being the limits of mental substance controlled by the king of mental substance.

Mental substance is not bad. Mental substance is what it is: the limit of goodness. For it can be nothing else. This is why it is controlled by the limit of goodness. My friends, God, goodness, the Life and the Light, is what sustains the king below. Try to understand: "Who is the lord of my universe? Who is the law of my life?"

We, like a dewdrop, a part of all dew, believe when we see another dewdrop that we are different. Yet what is the difference? Only to the eyes who see first themselves and then the other dewdrop. And by viewing dual, they speak with a tongue that is forked. For in that moment dewdrop one views dewdrop two, looks back at itself and says there's a difference, there is a difference. It has already (dewdrop one) established the Law of Comparison. And you cannot experience comparison until you first deny. However, should dewdrop one look at dewdrop two and say, "Hello. I see we are both dewdrops. There is only one dew." That sees clearly. That's truth. That's joy. That's happiness. That's God. That's goodness.

So here we have, to dewdrop three, two dewdrops. And to dewdrop three, who didn't say hello, "I see you are me and I am you." So dewdrop three doesn't say hello to dewdrop one and two. For dewdrop three experiences its own denial, its own need, and it must protect itself from two other dewdrops that are on the flower of the dawn. So dewdrop three, from the experiencing of fear, does not communicate with dewdrop one, let alone dewdrop two. Yet dewdrop one and dewdrop two know they are dewdrops and, therefore, do not experience judgment, do not experience comparison, and they look with one eye. And looking at dewdrop three, they know they're over there, too. And because one and two dewdrop, looking at dewdrop three, they see in truth that dewdrop three is a part of them. And therefore, they do not experience pity, for they are united in one. They experience compassion. They view and they know that a part of them is suffering, a part of them is sad, a part of them is lonely, the effect of over-identification with dewdrop three. Over-identified with its limited form, it's experiencing all the fear, all the want, and all the need, the payment of judgment, the payment of denial.

Divine right of choice is the law that governs the individualization of the eternal being. Divine right of choice. God, in the infinite wisdom of this Divine Intelligence, this great Principle of Good, the law grants to all who enter creation the divine right of choice to believe that they are unique, separate. Viewing with two eyes and speaking with a forked tongue is the divine right in the process of individualization or limiting of the Divine Spirit. And so ever in keeping with the expanding consciousness and the evolutionary evolving soul, you enter your earth and either your minds are programmed in keeping with the laws you have established in evolution, early programmed to believe you are different, to believe you are unique, to believe you are special, and ofttimes to believe that you, the limit, being the limit, are perfect. Hmm? The price, my good friends, is very great.

Whatever your talent in life is, it is only the expression of the God within you, that which you are. All things, all things are possible to what you are. All things. For you are greater than things, and because you are greater than things, you are the power that sustains things. And because you are the power that sustains things, you are greater than things. And because you are, things, that which you have power over, things you cannot be! Thoughts are things. You are not thoughts. You cannot be thoughts. You can only believe for a time that you are thoughts. Only for a time. For time is the domain of the realm of delusion; therefore, delusion, like an obstruction to the light of truth, casts its shadow for a time.

So whatever it is in your minds that you believe you are, be rest assured it is a shadow for a time. For what you are is not subject to nor dependent upon belief, which is bondage, controlled by the king of creation.

And so in speaking of the many religions and philosophies of your world, we find that when religion entered the mental realms, the mental realms offered to religion, that dedication to the Principle of Good, called God, dedication to the truth, when the minds of men and the thoughts they form slowly, but surely, gained control over religions and churches, that was the beginning of discord, division, falsehood, and disease. And so we find in your world, as many have found, the disease of so-called religion. Diseased by the dictates of the human mind. There's one way, so many religions say, in your world to find God. Without that way, you cannot find God. It's a wonderful way, I admit, to build the membership of any organization for it instills within the human mind what needs to be instilled in order to control it: it instills fear. And that which we fear is that which we serve. Let us not fear, for in so doing we deny truth.

When you believe that you must do something outside in order to enter heaven inside, then it's time to join the gophers in their efforts to dig below. For the only thing necessary—only necessary because of belief we are the thoughts of our mind—the only thing necessary is to be what you are, and stop trying to be what you believe you are. Searching and seeking for a moment of goodness. Searching and seeking, told by the thoughts, the children of your mind, what you must do to experience God. When we all know in truth what we must do is to control our own mind and take and set it on the shelf for a time. Try setting it on the shelf, perhaps for nine seconds.

And someday because some of you latter students here, in these classes, have not received the controlled breath and, therefore, are not establishing the necessary chemical changes in order to control mental substance for a moment, someday in the near future in your world I shall once again share that with you. I shall also say everything we receive in life is in keeping with the laws we have established. You have paid in mental realms in creation by believing you're a part of it; you have paid dearly for what you have received in life. Be practical with your payments. Be not attached to them. Be practical. Do not glorify mental substance by giving to the uninitiated, for in so doing you take from yourself. And the law clearly states you have a duty, a duty to qualify yourself before glorifying in what you have accomplished by speaking forth to those who have yet to earn what you have earned. You have a duty unto yourself. Oh, be not concerned with my work. I graciously make, and so does my channel, any payments that are necessary. But try to understand, my friends, to pay what is necessary to truly be free you must gain control of your mind.

No matter what it takes, you have everything necessary. You have will power. Not will force. You are will power. That is the lord of your universe. That power of will for the good of all is greater than any thought. It is greater than any torture. For, you see, my friends, when the senses suffer—senses belong to the man below—and when they suffer greatly, they are tempted, tempted unless you use the power of your will in service to the Principle of Good. It is one thing to be tempted; it is something else to serve it. Of what benefit can there be to serve in the belief that you will be freed from torture and suffering when you know beyond the shadow of any doubt the tempter wants to loan you for a time what your mind knows as satisfaction? And we all know what satisfaction truly is: the slumber of the light of reason.

So suffer well, O servants of the king below. Suffer well and rise in dignity. Rise in the dignity of the only God there ever was and ever will be, greater than all the things and limits of your world of creation. There is something greater. And how blessed are those who suffer, who suffer while yet in the limit of the forms that are controlled by the king below, for they have been granted in their evolution to be the living demonstration of what God can do. And God can do so much more than any thought you could possibly conceive.

And so I've shared with you to put God in it or forget it. You all know not only what that means, you all know how to apply it. You do what's right, for it's right to do right. You're not interested nor concerned with what the receiver does with it for you have given what you have to give, and in so doing you are free.

And so this wonderful process of the expanding consciousness. To those who pause and refresh themselves in the great peace that passeth all understanding, they're on their way home, to a home worth going to. So many people think of home in the realms of so-called heaven, where they can relax, sleep, be waited on, satisfying all their sense temptations, every one [of their temptations]. That's not the heaven of which I speak. If you can call a home like that heavenly, then there's a long ways to go. Heaven is not like that. Harmony is not like that. How could you possibly tell yourselves, "Heaven is where I get everything that I want; my desires are all fulfilled," when want, need, and desire is not harmonious? It's the opposite; it's discordant. So those things don't exist in the Light, the heaven that is. They exist in the dream world of mental substance. No, heaven, a state of harmony, is not oblivion. No, no, no, no, no. Oh, no, my friends.

Heaven is where you experience the joy of living. Heaven is where you're not limited. Wherever you want to go, you are transported in that instant. Whatever you want to see, you see. Whatever you want to do, you do. And the reason that you see and you do all that is because you have no want. That's why it all *is*. You have no want. You simply express harmoniously. Everything *is*. But to your minds, in order to relate, if you want a new car, it exists because, you see, you don't have any want. You are aware you are. And there is no experience in consciousness to see anyone, to hear anyone, to do anything, for you hear, you see, you do, you are *everything everywhere*. That's heaven. That's harmony. That's truth.

And so when your minds think, "Oh, I will get to see so-and-so and so-and-so and so-and-so. And it'll be so nice to do what I used to do," remember that's not the heaven that is. It is, however, the way station on the way. The slumber lands, part of the evolution and expanding consciousness. That's where most souls encased in forms on your planet, that's where they go. But remember, if that's your desire from your want, from your need, from your judgments—and in keeping with the laws of evolution and what you have earned, you shall pass through that. Oh, yes. It's nice to stop for a moment at the way station in the slumber lands and say, "Hello. Isn't it nice we are? And isn't it nicer I am?" Then, there's no division. There aren't two. There aren't three billion, trillion, or zillion. There's one. And that's you. There's no yellow, no green, no black, no red, no white. There just is.

Isn't it truly in peace? Isn't it better to think, "That's what I am"? Well, how about getting there? The sooner the better. But sooner and better is dependent on how graciously you are accepting the lessons you have learned that are necessary for you to get there. Don't try to escape. There isn't any escape. Don't entertain those thoughts. What you have to pass through, you shall pass through and, in so doing, free yourself from that particular thing you're passing through to tempt you again.

Ofttimes in your world of creation you seem to demand that the lesson be repeated many, many times. One was not enough. Not even two, three, four—why, I can count by many numbers how many times repetition has knocked at your door for the lesson once again. You see, my friends, it's only a seeming different form bringing to you the same old lesson. And sooner or later you will no longer see a difference. You will no longer be deluded. "Well, this one is a blonde. That one was black-haired. This one has freckles. That one doesn't. And this one is red-haired. This one is something else. This one is younger. That one is older." Why, sooner or later you will say "Thank you, God, O Principle of Good, it sure took me a long time to learn that simple lesson. Why did it take me so long?"

I have great compassion—and vice versa—[when] I speak of people and their needs. When we have paid our price—and we set the price tag on things—and then we think we've paid what we think the price tag we judged was going to cost, and then we suddenly, surely, awaken and say, "Just a minute. That's not the price tag that I agreed upon!" Oh, of course, it wasn't. That was what you judged it would cost. And, like you might say, [it] seemed like a good deal. But you forgot. You were being loaned that by someone who was going to collect that debt tenfold.

And then we find, along down the road, we say, "That wasn't worth that at all. That cost me a lot more than I figured." And you're telling yourself, "That cost me a lot more than I judged it was going to cost me. I don't appreciate it." And then you get angry. Not at the one you called forth to learn the lesson you have to learn. No, no, no, no, no. You are angry at your own mind because you made a judgment how much it would cost and finally awoken that you had borrowed that substance and he came to collect.

And it's all inside. We all know that.

We need something because we believe we don't have it. And when we believe we don't have it, it's the effect of not accepting God. We accepted something else by denying God. We glory in our denials for they serve us to be different. And we have great need to look around and to tell ourselves, "I'm different." Well, if you see with two eyes, of course, you're different. If you see with one, there's not even the thought of that; therefore, there's no price to pay.

Now we're going to take a few moments—I see we have a few moments left here. Perhaps if I got some assistance from back there in your world. *[The teacher is asking the recording technician how much time remained on the tape recording the class.]* We have a few moments for—I didn't even get any assistance except a little nod, but it's all right. Someday my students are going to do their share.

Now let's see here. I'm going to let you ask a few questions before we conclude this seminar this evening. And let us think. Let us think and think. And let the question rise within the consciousness because, you see, my friends, without your question, you do not expose what you should expose for exposure frees the soul through revelation. Now do we have any hands or do we all feel and believe we're something else, that we are not.

Yes.

*I'd like to ask, What is the best way to encourage ourselves?*

The question is a very good question. What is the best way to encourage ourselves? First of all, there's one way. Some could consider it best, and some could consider it worst.

Encouragement is a faculty of what you are, not dependent on anything.

Now when a person believes they are discouraged, they must accept the demonstrable truth: they are not experiencing at the moment of discouragement what they believe they should be experiencing. And because, my dear child, they are experiencing what they believe they shouldn't be experiencing, they must work diligently, through the power of will, and separate that which they are (truth) from that which, being human, they believe they are (creation). And so that requires, of course, certain faculties, beginning with faith, poise, humility. For duty, gratitude, and tolerance, of course, already are. They are, for duty, gratitude, and tolerance are revealing themselves to be directed or stolen by mental substance. Does that help with your question?

*Yes. Thank you.*

And so, you see, in those moments we are tempted to believe what we are not and through the repetition of any torture, suffering, or experience we are tempted and we must use that which we are: the power of God. And the power of God that we use is free, of course, from any dictate—when will it begin and when will it end—free from all of that. For you are what you are. Does that help with your question?

*Yes. Thank you.*

Yes, please.

*How does one break the habit of sleep versus rest?*

In reference to your question, How does one break the habit of choosing sleep over rest?

*Of choosing rest over sleep.*

Oh, thank you. "Of choosing rest over sleep." First of all, one should pause and when the form known as need—for a form of need to sleep, it is a form created by our minds in our days of ignorance—when that form comes into our consciousness and tells us many things and justifies those many things that we must serve it—and not only does that but talks to as many people as possible to get all of their forms to support them—then a person takes the wise path, slowly but surely, and reduces or puts this form they have created, known as need to sleep, one, slowly but surely, puts them on a diet, like five minutes an evening for perhaps the first five weeks. And once one is strong enough, through the power of their will, they may increase another couple of minutes for the next two months. And slowly but surely gain control over the form they have created in their days of ignorance. And those who wish to rush and suddenly make the change are doing so by a form created in the mental world that they are trying to be freed from. Does that help with your question?

*Yes. Thank you.*

Why substitute the dieting of the sleep form at the price of creating a glory form? Only to fall back to the sleep form more than ever before? Did that help with your question?

*Yes.*

We have time for another question. Yes, the lady there, please.

*There are a number of organizations that are encouraging people to donate tissue and organs at so-called brain death. And I would appreciate your understanding and recommendations regarding that practice.*

Yes. Well, in reference to the tissues and organs of the house of clay, the temple of God while the soul resides in it, in reference to that, we should first consider how attached to mental substance, to the belief that the individual of whom you speak, or individuals, how attached, through belief, are they bound to the flesh of clay. If, beyond a shadow of any doubt, they are not attached and they are free from the belief that they are the flesh, then all things do return unto their source, if we don't try to hold on to them. So a person, who, freed from their form and freed in consciousness before their soul leaves that form, then there's no difference to the use of those tissues and organs than there is to grafting a plant or using anything else for the good that creation has to offer. Did that help with your question?

*Yes. Thank you.*

Yes. Now the gentleman next to you, please

*How can we, when we become aware that we're living in a state of frustration, begin to become aware of the judgments that are causing that?*

Thank you. Well, in reference to an awareness of a state of mind known as frustration, the first thing one should consider is through the use of the lord of their universe, known as the power of will, is to take control over the mind. Through proper exercise and proper control, daily, of the mind, one can and does gain control over it so that no new thought enters. Now if, you see, in the experience of frustration you first control your mind that you no longer for a moment have any experience, you understand, within consciousness—you see, it appears to be difficult to the mind, doesn't it?

*Yes.*

All right. Frustration, a multitude of forms, the effects of judgment, playing house in your little mind, going wild, so to speak, undisciplined, all demanding and screaming for their feeding. One thinks, "How can I gain control over all of that?" Well, my friends, through proper control of the mind, which is available to all of my students—including my channel. And ofttimes it's very difficult; however, he still gains control over it. Because sometimes the mind, you know, gets such control, then it doesn't even permit, into the mental consciousness, exactly what to do. So we want to work to nip these things in the bud, you see. By proper breathing you are aware of one thought; that's one form you have to work with. No other forms enter your consciousness. Now one you can battle with through the power of your will. And you could battle with the many and it doesn't seem to work. It doesn't work because you're not encouraged, you see. It's like going to war. You're one against the Philistines. Only God shall free you.

And so it is with the human mind when the battle rages. They're all at the table screaming for their feeding. Well, you can't feed them all at once. Because there is within you a faculty of reason to your conscious minds. No, you just can't do all of those things. It is not possible for you all at the same time. Correct?

*Yes.*

All right. So you take control through proper breathing and now you have one form to battle. Now that one, you can do something about. And so once you have slaughtered that one, and you continue on and feel that moment of peace, do not permit your mind to be satisfied or pleased with itself for you, once again, open the trap door and they all rush in because they're all down there waiting. Does that help with your question?

*It does. Thank you, sir.*

Yes. Now we had another question. The lady there. I'll be right with you, thank you. A lady here had a question. Yes.

*Yes. When we're creating a new form in our consciousness, new way . . .*

Ah, may I understand one thing?

*Yes.*

Do you mean to tell me that you consider a new form a new way? And, if so, may I ask a new way to what?

*A new way of thinking. A new way of experiencing certain . . . of life. A new way . . .*

I see. Then you are speaking to me, first, on the controlling of the mind so that you may consciously create the forms that you judge will bring you the goodness that you desire by believing that you do not have it. Is that what you are telling me, please?

*Well, I think, I believe so, when I'm dealing with my mind and keeping . . .*

Well, my dear child, whoever deals with the mind deals with judgment. And whoever deals with judgment is denial. And whoever is denial must pay the price and be destined to the suffering that creation has to offer. Does that help you with your question?

Now, should you be sincere—and I know that you are—in freeing yourself from the mental world and seeing life as life is, singular, freed from want, need, and desire, then, you see, you'll be freed from bondage of belief that you don't have what you need. For you will awaken that you don't need it because you are it. Now, how could anybody possibly need anything that they are?

You see, my friends, give it to God. And in the giving [of] it, the form, the judgment, you see, you're freed from the destiny of denial. Give it to God. It is in keeping with the laws of form, you see. Say that you desire a bouquet of flowers. That's fine to experience that desire, for desire is the divine expression. Now comes the step, "That would be nice. Thank you, God." And it's gone. God shall return it unto you in keeping with the law that you alone establish. If you permit yourself to say, "Now let me see, when is that coming? Can I be sure that God will bring that to me?" Do you want it if, from having it, you experience the opposite of goodness? Ah, then whatever it is in your evolution in your experiences of judgments and denial, give it to God. God knows what's good for you, for God is good.

So, yes, let's use wisely those, if you can say "those," who are qualified, who have it to give. God not only has it to give, is waiting, waiting for your acceptance. Thank you.

Now I have time for one more question right here in the front row, please.

*Thank you. In one's dreams one can receive messages, ideas. Is that the subconscious or is it something else?*

Well, there are many things it could be. One of the most common things is the unfulfilled desires of the subconscious. That is not restricted to that. There is also the interpretation by the human mind of an experience affecting the physical body, such as a draft and things of that nature. There are the experiences of one's own spirit and soul revealing unto them that which they should be doing that they are not doing, ever in keeping with their faith in God, the Good, the Principle of Life. Does that help with your question?

*Yes. Thank you.*

Thank you very much, friends. It does seem that our time has passed. And good night.

JUNE 13, 1985

## A/V Seminar 4

Good evening, students, and welcome to our class this evening on the subject of living.

Within the human body there is a physical substance, known in many philosophies throughout the ages, called, by some, *prana*, by others as the coiled serpent, and still by others as vital energy or life force. In this philosophy it is known for what it is: living light. This fluid is a stream of consciousness that flows from the north to the south pole and from the south pole to the north in your body, in your universe. It is the manifestation of infinite, intelligent Energy. It is indispensable to all beings, be they human, animal, or plant. This living light is the substance that is available to all beings.

It is with this substance, when it enters the plane of consciousness of creation—which in other religions and philosophies are known by many names, such as *chakras* or centers. In the Living Light Philosophy, we know and understand them to be the nine planes of consciousness, which each contain nine spheres of action. These so-called centers, which are planes of consciousness, are known as earth, fire, water, and air. That is four of the planes of consciousness. They control the functions of being in a world of form or creation. It is not only the responsibility but the duty of all intelligent beings to use this living light intelligently for the good of living. Ignorance of its existence or abuse of the purpose of its design brings to man struggles, suffering, denials, and destinies and ever a lack of fulfillment.

And so it is that man in his responsibility to the proper use of its true design in awakening to what it is he is responsible for uses that Infinite Intelligence for the purpose of its design: the Principle of Good.

The question has been asked at some of my classes in reference to what is known in some religions as virgin birth. At the time of the question I gave an answer. I answered it in keeping with the law and the revelation of truth. Virgin birth is birth or formation absent of what is known to the human mind as lust. In order to be an instrument through which there is a virgin or pure birth, it is necessary to understand and apply the Living Light, which you, in truth, are.

We sit here, in this class, and we believe that we are the bark of the tree and not the tree. And we go through our experiences in life ever changing our faces, never changing what we are. And so it is that the bark of a tree is like the belief of a man; it grows, it changes, and finally it falls away to reveal what we are, not what we believe that we are. And so we find ourselves, one moment we believe we are happy. The next moment we believe we're sad. One moment we believe that we have the goodness of life, only in the next moment to believe that we have lost it. The truth reveals itself: you can never lose what you are. You can only lose the deception that you may, for a time, believe that you are. For the human mind is designed to conceive. It is governed by the first four planes of consciousness. They are the domain of functions. They govern form or limit. That is appearance. That is subject to the Law of Conception.

And yet that which you are is another four planes of consciousness, governed by intelligent, infinite Energy, an awakened consciousness where you perceive. And those who perceive are free to wisely choose, for a time, what they desire to believe for a time.

When you permit your mind to be directed to the lower four planes of consciousness (earth, fire, water, and air), then that is where you form, from this manifestation of living light, the various forms that you create. You create your thoughts. You form them in keeping with your motives. When you believe what you have created is you, then you begin to serve that which you have created.

Some time ago I spoke to you on the rapid advancement of science and technology, far advanced over the spiritual awakening of mankind. And so in keeping with the laws made manifest in your world, you are living to awaken to the demonstrable truth that whatever man conceives, man depends upon. And whatever man depends upon becomes man's master and man's false god. And so you depend, ever in keeping with the laws made manifest, on various technological advancements. You depend upon them to do things that you yourself, by choice, permit them to do for you. And so you live in a time and age when you will witness few people will be able to read, let alone to spell. Fewer still will be able to do mathematics by the intelligence within them for they have created machines to do that for them.

Now the machines are not the problem. Man's dependence upon his creations is the problem, for whatever man permits himself to depend upon becomes the god he has created.

And so man, depending upon the thoughts that he creates, solidifies them within his consciousness and, therefore, becomes dependent upon them for his happiness, for his fulfillment, and for the abundant good. The lack, he experiences from denying this truth, this Living Light that he is.

You are formless, free Spirit that is manifested in the river of consciousness, a fluid that is passing from the north and south pole and the south and north pole in your physical being.

Years ago in your world I clearly shared with you that the sole and only purpose of the release of this energy, this living light fluid, was for the sole purpose of creating forms (procreation) in your physical world. Now in order for you to be an instrument through which a soul enters your physical world, you, your consciousness, identifies with the lower centers: earth, fire, water, and air. Therefore, you are not instruments through which an immaculate conception is possible.

An immaculate conception takes place when the stream of consciousness, the fluid, rises through the remaining four centers, at which place form is designed in realms celestial. It descends on the river, southward bound, from the celestial to the ethereal, and from the ethereal on down until it reaches the odic. Now this, what is known as odic, is the formation realm of consciousness through which this fluid, this living light, begins to take shape.

Most and all births are through an identification with the lower centers, specifically, the fire center. Whoever believes they are in need has identified in consciousness with what is known as the fire center or the second plane of consciousness in evolution and, therefore, [is] governed by that king of creation. A dual law must pay the price for the ignorance that they choose to demonstrate for a time until their law is fulfilled.

The movement of this living light, that you are, is a natural movement. The river does not stop because you tell it to. Your identification, your belief that you are separate and individual is your raft on the river of life. You place that raft on that river in the plane of consciousness that you choose at any moment to identify with.

And so it is, it is your identification with limit or form that places you in whatever plane of consciousness that you find yourself at any moment. Now, for example, you have a thought. You form and you create it. Should you at the time of its formation permit yourself to believe that you are either on the first, second, third, or fourth plane of consciousness, then your experiences, the return of the form you have created, shall return unto you on the first, second, third, or fourth plane of consciousness. It shall return unto you for that is the law, the Law of Creation, the Law of Conception.

We seem to have no problem in viewing our electronics, our technological advancement. We seem to have no problem in being fascinated with what machines are able to do.

All students shall kindly open their eyes, for I am not here to help you sleep. I have come to help you awaken that which you are, not that which you believe that you are.

And so you create many things and, therefore, are responsible for many things. It is the power of your will that directs your identification with any plane of consciousness. We all know from years of experience what our will power can do. Now let us understand that Power is God, that will is the movement or the action of God. For us to experience the power and action of good we must make a change in our consciousness, for you have already received what the action or will of God, the Principle of Good, is. You all know what it is. The will of God is total acceptance, for that is the living demonstration.

God, goodness, cares for the blade of grass as well and with as much consideration as he cares for you. The blade of grass is not different in the eye of God. How could it be? For God, the Principle of Good, is not deceived. God, the Principle of Good, perceives, and it looks through and into the blade of grass. And it sees within the blade of grass what you know as life force, *prana*, vital energy, and what we know as the living light. God, the Principle of Good, sees itself. Seeing itself, of course, God knows itself. So when you apply the will of God, which is demonstrated for you moment by moment—nature constantly reveals the will of God: total acceptance. It does not shine on the daisy and forget the dandelion. It shines in keeping with the law, and all of those that are within its rays receive its benefits.

And yet we permit our minds to deny the right of the Principle of Good and expect to experience the Principle of Good after establishing our denial of it. A house divided cannot stand and that is a demonstration of division. And division is the Law of Destruction. Divide and conquer is something that all minds are familiar with. They do not seem to understand the law that is so clear. Unite and control that which is within, by divine law, your rightful domain. Unite and control; the effect of experience of that is freedom. For years we have taught you that the effect of self-control is the experience of freedom.

But you cannot control what is divided. You cannot permit your mind to tell you to use your power of will for this at the expense of denying the right of that, for to do so is division; and division is discord; and discord is disease. You cannot ask the Principle of Good, known as God, for health, wealth, and happiness and blatantly demonstrate the laws of the opposite: poverty, disease, and misery.

To those who know the way, the burden of responsibility is in keeping with their unwillingness to change. The more unwilling we are to change (the Law of Evolution), the heavier is the weight and the burden that we place upon our shoulders.

We are given, in this school, the opportunity to experience, through living demonstration, our willingness, our ability to spontaneous change. For that is the spirit of the law. It is the letter of the law, it is conception that killeth. It is not perception. Those who perceive know beyond a shadow of all doubt they are the stream of consciousness. They are moving ever in keeping with the direction of what they know as identity. They identify with that plane of consciousness and, therefore, experience what it has to offer.

Man's responsibility is to not only know what his future is, man's responsibility is to apply the law in the moment of his conscious awareness. And in the application of that law, man's future is no longer a mystery. Mist and mysteries [are] designed by the minds of men to control other minds of men for selfish needs of mental substance.

The law reveals so clearly: beginning students, advanced students, intermediate students are not dependent upon years, weeks, or months of studying. That is not where it is. It's not a matter of how much time. It is a matter of perception. For many students study, in life, many things for many years, and they end up with a warehouse in their consciousness filled with forms they have conceived. That, to me, is a beginning student. Then there are students who, receiving, take control of their mind and perceive, and that, to me, is an advanced student. And so, my good students, when you want to know where you are, all you have to do is to pause, be honest with yourself, ask yourself the question: how joyful and how willing are you to change? If you find change difficult, if you find change an emotional experience of trauma for you at the very thought of change, then be rest assured, you, at that moment in your life, have fully identified with one of the four planes of consciousness of the functions of form, your form.

And so change, the Law of Evolution, through repetition, and the spirit of spontaneity offers to you great opportunity to experience personally for yourself where you are at the moment you have earned that opportunity. To tell a person what is going to happen (that represents a change for them) is to permit the person to work on all of their judgments that they believe that they are and then to demonstrate the letter of the law that killeth, not the spirit of the law, which is the spontaneity of life itself. And so when the four planes of consciousness do not receive what they judge is a forewarning, they react and they tell you where you are at that moment. They not only tell you where you are, they tell you what you believe you are. And you experience their resentment, their retaliation because they did not know in advance. My friends, knowledge knows much; however, wisdom knows better.

So let us not forget the goodness that we are. Let us spend a few more moments in our daily activities declaring the truth of what we are, refraining from the laziness in consciousness of believing the shadows that have passed that only can move in your consciousness when you direct that which you are, living light, the stream of consciousness, the river of life, when *you* direct it to it.

Now I have one announcement here to make before we get to our question time. And that announcement is that I will, for a very short time, take applications for new private students. For a very short and limited time. To those of you, if any, interested in my private teachings, which are weekly, you will kindly make your arrangements with our secretary of the organization, who, in turn, has a responsibility to bring them to my channel, who I know beyond a shadow of any doubt will bring it to me.

Now we'll take a few moments for you to raise your hands and ask your questions. Kindly speak clearly because I think that boy back there, called a technician, doesn't have a microphone out there. But don't be concerned with it. Fine. Oh.

Go ahead, please. The lady there, please.

*The living light moves north and south, and then south to north. Does that represent the two sides of our body, like the electric and the magnetic?*

I—in reference to your question, the stream of consciousness known as the river of life, the living light, that which you are, moves from the base of your spine to the top of your head. That is its flow and return. Does that help with your question?

*Thank you.*

You're welcome. The gentleman there, please.

*Yes. During the day when we become conscious of levels that we are serving that are not to our best interests and we are firm— or we want to affirm the truth that we are, I have had experiences when I was, when I affirm the truth that I that, that we are taught that we are, that I am, of that form, whatever it was, siphoning off the energy that I was trying to affirm.*

Yes, and what may your question be?

*I would like some help or some guidance in my efforts to affirm the truth that I am, that that won't happen.*

Yes. Well, the only way that a created form in mental substance can siphon off your energy, that which you are, this living light, this fluid in your being, the only way that is possible is because you would continue to identify with it through a belief that you are it. And so that's known as a house divided. You are battling against what you believe is yourself.

You see, that's like a man saying, "No, I'm not going to talk to these thought forms here. That's ridiculous. That's, that's not sane." Because, you see, a person who believes that they are the thought that they have created would say something like that, you see. So when you experience—say, for example, you want to be free from an attitude of mind, which is the effect of the thoughts, which create thought patterns, creating attitudes of mind and solidified judgments, then you must refrain from the slightest belief that you are that which you have created. That help with your question?

*Yes, it does.*

You see, you see, it will not leave your universe until you—you are a private student, then you know the way through proper breath control, etc. Thank you.

Someone else have a question, please? *[After a short pause, the teacher continues.]* Very enlightened class this evening. I'm so pleased. Yes, the lady here, please.

*I'd like to know if the light—*

I didn't state which light. Thank you.

*I'd like to know if the light of reason is found in the first of the four centers, and, if so, is it related to conception?*

The light of reason, in reference to your question, the light of reason is the very power that transforms our being. Therefore, it could not possibly be under the control of the first four planes of consciousness governed by the dual laws of creation. Does that help with your question? Yes.

*I'd like to ask if there was any reference before regarding the light of reason and air.*

Indeed, of course, there's been much reference to the light of reason and the highest of the four centers of the functions. Yes.

*And so I'd like to ask for some clarification with that connection.*

Well, in other words, you want to find a way to use the light of reason for what, of course, we all would understand to be the fire center or conception. Is that correct?

*No. I just wondered since it's considered to be that which transfigures us . . .*

I see.

*And there's mention of the air center. I don't get the connection.*

Very well. Very well. Transfiguration or transformation takes place when you move from one plane of consciousness of the higher consciousness of faculties into the first plane of consciousness of the functions. So, in other words, when there is an amalgamation, when—you see, heaven comes to earth when the faculties of the soul are perfectly balanced with the functions of form or the functions of the being. Does that help with your question? So when you bring something into balance, you unify or unite it. Is that not correct? And that which is brought into balance is unified, becomes one. Is that not correct?

*Yes, sir.*

And so you no longer have division. You no longer have difference. You no longer have separation in consciousness. Do you understand it that way?

*Yes.*

All right. And so your question is really relating to the immaculate conception or virgin birth. Yes. I hope that's helped with your question. You're a private student, also, aren't you? That'll be covered in private classes in the future.

*Thank you.*

You're welcome. The lady here, please.

*Yes. I'd like to know where the celestial, ethereal, and odic centers are located.*

Yes. I'd be more than happy—you're a private student, aren't you?

*Yes, sir.*
That'll be answered in private classes.
*Thank you.*
Any other questions pertaining to this evening's discussion? The gentleman here, please.

*Thank you. The centers you talk about, now these are large items, like fire of the mountain and air all around us, like, are we discussing that within us? Like a fire center in ourselves? The water center in ourselves? Like . . .*

Yes, maybe I can explain it this way. You see, without earth, fire, water, and air, you do not know what you know as you (your form).

*Yes, sir.*
Is that not correct?
*Yes, sir.*
For within you burns a fire, dim or bright, depending on your mind and what you do with the power of your will. Is that not correct? Sometimes your fire burns very brightly. And ofttimes the fires of the fire center, we are deceived and for a moment believe they are the lights of heaven.

And so these fires, and this earth and this water and this air is within your being, your physical being. Now, for example, you will find that laziness in consciousness is very subject to temperature of a person's universe. Do you understand that?

*I'm not sure.*

As the temperature increases within a person's universe, they become more sluggish and more lazy in their movements, mentally and, therefore, physically. Does anyone not understand that?

Because, you see, my friends, the four planes of consciousness, governed by creation, the functions of being, are in the southern pole at the base of your spine. Do you understand?

*Yes, sir.*

Now as you move to the north pole, the temperature is not as warm. It begins to cool off. Hmm? In fact, based upon scientific knowledge in your earth realm at this time there are those who firmly believe that they can, when transition takes place, that they can freeze, wait, and reanimate. The only thing that your scientists are unaware of is that the flow of the river at the moment the Isle of Hist separates, this river leaves your body through what you call the soft spot in your head.

And so for eons of time, this odic force leaving the physical body is shown as a light, a golden light over the head. Now that the artist painted eons ago to represent that that particular being, leaving a world of creation, was entering into this perfect circle of golden light; and that's known as sainthood or saintliness. And so it is rare and there is only one in your world of art, religious art, that reveals this so-called aura or golden light is completely around her entire body, and it's known in your world as the Virgin Mary. That is done by the artist to reveal to the world that this lady, known as the Virgin Mary, was an instrument through which there was a virgin birth or immaculate conception.

Now in my private classes, I explain in vivid detail how an immaculate conception takes place. It is not a question for a public class or seminar. Does that help with your question?

*Yes. Thank you.*

You're welcome. The gentleman there had a question, please. The gentleman with glasses. Yes. Did you forget the question that you wanted to ask earlier?

[After a pause, the student responds.] *No.*

Oh, then you may ask it now. You know, I can't get to everyone at once in your limited world. Go ahead.

*How is kindness the bridge to the subconscious?*

Kindness? I see you don't have a child, physical.

*Yes.*

Perhaps you may understand that you can gain more control through understanding than you can through force. So when you want to control something that you have created, you use understanding, your understanding. And understanding contains these various things; one of which is consideration, kindness, compassion, and all the soul faculties. For it is not the soul that you seek to control. It is the form that is your rightful domain to control. So when your hand does not do what you know it is designed to do—an instrument of action to bring good into your life—then it is best that you cut it off. Does that help with your question?

*Yes, sir.*

So by using understanding you offer, to the children you have created, kindness and consideration for they exist as your children. You have created them. To deny one's creation is to tempt oneself to escape personal responsibility, and there is no escape. For that which is created by you shall pound at the door of your consciousness until you let them in and educate them. Does that help with your question?

*Yes. Thank you.*

You see, to experience a form and have it drain your life vitality, your living light from you, is a battle that is taking place; you're trying to deny your children. And they pound louder and louder at your consciousness, and you become more and more identified with them. That's not the way to get them on to school and to grow up. Do you understand?

*Yes.*

Any parent will tell you that. Anyone that is a bit awakened. Does that help with your question?

*Yes, sir.*

You're welcome. Yes, you may ask your question, the lady there.

*In the returning of the law—you spoke a while ago about the centers in which it returns to.*

The one you create it on, my friend.

*I see. So if you have changed your consciousness upon the return of the law, that does not neutralize the law.*

Oh, no. It waits until you go down again [to] that plane of consciousness. You know, it just waits. And the longer it waits, the more aggravated it gets, the more irritated. And when you finally go down there, it is a screaming demon. Yes.

*Thank you.*

Remember, I told you, in our private classes, that demons cannot walk straight lines. Yes. Is there any further question on that?

*Thank you.*

You know, when you have a desire, you'll wait so long for what you call its fulfillment. And depending on the control you have of your mind, depends on how long you will wait. And the longer you wait, the more anxious you get. Would you not agree?

*Yes.*

And the more anxious you get, the more determined and frustrated you get. Would you not agree?

*I would agree.*

And then finally you pass through a phase, "Well, it looks like I'm not going to get it at all." And then you pass through along another phase, and you feel sorry for yourself because you're not going to get what you think you should have and have a right to. Is that not correct?

*That's correct.*

And then finally you get so discouraged that a change takes place in your consciousness and you say, well, it wasn't worth having anyway. And you move on to the next one. Right? Well, that's how your children act. Yes. That help with your question?

*Thank you.*

You're welcome. Yes, please, the gentleman there. Yes. I see you, but I will move so you can see me. Thank you.

*If, as you spoke of a spontaneous insight occurs when faced by the forms, does that mean then that by using the spontaneity of your understanding to overcome the forms in a moment that you have to return again and again to confront them?*

Well, in reference—you see, it is possible for all people, all people to make a change in consciousness, an instant change within their consciousness and not experience the return of their children. However, it is not possible in the present state of evolution on the planet Earth, the fifth planet, to remain there. We experience the spirit of spontaneity as a spontaneous moment. Would you not agree?

*Yes.*

And one does not find it possible for them at present to maintain that level of consciousness, that awareness over a period of a full day. Would you not agree?

*That's correct.*

Now, therefore, when one is in a state of consciousness of a light of reason, one then makes intelligent choices and decisions and says, "Well, in keeping with the law, these are my children. They will return. Then, I am there to face them intelligently." And intelligently is by not believing that you are them. That's known as the separation of truth from creation. You are truth and believe you are creation. Do you understand that? You are truth. You believe you are that body that you are using. Is that correct?

*That's correct.*

There are times when you wished you didn't believe that you are that body that you are using. Is that not correct?

*Frequently.*

Yes, there have been moments. Therefore, that is a very good experience as being instrumental in helping you to refrain from over-identifying with it and believing that it is you. Would you not agree?

*Yes.*

However, we have in our evolution earned the bodies that we have to use on this particular planet. You do understand that, don't you?

*Yes.*

That's the body you have that you have earned. You have a responsibility to it to use it wisely. You have a responsibility that it serve you well. You understand that, don't you?

*Yes.*

So when it doesn't do what you guide it to do, you must use the power of your will to see that it does so. You understand that? Now you have the will power. Would you not agree? You have no problem when you decide you're going to do something to do it. Is that not true?

*That's right.*

That is an exercise of the power of your will. Now if you make the effort to put God, the Principle of Goodness, in the movement of this power, you understand that—that means that the will, the movement of this power, must be in total acceptance, you understand, for that is the movement of God or good. And when you do that, you'll not have the problems nor be one bit discouraged of the fine vehicle that you have earned to drive you around your Earth planet. Do you understand?

*Yes.*

For it has been designed by the Divine Architect in keeping with the evolution of your eternal being, known as your individualized soul. Do you understand that? Pardon?

*Yes.*

Yes. And so it has been designed to offer to you the necessary lessons for you to grow, to awaken, and to control your life. Now whatever lessons in your evolutionary incarnation that you played hooky on in eons past, in times past, they're with you in your little vehicle today so that you may pass the test that you have imposed upon yourself, like everyone else, to know beyond a shadow of any doubt, "This is the automobile, the vehicle, the body that I have earned. Now, body, you are not me. You are here for me to use for the good of my life." Do you understand that?

Yes.

And you also must learn that that body is designed to serve you and offer you the, what you call, temptations. And the temptations it offers you—the greater temptations it offers to you reveals to you the lessons you flunked in your evolution. Do you understand?

Yes.

Yes. I do hope that's helped with your question.

*Yes. Thank you.*

Yes. The lady here, please. And I'll be with you in a moment.

*There's a point at which, when we're working with our children, we're kind and understanding. Then there's a demarcation line, it seems, where if they cross over, discipline is offered to them. And in working with the children, our forms that we've created in our mind—*

Yes?

*I'd like to ask how we discern to step in beyond kindness with firm discipline to deal with these thought forms that we've created.*

You will have no problem in using discipline if you demonstrate within discipline. Now discipline is absent of the first four planes of consciousness. There is no self-interest at all. There is no earth, fire, water, or air. And therefore, God is in it and only good can come from it. Does that help with your question?

*[Thank you.]*

You're welcome. Now the lady, there, has a question, please.

*I have two brief questions. One, is there an optimum degree that would be good for us to be in, like at the time we meditate. You spoke of the degree of temperature of the air . . .*

Indeed, yes.

*In the center . . . consciousness.* [The student and teacher speak simultaneously, and it is difficult to accurately transcribe the student's remarks.]

Brief answer: indeed, yes. Next question.

*Could you tell us what that is? What the degree that would be good for us is?*

That is very individual, depending on your evolutionary experiences and your present incarnation and the lessons you have to learn. Yes. Brief question, brief answer. Yes.

*The direction, you spoke about north to south, south to north. When we're meditating would it be beneficial to face in a certain direction?*

Yes, yes, it would.

*Would you be willing to reveal that direction?*

You're a private student? It'll be revealed in private class. Yes. Were there any other questions?

*That's all.*

Thank you. I tried to keep my answers as brief as you requested with your brief questions. Yes. *[After a pause, the teacher continues.]* Everyone is so illumined. I'm so happy. My, if I could only be dependent on appearances, I'm sure I would be thrilled. *[Some of the students laugh.]* Yes. The lady there, please.

*Could you speak on leadership?*

Leadership.

*Yes.*

I have spoken a full discourse in *The Living Light* book, which you should be studying on leadership. I also have, over these years, offered an entire class on that one subject. Have you studied that class?

*In* The Living Light *book, I have.*

And the audio tape that is available for you?

*I don't think I have that.*

Yes. Check with the secretary of the organization so that you may study that. And then from that, you will be able to ask a question specifically concerning leadership. All right? Thank you.

*[After a pause, the teacher continues.]* Well, of course, I could present my own questions, but I'm not. That's your responsibility. It's known as participation. You know, we get out of a thing what we put in. Little in is little out. Thank you. The lady there, please.

*Is it possible to work with those, the four basic levels, within ourselves to create balance or harmony so that they don't get in the way? Do you know what I mean?*

Well, I accept that you know what you mean, and therefore I respect that. Now you don't want these four planes of consciousness to get in the way. They're not in the way. We're in the way. Our belief is in the way. You see, our foot is not in the way. Our foot is designed to serve us, to move us from one place to another where we choose to go. You see? It is designed for that purpose. So it is not the functions that are in the way. It is our belief that we are the functions; that's what's in the way.

You see, when *we* grow in consciousness and awaken, [we say], "I have a hand. It is designed to be used at my direction. To lift a glass of water. I have a mouth and a throat. That's what I have. That is not what I am." Now when you separate truth from creation and you awaken within that you have a hand to use, a foot to use, a mouth to use, nostrils to use, but you are not them. They are designed in keeping with the laws of your evolution for you to use. They are not to tell *you* that *you* are to be used by them. Does that help with your question? So it's our attitude towards the functions that is the problem. The problem is our attitude. The problem is our laziness in consciousness that permits us to depend upon the form for the goodness that we are.

By denying what we are, we believe what we are not. So when the hand is removed, we believe we have lost a part of our self, when all we have lost, if there is any loss, is a part of a vehicle that we are using. And, you see, it is our belief that we are limit, an effect of denial of the truth, the limitless Infinite Intelligence that we are. Does that help with your question?

*Yes, it does.*

The functions are not in the way. Our absolute insistence that we are them is what's in the way. That's the only thing that's in the way. Now when you use a function and through the laws of abuse (overuse of that function) you begin to believe that you are the function—as I stated so long ago, when the worker believes he is the tool, then he begins to serve the tool. So when you permit yourself, through laziness in consciousness and abuse of the functions, which are designed to serve you, your soul, then you've got a problem, and *you* are in the way. Does that help with your question?

*Yes.*

The functions are not in the way. No, no, no, no. They're not designed to be in the way. They're designed to serve you. That's like saying, well, you get into your automobile and it says, "No, I don't want to start today." And it won't start for you. It won't go. And no matter what you do, it refuses to go. How would you feel?

*Upset, probably.*

Yes. And what would you do?

*Try to find a way to make it work.*

And if you couldn't, what would you do?

*Do something else. I mean, I—*

And what would that something else be?

*Walk.*

Pardon?

*Walk. I mean, find another way to, another vehicle.*

Find another vehicle! Now, you see, this is what I'm talking about. The functions are not in the way. Our attitude and belief is in the way. The dependence on something outside for the goodness that we are inside. So when we depend upon the hand, our hand, for God, when we depend upon our ear for God, when we depend upon our toe for God, and whatever else on the little temple of God you want to choose, and you know what I mean, then we've got a problem. Would you not agree?

When a part of the temple of God, designed by the infinite Divine Architect, is designed for the sole purpose of procreation and you use it [for] something else, that's like taking the tire of your car, removing it, and expecting your car to fly! It doesn't have wings! You see? It proves it's not an angel, yet. That help with your question?

*Yes.*

You're welcome. Yes, the gentleman there, please.

*What is belief?*

What is belief? Absolute dependence on what you cannot control. Contrary to divine, natural law. That's belief. Depend on whatever you will, you guarantee to believe you're it. Depend on your finger, and you will soon find you believe you are your finger. And when your finger does not rise when you want it to rise, you will reveal to the world how you believe you are your finger. Does that help with your question?

*Yes, sir.*

Thank you. The lady here, please.

*I'd like to ask, What are the steps that we can use to get out of belief, which is limit, and come into the limitless spirit that we truly are?*

By refraining from the type of thinking that tells you that you must do this or that to experience God, that which you are. Refrain from what you know as fear, for it only reveals an absolute dependence on a limited mind. Do you understand?

*Yes.*

So whoever is ready and willing for the truth, the experiencing of the truth that they are and the freedom that it offers, will have to take control of their vehicle, including, especially, their mind, which their physical being responds to; and say, "Just a moment. Don't tell me what to do. You have been designed by the Principle of Goodness to serve me. I will tell *you* what to do. And I will tell *you* when to do it." So you must learn to take control of your mind, which includes your spoken word, which releases into the atmosphere the living light, which creates forms. You must take control of the mouth; take control of the eyes, the nose, the ears, and all other parts of the temple of God. That help with your question?

*Yes. Thank you very much.*

And not permit the mind, the vehicle, to tell you unless you do such and such you cannot experience God or goodness. And never permit this vehicle, the mind, to tell you your way to goodness and abundant good is dependent upon anything you, by divine law, do not control. Do you understand that?

*Yes.*

Yes. I hope that's helped with your question. *[The teacher continues after a pause.]* You know those of you who have the benefit of these fine videotapes, I know, do not appreciate long pauses. Hmm? There's something about the human mind: it has difficulty with silence. So remember that, those of you, when you receive your videotapes. Well, I could talk to you about some mundane things; I suppose it would be of more interest to some of your minds. Yes. Yes, the lady there, please.

*We've been advised to keep our spine upright in regard to this living light, this fluid within us. And I'd like to ask, Would it be advisable at the time someone was trying to leave the earth realm to have the position vertical rather than horizontal?*

I have stated, privately, to you students that a 45-degree reclining position is the most advisable, and I think that covers your question for this particular seminar. Does someone else have a question? The lady there, please.

*In learning how to accept change, if one perceives that as a problem within oneself, in learning how, what would be the greatest benefit in changing that in your consciousness?*

Well, first of all, the problem is not in learning how to accept. The problem is in the blatant refusal to accept. There is no problem accepting. Man accepts many things, and then there are many things man blatantly refuses to accept.

Now the will of God is total acceptance. That is the demonstrable will of God. [If] you want goodness and God in your life and all that goodness and God have to offer, then you must demonstrate through the power of your will the will of God. Now what happens in your mind when you say, "I want to demonstrate total acceptance"? What happens in your mind? I guarantee what happens in your mind. You know what happens in your mind. Every judgment you believe is you rises up screaming. Those are the very things that keep you from God.

How do you know—does God become limited to the form of the blade of grass by accepting the blade of grass? By accepting the blade of grass does God then become the form of [the] blade of grass? I don't see anyone worshipping the blade of grass that God is expressing through.

And so it is not in how to accept, my friend; it is simply in accepting. And when you go to make the effort to accept, that which is contrary to your prejudices—because, you see, a person in their effort to demonstrate the will of God, total acceptance, instantly faces their prejudice. And they find that prejudice is prejudgment, that which you have previously judged. And so they face their own prejudices, and all these judgments rise up and deny and put in to your experience what you call fear that you will become the flower because you accept God is expressing through the flower. That only reveals conception's in control, not perception. Does that help with your question?

*Yes.*

Yes. Yes, the gentleman here, please.

*In speaking of the Virgin Mary, commonly called Mother of God, were there other Virgin Marys or—*

Indeed, there are fourteen in recorded history in your particular planet, in your Earth planet. There are fourteen that have preceded in history the one of which you speak, the Virgin Mary.

What does Mother of God mean to anyone who is in that acceptance? Does it mean the mother of goodness? Does man believe that God is the Principle of Goodness or does he believe that God is a judge, giving this and giving that in keeping with whatever you give to Him? For that kind of a belief—to believe in a god that gives you what you give to him—that's a terrible, selfish god. Would you not agree? Oh, why, of course. Then, if you have someone who demonstrates the principle of goodness and it is a woman, then it is understandable that she is the mother of goodness. Would you not say?

*Oh, sure.*

Well, I don't find any in your planet, yet. But to God all things are possible. All things are possible. Hmm? Now, yes. Now go ahead with your question. Most interesting.

*So she, from my reading, she was a very special, chosen person.*

Special? There is no doubt about it. All of the virgins were special. There's no question about that at all. Special in the sense that they did not experience the denial of the Principle of Good and, therefore, had no awareness of the need. And when you have no awareness of need, there is nothing to seek, to search, to depend or rely upon that is outside of your being. Is that not correct? Why, yes. Absolutely. Their history in your world—the Earth planet has not had too many or let us say there's been very few. And therefore, that which there are few demonstrating would be considered special. Would you not agree? Definitely. Absolutely special. Yes.

Yes, the lady there, please.

*I would like to ask, the word* virgin *has usually been used to refer the feminine aspect. Is it necessary to have the masculine aspect also in that state of . . .*

Why, absolutely! Otherwise, there's no virginity. There's nothing pure or virgin if only the female is the virgin. My goodness' sake, no! Yes, I hope that's helped with your question. Absolutely! My!

Ah, it would be nice to experience only virgin thoughts. Pure and simple. The lady there, please.

*Could you speak on prayer and meditation?*

Yes. In reference to meditation, one should choose very wisely their time and place for so doing. One should demonstrate their value of their efforts to attune themselves to the goodness, the God, that they are within their being. And that value is demonstrated by effort, by a repetition of a set time that they have set aside, out of twenty-four long hours, for the experiencing of good or God. Therefore, without discipline, there is no meditation that is worthwhile. One should not exceed twenty minutes in any given twenty-four-hour time for meditation, for so easily the mind takes one into what in your world is known as a type of self-hypnosis. That, on meditation.

Now in reference to prayer, one so often confuses prayer by believing that when they can't make something work, they will pray and, therefore, possibly something else will happen. We understand that, don't we? This is a very common thing of the mental world of all people, you see. When they've tried and judged they've failed—which is really ridiculous because failure reveals success. We were successful in doing what we really wanted and forgetting what it was when we made that choice. Therefore, there is no failure; there is only successes. So prayer— so often a person, you know, they turn to God or the Principle of Good because everything their mind has tried hasn't worked. Or they think and they believe it hasn't worked. And usually they reveal they have not had the wisdom of patience, you see. Now that's not prayer in the understanding of the Living Light Philosophy nor in mine.

Prayer is an aspiration of the soul, this covering known as soul, individualized soul, the covering of this Divine Spirit. It is an aspiration of the individualized soul to the Allsoul, a return to that realm of consciousness. You see, when a person truly prays, there's an aspiration. They experience a total acceptance. They no longer have any interest nor concern with that which they have prayed, you see, because they have risen in this realm of consciousness to these higher planes within their being, and there they experience the allness and the truth, that which they are. Now they return and have to re-identify with these other four centers, and they bring with them a certain feeling of goodness at that moment. Their responsibility is to keep that little spark alive in their consciousness. Does that help you in reference to prayer?

*Yes.*

You see, you have accepted, you see? You have totally accepted. You have demonstrated the movement of the divine Principle of Goodness, and by doing that you benefit from the effect thereof. You can only experience goodness, you see? There's nothing disturbing. For, you see, the mental world is calmed for a time and healed. You see, you no longer experience denial. Therefore, you no longer experience need. Therefore, you no longer experience frustration for you no longer experience the limiting of the divine expression known as desire. Yes.

*I was going to ask, What was the difference, therefore, in meditation and prayer?*

Well, the difference in meditation, in that respect, you see, meditation is designed to take control of the mind consciously, and through the power of concentration, you understand, which is directed by your own will, you consciously rise through to higher levels of consciousness. You understand?

*Yes.*

Now prayer is another way of entering those higher realms of consciousness and, you see, prayer requires total acceptance. There's no other way to enter those celestial realms without the movement of the Principle of Goodness. And so, you see, anything that you deny within your consciousness, no matter how small or how great, keeps you from moving into those higher realms. So all one really needs to do, honestly, is to say, "Now let me see, what is it that I deny? Help me, God, but please reveal it to me slowly, for there is such a mountain, I will collapse under the weight." All right? *[Some of the students laugh.]* It's called prejudice, my dear. Yes.

*Thank you.*

You're welcome. The gentleman next to you, please, has a question. I know you had to wait a few moments, but yes, you may speak your question now.

*Thank you.*

You're welcome.

*The—would you tell me how fear arises in me and what I can do to overcome fear?*

I will be happy to share with you the law that is demonstrable. The only reason a person ever experiences fear—ever—is by believing they are the thoughts of their mind. By depending upon the thoughts of our mind, we believe we are those thoughts. And in keeping with that, we experience fear. It is not you that fears. It is the forms *[At this point, based upon the sounds of the recording, it seems that one of the students dropped something, perhaps a notebook.]* created by the mind, created by the mind, created by the mind that believe, that you believe are you. You are not that. You are that which has created it. Do you understand that?

So what is there for *you* to fear? You are not the hand; you cannot fear losing it. You are not the toe; you cannot fear losing it, for you know that is not you.

Now what does one threaten when one threatens another's life? They only threaten what the person believes that they are in a mental world. You do understand that, don't you? So ask yourself—when you experience fear, remember, it is the effect of a judgment that, for a time, you believe that you are and, therefore, are dependent upon it. Do you understand that?

*Yes.*

Now that is not what you want, is it?

*No.*

You don't want that effect known as fear. Is that correct?

*That's correct.*

There's no problem. All you have to do is to apply the Living Light, that which you are. The steps are very clear. All you have to do is say, "Now that's it. I'm experiencing fear. Fear. I don't like this experience." Pause. You will see clearly in your mind there's a judgment that you believe that you are by depending upon that judgment that you have created, you see? That is not you. But that judgment is a child you have created. And that judgment, that form is what is afraid. And it is trying to survive. Do you understand that? It has made a judgment that it may be annihilated, you understand? And it doesn't want to be annihilated. For, you see, it depends on you as its sustenance, and without you, without the Living Light that you are, it disintegrates and returns to the mental substance from whence it has been created. Do you understand?

So if you don't want to experience fear, then do not believe and depend upon what you have created, you hear? So anytime you think that you're afraid of something, pause and be aware of the very form that in that moment you believe that you are. Tell the form—I know, we have a few minutes [of tape] left—tell the form that, "I created you. I am your father. I am in control by the divine, just law that I have created you." Do you understand that? And when you do that, [the] next moment you'll be aware, "Well, there was nothing to fear at all. That was never me."

Thank you, my good students, and I see that it's now time, there, for refreshments. I put that little thing away there. *[The teacher removes his microphone]*. Sometimes I forget it, being down in this old world with you—*[The recording ends.]*

JULY 11, 1985

# A/V Seminar 5

Good evening, class, and welcome to this seminar. This evening's discussion: experience and why we need it.

First of all, we'll discuss what experience really is. We understand that the thoughts of our mind and our belief that we are the thoughts of our mind establish the laws necessary that those thoughts created by our mind shall return unto us as experiences.

Now all thoughts of the human mind, their formation, their creation, are dependent upon the breath of life for their very form. And so the control of one's experiences in one's life, of course, is dependent upon the control of the breath of life, that which is indispensable to the creating of a thought or thought form. When we desire to change the experiences in our life, it is therefore necessary and absolutely essential that we gain control, through our will power, of the breath of life.

Each thought created by the human mind and dependent upon what is known commonly as the life force registers and is formed on a certain frequency on a certain rate of vibration. It is therefore necessary for us to enter the rate of vibration, the frequency, on which the thought or thought form has originally been created. Whenever the effort is made to gain control of one's breathing, then one, slowly but surely, shall gain control of their experiences, for they will then choose wisely what they will create and, therefore, know beyond a shadow of any doubt what their experiences will be.

Why do we need experiences? Why are we dependent upon them? In order to exist as an individual, so-called, that is, in order to exist in form which is limit, it is necessary to believe in the illusion which is, of course, limit or limitation. So man, in his belief that he is the form, the limit, the thought of I, finds it necessary, in fact, is totally dependent upon the illusion or experiences that he believes that he is.

To gain control over those experiences is not only a wise path, it is a necessary path and one that is guaranteed in evolution. For the limit is in a constant process of changing, of expanding and contracting. For all limit expands in its birth and growth and contracts in its descent and so-called death. So we find in our daily activities, we find in keeping with our belief that we are the thought of I, the limit, and the form, we find that we are ever on a path of so-called happiness only to enter, in the next moment, one of disappointment, sadness, and distress.

When we pause in those moments and we make the effort to gain control over our breathing, we quickly find that the experiences that we are having seemingly change by themselves. The created forms which are returning to their creator, that is, ourselves, they do not change. We simply change our rate of vibration, and we experience in that change other forms, other thoughts, other feelings, other attitudes of mind.

And I'm going to pause at this moment so that you may ask a few questions in reference to what has just been stated, for without your participation you cannot possibly benefit. For the law reveals, as has been stated so many times, that in life, as in anything, we get out of it what we put into it. When you speak, when you release from your universe the spoken word, you release a created form. You release a form that you have not only created but one that you believe that you are. When the form, which is released from your universe, returns to you, it returns, and you experience what you believe is satisfaction, dissatisfaction, or all of the other created forms that you have already mothered and fathered in times past.

We seem to live by free choice. If you understand that free choice in creation is only a delusion created by your mind, for to believe that you are the separate, the limit, to believe that you are creation binds you to illusion.

And so when you speak the word, the form leaves your universe; it returns to you with other forms. They are either, as I have just stated, happy or they are unhappy for like attracts like in the universe. And so whatever you send forth returns unto you, and your experience, of course, is dependent on your belief that you are what you have sent forth.

Now in order that you may awaken to what really happens in life, it is necessary for you to communicate with the many thoughts that you have created already. And those thoughts, you are responsible for. If they are not satisfied with what you are doing, they will rise up in your consciousness and the battle goes on within one's own mind; and one believes they are those forms they have created. To spend time and effort to understand anything you must put energy into that which you desire to understand, for one cannot guide, let alone control, that which they have created until they are ready, willing, and able to communicate with their many children, which you call thoughts.

And so, as I said, we will pause for a moment for your questions. You will kindly raise your hands. The gentleman there, please.

*What determines how quickly our thoughts return to us?*

The awakening of one's own true being. The more awakened one becomes—and by *awakening*, I mean to say freedom from belief that they are the thought. If you believe that you are the thought of your mind, the return of the thought form takes much longer to return unto you. If you have, however, in your awakening, grown in consciousness to an understanding that you have created the thought, you are responsible for the form that you have created, however, you are not the thought, then the return of it is much quicker and much sooner. Does that help with your question?

*Yes. Thank you.*

You're welcome. The lady there, please.

*Thank you. In this philosophy it said the hissing hounds [come] before the victory. When you're in the process of that and you have been trying to direct your energy to other forms and it seems like those forms are screaming for energy, what—I'm not sure what exactly is happening.*

Well, first of all, in order to be aware of the experience, in reference to your stating just before the victory come the hissing hounds of hell, now, in order to be aware of that, you must be in a rate of vibration or frequency upon which they have been created. Now in order to enter that frequency or rate of vibration, you must identify with what you know as self. For whenever a person thinks of self, they reveal that they believe they are all of the thoughts, the feelings, and the attitude of mind that they have already created. Therefore, they, in that respect, become the servant of their own creations. Their creations demand their sustenance.

Whereas, you have, by the life-giving energy of your own breath and in that you have created the form. You see, a person may say, "I had a thought, but I did not speak it." You cannot have a thought without a breath. It will not form. It is physically impossible, impossible to create a thought without the movement of what you know as the breath of life. Does that help with your question?

*Yes. Thank you.*

You're welcome. The gentleman here, please.

*Thank you. You mentioned controlling the breath to affect your experiences.*

Correct.

*In what way is that done?*

Yes. For example, when you have the return, which is known as experience, when you have the return of the thoughts you have already created in your mind, when they return to you, you call that an experience. Now if you like that experience, then you wisely choose to continue to identify or direct intelligent energy to that particular frequency on which they were originally created. If, however, the experience that you have is not one that you desire, it is not one that you consider pleasant, then it is necessary for you, for anyone, to control those experiences by a control of your own breath. Now you've had experiences, I know, in your life whereas rather than to express what you know as your temper, you have chosen, however, to hold your breath. Is that not correct? Perhaps you learned that lesson when you were a very young boy. When your mind told you, if you permit yourself to express this particular thought, you will not have a pleasant experience from that expression.

So you all have experiences in your very early life when, you might call [it], you bit your tongue or you held your breath. By so doing you did not become the victim of the return of the forms that you had already created, for by holding your breath you managed to stay in a frequency on which those experiences could not return to you. Do you understand that?

*Yes.*

Now, you know what experiences you have. If they are ones, as I said, that you do not like, one, through honesty, will find what thought patterns, what attitudes of mind—remember this, all experiences in life are effects of the denial of truth. All experiences in life are an absolute belief in the illusion of limit. Now when we believe in limit, we guarantee the experience of need, for the belief in limit is the denial of truth. So whenever man denies truth, he must pay the price of the denial of truth, and that's known as a belief in limit. And as man believes in limit, he constantly is in need. Does that help with your question?

*Yes, sir. Thank you.*

You see, we don't stop and say to our self, "Now let me see, how can I best believe in limit today?" We don't do that. We're much more cunning, our minds, and we're much more clever than to speak to ourselves and say, "How can I believe in limit today?" No, we do not do that. We believe in the thought of I; that establishes the principle and the law of the belief and the bondage of limit, the denial of truth, the experience of need, and all that it has to offer. Does that help with your question?

You see, if a person, when they are experiencing what they call need, if a person will speak the truth to themselves, "I accept the possibility of something greater"—do not specify what the something greater is, for to specify what the something greater is, is to continue in the law of limit. So one has experiences, usually daily, when they believe that they're in need of this, they're in need of that, they're in need of something else. All they have to do is to declare the truth: "I accept the possibility of something greater." One must never permit themselves to be tempted to declare they accept the possibility that this or that is going to work out, for they just perpetuate the law of limit and continue to experience need, the effect of denial. Does that help with your question?

Yes. The lady there, please.

*Is it a possibility to believe that you're some thoughts and not others?*

Absolutely. In the process of evolving and awakening, the ones that have never had the strongest registration, the ones that we do not frequently visit in frequency and in vibration, those are the ones that go first. And slowly, gradually, but surely, we free our self from the shackles and the burdens of belief that we are any of them. Does that help with your question?

*Thank you.*

You're welcome. The gentleman there, please.

*When an experience returns to us at a time in which we're at a different vibrational level than the one in which the experience was created, the original thought was created—*

Yes? Yes?

*And that vibrational level is higher, does the need to confront that experience exist?*

No. The need does not exist, for you are on a different frequency. You are aware that the experience or the return of the thought you have created at some time in your life is returning. It does not have the value to your mind. You are aware of the experience. You do understand that? However, you are aware, but you do not express. You do not react to it. That reveals to you that you no longer believe that you are it for you are now on a different frequency. Does that help with your question?

You see, that's one of the great values of proper daily meditation and proper breathing, for through that daily effort you rise to higher frequencies in consciousness, and things that might have disturbed you at some other time do not disturb you at all. You see, the law reveals that which disturbs us in life is that which controls us. And so when you are not on the frequency where the thought form has been created (you are on a higher frequency), it does not disturb one. Therefore, it does not control one. Does that help with your question?

*Yes.*

Certainly. The—yes, the lady there, please.

*Once a person awakens from the illusion . . .*

Yes?

*What is their responsibility to another person who is still living in the illusion, to free them from that?*

Yes. That, of course, is dependent upon your understanding of the Law of Solicitation, for unsolicited assistance, unsolicited help is ever to no avail. Therefore, one must awaken within their own consciousness and understand the Law of Solicitation. Now presence is the Law of Solicitation. If someone presents themselves to your universe—you understand that?

*Yes.*

You have, in keeping with the Law of Solicitation, a certain responsibility. You have that responsibility to yourself, for you are responsible for all things that you create and all things that you attract, for that which we attract in life (like attracts like) is ever in keeping with what we are creating or have created. Therefore, presence, the Law of Solicitation, one must exercise personal responsibility. And how does one exercise their right and that personal responsibility? In keeping with the law, we grow in life or we go in life. Does that help with your question?

*Yes. Thank you.*

Yes. Now, in understanding that—and ofttimes it is so difficult for two people, from lack of honest communication within themselves, they are not qualified to communicate honestly with another. You see, the lack of communication with another only reveals the lack of communication with oneself for we cannot in life grant to another what we have not first granted unto our self. And this is where the teaching comes from, "O physician, heal thyself." So if we find in our experiences with others that we are having problems in communicating with another, we should pause, be honest with ourselves, and look inside and find where our own lack of communicating with our self really is. For outward manifestations in life are simply revelations of inner attitudes of mind. Does that help with your question?

*It does. May I ask another?*

Certainly.

*Is there, then, a price involved with being honest and open with someone who is not on that vibrational level?*

Oh, yes, indeed. Indeed, there is. However, one takes a look at their life and they ask themselves the honest question, "What is it or is there anything that I want from someone else? If I want something, anything, from anyone else, then I reveal to myself a need that I believe that I am from a denial that I have established within my own consciousness." Now the price to pay is the forms known as retaliation, which are the expression of an inner attitude of mind known as rejection. If you tell a person what you really think, you must first be willing to tell yourself that truth in order to offer that to another. Now once you do that inside yourself, in communicating with yourself, and you offer that to another, you accept they will grow or go. Does that help with your question?

*Thank you. It does.*

You see, also [it] is a great benefit because it reveals to a person how much they have denied the Truth, God, the Principle of Good, in their life. It reveals to anyone how prejudiced they are. Prejudice meaning prejudgment, how a person prejudges that their God, they may experience through the limit of this person or that person or something else. Does that help with your question?

*Yes.*

Yes.

*Thank you.*

Freedom has a great price tag. A great price tag. It is a great price tag to one who believes they are the limit. However, through an application of the philosophy you have received over these many, many years in your world, through a daily application of that philosophy, which will prove beyond a shadow of any doubt, unto oneself, that the price of letting go is not at all very great to one who knows, deep inside and permits that awakening to rise in their consciousness, that no thing can replace the goodness that they truly are.

You see, speaking on that, relationships and what you call, people call love, it is only—love is only a reflection in another of the goodness that is in oneself. Now it is our mind and our belief that we are the thoughts of our mind that limit us to believing that this or that, they can reflect the God that is within them. You see, the mind reflects. We are not the mind. When we believe we are the mind, we believe, then, that we are the mirror of life instead of life itself. And so we believe that we are the mirror of life, and we look to find a nice, polished mirror that will reflect the goodness that is within us, you see?

We must experience good. We *must* experience good. It is absolutely essential to life for no form continues without the Principle of Good or God. Therefore, man, for his own survival, must experience good. How man will permit himself to experience

God or good is ever in keeping with man's own belief that he is the thought of I. Does that help with your question?

*Yes.*

You're welcome.

*Very much.*

Yes, the lady there, please.

*How does one determine what one is getting out of a repetitious experience?*

If one is freeing themselves from an experience—now try to understand that all experiences are repetitive. They always come back to their creator for their feeding. You see, as you, your limit (your form) is dependent upon sustenance for its continuity, the thoughts created by our mind are dependent upon sustenance for their continuity. So when they do not receive that sustenance and we permit our self to be on the rate of vibration or frequency, which, of course, is ever dependent on our own breathing and our efforts to control it, we permit our self to be on that frequency, we then experience and, by being on that frequency, believe that we are the thoughts that are returning to us as experiences. And so how does one know if they're making any headway with their efforts, is that the question?

*Well, the question . . . Is it so that one's getting something out of the experience? Like, is that a clue to how it keeps happening over and over and over again?*

Well, the return—by believing that we are the experiences of life, we continue to stabilize and believe we are secure from those experiences. Now, for example, when we permit our self to believe we are the limit, the thought of I, it requires support to sustain that belief. Now that support we receive in what we call experiences. If you tell a person that their hand has betrayed them and to cut it off, you will quickly find out how much they believe they are their hand. And yet by believing that we are the hand, we do so at the sacrifice of believing that we are something else.

So if a person only believes that they are their hand and their hand is betraying them repeatedly, then they have a serious problem. Now if we believe that we are our ear and our ear is deceiving us, then we have a serious problem. You see, to pluck out the eye or the ear that deceives us, to cut off the hand that betrays us is a terrible experience when we believe we are those things. And yet to remove the hand, the only change that has taken place is a change in our own beliefs. We continue to live. We continue to experience. And we prove to our self, again, "No, I am not the hand. I'm still walking. I'm still breathing. I'm still experiencing. Well, I have other experiences where I used to use this hand." For those forms that have been created, you understand, which are dependent upon you, which the hand was in use at the time of creating—you understand that?—they don't get the feeding they used to get for the hand is not there to be used by them for their sustenance. Is that intelligent to you?

*Yes.*

Does that help with your question?

*Yes, it does.*

You're welcome. The lady here, please.

*It seems as if it's the breathing that follows the thought, rather than vice versa.*

That is absolutely incorrect. The breathing does not follow the thought. The thought cannot be formed without the breathing. For example—I would like to clarify that. When we breathe we are not—no longer consciously—not consciously choosing the frequency on which we shall breathe. In your world there have been eons pass that that was a natural process for mankind on earth. Those eons are long gone. We do not pause and make an intelligent choice and breathe accordingly. We do not do that anymore. We do not consider the frequencies that we are entering just from our breathing. Therefore, when man controls his breath, while the breath is controlled, man, receptive to the Principle of Good at that time, releases the form and only good thought forms can use that substance. Therefore, man can only experience the goodness of life that he is. Man, then, is no longer dependent upon the mirrors of life, the reflections of the goodness that they are. Does that help with your question?

*Yes.*

You go ahead with your next one.

*I was thinking in terms of, like rapid breathing when there's an experience that's very traumatic and emotional. It seems as if...*

Yes.

*It's automatic.*

Yes, in the sense that those forms were created on that frequency. We have entered that rate of vibration or frequency, and therefore it appears to be automatic. One might even liken it unto what you would call a habit pattern.

*Right.*

Yes. And yet the breath of life, without the breath of life, your existence as you presently know it and believe that you are does not exist for you. Yes. That help with the question?

*Thank you.*

Yes, the lady here, please.

*Does the fetus in the mother's womb use the oxygen, like, in her bloodstream for its breath of life or its thought?*

Indeed, it does. From the moment of conception what you know as thought forms are impinging upon the growing consciousness. Yes, absolutely, from the very moment of conception.

*Thank you.*

You're welcome. The lady there, please.

*Yes. From the conversation about rapid breathing and what happens, I'm wondering if part of controlling the breathing would be to teach oneself to slow down in numbers of breath per minute. Is there a merit to that?*

Well, let us look at it perhaps in another way. When you are experiencing a good feeling, when you are, after that experience, free from exhaustion and the drain of vitality or energy, what would you say your breathing was during those experiences?

*I'm not certain. I don't, I don't feel that I'm really thinking about it.*

I see. Do you have something, perhaps—yes, you do—when you felt very good?

*Oh, yes.*

And after you felt good, you did not feel as though you were drained of energy or vitality? In fact, you felt rejuvenated after the experience?

*Yes.*

Well, if you will pause for a few moments, you will find within your consciousness that your breathing was very harmonious.

*Oh.*

You see, long ago we stated to you: health is the effect of the Law of Harmony. Well, one cannot experience health—What is health? Health is all things in harmonious motion. What is health? Health is an expression of the Principle of Goodness. You have the health of your finances. You have the health of your body. You have the health of your mind. You have the health of your environment. It is dependent upon the Law of Harmony.

Now a person cannot breathe discordant and inharmonious and expect to experience health, wealth, and happiness. It is not possible. Does that help with your question?

*Yes.*

You're welcome. The lady there, please.

*If a person is not very aware of the forms that they're creating, how can they increase that awareness?*

If a person is not very aware of the thoughts of their mind, which are the forms they are creating or servicing—for many forms or thoughts have already been created; they only come back for their sustenance or what you call their feeding. How can a person be more aware? Let me state this once again: the intensity of density is measured by acceptance.

Now we all understand that acceptance is the will of the Principle of Good, known as God. The more acceptance in life we have, the more awareness we have. So when we reach that place in evolution, accepting the divine right of all expression, for God, that Principle of Good, sustains all thoughts—even the thoughts of denial the Principle of Good sustains. So if we want to experience the goodness of life and we want more awareness of the thoughts of our mind and control of their return, which is known as experience, then we must expand our consciousness, broaden our horizons, and demonstrate the will of goodness, the will of God, known in this philosophy as total acceptance.

You see, each thing that we deny in life we destine our self to it. So we deny the expression of this person. We deny the expression of that person. We deny the rights of this to live. We deny the rights of that to, what you call, die. When we do that, we destine our self by the very law that we are establishing.

Now there are many things that man does not wish to experience. If he does not wish to experience them, then man should wisely refrain from denying their right of existence. You see, we say that, "Well, I grant the right, I grant the right of that person doing that, but I would never do such a thing." When you make that type of a statement, you have instantly established the Law of Denial, the destiny for yourself. So you cannot say that, "I grant that person the right to do that. However, I would never do such a thing." For the Law of Destiny—that Law of Denial is the Law of Destiny. We only guarantee in principle the experience. We do not guarantee the exact formation of it. However, we guarantee the experience. Does that help with your question?

*Well, I have one more now.*

Certainly.

*If so—if you say I grant that person the right to what he's doing, is that as far you go then, rather than the continuing on?*

No, no, that's not the way to do it. First of all, to state, "I grant that person the right to express in that way," you have immediately in consciousness entered into limit, formation, person, and personality. When you view experiences that within your consciousness immediately a judgment rises up to express itself, you declare the truth: the divine right of all expression. Period! You will, slowly but surely, gain control over destining yourself to identically the same experience in principle. You see, first of all, by permitting the judgment to rise within the consciousness, we have already entered the limit and the formation of the throne of judgment. Now no one with any awakening at all could possibly believe that God is a doer or a giver. God *is*. Whether or not we choose to experience, without dependence on that which we cannot control, this Divine Principle, known as God, is entirely up to us. You don't need to move limit in order to experience God. That is not necessary. That is totally dependent upon illusion. So when we tell our self, "I need a vacation in order that I may feel good and feeling good is knowing God," then our God, for us and for us to experience that goodness, is dependent upon the laws of limit, known as creation. Does that help with your question?

*Yes. Thank you.*

Yes. You see, to look at the flowers and say, "The buttercup has no right to be here. This is a field of daisies." We only create, within our own consciousness—our world, our world is just exactly the way we make it and exactly the way we take it. We don't take it very well. We don't seem to have much of any problem making it. We don't seem to have any problems forming thoughts. We seem to have no problems creating all kinds of forms from our thoughts and attitudes and beliefs and disbeliefs.

Our problem is in our willingness to accept what we have no problem creating. So that's where our real problem is: accepting "That's what I created. Now, thank you for your return. You are helping me to inspire me to create no more of you. Or to make greater effort in my consciousness to rise to different frequencies."

Now remember this, you cannot continue to create forms that return with distasteful experiences and stay in a state of meditation or higher frequency twenty-four hours a day; it's not possible. Now you can do many things for so many minutes or perhaps hours of a day, but there is no way, while yet identified with the limit, that you can remain in meditation twenty-four hours a day. Does that help with your question? So, of course, reason alone reveals, "Just a moment. I can only stay in meditation so long in a twenty-four-hour period. Therefore, I must make greater effort not to create those forms that I don't appreciate when they return." You see, we must have the same lack of appreciation in creating them as we already have in their return to us. And then we'll have no problem at all. Thank you.

Someone else have a question now? The lady right there. There. Yes.

*When you talk about control, are you talking about the diaphragm, control of the diaphragm as in singing or . . .*

The control of the breath. Now, you see, we seem to have this belief that the breath of life should enter our being, stop at the chest, and go back out. We seem to totally disregard the rest of the temple of God. The breath of life is life. Our toes, our feet, our legs, our knees, they all have a right to that life and that vitality. So when we permit our self, which is an error of ignorance, an effect of laziness in consciousness, to believe that the breath of life goes in and out of the lungs and no place else in the human body, it's absolutely ridiculous. Does that help with your question? So if you want to be a whole person, then you must make the effort to breathe harmoniously, which, of course, is rhythmically, and to breathe wholly and fully, and not leave your toes out. Thank you.

*Thank you.*

The gentleman in the back, please.

*Can the breath of life be done at a more rapid pace?*

More rapid?

*Say, if you were in a, in a laborous mood?*

Your "laborous mood"? Well, if you enjoy the forms of what you call a "laborous mood," then, of course, you are experiencing an effect of a certain frequency or rapidity that you seem to enjoy. Now many people truly believe that they experience God or goodness through certain thrills. Well, there are many things that thrill the human mind. The question is, How beneficial are those thrills or rapid, so-called, experiences to the whole being? That's the question that one should ask themselves.

Someone else have a question? The lady here, please.

*How can we know or tell when our toes are getting the benefit of the breathing exercise?*

Well, everyone can feel their toes when they choose to feel them. Because, without your feet, you would not be very happy.

*Right.*

I don't believe that you believe you would be very happy without your toes and without your feet. Then, you have a responsibility in appreciation that you have them to see that they are properly nourished. Now you want to know how you can tell when the breath reaches your toes?

*Yes.*

First of all, you must be aware that you have toes before you start breathing. Now when you make the effort to be aware, "Yes, I have toes. Yes, I can feel my toes." You see, you must learn to feel your toes without moving your toes. Now that's part of an exercise that I have given to some of my students. You be perfectly still; you send your consciousness to your toes and you will be aware of your toes. Now you have a moment to do that. *[After a very short pause, the teacher continues.]* The moment has passed. You feel your toes? Don't move them.

*Yes.*

Yes. You are aware that you have toes?

*Yes.*

Yes, of course, we're aware. We're aware of anything and everything that we put our attention on. So, first of all, we put our attention on our whole being. Now after we've put our attention on our whole being, then we do proper breathing. And then you won't have to worry about how you're going to know if your breath is getting to your toes for your toes will tingle, just like all of the rest of you.

*Thank you.*

And if they don't, then the breath's not getting there. The vitality and the nourishment is not getting there. You see, man is not just an animal; he's like a plant. If you don't water it, you don't care for it, then it doesn't get nourished, then it does not survive. It does not flourish. Do you understand?

*Yes, I do.*

Yes. And so one so often, you know, they will, in consideration of limit, only think of the limit of the physical body, not thinking of the limit of the mental body. You know, it is rare that a person will say, "Oh, I didn't think about eating today." It is extremely rare that a person will say, "Well, last week I didn't eat at all. I never gave it any thought." And I'm sure you will find it's very, very rare that a person says, "You know, it's just dawned on me that I haven't eaten anything physically for the past six months." No. No, no, that's very rare. And yet we find, in your world, people going not a day, not a month, not even 6 months, 6 years, 10 years, 20 years, 30 years, 40 years, 50 years, 60, 70, 80, 90 years and never once giving consideration to the nourishment or the feeding of their vital body, of their mental body, of their astral body, to none of those bodies of which they are using all the time. Using those bodies, however, totally ignorant, and yet, complaining and very unhappy when those bodies register experiences that they judge they never deserved. Does that help with your question?

*Yes.*

You know, ofttimes a person meets another person and they say, "That person had no right to be so nasty to me. They had no right to talk to me like that." We rarely ever say, "That's very interesting. I sent out into the universe a thought, a feeling, an attitude, and a form. And that person came in to show me what I had done. And now I'm blaming that person from my lack of effort and my ignorance of the forms that I sent out, that through the law that like attracts like, that person has brought to me." Did that help with your question?

*Yes.*

You see, it's like, you know, it's stated so long ago: the stone the builder rejects becomes the cornerstone. We are blinded by the vehicles which are used to return the laws to us. We look and we see the form. We refuse to see the law expressing through that form at any given moment. When we look in life and we go beyond the limit and we say, "I didn't like that person at all. I didn't like the way they acted to me," stop at that point for that's delusion. By believing in illusion, you become the delusion. All right. So you pause and you say, "Let me see, terrible. Very nasty. Now those are forms I sent out. I don't like their return. I had no problem in sending them out, but I don't like them returning to me. I'm going to make more effort to be more aware of what I'm doing and what frequency in my life I'm expressing on." Does that help with that?

*Yes.*

You see, when you permit yourself to be disturbed by anything that you cannot control, what you reveal is a blatant denial of the truth that you are. So when you allow yourself to be disturbed and you then tell yourself, "This is beyond my control," then you deny the truth that you are. For it is your mind. It is in your domain. It is not only your divine right, it is your responsibility to control it. You are not dependent on someone else for the experience. If that person didn't bring you the experience, the next person would. So how many people in your world say, "Well, that marriage didn't work out. I'll try another"? Second one they try, that doesn't work out. They try the third one. That doesn't work out. They try the fourth. That doesn't work out. They try the fifth. That doesn't work out. They finally say, "It's just not worth it." Well, it's true: it's not worth it to continue to believe and to delude oneself that those, all those people, it's all their fault. They are only the bearers of the law that we send out. Does that help you?

*Yes, sir.*

You're welcome. *[The teacher continues after a short pause.]* Silence is golden, but I don't see everyone here golden. Thank you. The lady there, please.

*Why is it so seemingly difficult to be honest with oneself? What is the obstruction?*

The obstruction to be honest with oneself is the bondage of believing that we need something from them. You see, anyone who believes and from belief in self is tempted—for one tempts oneself by believing that they are this limit, then they are tempted. For, you see, when you believe you are that limit, that thought form of I, when you believe that, then you have denied what you are, and therefore you have the experience known as need. When that happens, that need must be filled, for no one lives long in the experience of need, for no one can long endure that way. It's an imbalance within the mind. So a person [who] experiences need, the effect of denial, is absolutely convinced what they must have: the fulfillment. Someone else has it. Someone else has to have it, for if they had it, they are convinced, they would not experience the need. You understand that? Therefore, the price to be paid is to search the world, constantly searching for someone to fill the need. You experience the need because you're convinced you don't have it. Because you don't have it, someone else *must* have it, for you are experiencing the need of it. Because you experience the need of it, you know beyond any doubt in your mind. You have convinced yourself it's got to be filled. [You have convinced yourself] there is someplace, somewhere there is someone that has the ingredient necessary to fill your need, which is your own denial. Do you understand that?

Now, so you search out for someone to do that. And you make the judgment, "Ah, this person, I believe, has what I need. They will fill this need of mine." And for a time, you delude yourself. For a time. And how fortunate you are and how beautiful life truly is; it only lasts for a time. Does that help with your question?

*Yes. Thank you.*

Yes. Yes, the gentleman here, please.

*The Lord's Prayer says, "Forgive us our trespasses as we forgive those who trespass against us." Can we speak on forgiveness? And—*

Yes?

*What is the best way to forgive?*

To give forth. *Forgive* means to give forth. All right. Who, you, you—one must ask oneself the question, If one is having an experience they wish to be free from, then because the experience within their mind was dependent upon another person—you do follow me, do you not? I hope so. All right. Because it was dependent on another person, they cannot forgive or give forth without honest communication. It's not possible. For, you see, within their mind, when they go to give it forth, it reaches a wall which they cannot penetrate. Do you understand that? All right. Now, so depending on the belief of a person that they are the limit, they must speak to the person who is involved with what they are trying to free themselves from. Now as a person evolves in consciousness, they can forgive or give it forth to God, the Principle of Good. But that's dependent on how much a person believes that they are the limit. Does that help with your question? A wise man forgives; while yet in form, he does not forget.

For a person to remain in form and in limit, they must believe in illusion in order to identify. Therefore, by believing in limit, man cannot afford the luxury, while believing in limit, to forget. To forgive is the path of wisdom, and freedom, of course. To forget is not. You see, to forgive is human. Ah, to forget is divine. So one should not forget until they experience the fullness of the Divinity. And when that happens, well, we'll not be here communicating in this limit, will we? Does that help you?

*[Thank you.]*

You're welcome. Yes, the gentleman there, please.

*Yes. Does man know how many parts there are to the brain?*

Well, an awakened man knows not only the brain but every other part of the temple of God for which he is responsible. Yes.

*An awakened man.*

Yes. You asked me if man knew all the parts of the brain. And I said an awakened man not only knows all parts of the brain, he knows all parts of the temple of God for which he is responsible while residing in it.

*Thank you.*

Did that answer your question?

*No, sir.*

Did you want me to speak on what an unawakened man knows in reference to the parts of the brain?

*Yes, sir.*

Well, then I can tell you right now they know approximately 40 percent of what actually exists. Yes, just in reference to the brain. Forty percent.

*Yes.*

Yes?

*Does each part correspond to a body, one of the bodies?*

A body or to a part of the body?

*A part of the bodies. You say we have a mental body . . .*

Oh, absolutely! Astral bodies and etc. Absolutely. Definitely. The brain is a physical substance through which those bodies express. Yes? Was there some other question you had there?

*Yes, but it hasn't come clear yet.*

That's all right. We have time, I think. The lady, please.

*Through the rhythmic breath of life does all of the emotional bodies and, do they all get cleansed at once? Is there, is there . . . a way to—*

Well, yes, thank you. I think we have your question. In reference to what we were discussing on controlled and proper breathing, all bodies for which you are responsible would, of course, in that respect be benefited. Yes.

*Thank you.*

You're welcome. The lady, please.

*How is bodily disease created? What is it an expression of?*

Yes. An imbalance between the faculties of the soul and the functions of the senses or the body. And that imbalance creates discord, which is known in this philosophy as disease, the opposite of health.

*Yes.*

You see, for every function there is a corresponding soul faculty. And when those are brought into balance you have harmonious expression. Yes.

*Well, on, on a physical level—*

Yes.

*This society gives credence to foods that cause cancer and that type of thing. I was wondering how that translated into the harmonization of the soul, mental and physical?*

In reference to what you were speaking on cancer, which is a discord between the blood cells, you understand, the red and white corpuscles, there is an imbalance, which is the direct effect of an imbalance between the faculties of the soul and the functions of the body.

When you understand that the fluids of the human body flow in keeping with the harmony of the mental body which controls them—now try to understand, we're not speaking about what you know as psychosomatic medicine. We're not speaking on that at all. We are speaking at this time on the natural flow of the fluids in the human body. Now man obstructs that natural flow from deep-seated inner beliefs and attitudes of mind, very deeply seated. Deeply seated in this respect, your form, presently, is an effect. It's a house. It's a temple of the Principle of Good or God.

Now the lessons in evolution—this philosophy teaches evolutionary incarnation. You enter your Earth planet; your parents are effects of laws established in your evolution, and they are effects of those laws. You could not have entered Earth through any other parents, for their combination offered to your evolving soul the necessary lessons in keeping with what you had passed in your lessons in form in other times, other places, and other planets. So you have certain color eyes. You have certain color skin. You have certain color hair. You have a certain size. You have certain strengths and certain tendencies and weaknesses in your physical body. Do you understand?

*Yes.*

Now, because each and every part of the temple of God represents a soul faculty and a sense function, through an understanding of that, one can learn what the lessons are that they have to learn in their present incarnation. Now when you, the true being, identified or dented the consciousness and became form or limit, when that happened, as you strengthened your conviction that you are the limit or the form, you do so at the expense of your own awakening and your own knowing of the lessons that you are in your particular planet to learn. Does that help you with your question?

So, you see, no one enters any form by what is known as accident. There are no accidents in the universe. What appears to be accidents or miracles is nothing more and nothing less than our lack of understanding the laws by which they are controlled. And so when a person has an experience in their life [and] the experience repeats itself [and] they have great difficulty in not having those particular experiences, it reveals to them the lessons in their incarnations in evolution that they, so to speak, have flunked.

And so those experiences continue to repeat themselves for repetition is the law through which change is made possible.

*Yes.*

Now it's like a person who becomes dependent. Say a woman becomes dependent on a man and the more dependent she becomes, the more difficulties she experiences, which is her own freedom. It's the same way with a man. He becomes dependent upon a woman for the goodness of life. And so he has many experiences, and the more distasteful the experiences are to him, the freer he gets. Does that help with your question?

*Yes.*

You see, you see, if we depend on man, we do so at the sacrifice of our reliance upon what we are, the God that is within us. So the more we depend on something outside, the smaller our God is inside. Does that help with your question?

*It does.*

You see, "All things I am, can do and be, for I am the goodness that you see." So you talk to yourself. You see, when you look in the mirror, declare the truth: you are the goodness and all things you are, can do and be, for you're the goodness that you see. So when you look at this reflection, look in the mirror, you will experience that because that is what you are. That is not what you believe. That is what you are, you see.

And when a person is what they are, it's a beautiful world. It *is* a beautiful world. It is up to us to let that beauty in, but that comes at a cost of freeing our self from dependence on anything that it is not our right to control.

*Yes.*

A wise person depends only on that which they can control. And that's known as putting God in it or forget it. If you see something there and you believe it's going to fill your need, then it is not—it is something outside of you, then be rest assured, forget it for God cannot be in it. It's only a temporary experience of delusion.

So no matter—you know, when it is stated, "O suffer senses not in vain for freedom of thy soul is gain," it seems difficult if we believe we are those senses. But once we understand that we are the worker, we are not the tool—when we believe temporarily that we are the tool that we are using, then we suffer from the belief of the denial of what we are. We are not the tool. We are not the eye. We are not the toe. We are not the hand. We are not the foot. We are that which uses the eye, the toe, the hand, and the foot. To permit ourselves to believe that we are the tools that we are using is a path of great suffering for all minds. Does that help with your question?

*Yes. Thank you.*

You're welcome. Now the gentleman here, please.

*Yes. May—I'd like to ask what body corresponds to creation, to earth?*

All bodies correspond—in fact, all bodies are creation, for all bodies are limits. You see, "I am Spirit formless and free, / Whatever I think, that will I be." You are not a body. You are that which uses a body. You are that which is responsible for what you use. You are not a body. You only use a body. The body does not belong to you. The body is loaned to you to be used for a time. To those who believe they are that which has been loaned them to use for a time suffer greatly when the time comes for that which has been loaned to them to return to its source, from whence it was composed.

And so when man permits himself to believe that he is the thought of I, which is the limit of the true I that he is, then man suffers. Man only suffers by trying to steal what has been loaned to him. His body is loaned to him. The thoughts are loaned to him. Experiences are loaned to him. He uses them and unfortunately, by believing that he is them, he abuses them. And it is through that abuse that man suffers. Does that help with your question?

*Yes, sir. Very much.*

And so the place to work, of course, is to work through control of our mind. To work through these frequencies and these vibrations and to declare the truth: "I am that which uses this limit. I am not the limit, for if I was the limit, then I could only limitly use it." You see, you are not the limit. When you permit yourself to believe that you are, that's when you become it. You only become it for a time. So when you have a thought and you believe you are the thought, and when you have, from that thought you have created, you have the experience of need and you further that need by believing someone else is going to fill it, then you have to pay a dear price for that, for you have lied to yourself. However, it's only temporary, but you have lied to yourself for a time. Now does that help with your question, young man?

*Yes, sir. Ah . . .*

No, not yet. Go ahead.

*OK. What, what is the purpose of, what is it and what is the purpose of our subconscious?*

Of your subconscious?

*Yes, sir.*

What is its purpose?

*Yes, sir. What is the purpose of it?*

Well, the purpose of it is quite simple. The purpose of it—it is the warehouse where all of these forms, you see—you want to know—you see, you have many thoughts, is that correct?

*Yes, sir.*

In the course of an hour you have many thoughts.

*Right.*

Well, they're all stored in what you call the subconscious. They all wait down there, you see. They wait for that moment when they say, "Oh, our chance is now! Now I've got a chance to get food. I haven't eaten for weeks! Perhaps even months!" They're all waiting down there. Yes, that's where they're stored. You see, the subconscious, you see, has no faculty of reason. The faculty of reason only exists in the conscious mind. So one should not—it's—the subconscious, that's where you put all of these forms you've created. [If] you want to get new forms down there, well, then you best be quite intelligent about it and never let your conscious mind be set aside so that you're controlled by the forms that you, from belief that you are them, that they can rise up and take control of your life. No. Does that help with your question?

*Yes, sir.*

Yes. It's quite a—what do you call it?—it's quite a can of worms down there. I wouldn't be tempted to go down there to live. I mean, it's one thing to take a look at it and try to get some reprogramming done, but it's not the place to live. I find—you know, where—you have these experiences, I know that you do, in what you call emotion. Right?

*Yes, sir.*

Well, what is emotion? It's only the expression of forms that you believe that you are who are determined to have their own way and they temporarily have an obstruction. Pardon?

*Right.*

Well, yes, but at least, be it in Divine order, you know that that is not what you are. However, you are responsible for them, but that is not what you are. Does that help?

*Yes, sir. Thank you.*

Yes. Yes, the gentleman here, please.

*Faith can apply to a task, can it?*

Faith?

*Faith. Like I have faith that I can do this or . . .*

Yes, I think, perhaps, you might use that in terms of conviction. For, first of all, you see, to say, "I have faith that I can do this," we have already entered the realm of limit. Therefore, one may be convinced that they can do something. However, faith is far beyond that. You see, faith is not controlled by limit. Faith *is*. You see, a person has faith in something greater in their life. To specify is to limit. Therefore, a man may convince himself of what he is able to accomplish. However, faith is not dependent. Faith is above and beyond limit. Faith is an expression of what you truly are in the universe. That's faith: what you are. It's not subject to belief and therefore, absolutely and positively, it is totally freed from limit. Does that help with your question?

*So it's an opposite of confidence or conviction, I should say.*

Yes, well, when a person—well, a person may say that, "I'm using faith in that way." Then one would have to call that conviction, for it is this power within one that they are limiting by the human mind because of their belief in the Law of Limit. Does that help with your question? So a person, one has faith in God, but one is not so foolish to say, "That's God and that's what God is like." One is not that foolish. God just is. So one has faith in what *is*, and by having faith in what is, one is freed from what one is not.

Now I see that our time is up. Thank you very much and enjoy your evening.

AUGUST 8, 1985

## A/V Seminar 6

Good evening, students.

And at this evening's seminar we will be discussing experiencing what you want in a world of creation, a dimension of duality, by accepting what you do not want. It is known as the Law of Contradiction, the Art of Control. This may seem a bit surprising to some of you only in the sense that you may not be aware of what you are already so proficient at.

A wise man would rather carry a big stick than to cast a giant shadow. For shadows, as some of you are well aware, are merely forms created by what you know as an obstruction to the Light. For that which obstructs the Light that you are, in truth, absorbs the Light that you are and, therefore, through that absorption of the Light, creates a form which you know as a shadow.

By accepting what you do not want, you free yourself from the control of what you claim that you do want. For example, the direction of attention to anything gives life-giving energy to that which you direct, through the Law of Attention, that energy to.

Ofttimes in your experiences in creation you feel discouraged and disappointed that things have not worked out the way that you believe you wanted them to work out. They always work out in keeping with what we truly direct the energy to. So that reveals to us that our adversities use more of our energy and, therefore, by the use of that energy, become our attachments or obstructions. For all adversities and all attachments are in truth obstructions.

Do not be concerned with my little student here. He's doing just fine. Mr. Red, come along and say hello. He's had major surgery within the last twenty-four hours. And so if he just stands and doesn't do anything, you will understand he's under the influence of what some people think is a necessary high. *[The teacher refers to the church's dog.]*

Now we look at our life and we see so many things; they don't work out the way we planned. That's what we believe. And yet when we're honest and we take stock of where our attention has been, we will find that in the course of a day we spend more thought and more energy on the things in life that we do not wish to experience. And by so doing, of course, we create those things.

This, in truth, creates a contradiction within the consciousness. And that which is contrary is, in truth, controlling. We are not controlled when we are peaceful. We are, of course, peaceful when we are not concerned. We are concerned when we view our obstructions. We are never concerned when we view what we believe is our way. Concern only enters our consciousness when we place our attention upon what we believe is our obstructions.

In these seminars and in these classes over these many years, students have seemed to have had great difficulty: difficulty in asking the questions they want to ask. And it is important, as students, that you understand the cause of the difficulty. When one speaks, one reveals. Ofttimes they do not reveal what they wish to reveal. But by the spoken word, because it is life-giving energy, we do reveal what is to be revealed. And so in one's life's experiences in creation, one soon learns not to ask, for to ask is to reveal, and to reveal usually is not what one wishes to do.

Creation is a world of images, for that's what creation is. The images change moment by moment, for that is the nature of images. They are not stable. They cannot be relied upon, for depending upon the light, reveals the image and its rapidity of change. For example, a person looks at their image in a reflector. Depending upon the light that is being cast, depending upon how much of that light they are absorbing, so be their image at any given moment. Sometimes a person will look at their image in a reflector and they will be pleased with what is revealed to them as a reflection of what they believe they are: their image. That reveals, in truth, that they are less of an obstruction and, therefore, absorbing less of the Light that they are. Therefore, they are pleased with what is reflected back to them.

For example, we take, here, this evening and this seminar. One of my students has been kind enough to set the lights in keeping with the limits of your world and what is available for you at this particular time. The cameraman was instructed, prior to this seminar, to check what you know as a white balance after everyone was present. The reason for that, for your world reveals, and the reason for that is that those objects, people absorb. As objects absorb vibration, they absorb color, they absorb sound, and, of course, they absorb light. For light is color and light is sound.

You hear sound not by pure Light, only by what obstruction is in the way of pure Light. You see objects or people not by the pure Light that you are, only by the obstructions that are in front of the Light that you are. So when we believe that we are not experiencing what we want to experience, we go to work on the obstructions that are absorbing the Light that we are. And we do that by accepting the obstructions that are in the way of our Light that we do not want. Now that is known as a balance or neutralization in a world of creation or form. For whoever accepts what they do not want establishes the law to experience what they do want. That is contradiction. That, also, is control. For when man accepts what he does not want, he frees himself from identification with the obstruction to what he does want. Now you've been given that in so many different ways and especially in the Law of Gratitude, which is the guarantee of supply.

So to be concerned and to be worried is only to create greater obstructions. For when a person entertains the possibility of experiencing what they do not want in life, fear rises and controls what they are. When one accepts the possibility of experiencing what they do not want, one frees themselves from the self-created obstruction.

Now it's time for you to ask your questions in reference to the little discussion that we have already had, if you'll be so kind as to raise your hands. Yes.

*We were encouraged to accept what we do not want in life and, at the same time, not to be a blade of grass to be mowed over by the people we encounter, how—*

May we pause at that moment?

*Yes.*

We, of course, do not wish nor desire to be a blade of grass to be mowed over by someone else. We cannot experience that thinking without first believing that someone outside of us is controlling us, which is, of course, a denial of the Law of Personal Responsibility. Go ahead with your question, please.

*Thank you. My question was, How can we discern the difference between those two situations?*

In reference to discerning the difference between two situations, one which is a belief that something outside of us controls us, the freedom from that belief is in the acceptance of personal responsibility. You see, personal responsibility, the only path to freedom, clearly reveals that nothing beyond our control controls us. Now when we accept in our consciousness what we do not want, what we in truth are facing is the shadows of the past. We in truth are facing the judgments that we have made, the obstructions we have created. Now when we accept a judgment that we have made, we free our self from the control of the judgment, and by freeing our self of our own self-creations, we then control ourselves. But we cannot possibly believe that we control ourselves when we permit ourselves to be victims of things we have created. Does that help with your question?

*Yes, sir. Thank you.*

Yes. You're welcome. The lady there, please.

*What causes a person to be impulsive? And how can it—and how can it be . . .*

Yes. What causes a person to be impulsive? The lack of effort on controlling the judgments of the mind. They're using our mind as a freeway. There are no cautions, no stops, only goes. Does that help with your question?

*Thank you.*

Pardon?

*Thank you.*

You're welcome. The lady there, please.

*In, in accepting, are we accepting the right of that expression? Is that what we're doing?*

We are accepting the divine right of all expression. And we are accepting what we have created, which are judgments, which are obstructions to the Light that we are. You see, denial is our destiny. And so our experiences in creation of not getting what we believe we want to get is simply the Law of Denial. We have denied what we have created. To accept what we have created is to free our self from our creations.

Yes. My friend, here, he's gone to rest. *[The teacher again refers to the church's dog.]* Yes.

*Thank you.*

Thank you. Does that help with your question?

*Yes. Very much.*

Yes, please, the gentleman there.

*Yes. Is any mental recognition an obstruction?*

Pardon?

*Is any mental recognition an obstruction?*

Well, it depends on what you mean by *recognition*. Now we recognize, here, and we judge that to be, based upon our experiences and our training, to be a glass that's filled with water. Now we recognize that, would you not say that?

*Yes, sir.*

Would you consider that an obstruction?

*No.*

It could be an obstruction, couldn't it?

*Yes, sir.*

If you wanted something else there, then you would want to move that so that you could have something in its place. And if it refused to move, then you would have an obstruction to your desire. Is that not true?

*Yes, sir.*

So whatever we recognize can be an obstruction; it depends upon how much control of our own desires we have at any given moment. Do you understand?

*Yes, sir.*

So one person looks at something and they find that to be no obstruction at all. It does not bother them. What they are telling you [is], "That doesn't control me at all." If it bothers us, if it disturbs us, then, of course, it is controlling us. For when it is moved, we are no longer disturbed and we return to the peace before the disturbance. Do you understand that?

*Yes, sir.*

Therefore, what is an obstruction to one is a way to another. However, we must understand that we have created the obstructions, which are absorbing the Light that we are and convincing us that we are the shadow that it casts. Thank you.

*Thank you.*

Someone else have a question? The gentleman here, please. Yes.

*Thank you. It's been my experience that when an object is placed in the path of light, it not only absorbs the light but it also reflects, to a degree, the light. And what I'm asking is, If we can recognize that it also reflects the light, is that like seeing the good in, in the obstruction?*

That which reflects the light does not absorb the light, would you not agree?

*Yes.*

Therefore, by accepting the light, the light is reflected; by denying the light, the light is absorbed. And so if you take a look at any thought that you have and you find that which you deny is absorbing—and by its absorption process creating and, therefore, what you understand, casting a shadow—that energy (that which you are) is being used to convince you of what you are not. For that which reflects the light is not absorbing the light. For it is a light equal to the light that it is receiving. And by being equal, it therefore reflects or returns the light that it is receiving. Does that help with your question?

*Yes. Thank you.*

Yes, the lady here, please. And I'll be right with you over there, yes.

*Could you please speak in that same regard to the moon as being a reflector and how that ties in?*

Well, in reference to the moon, the moon, as you understand in this philosophy, is the reflector of the true light of the sun. However, the moon as the reflector of the true light is also the controller of the emotions or the lesser light.

*Could you expand on that a little bit? I'm . . .*

Well, for example, when you have a lesser light, man is convinced by illusion. Illusion is made possible by a lesser light. The brighter the light, the lesser the illusion. And so the moon as a reflector of the true light controls what man believes he is [and] does not affect or control what he truly is. So if a person chooses to believe that they are the shadows of their own judgments, people of that type therefore are affected or controlled by what they understand is their emotions. Emotions are totally, wholly, and completely dependent upon the conviction of a person's mind that they are the shadows that their own judgment has created. Does that help with your question?

*Thank you.*

Therefore, a person in emotion does not see the Light that they are, only the light that they have convinced themselves that they are and, therefore, are dependent upon something outside by denying what they are inside.

Now the lady back there has a question.

*Would the first telltale sign, then, that you are becoming the obstruction, would that be the discomfort, since it can be so elusive at times?*

Yes, a person, of course, is not comfortable when they are experiencing the belief in what they are not. They do not feel good. They do not feel comfortable because they are being bothered. You see, no one consciously—and that's where the faculty of reason expresses itself, in our conscious mind—no one makes a conscious choice to be bothered or disturbed. They make a conscious choice to deny what they have created and, from that denial, are destined to the experience of being controlled. So when one refrains from denial in consciousness, one moves to the opposite, which is acceptance in consciousness. And whatever we accept, we then control.

You see, as I started this seminar this evening in denial and acceptance: accept what you do not want and experience what you do want. For by so doing you remove the obstruction that you have created, and when you remove the obstruction in consciousness, you experience what you are. And what you are does not experience denial. And not experiencing denial, it cannot experience need. Does that help with your question?

*Yes. Thank you.*

Contradiction—the art of control. Yes. In a world of creation.

Yes, would you—I have—the gentleman in the back row has been waiting. I'll be right with you.

*How can I best provide the relationship that she wants from me?*

Do you desire to provide a relationship?

*Yes.*

Then, therefore, you believe you have need. Correct? One does not desire what they know they have. One only desires what they have denied. So you are asking how you can best provide what someone else wants or are you asking how can you best provide for what you want? There is a difference.

*How I can provide what I would like.*

What you'd like or what you want?

*What I'd like to be able to provide for some relationship.*

For your relationship, is that correct?

*Yes, partly . . .*

Because, you see, if you are not satisfied, if your judgment of what a relationship is, is not satisfied, then there is no lasting relationship. There's hardly even a beginning one. Pardon? If we'll only be honest and tell our self the truth: "I have denied that which I am. From that denial I now experience need. My denial or need is taking the form of what I believe someone else has for me. I call that a relationship. I expect them to give to me what I have denied myself." Does that help with your question? Now if you're honest—and be honest with yourself and say, "I have denied that which I truly am. From that denial I am experiencing a need. I believe that this person can fill my need." Now you speak to the person and you say, "This is what I am experiencing. I have this belief that you can fill my need. Are you willing to do so, and how long will you be willing to do that?" Pardon? That's known as an honest relationship. The other type of relationships are not worth the energy of the spoken word, child. Thank you.

The lady there, please. Yes.

*I'd like a little more understanding. In tonight's class was mentioned that vibration is color and sound and . . .*

Yes?

*When we create obstructions to the Light, they're colors. And—*

They absorb colors, yes.

*They absorb colors.*

And sound.

*They absorb the colors and sound . . . I'm still formulating what . . .*

I understand. Well, for example, you're sitting here, this evening, at this seminar in this room. You look around and you see various colors. Now in your world these colors are created by what you call filters. That light there has an amber filter. That light there, it has a rose filter. That one is what you call white. That one is what you would consider an ice blue. So you have these different colors. Now these colors and this light temperature—and I'm not speaking of heat; I'm speaking of light—this light temperature has been adjusted by one of my students, and it has been tested and showed and [has] excellent balance. However, when there are more objects or more people present, those colors in the atmosphere are absorbed by those objects and people by their apparel and by their own vibration. Therefore, one must balance your little picture box [a monitor], there, after everyone, all objects, have been introduced, for there is a change in the color in the temperature of the light. Does that help with your question, to help form your personal question?

*Yes.*

All right.

*Therefore, when each thought has a color and a vibration and a sound.*

That is correct. That is correct.

*I'm still thinking.*

Well, that's fine. I'm happy to hear that. We should all consider thinking and thinking more deeply.

*Thank you.*

Yes, please, the lady there.

*Thank you. What color absorbs the most, I mean, absorbs the most light? And what color doesn't—absorbs the least light?*

What color absorbs the least light?

*Yes.*

White. What absorbs the most light? Is that the question?

*Yes.*

Black. Does that help with your question?

*Yes. Thank you.*

You see, that's why I'm fond of daisies. They're white. Yes. Yes, the lady here, please.

*In the last class you were talking about rates of vibration and controlling our thoughts with our breath, first with our breath.*

Yes.

*And now, tonight, you're speaking of vibration and color.*

Yes.

*And, also, how would this correlate with our thoughts, so that we can be in a peaceful, harmonious vibration when we come upon, maybe, an obstruction that we are trying to accept?*

Yes. Well, first off, you cannot have a thought without a breath. We've already discussed that, I think, in our seminars. And the reason that you cannot have a thought—for a thought is a form; it's a form of energy. The thought, the process, it absorbs energy at that very time. At the forming of the thought, you see, you are absorbing energy in order to create the thought. So the breath of life is inseparable for that process of creating. Without the breath of life, you do not have creation.

Now a person will say, "Well, now this is a wooden table. This doesn't have life. It doesn't breathe." But we know that that is not true. We know that the wood breathes. Now the question is, When you remove the wood from its root and from all of the rest of the tree, does it continue to breathe? No. It does not continue to breathe, no more than your physical body continues to breathe after the life force has been removed from it. So when you remove the piece of wood from the tree, you remove it from its own life force. When you do that, the life that is within it, having left it, you must do something to keep the wood from what you call a decaying process. If you wish to preserve it, you must use preservatives, you see. You must introduce preservatives to it.

So when you create a thought, you see, you use the life-giving energy of your breath to create it. Now it has, at the moment of its creation, it contains not only the form of the thought, it contains the motive and all of the intelligence of your mind, do you understand? Now that form must be fed. Its lifeline is its creator. As the leaf will die without the branch, the branch will die without the trunk, the trunk will die without the root, so each and every one of your thoughts, they die without your attention or your energy.

Now they, having the intelligence of your human mind, have found many, many cunning ways that they may survive. One of those many ways is to knock at the door of your conscience and tell you to be concerned. And so as you're concerned, they start thriving once again. Another way that they continue on with their survival is from impulsive thoughts, acts, and deeds they absorb energy for their continuity. A person who is greatly identified with denial, which, of course, is limit, is a person who is frequently drained of vitality or energy. For these forms, containing the intelligence of your mind at the moment of creation, also contain your great desire for survival, for self-preservation. Now what is your question there, please?

*What I was asking is, How we can control our rate of vibration through our breath?*

The control of the rate of vibration through your breath is to use your breath in keeping with the classes you have already received and to use it when your mind tells you it doesn't work anyway. You see, if you want to know how well something works for you, listen to your mind when you're thinking about yourself and it will tell you, your mind, "That doesn't work. I've tried this. I've tried that. No, no, no, that doesn't work at all. I gave that a try." Maybe you've tried it for three days, possibly even three weeks. Maybe you tried it now and then. Because, you see, if you will only listen—listen when your mind, you believe you are filled with concern. Listen when you feel that things aren't going your way. Listen when your world seems to be falling apart. Listen attentively. Listen carefully. For those things that are speaking are telling exactly what you should not be doing, you see. So if you do what the opposite of what they tell you to do, you will find yourself on the path of freedom. Does that help with your question on controlling thought?

You see, don't say, "Oh, go away from me. Get behind me," and all of that, you see, because you identify, then, even more, and you give them more energy and they become stronger. You see, to, to fight and to battle with what you believe you are is a divided house that cannot be successful in that respect. You see, when you experience a thought that you don't like, remember, it's another thought form in your mind at that time that's most unhappy with another thought form on another level of consciousness that's getting fed. You are not either the one of that level or that level, but you, of course, are responsible for all of them. And because you are responsible for your own creations, stop denying that which you have created. You created your judgment. You created your prejudgment. You created your prejudice. Stop denying that you have created them. Accept them that you may be free from them.

Now no one, surely, can say that God is controlled by the minds of men. No one could ever, certainly, say that he controls the light of even the sun. No one can say that. So why, why deny what you have created and from the denial be controlled by it? Do you understand that?

*Yes.*

You see, you see, for a person to say, "Oh, this thought is just terrible! Where did this thought come from?" Well, then one pauses and says, "Well, it's my mind. Wherever it came from, it got into my mind. It couldn't get into—if I refuse to accept that

I have created it at some time in my life, the least thing I can do is accept that I've got into a level of consciousness, through the law of like attracts like, in order to experience it." Accept that you are experiencing it. Stop believing that you are it by fighting with it. You see, to, to deny, to blatantly deny what you do not want to experience is to give energy, power, and control to what you really don't want. The moment you accept it, you will be free from it. And if you don't find yourself free from it, then you know very well you haven't honestly accepted it. Pardon?

*Yes. Thank you.*

You see, because it's taking place within our own mind. Because it's taking place within our own mind, it is subject to the demonstrable Law of Personal Responsibility. We somehow got it in there. And because we got it in there, to deny its existence, when we're the ones that got it in there, is foolhardy. As I said earlier, a wise man would rather carry a big stick than to cast a giant shadow. It is a great shadow that one casts when they deny what they have created. You see, *we* have created our judgments. We have serviced them. We continue to service them.

Now our judgments are enough of a cross to bear in life. It's something to accept that we alone have created them. Fine. But to move on and to permit a judgment to become a prejudgment, to automatically be prejudiced to anything one sees just because it is not the way they believe they are at any given moment, depending on what level is in control of that, that is indeed a bondage. Would you not agree?

*Yes, I would.*

Yes. Thank you. Yes, the lady in the back, please.

*If you have a thought and you say, "I accept that this is my thought," but there's resistance to the acceptance, but it's not on that level of thinking and saying. How do you dissolve that resistance so that the energy goes to the good and the thought is relieved of its power?*

Thank you for your question. If you have a thought, you may be rest assured that it is yours. For the law will not fail us. If you have a thought, somehow it got in your mind. You are responsible for what gets in your mind, and you are responsible for what leaves your mind. That is the Law of Personal Responsibility. So if you have a thought, you are the one who let it in and you are the one that is responsible for what you do with it. You have a thought and you do not like the thought, is that correct?

*Yes, that's, that's correct.*

Fine. First of all, you recognize the thought and you say, "I do not like that thought," is that correct?

*Yes.*

Accept that this is a thought that you alone have created. And because you alone have created it, you alone have the power to do something with it. Do you understand that?

*Yes.*

For you have the power to do with what you have created what you choose to do. Now if you do not exercise that power, which is your divine right, then that which you have created will exercise it for you. And what does that mean? It means that the thought that you now decide you don't like, even though you are responsible for having created it, is now exercising what is justly your divine right, and it's telling you what to do. Do you understand?

*Yes.*

Like an undisciplined child, you have to take and make effort. Accept, first, that it's yours, for it's taking place in your mind, and you are responsible for what takes place in your mind. For whatever takes place in our mind, we alone have created. Now because we don't like—ofttimes in life we do not like what we have created, [but that] does not free us from the responsibility of having created it. Ofttimes in our experiences we create many different types of relationships. And at some point in so-called time, we decide we don't like the relationship at all. It didn't work out the way that we wanted it to work out. It *did* work out the way we really wanted it to work out. It's just a matter of so-called time, which moves us through a world of illusion, 'til we can open our eyes and say, "Well, thank you, God, I never did believe—it seems strange to me now—that that is what I really wanted. But, O my God, I'm so glad it was, though I couldn't recognize it at the time." Does that help with your question?

*Yes.*

Certainly. Yes, the lady here, please.

*What is the motive—no. Is the motive the nucleus of the thought?*

The motive is where the law is established in order to form or create the thought, the motivation. You see, something cannot come out of nothing, not even the thought form of thought. There is something that prompts and motivates us to creating that particular type of a thought or thought form. So the motive is the law that moves us in consciousness to the creation, yes. That help with your question?

*Yes.*

Yes. The gentleman here, please.

*Thank you. You take an experience like procrastination . . .*

Yes?

*That's blocking the way to something. Is the way to eliminate that to accept it or to understand why it is being created?*

Thank you. We cannot understand what we do not first accept. For if we do not first accept that we alone have created the obstruction, then we cannot understand it for we do not qualify our self to understand what we do not first accept.

So first we accept that we have experienced and perhaps recently experienced what we know as procrastination. Do you understand? Now by accepting that we have experienced that, by accepting that we have created it, we begin on the path to understand the motive, the law established, that expresses itself in what we understand to be procrastination. In other words, we want to do something, we know that we should, but we put it off. What it reveals is other priorities, other forms, rise up and convince us that we are those forms, and that that over there, which we know we should be doing, well, that's not as important at this time. Do you understand that? Well, those are forms created by our mind which have convinced us, and we believe that we must do this or that in order to experience what we believe we need to experience in our tomorrows. Did that help with your question?

*Thank you.*

So, you see, by accepting, "Fine. I have procrastinated. I didn't want to, but I did." By accepting it, we begin to understand it. For we cannot understand what we do not accept. Would you not agree?

*Yes.*

You see, there is nothing in life, in creation, that we can understand until we first accept. Because we cannot honestly examine, analyze, and study what we do not first accept. And so we find our self in many schools and many different philosophies, and there is a little bit of us that accepts. Well, if we make the effort, and the Law of Continuity will reveal to us, from that small acorn and from our effort of continuity, that little acorn starts getting bigger and starts to grow. And someday we take a look and we [say], "My, what a great tree that has become. Now it will serve me well." And it always does.

So there is nothing wasted in life. Everything is serving a purpose. It is serving the purpose of its original motive, which is the law of its design. Did that help with your question? Yes. The lady there, please. Yes.

*Me?*

Yes.

*What is your reference—I was wondering about your reference to a big stick.*

What would you do with a big stick? If you had a choice between a giant shadow or a big stick, what could do the most for you? What could do anything for you?

*The shadow couldn't, I know that.*

Do you mean to imply that the stick can? Can you use a stick? Can you use—

*Well—*

Can you use a stick as a tool?

*Yes.*

Can you use the shadow?

*No.*

It has no substance, has it?

*No.*

Well, tell me something, that which has no substance, does it have reality?

*No. Only the reality of the mental substance.*

The reality of an illusion.

*Yes.*

Well, if a person believes in illusion, then, of course, a person will be the servant of a shadow, for that is the world of illusion. That's where shadows live. Shadows are not reality. Shadows are illusions. So people who do not make effort to live must therefore be victims of worlds of illusion and servants of the forms therein, which are known as shadows.

Now, for example, a person sits down; they look at a picture. They look at that, that box called a television. They look at that and what are they doing? Are they consciously aware of a world of reality? Or are they escaping from a world of reality and entering the land of the mist? Are they uplifted after their viewing? Is their vitality improved? Is more accomplished in a world of substance and reality, or is less accomplished? Is their health improved? Is their wealth improved? You see, when we, through denial, experience reality as a struggle, a cross to bear, we tempt ourselves to enter a world of illusion and finally are convinced, by the forms in that world of illusion, that we are them.

A person may pause [and say], "Oh, how beautiful it was in 1967." You remember 1967, do you?

*Yes.*

Yes, you should remember 1967. And they say, "1967. Oh, what a wonderful year that really was. Remember? There were many good things that took place in my life." Now one could not call that reality; it is now a shadow. It is something that has passed through reality.

And so if one does not accept illusion and the shadows for what they truly are, then one becomes convinced and one lives, not in reality, not in the eternal moment where the power of goodness is expressing, only in an illusion. They escape into the picture box. Does that help with your question?

*Yes. Thank you.*

But someday, you see, we all must come out of the picture box. Someday. And when we come out of the picture box, we're not happy. Because, you see, we believe when we're in the mist and in the shadowland of illusion that we are in control. Everything is doing exactly what we want it to do, and everyone is doing what we want them to do. What we do not realize at that moment: they are convincing us that they are doing what we want them to do. And through that conviction, we believe that we are them and escape from responsibility, you see, which is known as reality. Reality is responsibility. So if we want to know how firmly our feet our planted into reality, all we have to do is see if we have a love for personal responsibility or an adversity. If we are adverse to personal responsibility, then we know that our feet rest very lightly in reality. And so when, by the laws of responsibility, we have to face reality, we immediately want to escape back into the picture box. You see, all boxes are picture boxes for they restrict and they contain. Now whether you're talking about a sandbox or a water box or a toy box, they are all picture boxes of illusion. Does that help with your question?

*Thank you.*

You're welcome. The lady next to you has a question, please.

*Yes. A little earlier it was said that there is no understanding without acceptance. And in a previous class it was said that the return, the quickness of the return of the law is dependent upon the awakening of an individual.*

Indeed, yes.

*Is that the same thing as the will of God of just acceptance?*

I would certainly consider that the movement of the Principle of Goodness, known as the will of God, is total acceptance. It is the teaching of the Living Light that the will of God, the movement of the Principle of Goodness, is total acceptance. So whatever you deny—don't you understand, what you deny, you not only destine yourself to, but whatever you deny or do not accept, you go against the movement of the Principle of Goodness in your life, known as the will of God. You see, in order to move from a world of illusion—for that is what the realm of duality is; it is a world of illusion—in order to move through a world of delusion, you must enter the will of God, the movement of the Principle of Goodness. And that is dependent upon the totality of your own acceptance. Do you understand?

*Thank you.*

You're welcome. Yes, the lady there, please.

*What role does predestination play in our evolution and, therefore, the thoughts that we create that provide the obstacles in our reality?*

Man experiences what he knows as what you call predestination, an effect of his denials. So, you see, what you deny yourself today, what you deny in your consciousness, you predestine yourself to. So a person has no problem understanding or knowing their predestination, for they do it moment by moment by their denials. You see, one says, "Well, I don't deny that person that way of thinking. I do not deny that person that way of living." They deny it in their consciousness. Now to deny in one's consciousness—do you understand?—is to deny the Divine Principle that sustains everything.

You see, fear does that. Fear is man's belief that he is mental substance. And when you believe that you are mental substance, then you believe you are limit. When you believe you are limit, you fear that which is different, that is not within the boundaries of your limit. You see, when a person believes they are their mind, then it clearly reveals they believe they are the limits of their mind. We understand that, don't we?

*Yes, sir.*

So when we believe we are this limit—and within this limit is contained many things. Now beyond that limit is many other things. Because they are not within our limit, we believe we cannot control them. Do you understand? And because what we cannot control we fear with our mind—do you understand?

*Yes.*

Man fears anything that isn't within his own limits, and he says, "It's different and that's why I fear it." What he is truly saying [is], "It's not within the domain of my control. Therefore, I fear it." Does that help with your question?

*So in, in reference to predestination . . .*

Yes?

*Each soul creates their destination moment to moment then.*

Moment by moment. You see, the moment the, the Divine Spirit identifies, it dents into what you know as form. The moment that that happens, the Law of Denial is established. The Law of Denial is established by believing you are the identification. Whoever believes they are what they identify with is controlled by that which is within the limits of their identification. Does that help with your question in that respect?

*Yes. May I ask another?*

Yes, go right ahead. Certainly.

*So if we accept our obstructions . . .*

Yes?

*In order to diminish them, what steps can we take in order not to identify with creation?*

The thing is, you see, we must identify with the vehicle that we are using to express the true being that we are. To completely free our self from the identification is to free our self from the limit. So we have a responsibility to the vehicle that we have earned in evolution; therefore, we do not want to deny the limit that we have identified with. Our work is to expand the limit through a broadening of the horizon by accepting that which we deny. By accepting that which we deny in our consciousness, we broaden our horizon and expand our consciousness, do you understand? From an expansion of our consciousness, that which we have denied comes under our control. And so this is the art of control, the Law of Contradiction in a world of creation.

You see, it's like a businessman. He has a competitor. When he accepts his competitor in consciousness, he moves on the path of controlling him. Do you understand? You see, that which we fight, we are controlled by. For that which we fight bothers us in order for us to be challenged to fight it. So we don't fight it; we accept it. And that which we accept, we absorb. That which we absorb, by the Law of Personal Responsibility, we control.

*OK.*

You see, the moment that you deny anything, you keep it outside the limits of your control. And whatever you keep outside the limits of your control, you fear. Does that help with that question?

*Yes, it does. Thank you.*

Yes. You're welcome. The gentleman there, and I'll be right with you. Yes.

*When we focus our mental energy . . .*

Yes.

*On an identification with an obstruction, is it helpful to speak, to use our voice to discuss that obstruction with someone else or by ourselves to allow ourselves to overcome the obstruction? Or is it best not to verbalize and to keep the energy only mental and not verbal?*

No. The verbal, the spoken word is life-giving energy. One, however, should not speak it forth to another until one understands themselves, for each person has the limits and the boundaries in which they have already believed they have control. And so one speaks to the creation for it is their child. And you speak forth the life-giving energy, not within the hearing distance of another person, for then you must pay for their forms that are within their limits. Do you understand?

Now, so when you speak forth the word, you free yourself from the control of it. And the more you speak forth the word, the freer you become. Does that help you?

*Yes.*

But one should choose wisely anyone that is within hearing distance because they must pay the price of the forms that rise in the belief of the listening ear. Hmm? You see, when a person is honest with themselves, they say, "Now let me see, I deny this and I deny that and I deny that and I deny that." At the very moment of accepting what you deny, you experience fear, would you not agree? You see, you just stop and you [say], "Now let me see, I don't want that, that, that, and that. And I never did want that, that, that, and that. I now accept it." All of this—you find this experience come over you, known as fear. But that reveals how you are being controlled in life. *You* are controlled. You deceive yourself to believe that you are controlling, when in truth you are being controlled. You're being controlled by the limits and the boundaries that you have established in consciousness.

You see, the success of living, just like business—the business of living—you take a look at business. You look at those who battle their competitors, and you look at those who absorb them. Those who absorb them are those who accept them. So whatever you accept in life, you establish the law to absorb it. So accept it and absorb it, and find out what you are. It's far greater than what you believe you are.

Is there any other question? Yes, now the gentleman here, please.

*Yes, I would like you, if you would expound on the principle of how viewing is possible, if it's possible, without mental recognition.*

How what? Thank you.

*How viewing...*

Viewing?

*Yes, sir. Is...*

In keeping with the Law of Identification man sees or man views. Now we view life from a so-called vantage point of total consideration. Total consideration does not exist in a mental world, for a mental world may expand the boundaries of its limit, but it cannot, *it cannot* go beyond limit. So man sees with his mind and views with his soul. Does that help you?

*Yes, sir.*

So if man wants to view, then man must walk the path of total consideration by establishing the Law of Total Acceptance. One cannot totally consider what one has never totally accepted. Then the question must be asked, And who is man to believe that he is greater than God? Man suffers from his belief that he is greater than God. And man insists on believing he is greater than God by denying that which is. So whoever denies that which is has established the law of believing he is greater than God.

Now what happened to the angel that sat next to God? He believed that he was greater than God; and so God, in total consideration in total acceptance, gave him an entire domain. It's called a world of illusion. Did that help with your question?

*Yes, sir.*

So that same law has not changed. Whoever believes they are greater than God is given the domain that Lucifer was given. That's his domain. Limit is the domain of Lucifer, for denial is the domain of Lucifer. Bondage is the domain of Lucifer, for belief is the cement of Lucifer and faith is the freedom of God. Thank you.

*Thank you.*

You're welcome. The gentleman here, please.

*If we make an effort to accept more of the thoughts that are not pleasing to ourselves, will that help us to grow in tolerance?*

It will not only be instrumental in one's expansion of tolerance but one's success in life. For success, what you understand as success, abundant good and no obstruction to anything in your world of creation, is totally dependent upon your own tolerance. The less tolerance you have, the more obstructions that you service. That help with your question?

*Yes, sir. Thank you.*

For tolerance or intolerance is only an expression of the limits of our own acceptances. And what we do not tolerate today, we only guarantee to experience in our tomorrow. So if you have difficulty in accepting that which you do not want to accept, just remember, you're establishing the law of total attachment. A wise person in a world of creation, certainly, doesn't say never. For never is a guarantee of sooner or later, for sure.

*Thank you.*

Hmm? When God has not declared never, who is man to do so? Yes, the lady here, please.

*I'd like to ask you about inaction and action. It seems that if we are in total acceptance and no denial, then there's no need or reason to move. And it seems like whenever we start out to work on a project, it means we're in a desire, which is need and denial. So I'd like to ask, How do we ever move in creation without being in denial?*

Well, my dear, there's no problem at all. It's known as the Law of Personal Responsibility. That is the motivation. You have already entered form and are responsible to the form; so you have no problem at all. Just accept personal responsibility and the Law of Motivation will fulfill itself. Yes.

*And then I'd like to know how are we guided in a direction to know that it is the right thing to do and not just a desire that we're following through based on our own denial.*

The question does not exist when we are what we are. The question only exists when we are tempted to believe what we are not.

*Thank you.*

You see, when we have accepted what we are, there is no question.

*OK.*

The question can only exist when we believe in what we are not. For that's the only place that limit exists. You're welcome.

*Thank you.*

Yes.

*I'd like to know if I can ask a prepared question that is not specifically with this class.*

As long as it does not refer to my private classes.

*No, it doesn't.*

Then you may go ahead.

*Thank you. If a soul is in the Halls of Repose, does that mean they followed the Light at transition and avoided being trapped in the lower levels that they are serving or have been serving?*

In reference to your question of a soul departing from your planet and entering the Halls of Repose . . .

*Yes.*

And you want to know if they have avoided other realms of consciousness?

*I guess what I'm wondering is, Do they go to the Halls of Repose first and then go back to the realms of consciousness?*

Ofttimes yes, for they are better prepared to pay the price of what they have thought they got for nothing.

*I see.*

Yes. You see, when you pray for the soul, you put another little candle lighted on the pathway through the darkness of the realms of belief, you see. Now ever in keeping with the soul's evolution, ofttimes they leave the earth realm and those who care for them are there to meet them, if possible, in keeping with the law. Or there are other helpers and rescue workers who take them on to the Halls of Repose for awakening. And after awakening in the Halls of Repose and learning something about personal responsibility, they are better prepared as they work their way through the realms of belief that is controlled by the king of creation [and awaken] that that is not them. And they serve their time and free themselves from the purification realms or what you know as purgatory. For man is freed in hell, saved in heaven. Yes. You're welcome. The gentleman was waiting with a question. Yes.

*I would like to ask, What part of us is electromagnetic?*

What part?

*Yes, sir.*

You mean of your body?

*Well, I'm not thinking it's our body. I'm thinking it's the* prana *that runs through our body, that goes through our body.*

Whatever is form is electromagnetic in order to be form. Yes.

*Our mind is included in that, too, right?*

That's correct. Now some people are more electric than they are magnetic, and some people are more magnetic than they are electric. Some people are more electric in a physical form, while they're extremely magnetic in an emotional form or mental form. Now some people are very, very magnetic in a physical form and extremely electric in a mental form. Does that help?

*Yes. Ah . . .*

Wouldn't you say that you are quite electric in physical form?
*Yes.*
Wouldn't you also say that you are quite magnetic in an emotional form?
*Right.*
Well, let's put it in another way. A person who is easily tempted to express their emotions is a person who is easily affected and magnets—the principle of magnetism is that which is affected. Hmm?
*I agree with all that.*
Thank you. That's kind of you. *[Many of the students laugh.]* Yes, you have another question. So kind of you. It's so rare that I have a student agree with me. But I have spent eons in the battles, so I [am] always prepared, one might say. Go ahead. When you're sailing, you know—and that's what we're doing in this so-called world is sailing through form—then, *siempre preparados* I think is a wise, the wise motto to have. Yes, go ahead with your question.
*I...*
And thank you for your encouragement to me. Yes.
*You answered all. Thank you.*
You're welcome. Someone else have a question? The lady here, please.
*Yes, I'd like your understanding, if you'd give it, please, on how we greet each other. We say the word* hello *and I'd like to ask your understanding.*
Yes. Well, ofttimes in our work in your world of creation we find that word, you see, *hello*, and sometimes they even shorten it to "hi."
*Right.*
I see. I note they don't say "lo." *[Many students laugh.]* Yes. Well, usually what it means is, "What do you want from me now?"
*Oh!*

So I think in your world it could be more honest a greeting to say, "Yes, what do you want from me now?" And there would be a new world awaken, you see. And then we could all say, "They want this from me, that from me, that from me." And then a person would say, "And, yes, what are you willing to pay?" And then if a person, with this greeting, "Hi, there. And what do you want from me today?" [says] the person that's receiving the "Hi," and then that person says, "Well, how much are you willing to pay?" I think there would be a great deal more honesty expressed, don't you think?

You see, if a person says, "Hello," and if the other person doesn't give them something back, the person that said "Hello" immediately has the experiences that they didn't get what they wanted. So, no, seriously, I'm being honest with you. You walk down the street and you see someone that you know and you say, "Hello," and the person looks right past you. You have a strange experience, wouldn't you say? Well, the strange experience is an effect of what you wanted out of them that you didn't get, you see. So if you go around the world and you say, "All right, what do you want out of me? Hello." *[Many students laugh.]* Yes. "What am I willing to pay? Hello." Yes? Wouldn't that be helpful?

*Yes.*

Do it only, please, with the two-legged animals. The four-legged ones don't go around saying "Hello."

*When we say "Good night," the word is "good," and I'm wondering if the Spirit has a recommendation for us to greet each other that would be, again, a higher vibration than "Hello."*

Well, considering a world of creation that denies the truth in order to be limit or a world of creation and considering the king that controls creation, that is a question that I think we should consider. First of all, we cannot walk around saying, "Light," because not everyone is sure of how bright that light may be.

And some may agree with the light. And some may say it's too bright. Some may say it's too dim. And we're not really very satisfied that way. Besides, I think in your world they might think you were a bit odd, different, and that which is different is feared. And that which is feared is denied, and so the problems would, indeed, therefore increase.

However, wouldn't it be nice to wake up in the morning, you see a two-legged animal and say, "What did you want out of me today?" *[Many of the students laugh loudly.]* And then the person could say, "Let's see, now I want to be sure. Is there anything I want out of you today? Oh, yes, this is what I want out of you today." And then you could say, "Well, how much are you willing to pay?"

You see, in a world of limit you have to consider minds which believe in payment and attainment. That's a world of duality. So we therefore must work with denial and need. So when you say, "What do you want out of me?" then the person can react with their need, and there can be an honest conversation. However, I understand it would be difficult in your world.

What can one say as a greeting? Well, the eyes reveal not where a person believes they are, but where they are. Silence, known for ages to be golden, which, of course, we know in this understanding to be wisdom. The eyes say everything that should be said. The interpretation of what they are saying may be something else to someone else. And so a person reveals in their eyes what they have denied. A person also reveals, yes, in their eyes, what they have accepted. And so the best greeting, the best greeting one could have is to be still, to smile, for those who need a smile, but to look into the eyes, which reveal the soul. And for a person to remember that as one looks out into the world, one is seeing through the censorship of their own judgments. Did that help with your question?

*Yes. Thank you.*

You're welcome. Time passes quickly. Yes, I know. That's why I told you, "Time passes quickly," so you would give me those five fingers, which you had neglected. *[The teacher addresses the technician recording the class.]* Yes, the lady there, please.

*Is it wise to aspire to anything in creation?*

The soul aspires; the mind perspires. And so the choice, really—my good friend, Mr. Red, yes?—the soul really has no problem. It is the soul that aspires. The soul doesn't need creation. The soul is expressing through creation, for the soul, the Principle of Goodness, couldn't possibly need, and even if it could, it certainly wouldn't need that which is limited. You see, here's the Divine Spirit, limitless and free, expressing through soul, which in turn is expressing through all of these other forms. So remember, the soul aspires; the mind perspires. And so the more the mind perspires, someday it wears out from within, and the little soul gets to shine like the sun at high noon.

Now I think I'd best say good night to this little seminar here. And thank you all very, very much. Good night.

SEPTEMBER 12, 1985

## A/V Seminar 7

Good evening, class, and welcome to these continuing seminars on the expanding consciousness. This evening we shall discuss piercing the layers of experience with the pen of reason, from which floweth the Light of eternal truth.

In keeping with our priorities of belief, we ofttimes in life find it difficult to maintain and to sustain balance, the effect, of course, which is harmony, health, and the happiness which is our birthright. We find this difficulty as we have experiences, the last one registering in our consciousness seemingly having the greater impact. These layers of experience, that we sometimes in our life believe that we are, are pierced by the pen of reason, which is covered with the shell of logic. Therefore, it is necessary in our evolution to remove the logic, a function of mental substance, which is dependent upon and a servant to the experiences that we, at sometimes in our lives, believe that we are. And so a balance maintained between the mental substance and the spiritual essence offers the abundant and joyful living.

It does seem at times to be a struggle to enjoy the good that we are. It is only a struggle when we identify with these layers of experiences, which, as we all know, are but obstructions casting their shadows and, therefore, temporarily blinding us to what we are, where we are, and who we are.

Now I'm going to take a few moments here to respond to the many questions that you have prepared. And so at this time, please speak forth your questions.

*What is the process the soul goes through when it leaves this body?*

Well, in reference to the process that the soul, which is, of course, the covering or the individualization of substance, which is the expression of the spiritual essence (that which we are), the process it goes through is to move through all of the experiences that one has encountered while identified with limit or form or creation. As it moves through these various realms in consciousness, in mental substance, it serves to raise the consciousness that has been imbued in the mental substance by an identification with mental substance at various times in our lives. Many philosophies and religions have called that process purgatory. Many philosophies have referred to it as the purification of the being.

The process, if one continues to believe that they are what they experience, serves as a bondage to the evolving soul. For when one believes in anything, one becomes the servant of that which they believe in. Therefore, a wise and reasonable man accepts belief for what it truly is: a creation and form in mental substance born from the denial of truth of what one truly is to serve to fill a need for a time in the ever-expanding consciousness.

You may speak forth your next question, please.

*How may we free ourselves from being trapped in the mental level?*

As long as man (his mind) permits himself to believe that he is experiencing need, the effect of denial of what he is, then man traps or binds himself to the filling of the need. Because man permits himself to experience need, he gives birth to the delusion, the belief that it can be filled by something outside of himself. For we cannot experience need until we deny the wholeness that we are. And so a person who does not wish to be bound or entrapped in those realms of limit must pause and accept what they truly are and refrain from believing what they are not.

*Please explain the friction in duality, saying one will do one thing and meaning the opposite?*

Well, ofttimes in a person's experience they have good intentions. However, the fulfillment of their intent is ofttimes thwarted by what they call experiences beyond their control. Circumstances that one cannot control in one's life reveal a denial of what they are, a belief in what they are not, a dependence on something or someone that by divine law they cannot control.

*When a person feels like they're making nothing but mistakes, how can they continue to encourage themselves? Also, what is the significance of a mistake?*

Well, in reference to what one considers a mistake, what one considers is a mistake in their life is a lack of acceptance of the Law of Personal Responsibility, a dependence on what they cannot control. For example, one believes that they made a mistake after they had an experience that they consciously desired and chose. One believes they made a mistake rather than to accept that they alone established, by denial of what they are, a need to fill what they are not. Now in a situation of that type, one has denied the Law of Personal Responsibility.

Then we have the consideration of one's awakening that they knew the way for them; they were tempted, which is an expression of a weakness in the fiber of one's character, and they had an experience. They feel badly because the experience did not meet their expectations, for they are dependent upon the judgments of the mental substance of their own consciousness which they believe at times that they are. And so a person who permits themselves to be discouraged and to feel sorry for an experience that they alone in their lives have established is a person who is continuing to deny the demonstrable Law of Personal Responsibility and wants the path lined like a bed of roses.

*What is the spiritual definition of* innocence *and what is its value?*

Well, in reference to the question you're asking on the spiritual understanding of *innocence*—is that your question?

*Yes.*

And you're asking in reference to its value?

*Yes. Thank you.*

Well, in reference to *innocence,* one could liken the word in your world (*innocence*) to ignorant. When one is ignorant of something, they are innocent; they are not aware. The purpose of the expanding consciousness and the soul's entrance into mental substance is to experience, to learn, to grow, to prosper, and to accept that which they are. Now that takes place as a person using the vehicle through which their true being is expressing in a wise, intelligent, beneficial way. For as one uses wisely what they have earned in evolution, they establish the Law of Fulfillment and, in so doing, move on and experience [an] ever-evolving and refined expression of that which they are.

*Thank you. How do we create our own opportunities?*

Opportunity, like the hands of a clock, by the law governing the mental world—for, you see, opportunity moves ever in keeping with the moments of our acceptance. As we in mental identification accept and deny only to accept and to deny again and again and again, we are moving in a cyclic pattern of our own creation to have experiences. Now a person, pausing in consciousness, becomes aware that each moment, each and every moment is opportunity. Opportunity is like [the] hands of a clock, which express and reveal to a mental world of identification the Law of Time. Time does not exist in the world and with that which you are. Time only exists in what you believe that you are. And whatever we believe that we are, is the effect, the expression of denying what we are. And so it is that we seek opportunity, which reveals our need for it, an effect of our denying we are, moment by moment, opportunity. For we, man, humanity, we are a law unto our self.

Some time ago I spoke to you in reference to, "Man, what are you doing with the law that you are?" And so if you have a question, if there is something you think that you need, pause; become aware. You already have it. You have always had it, for all that you are is a part of the whole. You cannot move outside of the whole. You can only temporarily believe that you are separate, different, smaller, larger, greater, or etc. You can only temporarily believe the illusion.

*What is friendship and what is its value?*

Friendship, as has been stated so many times, true friendship is use, not abuse; respects the rights of difference; weathers any storm. True friendship is sharing one's experiences in life for the benefit of oneself and the friend with whom they are communicating. Friendship does not contain need or greed.

*Thank you. Why does it seem, when obstructions manifest (the result of laws we have set into motion) that they come many at the same time?*

It is indeed seldom that we accept that we alone have established all experiences in our life that are and yet to be. And so—my little student, here, wants to be more comfortable. *[The teacher refers to Reddy, the church's dog.]* And so we alone accept the experience seldom, frequently deny that it is just, and frequently believe that someone else has been and is the cause of it. Yes.

*Thank you. When we accept an obstruction that we do not want and free our self from the control of it, is this the same as redirecting our energy?*

Well, it's different in the sense that ofttimes a person will choose to identify with something so that they do not have to face the obstruction that's seemingly in their path for they judge that it is too heavy a cross to bear. So there is a difference in that respect. A person facing an obstruction in their life by accepting that a part of their mental substance at a time of their life expressing its denial, known as need, believed temporarily that they could fill their needs by transgressing the natural Law of Personal Responsibility. In other words, that someone else could fill their cup for them, and they would not have to make such an effort to do so. Now, by accepting, "This experience has come to me in my life, an effect of laws that I have established. I do not like the experience. And when I do not like it sufficiently—in other words, direct sufficient energy to disliking it, as I directed energy to desiring it as an expression of my need, which was an expression of my denial of what I am—when the energy levels are balanced, they will be neutralized." One will experience personal responsibility and the freedom from the obstruction.

*Thank you.*

Yes.

*How may we overcome mental lethargy to allow our minds to react quickly to circumstances as they unfold about us?*

What you call in your world mental lethargy [is] the lack of desire to make changes, knowing that in order to change your experiences the changes must take place within the consciousness. To work through that type of thinking, one should consider that the longer they permit themselves to refrain from making the changes that they know are necessary in order to have what they consider better, more harmonious experiences in life, the longer one procrastinates, one finds themselves in time a molehill that, to them, has become a great mountain to climb. And so when one knows inside that changes for them in their consciousness are necessary to experience greater good more often in their life, then one moves quickly.

What does it take to inspire a consciousness that is experiencing what you call mental lethargy? It takes ofttimes what you call the bottom of the barrel. For some of the greatest inspiration comes when our priority values, our beliefs no longer serve us well. And so, O suffer senses of the mind and suffer well for freedom of the soul is not only well but it is the Divinity that you are.

*Thank you. In this busy life we live, how can one best pause so that one can gain control?*

Yes, in this seemingly extremely active life that one has on earth, how can one pause to gain control? As the body runs, a mind that has opened up the door to reason may fly or may walk, may sit, may swim, or may float. It is only to the mind that believes it is the form that it uses that one finds a life so busy there is not the moment for the pause to gain control. And so for those moments of pause, which are available to everyone in every universe, one simply needs, in their mental world, to put the brake on the belief that they are the form that they are moving. And so in separating truth from creation, one finds the movement of the limit, the stillness of the truth.

*Thank you. When someone gives us the creeps, so to speak, that we meet, is this a meeting of the forms?*

When someone gives out what?

*When we meet someone and they "give us the creeps," is this a meeting of the forms?*

Well, of course, that would be dependent upon what the questioner means by *creep*. Do you mean, by *creep*, an insect that moves slowly? Or do you mean, by *creep*, something that is undesirable for you have judged that it can move in ways that you cannot?

*This was in reference to meeting someone who makes us feel uncomfortable.*

I see. Well, now we meet many people in our evolution and to those who experience what you call the creep, reveals a person who is wanting in self-control. For example, a person looks out at nature; they see various little forms. And some of those lovely little forms, they say, "Oh, that gives me the creep!" It gives us the creep, you see, for we do not understand their form. And we believe that we are our form. And because we believe we are our form, our body, our flesh, our bone, we can only accept that which is of like kind. And so we find in our ever-evolving consciousness that many things give us what you consider the creep.

Now we have experiences early in our life. They frighten us. Try to understand, that which frightens us is that which controls us. And it only frightens us because we believe we are the limit. We believe we are the form. And the form is different. And whatever is different, unless we make the effort to understand our self, we cannot tolerate that which is alien to us. And that which is alien to us is ever in keeping with our over-identification with what we are not. I do hope that's helped with your question.

*Yes. Thank you. It has been said that World War III would be, and is, a war between ideologies, a war for control of men's minds. Is this the same war that took place on this planet in Atlantis? If so, how is man doing this time? And what role do we as students of the Living Light have in this war?*

Well, in reference to [what you] call World War III, and in reference to your question, Will it be a war similar to the descent of Atlantis? Atlantis and its descent was not an effect of war amongst people as you know war. Atlantis and its descent was an effect of the advancement of technology. It was an effect of the use, the awakening to the power within the being. A use of the power and a slow, but sure, descent to need it. For example, as one in their evolution slowly, but surely, awakens to this power within them, they are ofttimes tempted to believe that that is them. However, that which is doing the believing is the covering of the power and not the power itself. And so when that which is limit, that which is mental substance, that which is form believes that it is the power, that is when the great descent begins.

Now in your reference to World War III, be not concerned that such a war of destruction of that type of physical substance is taking place, for it is not. However, if you consider war [as] vehicles of fine intellect to which you slowly, but surely, are tempted to serve, then in that respect, yes, war is already here. For example, the human mind, the intellect, designed to serve the divine Light, is constantly tempted to believe that it is the Light. And in that temptation, it tempts to use the Light to devise and to experience power, denying the truth that force is the king of mental substance and power, the Light and expression of good or God. Now as mental substance, rising supreme, creates in a material world ever [more advanced] technological advancements formed from material substance and imbues that material substance with a part of their consciousness, as the minds of men design electromagnetic instruments to think as servants of the king of logic, as man is tempted to continue on with that great scientific advancement, man on your planet is destined to once again awaken to the demonstrable truth that he now is the servant and the slave of what he alone has created.

And so you're already beginning to find in your world that there are so-called instruments, equipment, you call computers; they think, for man has imbued them with a part of his own consciousness. Man has directed the substance to respond in ways of his own choosing in service to the king-pride of logic. So the Earth planet, moving along its evolutionary path, tempted, amazed, fascinated with what they believe they have accomplished, what they believe these many servants of machines are doing for them, will move on to the next step in evolution and awaken that these intelligent machines, having no soul, for they cannot be imbued—man cannot imbue his soul into another form, no! Man imbues his intelligence into the form. And man, as humanity, taking great pride in its accomplishments, shall awaken that he is now a servant of what he calls a machine. And he shall serve it ever in keeping with its logic.

Now let us think a few moments in reference to that. We can only give what we have to give. So man offers to the world what he has to offer. Man believes that he lives. In keeping with logic, man offers to the world, including the mineral world, the material world, man offers that which he has to offer: logic. However, the function of logic and its balance the faculty of reason—reason shall rise up and what man has created and what man tempted to believe is serving him, reason shall awaken him that he is serving it. For already in your world little children grow; they cannot add; they cannot subtract; they cannot multiply; they cannot divide. They are dependent on something that they temporarily believe they can control, which, in truth, is making them a dependent. And that which is dependent on something they cannot control is crippled for it is distorted. It is not healthy. It is not harmonious. It is not balanced.

When a person in their evolution, evolving, earning in their evolution a covering for their eternal spirit and for their soul, known as a mind, chooses not to use the mind in the way that it has been designed to be used and rather chooses to depend on something that in truth it cannot control, that is a growing world of unhealthy people. So man thinks, "Why should I stop to learn to add, to multiply, to divide, to subtract, to spell when there is a machine I can push a button and it will do it for me?" That's lethargy, and lethargy offers nothing but total dependence on something it cannot control. I hope that's helped with your question.

*Yes. Thank you. When we establish a rapport with someone, how can we stay in our own vibration?*

Well, first of all, in order to establish a rapport with someone, anyone, one first must establish a rapport with the level within themselves which, once having been established, ever seeks like kind. For example, say that a person chooses to identify with a level of consciousness of discouragement of self-pity. Once having made the choice within to identify with that level of consciousness, the law reveals that like attracts like and becomes the Law of Attachment. And so whatever level we choose to identify with and, therefore, bind our self to, we, sooner or later, by the law of like attracts like, shall bring that level into our lives. And so when a person desires to be freed from the experience or the effect of having attracted like kind into their life, all they have to do is to be honest within themselves and to look at the level of consciousness, the layer of experience within themselves that sought like kind in the world and make an intelligent choice not to identify with that level within. For levels of experience only offer denial of what we are. Therefore, levels of experience are filled with need. Does that help with your question?

*Yes. Thank you.*

You're welcome.

*In* The Living Light *book, Discourse 43, it states that the nature spirits begin to evolve and change as we, our spirits, make the daily effort to express light, love, and peace.* [A clock in the room where this class was recorded strikes as the student reads this question.] *Does this mean that the forms in the lower realms can evolve to higher realms to ultimately become angels of Light?*

Well, now if you would be so kind as to consider the lovely clocks that were timing away in your world of delusion and repeat the question, I will be most happy to share with you our understanding.

*Thank you.*

Yes.

*In* The Living Light *book, Discourse 43, it states that nature spirits begin to evolve and change as we, our spirits, make the daily effort to express light, love, and peace. Does this mean that the forms in the lower realms can evolve to higher realms to ultimately become angels of Light?*

Yes, indeed. All forms are sustained by one Light. Darkness is only a lack of understanding the lesser light. Nothing exists, not even the so-called midnight, that is not in truth a lesser light. The seeming difference you experience from high noon to what you call midnight is only degrees of lesser light. And so that which is sustained by the Light is Light; its expression varies. Does that help with your question?

*Yes. Thank you.*

You're welcome.

*Would you please share your understanding of the words divine grace?*

Divine grace. I have spoken to you before on divine grace. Balance is the law of the universe that governs all forms which are subject to the law of the universe. And so in our experiences and in our efforts there are times when we make effort to do something without thought or motivation of selfish gain. In other words, we do it because deep inside of us we know that it is right to do. We are not motivated by the function of denial which offers to us need. And not being motivated by the function of the denial of good, which we are, we do not experience need. And not experiencing need, we do not expect reward, fulfillment, or return, for that is not our motivation for doing it.

Now when we move in that realm of consciousness, we, like I said once before, deposit the goodness in what can be related to your world as our own bank account. And so we move on with our experiences, and we establish certain laws that have a return that is what we consider not beneficial to us. In times of what we consider is great need, we have, there on deposit, spiritual essence which can be used and is withdrawn for what you would call divine grace. What it is in truth, of course, is balancing the power with the force. It is not an escape from the law. It is a balancing within the consciousness between what we are and what we are not. Yes.

*Thank you. What is the spiritual meaning of an alignment of the planets, as in an eclipse? And is this meaning altered when different planets align?*

Well, yes, as different planets in the universe represent primarily certain faculties and functions, they have an influence upon the other planets, such as your Earth planet. When they are brought into an alignment, there is a balancing to varying degrees between the functions and the faculties. Now you might look at it in another way, that whenever your Earth planet becomes imbalanced with an over-population of a particular species, a particular form, there is a balancing through what you ofttimes consider a disaster. The divinity in that particular type of disaster is a balancing in creation. And that which is balanced is good, for that which is balanced is God. And that which is balanced is healthy and harmonious and abundantly good.

*Thank you.*

You're welcome.

*Is the power of woman the same as the power of man, the inner power, as the Indians have spoken of or are they different in nature?*

Well, in reference to the difference in nature of man and woman, yes, indeed, in form there's a vast difference. However, that which we are is not form. Therefore, it is not man, and it is not woman. That which we believe we are is form and, therefore, is different in nature, of course.

*Thank you.*

You're welcome.

*If the plants, trees, and animals could speak to us in our language, what would they want to tell those of us in human form?*

They would like to tell those in human form, "Speak to us in our language." *[Many students laugh.]*

*Thank you.*

You're welcome.

*What are the other two corresponding soul faculties to charity?*

When you consider charity [an] expression of encouragement, when you consider charity an expression of responsibility, then you will find the triune faculty of which you speak.

*Thank you. Please name the parts of our physical anatomy that three faculties are housed in.*

Well, in reference to that question, that requires further study of my private student, and as soon as they have accomplished that, we'll be more than happy to bring up the various parts of the human anatomy and what they represent in reference to functions and faculties.

*Thank you. Do 51 percent of our levels have to be in accord in order for a change to occur?*

If by change you mean beneficial experience—all experiences are in truth beneficial. If you desire a change within your consciousness for different experiences, then it requires a majority of the balancing within the consciousness. Yes, indeed.

*Thank you. When working on our acceptance of levels that are not in our best interest, what would be the beginning steps of that acceptance?*

Well, first of all, let us understand that what we consider at one moment is not in our best interest we only consider at the next moment to be in our best interest, which, then, in that state of evolution reveals an expression, of course, of need, which is the effect of denial. Therefore, a person, when they judge that experiences they are having they do not find beneficial, should make effort to look for the divinity in disaster. It usually comes as a hindsight. So often man sees the divinity of the disaster after it has long passed, rarely during its occurrence.

*Thank you.*

You're welcome.

*How do we bring those hidden levels into the light in order for us, first, to accept them in order to understand?*

Honesty. Whoever carries the lamp of honesty is walking hand in hand with God.

*Thank you. What truth has been given that would be the most helpful in the act of forgiving yourself and others?*

What truth has been given that would be the most helpful?

*That's what the question says.*

I see. And would you be so kind as to repeat the question for the questioner?

*What truth has been given that would be the most helpful in the act of forgiving yourself and others?*

Personal responsibility. For when one awakens that they are bound by that which they will not give forth or forgive, when one awakens that the price, indeed, is very great and the longer they refrain from giving it forth, the greater is the debt they have to pay. Yes.

*Thank you.*

You're welcome.

*Could you please discuss the difference between motive, the law established, and motivation?*

Well, in reference to motive, the law established, and motivation, we are motivated by two basic principles. We are motivated by acceptance. We are motivated by denial. Whoever is motivated by the will of Goodness, the law of God, known as total acceptance, is motivated along the path of inspiration and the harmony, the love, and the joy that is free from need, free from search, free from dependence. Now, however, if, in our awakening, we find that we are motivated by the Law of Denial of what we are, then we experience the strife, the struggle, the suffering, the ever-increasing need, the concern, the fear, the discouragement, and the pity of what we believe that we are.

*Thank you. Could you please discuss the design of the pyramid?*

If you're speaking in reference to the triangle, the equilateral triangle, that's what man is. That's what God is. Here, you have the divine perfect balance neutrality. And when neutrality divides itself, it has identity, the effect of division. For one cannot identify in what they are for it requires a reflection. For example, love is the reflection in another of the goodness in oneself. And so that which we are, God and goodness, is the trinity of truth. The expression of that offers us what we call positive and negative; however, the division of that which we are, by expression, offering individualization, which is covering or limit, is necessary in order to awaken limit. One cannot awaken that which by the law they have not identified with. And so be in creation and not a part of it. Identify and be identified. Use that which you believe; do not become it. For when one becomes what they believe, it is ever at the expense of what they are.

And so this triangle, this trinity that you are, you are evolving and returning to the apex, the oneness, that which you truly are. And so you have a world that reveals to you the base of that triangle: for every up, you have a down; for every good, you have a bad; for every day, you have a night. What does it offer to you? It offers reflection. It offers illusion. You are not the day for you are not the night. You are not the up for you are not the down. Experience is only an effect of the mirror you choose to look in. And so you have choice ever remembering what you are. Whoever remembers what they are knows who they are, has no question of why they are.

God, Good does not question. For God to question reveals an expression of need. God, Goodness does not contain need. Only that which has split from its source by identification, individualization, limit, only that contains need for it looks without and not within. Whoever looks without does so at the expense and the expression of the weakness of temptation; whoever looks without experiences need. Whoever looks within is joyous in fulfillment. For all that we are is within us.

And the movement from outside to inside is one that takes eons of evolving. It begins when we spend our days in declaring the truth: "I am responsible for my experiences this moment. I am responsible for my experiences each and every moment for I alone am choosing them in keeping with my own evolution. I am freed from want, need, and desire for I no longer believe outside. I accept that which I am inside."

Faith is the expression of what you are, and belief is ever the expression of what you are not. So whoever believes in what they are not is destined to experience need, for they've denied what they are and, in the denial, judges that someone has it. And so when we permit our self to believe, then we're ever seeking the one who we judge has the golden fleece on which we can lie our weary body, which we believe, unfortunately or fortunately, for a time that we are. Yes.

*As we're evolving to accept the Allness that we are, how do we discern if we are slipping into the dangerous point of believing we are the power?*

Whoever is freed from concern is not slipping into believing they are the power. You see, the belief that we are the power is an effect, an effect of a concern of what we're doing. And what we believe we are is the covering. And so whoever is concerned in reference to what they are and what they are doing (are they slipping into believing) is revealing, indeed, they are slipping by the very entertaining of the thought of concern. For the thought of concern can only express the belief in limit, for no concern exists in what you are. Concern only exists as an expression, an anticipation of fulfilling need, that which you are not. Yes.

*Thank you. Do adversities and attachments cast shadows because they deny the truth of what they actually are and dictate their importance to us?*

Attachments, adversities are obstructions to the Light that you are. For one cannot experience attachment to anything outside until they first deny what they are inside, for one becomes attached by denying the wholeness that they are. The attachment being an effect of the direction of intelligent energy to form outside the limits of their responsibility and control. Does that help with your question?

*Yes. Thank you.*

You're welcome.

*Can you use visualization to lift yourself out of lower levels and what image is most effective?*

The one that is the most desirable to the level in which you have become entrapped. For example, one finds themselves identified with and experiencing what they call need. In that level of consciousness, one has many forms to choose. One has other forms that they can service and, therefore, fulfill. And when that form is fulfilled in that realm, he or she will open the door after we have fed them so we can leave. Does that help with your question?

*Yes. Thank you.*

So it's a matter of choice. If you are having an experience and you believe that you need money, in the same realm of belief and need there are other forms that have been created and that also represent need and you are in a position to fill their need so the door in the consciousness can be opened and you can rise [to] higher realms of consciousness. Yes.

*Thank you. When many obstructions to the good in life are manifesting, how can one help themselves to maintain a feeling of good?*

Gratitude is the door through which supply continues to flow. Whoever is grateful for the experience of good in their life guarantees the law which brings about its continuity. Yes.

*Thank you.*

You're welcome.

*When one sorts out information to make a decision, it comes from the brain. What is reason in relation to the sorting out process?*

Well, in reference to decision, judgments are made by the brain by the limit for we find that a judgment is dependent upon past experience and is therefore limited in its consideration only to the forms of past experiences. Now whenever a person works to, to establish a decision, there is total consideration for they are in service and under the guidance of the faculty of reason, which considers all within and without.

Now our timing is rather passing quickly here. How's our cameraman staying awake here this evening? Yes. So let us go right on with your questions.

*The question is, I usually feel and am in touch with the outside. How do I help myself be inside and know what it feels like?*

Well, in reference to knowing what it feels like inside, of course, it is at the expense of refraining from need. You see, a person finds themselves in great need from a lack of effort in their life of spending the necessary energy through identification with the true being, that which they are. Now there are many different paths that are used by many people. Some have a daily time of meditation. Others have a time of contemplation. Others have a daily prayer time. So there are many different paths up the mountain where the Light of eternal truth ever shines. And so one should consider a daily time for them, and it should be the same time every day without exception, for it establishes with the consciousness the Law of Priority and value. And that which we value, by the very Law of Value, shall serve us ever in keeping with our priority for it. For in truth we get out of anything in life whatever it is we put into it. Yes.

*Thank you.*

You're welcome.

*In gaining acceptance so that one is not controlled by what one encounters, is this the same as what the Bible teaches in the phrase walking in another's shoes?*

Well, yes, indeed. Whenever we permit our self to depend on something that by the very law cannot be in our control, [which is] contrary to the divine law, then we are, of course, tempted to walk in another's shoes. And whoever walks in another's shoes, sooner or later, finds the shoes don't fit. Either they pinch for they're too tight or they're too loose and they fall off and they stumble along the path. Yes, indeed.

*Thank you.*

You're welcome.

*I don't have any more questions at this time.*

Well, that's fine because I see that our time is passing and we managed to, to take care of those this evening. Now before we close up our class for this evening, I would like to say how important it is for all of us to encourage our self. Whoever identifies with the faculty directs intelligent energy to it. And so when we take moments to see the good within our self, we will offer that to the world. And whoever offers good to the world can only experience good from the world. And so [we] must learn each day, every day, to speak honestly to what we believe we are and declare the truth: "The goodness is within me. At times I am tempted to believe it is not. And when I believe that it is not, I am thirsty, I am frustrated, I am unhappy. For by that temptation and weakness in the fiber of my character I believe someone else has it."

So if you must believe, then believe that you have it, until the next step is made when you move into that wonderful faculty known as faith, and then there's no more believing when you experience what you are. But while a world of bondage and belief is so important, and moving through that realm of bondage, believe, when it rises in your mind that you need this and need that, believe that you have it instead of being the victim and the servant of someone and something somewhere that, by the Law of Personal Responsibility, you cannot control.

Thank you, my good friends, and good night.

OCTOBER 10, 1985

## A/V Seminar 8

Good evening, class. Welcome to our seminar this evening.

Experiences in life repeat themselves until we no longer believe we are the judgments that have in truth created them. And this evening we're going to begin with the questions that you have submitted.

*Thank you. Is the purpose of pleasure and pain a necessary process for the soul to evolve to a higher state?*

The process or the experience that you call pain and pleasure is dependent, of course, upon the judgment that one believes that they are. It was therefore necessary for those in states of evolution who continue to believe they are the thought and the solidified thought pattern or judgment of their mind.

*Thank you. Is regret of what one does in life the mind's way of delaying and putting off the hard work and effort it takes to remain consistent on the path?*

Regret is used by the mind in order for one to continue to experience the hopelessness of effort to make changes. It reveals a person who is temporarily over-identified with their mind or mental world.

*Thank you. I'll pause for the clock. Thank you. Is there a greater sun that the galaxies revolve around, like a central sun or source?*

The galaxies are dependent for their sustenance upon a source, a light, and in that respect, that is correct. There is a greater sun.

*Thank you. Could you please share your understanding of the saying, "Work is God's love made manifest," and cleanliness is next to godliness?*

Yes, in respect to cleanliness is next to godliness and "Work is God's love made manifest." Cleanliness is a reflection of order. And the universe reveals to us that which is harmonious, that which is healthful, that which is healthy is orderly and, therefore, clean. Everything has a place in the universe. Every thought, every feeling has a responsibility to its original design. And whenever a person makes the effort to organize their thoughts, to put them in proper perspective in keeping with the true purpose of their original design, then one experiences the harmony, the health, and the abundant good which is, of course, their responsibility and their birthright.

Now in reference to work is love, God's love made manifest. The purpose of the design of the vehicles that are responsible to what we truly are is to work, to produce, to be active. For that which is not active does not serve its design as form or limit. Therefore, whenever the forms which are responsible to our true being are guided, disciplined, and controlled in keeping with the personal responsibility of our evolution, we experience the goodness that we truly are.

*Thank you. "The gift without the giver is worthless." Would you please share with us what is meant by the giver, and why the giver has such ability?*

"The gift without the giver is worthless." The giver has the ability of choice. One chooses to give or one chooses to loan. And so without the giver, the gift is a loan. For example, say that one feels impressed to give a gift to someone. If the person in giving the gift does not give the part of themselves that was inspired to give the gift, then the gift is without the giver and is, in truth, a loan and not a gift. Many people, in giving gifts, believe that they have given, when in truth experience reveals to them they have made a loan. For the thought formed in the consciousness impressed upon the mind to give the gift remains with the giver. Therefore, it is a loan, and the person is plagued with concern on what the person receiving the gift has done with the gift that they have loaned them.

*Thank you. Are there joyful celebrations and holidays in the higher realms? If so, would you please tell us of these?*

In reference to celebrations and joyous experiences in what you state there as the higher realms, there are indeed celebrations. For there are experiences with those who are studying, for those who are working to free themselves from limit. There are stages of evolution or what you may call graduations. And in that respect, there are times of celebration and joyous expression. However, they are not dependent upon what you may consider as the fruits of action or attachment. They are an experience of relief that that which has passed has passed. And therefore, they're able to move on to the next step.

*Thank you. Why did the Light choose this time to establish a temple of Light in the midst of creation?*

In reference to this temple of Light in what you understand as the midst of creation, try to understand that challenge in creation is a stimulation of what is known as the uneducated ego. In order to bring about a balance or an education of the ego, it is necessary to present it with what you understand as challenge.

When there is great disturbance in the atmosphere of any planet, it requires great effort in respect to the Light and what you understand as the limit or the lesser light. And so it isn't a matter of choice. It is a matter of evolution. And when the night is the darkest, that is when the Light shines the brightest.

And so in keeping with the many eons of evolution of the human species, as you know them, there comes a time when mental realms become highly refined in defending the limits that they represent. For example, the human mind, in its refinement and evolution, has found itself quite capable of defending, through justification, which is its defense, of defending anything that enters its realm. And so we find that on the Earth planet that the advancement and refinement and evolution of mental substance has reached such a point in evolution that the Light, that which you are, must enter the very being of what one believes that they are. For without entering into the very limits of one's belief, one has a corner, so to speak, in which to hide. And so the Light has come in this respect, and in many temples, but particularly in this temple, into the midst of creation. Therefore, in so doing man has presented to him a conscious choice for man has a constant reminder. A reminder in his own being of what he is and of what he is tempted to believe he is.

*Thank you. Would you please share with us the spiritual significance of the four seasons and their cyclic changing?*

The four seasons are in keeping with north, south, east, and west. The four seasons represent: the north, the winter; the south, the summer; the east, the spring; and the west, the fall. Now as man turns to the spring, as man turns to the east, he turns to the Light. As he turns to the Light, man is encouraged. As he looks back and turns to the west, he falls. However, if man stands and faces direct to the east, he will find he receives from the south, and he will find that he sends to the north.

This is very, very important to understand that man in his own being is north, south, east, and west. So man should remember in his consciousness which way to turn his attention. If he turns his attention to the east within his consciousness, he will find his experiences contain, without exception, good. He will see clearly that there is good even in the experiences that seem to him to be distasteful. An experience is only distasteful when man permits himself to turn his back in consciousness to the Light that he is. Therefore, whenever you feel there is something that you are not responsible for, remember, you have turned your back to the east, to the Light that you are, and, in so doing, are experiencing shadows and are falling from what you are to what you can only temporarily believe that you are. Therefore, whoever pauses in all experiences in life and declares the truth, "There is good in this experience," when that statement is made within the consciousness, one once again turns to the Light, to the east within them. And in the so doing, one rises in consciousness and experiences the good that they are.

*Thank you. For many people the holiday season, which is fast approaching, is a time of great emotional upheaval and not a time of joy or gratitude. Why is this so for so many people?*

In reference to your holiday seasons and in reference to emotional upheaval, it is when man looks to what has been and identifies with what has been and, in so doing, ties the ribbon of comparison to the present moment, that's when the judgments of the past arise, and man begins to experience what he understands as emotion. For he has fallen, by turning to the west. But he needn't fall, for in that moment he can declare the truth, "There is good in what I experience."

*Thank you. Would you please share with us your understanding of the price of genius?*

If you understand genius to be the refinement of the human intellect, then it comes at great price. If you understand genius to be an expression of the divine Spirit that you truly are, expressed through [a] mental world, then genius serves its true purpose. Genius, what you understand is genius, is not something that is acquired in respect to a person's study or mental activity. What you understand as genius isn't the expression of soul. Without the limit of the judgments of the human mind, it is the Light expressing itself clearly. That is rare in your world, but it does happen at times.

*Thank you. How can one express total consideration for themselves?*

One can express total consideration for what they are if one will make the effort to remind themselves of what they are. However, it is not frequent that one reminds themselves of what they are, for man is easily tempted when man does not make the effort consciously to remind himself that he is whole, complete, and perfect. That which he is, is whole, complete, and perfect.

However, from long patterns of use man is easily tempted to believe and to experience what he is not.

*Thank you. Why do we, after all these centuries, perceive things as in a straight line and so flat?*

All things are in truth a straight line. Everything that you experience with your eyes is a straight line. Is it flat? It is as flat as your judgments make it. It is as crooked as your judgments make it. The eyes of man are covered with the mist of what has been. They are covered with that mist and do not see clearly until man refrains from belief. For when man insists upon identifying with belief, then man cannot see clearly for the mist of judgments cloud his sight. And so pause for a moment and look. And if you will look, you will see how clear, how clean, how straight things really are. And if you find them a bit crooked, pause a bit longer, and you will see them straighten out, as you straighten out within your own being.

*Thank you. Should a person look for medical solutions other than surgery, since that definitely pierces the aura?*

Yes, indeed. Yes, indeed. There are many solutions to what you understand as medical problems, for medical problems are an effect, an effect of a discord within the consciousness and, of course, the body reacts to that discord. Things are not organized within the consciousness. And whoever identifies with what you understand as self is destined to experience that disorder or disease. Everything has its place. It is the responsibility of man to find the place, the proper place, in keeping with design, original design, for all, *all* of his thoughts and feelings.

*Thank you. After death, as we move through the realms, what do we say to the forms that will try to tempt us to their levels?*

"I am responsible for you for I have, in my days of ignorance, created you. I have created you as an effect of denying what I am. I no longer deny what I am. Therefore, you no longer exist in my consciousness." That declaration of truth is an instrument through which man frees himself from the old baggage of creation.

I do hope our cameraman, here, is checking the camera as well as all of these questions he's reading.

*Yes, he is.* [The cameraman responds.]

Hmm.

*Thank you. Does sexual intercourse on this earth's plane involve the penetration of the woman's aura? Does the entrance of the sperm?*

Yes, it does. And I think that all women would agree with me from the experiences that they encounter. Yes.

*Thank you. In Discourse 13 in* The Living Light *book it says if only you could see what is taking place when we use the telephone. Could you please share your understanding of what is happening and how one can protect themselves if their jobs require it?*

For whoever's work in life requires using that instrument (the telephone), the statement was made clearly in the book in reference to people who share, seemingly, their personal experiences over that gadget you call the telephone. Now the spoken word is life-giving energy. And when you speak forth a word, you release from your being electromagnetic energy. Now that energy takes the form created by your mind at the moment of releasing the energy. That form goes out into the universe and, for the telephone, it travels along these electromagnetic lines, those forms do, and a person [who is] receiving that over the telephone sends back to you their forms. Now there's an actual exchange of these forms between two people over these frequencies.

Fortunately or unfortunately, at those times your forms that you are sending out and the forms that you are receiving have added many other forms. Some of them are not in harmony. There are many ears that listen to what you think you say in private. There is nothing private when you release, through the spoken word, energy from your being. Therefore, a person should refrain from sharing personal experiences or taking so-called advice over these instruments of communication known as the telephone. To use those instruments in one's work, one should not in any way permit themselves to experience any emotional registration, for those forms would enter the water center and they, of course, would have responsibility for those forms that have been created.

*Thank you. It is said in* The Living Light *book that there is a method that is beneficial to us in making changes. This is the Law of Identity and to entertain in thought that we are another person, place, or circumstance that we find intolerable. How does this help us to make changes easier?*

That which we find intolerable in life is a revelation of that which we are adverse to. Whoever faces their adversities honestly, slowly but surely, shall gain control over them before they awaken to the attachment, which is in truth the final effect of all adversities. Now the adversity, what we understand as an adversity, is that which is a threat to the judgments that we believe that we are. And whoever permits themselves to experience a threat to their judgments is destined to experience the attachment, for one believes that they are their judgments. At one time it is an adversity, only to become an attachment because it is the child or judgment that they alone in truth have created. So whatever we find intolerable in life, whatever experience we consider to be that we are adverse to, we only guarantee the attachment to it because it is ours. We have created it; we believe that it is us, and the law fulfills itself.

*Thank you. Is the imagination something we should really develop? And does our imagination play an important part after our transition out of the form we are now encased in?*

Why, yes, indeed, our imagination is very important. For we image (imagine) many things. It is the avenue through which the creative principle expresses itself.

*Thank you. How do we find our birth number?*

Our birth number has been discussed before. For example, you know the month and the year and the day that you were born. Everything in the universe is mathematical. You could not enter your planet Earth, only at the particular time and date that you entered the Earth. For in keeping with the Law of Evolution, you're a five, a four, a seven, a nine, an eight, or one or two. Whatever number that you are reveals to you the frequency that you were on, and are on, in your experiences on the planet Earth. That does not necessarily reveal to you that you are more or less advanced spiritually or otherwise. It does, however, reveal to you certain characteristics of that frequency, and that is known as your birth number. However, like the stars in the heavens, they are there as indicators. They do not compel your life. They indicate certain tendencies that you have. However, you are greater than all tendencies, for in truth what is a tendency but an identification with the possibility of a temptation.

*Thank you. Why does it appear that the so-called chickens come home to roost all at once?*

Well, in reference to the chickens coming home to roost, if one understands their chickens as their adversities, if one understands what they think they're getting away with (the chickens that they have kept away from their conscious view and responsibility), then one would understand that the things that we know we should be doing ofttimes in life we just don't do. And because we do know that we should be doing them, we, sooner or later, face that all the things we knew we should have done have now returned: the chickens have come home to roost.

Man faces his responsibilities in life best at times of seeming disaster. When he's tried to get away and not face responsibility, he sends out these chickens. Only to experience at a later time, they've all come home to roost. They know who created them, those chickens do. They know who their parent is. And when they come home to roost, which they always do, they come home very hungry. For we're the ones that have created them and we're the ones that sent them out into the cold. And they're not very happy and they're very hungry when they come home.

*Thank you. Is the practice of drills for major disasters in truth helping to cause disasters?*

Man has a tendency in life to believe he is the human mind, which offers to him fear. Man ever seeks security and never seems to have enough of it.

Now in reference to your question, Is the preparation for disasters in one's life instrumental in creating them? As you believeth, so you becometh, as long as you insist on identifying with what you believe. So in that respect man prepares himself for days of financial disaster, man prepares himself for poor health, man prepares himself for marriage, man prepares himself for divorce, for man permits himself to believe that whatever happens to others is destined, possibly, to happen to him, with the exceptions, of course, of his adversities. Therefore, in that respect man is instrumental in an error of ignorance of bringing about the experiences, of course, in his life. For if that were not true, then we'd have to throw out personal responsibility.

Now if the person decides, "Now I best have some health insurance because I haven't been feeling too well lately. I'll go and get myself some health insurance." Well, then man has to face the judgment of letting go of the money to buy the health insurance. Now if he does not act wisely in consciousness, the judgment that he believes he is, in reference to his money, rises up, sooner or later, [and] starts to plague him in his mind, and says, "You spent all of this money for health insurance and you haven't been sick. And so you've taken and thrown away all of that money." This happens beneath the conscious awareness.

And so the money judgment is not a bit happy. And so it goes to work knocking at the door of man's conscience telling him that he spent money and is getting nothing out of it. Slowly but surely, he begins to think, "I think perhaps I've got a cold. Oh, it seems to be getting worse." The next thing you know he's not able to go to work he feels so bad. Within a few days or perhaps a week or two he has pneumonia. The next thing you know he has double pneumonia. Ah, the next day he is going to get his money's worth: he's got to go to the hospital.

And so if we understand when we believe we are these judgments and whatever we do in life is a threat to some of these judgments that we believe we are, we have these different problems. Now we go ahead and in that way we do create these seeming disasters. Of course, we create them. We experience them and we have personal responsibility for them. If we understand how we create them, if we're honest with ourselves and say, "All right now, I have these many judgments. Now right now I'm aware of these different judgments. I don't believe that I am these judgments, but I must remind myself when I go to make a change, such as spending money, that my judgments have not approved me spending."

You see, it's like being married. To believe you are the judgments of your mind is like being married to many wives. It's like a harem, you see, in that respect. And one of them will let you do this and one of them will let you do that, and another won't agree that you can spend the money this way or that way.

You see, man cannot be free as long as man believes he is these many judgments, because they all don't agree with each other. And whenever you go to make a change—and I know that all you have had the experiences, when you're in a store and perhaps you see something you would like to have and you pause for a moment and the next thing you know something's in your mind and you believe that's you [and it says,] "No, I don't need that at all. No, I don't want that at all." Or, another experience: you walk in a store; you see something; you immediately buy it. Then you go home or perhaps on the way home, you are very upset—you believe you are very upset because another judgment has risen up that was waiting for a long time for you to spend the money to fill that judgment, and you have turned around and spent the money to fill another judgment. And so a person, when they think of themselves, has to face all of that or experience the emotional turmoil in their mind. I do hope that's helped with that question.

*Thank you. How can one most effectively communicate the power of the spoken word through the written word?*

Honesty. Honesty. The power of the spoken word—and it is the power that is—can best be communicated through the written word when one is honest with oneself. Say, for example, that you are writing to someone. As you are writing, you speak to the person. You speak out loud to the person as you move your hand and you write the words that you have spoken. In that way you imprint upon the paper the forms that are being spoken and they go with the paper to the person that you send it to.

*Thank you. Are animals able to compose pictures, music, or other works of art without the use of the tools we use?*

Well, animals compose and create many, many things. They have not, in your world, been given credit yet. And that is only from a lack of understanding of the two-legged animal. Animals create many forms in the atmosphere; those that are pleasing and those that are happy. There are also forms created that are unhappy. They also express forms, at times, of denial, [but] nowheres near as frequent, of course, as the two-legged animal.

*Thank you. Do animals communicate symbols by imaging them?*

Well, in respect to symbols, animals do image. Animals have great imaginations. Animals communicate with a release of these forms that they have created. For example, a dog may lie and take a little nap. The time he's napping there are many forms that are being released into the atmosphere, and usually they are the desires of the mind of the animal, of the things that he would like to do, of the things that he enjoys doing. And in that respect, they release those pictures, of course, into the atmosphere.

*Thank you.*

You're welcome.

*What would be your understanding on working smart, not hard?*

Working smart?

*That's what it says.* [During this seminar, students' questions were written in advance of the class, submitted to a director for review, and read to the teacher by the vice president, who was also the cameraman.]

I see. Working smart, working smart, not hard?

*That is correct.*

Working smart—I want to understand the questioner's meaning of the word *smart* and the adversity to hard. Smart. Working smart. Well, if by the question the person means working for the best possible result, then I would say whoever frees themselves from concern of the fruits of action is a person who is working intelligently or smartly. A person who is concerned with their fruits of action from their labor of effort is a person who is not working smart and, ofttimes, working very hard. It is a freedom from self-identification, the lack of concern. Concern creates limit and is a service to what has been, and therefore the energy released by the person working does not produce the results in keeping with the energy released, for most of it is going to the concern of the human mind and an attachment to the fruits, which are yet to manifest themselves. I wouldn't consider that working smart. Yes, in that respect I would consider it working hard, but if you are concerned with what you're going to get from the labor that you do, that is not working smart.

*Thank you.*

You're welcome.

*What would be the best way to help oneself in relation to staying in charge while showing something to someone?*

By staying in charge? First of all, it depends on what you want the person to experience with what you have to show them. For example, if you want the person to have a good feeling from what you have to show them, then you must first enter that good feeling and not deviate or waver from your own conviction. And therefore, if you have, through self-discipline, gained control over your mind, then you will not only emanate that good feeling that you have created in your consciousness but through the discipline of your own mind and the ability of taking control over your mind that which enters your universe shall be affected by your universe.

*Thank you. How can one discern the difference between qualifying and pushing?*

Qualifying and pushing? Well, I think perhaps that refers to one qualifying or pushing. You see, there's something here we must consider. Is the questioner asking about pushing or qualifying themselves or pushing or qualifying another or being qualified or pushed by another? So we have many different ways of looking at that question. So please read it once again.

*How can one discern the difference between qualifying and pushing?*

Oh, I see. Well, the problem there is quite clear. To the judgments that one believes one is, when they are about to make a change they feel like they're pushed. Yes. Therefore, one should qualify themselves by effort to understand what they are and what they are not. For all judgments of our mind, if a change comes about, they always feel like they're being pushed. Yes.

*Thank you. Why would a person become intimidated?*

Why would a person become intimidated? Anyone who believes they are the judgments of their mind is ever a delicate being and can easily experience being intimidated for their judgments, which they temporarily believe that they are, are threatened.

*Thank you.*

Yes.

*How can we free ourselves from intimidation to be able to stay on top of a situation?*

One cannot feel intimidated unless one believes they are the judgments and, in so doing, must protect what they believe that they are. For what they believe that they are is threatened, and survival is the animal instinct.

*Thank you.*

You're welcome.

*Why do we have difficulty laughing at ourselves when we become stuck in a level which isn't really us?*

Because we believe we are the level that isn't us, even though we intellectualize it and say, "This is not me." We do not really accept that it is not us in the emotional center, which we are temporarily attached to.

*Thank you.*

You're welcome.

*When we feel from our heart and not from our—it says heart, but I believe they meant head—are we helping ourselves to become freed from the bondage of self-levels?*

When we feel from our heart? Well, it is our heart that feels, of course. Now are we helping ourselves to be freed from self-levels? Well, you know, one, first of all, can best help themselves from being freed by—from self-levels by personal responsibility. To declare the truth: "This is an experience that I'm having in my mind. This experience I alone have created. I can defend my judgments through justification and through belief that I experience this because of something beyond my control by what someone else has done." That is not the path to freedom.

First of all, state the truth: "This is an experience I am having within my own mind. There is good in this experience. The judgments that I believe that I am are not happy with this experience, and these judgments tell me that I am having this experience because of what someone else is doing outside and beyond my control." Try not to forget, whatever feeling, whatever thought, whatever experience that takes place is taking place within your own mind. You have not only the divine right, you have the responsibility to choose intelligently whether or not you want the experience to continue in your mind. And if you want the experience to continue, a guaranteed way is to tell yourself that it is an experience that is beyond your control. For whoever tells themselves that they are having an experience that is beyond their control is a person who is establishing the law for the continuity of the experience. Yes.

*Thank you. How may we help those around [us] become more harmonious within their levels?*

By helping our self. For example, if we want those around us to be harmonious, then we must gain greater control of our mind that we are the living demonstration of the harmony that we permit our self to believe that we are seeking. Harmony—in the midst of the Philistines the Principle of Good exists. We are delivered in the midst of the Philistines by a conscious choice to follow the light of reason, to turn to the east, where hope and encouragement fully reveal themselves in our life. Yes.

*Thank you. What is boredom a cause of? How can it be used to facilitate personal growth? What technique can be used to break through boredom?*

Well, in reference to boredom, I think if you will pause a few moments and accept the demonstrable truth that work is God's love made manifest, you will not experience boredom. I have yet to find a person who truly works who is bored. Now boredom is an experience that the mind has when it believes that it is trapped. It's bored. It has denied personal responsibility. We cannot experience boredom until we first deny personal responsibility. When we accept personal responsibility, we therefore consciously choose what we want and what we'll do. And no one consciously chooses to experience what you know as boredom. It is an effect of denial that you have control over your life. When you accept that you alone have control over your life, you will not experience boredom for the light of reason cannot flow in those realms of consciousness. And you are the light of reason, and you will not remain in that level or experience.

*Thank you. Are the forms that we create in our so-called sleep state as solidified as the forms we create in a conscious state of mind?*

Yes, indeed. They are indeed more solidified for they do not have the censorship of the conscious mind. And they express themselves vividly while you are experiencing what you call sleep. And sometimes you awaken and are aware of what you understand as nightmares, unfulfilled desires. And [during the day], you did not express yourself and tell the person what you really thought of them because you had the censorship of the conscious mind in the respect that—you see, in your sleep state, you express without the censorship [of your conscious mind] what you really want to tell a person. You wouldn't do that in the conscious state because in the conscious state you still have the fear that you may want something out of the person, and therefore you don't want to offend them. Yes.

*Thank you.*

You're welcome.

*Is concentration the key to power? And if so, what are the proper methods of concentration?*

Concentration is not the key to power. Concentration is the key to *all* power for there is only one Power. Now what you are is single. It is singular. You *are* Light. You *are* Truth. You *are* the Principle [of] Good. That is what you are. Whenever you accept what you are, you are therefore the Power, for you have accepted what you are. A person who is concentrated is a person whose I is single. Now the single I is not the I of creation, it is not the I of limit. You see, concentration is the I. Belief is the thought of I. So man believes he is the form of the I, and when he does that, he sees with two eyes. When man accepts that he is the I, not the thought of the I, the I, that is when man experiences that which he is.

Concentration is the key to all power. When you free yourself from believing, you accept what you are. That's faith. That is power. And when you spend a few moments each day, frequently, just a few moments to remind yourself, "This is what I am. This is what I am. For a moment I am experiencing what I truly am. I know that I shall turn, for that is my experience. I only pray that I will remember, when I turn, that this is what I believe; yet *this* is what I am." And when you have these many experiences that you have during the course of a day, remind yourself, "This is what I am. This is what I believe that I am, but it is not what I truly am." Yes.

That is concentration, the key to all power. You have the power of the universe; that is what you are. What you do with it is something else. What you are is one thing. What you do with what you are is something else.

*Thank you. How can we make Thanksgiving a more spiritual celebration?*

How can one make Thanksgiving a more spiritual celebration? The giving of thanks *is* a spiritual celebration. So if one is giving thanks in their consciousness, then one is experiencing a spiritual celebration. One can do it for oneself. One loses the giving of thanks by accepting need, which is denial of what they are. Ofttimes in life—I think I speak loud enough for you to hear me [over the chiming bells of the clock]—ofttimes in life one's giving of thanks is dependent on what someone else is doing; the someone else being beyond their power of control, beyond their right of control. The giving of thanks, which is a spiritual experience, the giving of thanks or thanksgiving is something that one should cultivate each day. You have a holiday once a year. If you spend 364 days of giving thanks, when that special day comes around, you will have qualified yourself with at least 364 days of effort. You cannot help but have a Thanksgiving

Day. Do not depend on what others do, and you will experience the spirituality of giving thanks.

*Thank you. Do they have such holidays of gratitude in the spirit world or is every day a day of thanksgiving?*

In the higher realms of consciousness every day is a giving of thanks. In other realms, in what you call Summer Lands, the lighter realms, the giving of thanks of the masses who come over to our side is their birthday. Their birthday is so important to them, for their birthday is the day they left the Earth planet. And they're so grateful and so relieved they truly celebrate that day. *[Many of the students laugh.]*

*Thank you.*

You're welcome.

*Is sleeping under an electric blanket detrimental, and why?*

Sleeping under an electric blanket is detrimental in respect to the balance of the electromagnetic vibrations depending on the person's state of evolution. Some people are not aware of the effect that it has, except they're warm. You see, whenever you permit yourself to become more dependent on something outside for the security you should be experiencing by conscious choice within your mind—try to understand, my friends, that warmth, in what you judge is a cold day, warmth is an emotional security, first. And when a person feels emotionally secure, they feel comfortable. Let's, for example, take a honeymoon; you can take them to Alaska in the midst of winter and if it's their second day of honeymoon, why, they're not concerned whether they have on a warm parka or not because they're so warm because they're so emotionally secure. They're comfortable. Someone might even have to remind them it's 20 below zero. You see, it's a matter of our attitude, our attitude of mind.

You know, a person who feels emotionally secure is less identified with what's going on outside. They're not as consciously aware of temperature changes because they're so comfortable with the temperature within. So, you see, the water center, in our consciousness and in our being, is a very important center because, you see, if we are not secure in our water center, then the slightest changes of temperature, we become very upset over. And so, first of all, seek the comfort and create a balance, an orderly balance, in the water center, in the emotions within, and then you will experience a more gracious adapting to the temperatures which your body is exposed to. Yes.

*Thank you. How may I overcome my poor memory? And does poor memory have any direct linkage to my inability to control spontaneous mental states?*

Well, in reference to poor memory, it has been my experience, for so long, that poor memory is not all-inclusive. There are some things—sometimes a person believes they have a very poor memory, and yet if they'll be honest with themselves, you'd be amazed what a beautiful memory they have in certain things in life. So it's a matter of expanding one's consciousness. And, first of all, accepting the demonstrable truth: with some things the memory's seemingly perfect. And just expand that state of consciousness into other things. I have found in my experiences the things we most desire, we don't have any problem remembering. It's the things ofttimes in life that we judge are responsibilities that we seem to have poor memories with.

But I do want to encourage that student who's asked that question. First of all, you have an excellent memory. It's only a matter of expanding it by not feeling emotional or feeling a burden with responsibilities. Look at those responsibilities with a brighter light, and you will find an expansion of that beautiful, excellent memory that you have. Yes.

*Thank you.*

You're welcome.

*Does the soul express itself during sleep?*

The soul expresses itself at all times. It's only censored by the human mind. And so, you know, those who have a peashooter mind, the soul gets what it can in its expression through the peashooter. And so it does so at sleep or awake. Yes, the soul, you know—if the soul did not express itself, there'd be no form at all: there'd be no mind, no form, [no] anything. So the soul is expressing itself. It's just ofttimes so censored by the judgments, some may ask if there's a soul there. Yes, there is a soul there. Of course, there is. Yes.

*Thank you. What does it mean to set a law into motion?*

We set a law into motion with each and every thought and every spoken word. So that's what it means. You have a thought; you set a law into motion. You speak the word and you give it strength, the strength of the electromagnetic energy or ectoplasm. And the form is created and out in to the universe [it goes]. And so that sets a law into motion. What law? If you don't know what law, that's not going to be any exemption from the return of the law for all laws return to their own creators. We are the creators and we do set laws into motion. We set laws into motion this moment, each and every moment. Our responsibility is to understand and to accept when the law returns, we set it into motion and start to make the connection of how we set it into motion. Yes. What thoughts we entertain. What attitudes. And, of course, what judgments.

*Thank you.*

Yes.

*Why do some husbands treat their wives rudely, even viciously, and why do some wives do the same thing to their husbands?*

They are insecure. They're insecure and they lack understanding of why they're insecure. You see, the soul is expressing itself through the limits of the human mind, which frequently, of course, is servicing judgments or past experiences. And whoever permits themselves to over-identify with their mind experiences the feelings, the thoughts, and the judgments that they've been unjustly treated. A child in the early, formative years, if effort is not made to guide them, they feel emotionally that they are unjustly treated for the effort has not been made to guide them, to communicate with them. And the child grows up and has this resentment in the mind that he has been mistreated. And so whenever he comes up against an experience as an adult with another person and there is any similarity and there is any connection in the consciousness that triggers that old experience in his early childhood, then they act, what you would say, rudely and not kindly to the person.

Now try to understand, those who, in our ignorance, we permit ourselves to become attached to—remember, we attach ourselves to the mirrors that best reflect the fulfillment of our denials, which we experience as needs. So a person can understand their denials from their attachments. One does not attach oneself to another unless the other reflects to them the fulfillment of their own denials, known as needs. So one finds themselves in life, in experience, dependent upon another person for they experience a fulfillment of what they have denied for themselves. That creates an attachment. And once the attachment is established, then, after a period of time, the person awakens that someone else is beginning to order their life and tell them what to do. So, you see, it works both ways. Here you have two people who have denied what they are and have found another person (each other) reflecting a fulfillment of their own denials. And, of course, two halves are never so perfect they make a whole, when a person is whole in the first place. Yes.

*Thank you. How does one accept another's right to express and yet not deny their own right?*

Personal responsibility. How does one accept another's right to express without denying their own right to express?

*That is correct.*

Well, if you understand that your right to express is not to go beyond your right of personal responsibility, then you have no problem. However, if you accept that your right to express is to enforce your beliefs and your dictates upon another individual, then you have a serious problem. Now when you have a group of people, like in a school or in a business or any organization, the right of the motive of the purpose of founding the organization is the supreme right. Otherwise, you cannot have anything organized. For example, your bees and nature and your animals teach you that law. Yes.

*Thank you.*

You're welcome.

*Does drinking a lot of liquids have a positive or negative effect on a person's health?*

Depends on what the liquid is. *[At this moment the teacher takes a drink of water. And a few students laugh.]* Thank you.

*Thank you. That is all the questions.*

Oh, indeed, and our time has passed. It is so nice to have spent this time with you this evening. So nice and comfortable. I mustn't take this off. *[The teacher refers to his microphone.]* I have a tendency to take this off before I finish talking, and I have been corrected several times. However, there's the clock. And I will say good evening to all of you. And I'm happy to see that you are thinking and presenting your questions and—because from your question, you are expressing a part of your own being, and in so doing it shall not return unto you void. Thank you and good night.

NOVEMBER 14, 1985

## A/V Seminar 9

Good evening, students, and welcome to our seminar this evening. And we'll begin this seminar with the many questions that you have prepared.

*Thank you. Would you please share with us the spiritual meaning of the horizon?*

The spiritual meaning of horizon, which is any horizon, which is limit to our view, is based upon conception, for our eyes see what we conceive, and our soul perceives what is. Based upon belief in limit, which is an effect of over-identification with limit, we conceive many things. One of the many things we conceive are horizons: the horizon as you look at the sky; the horizon of your success in any endeavor. And so it behooves anyone to perceive and to make greater effort to refrain from conceiving and conception.

*Thank you. Would you please share with us your understanding of a good starter and a poor finisher, and how we can correct this habit?*

Well, the habit pattern, what you know as a habit pattern, of a good starter and a poor finisher is, of course, based upon motivation. When we permit our self to deny the law of nothing in and nothing out, something in and something out, which, of course, is an expression of the Law of Personal Responsibility, then we will not be tempted by a motivation, the effect of which is a good starter and a very poor finisher. A good starter and a poor finisher is one who is tempted to get something in life with little or no effort. And that is known as a good starter and a poor finisher.

*Thank you. Why are men more emotional than women?*

In expression in your world on the Earth planet, your society, over a period of many, many eons of time, has accepted that it is a weakness of the female sex to be emotional, that it is more or less a part of their basic nature, which in truth is a very foolish way of thinking. And so society in your world has accepted the expression of emotionalism from the female sex and has also judged that it is not manly for the male sex to express emotion in the same or similar way. Consequently, whoever does not exercise or practice anything is not one who is proficient in it. And so men, having suppressed the expression of basic emotional instincts, have, therefore, not qualified themselves to express them efficiently, proficiently. And consequently, when they do express emotion, they are indeed quite foolish, little children.

I would like to speak for a moment on emotion, now that the question has been brought up. Emotion, which, of course, is an effect of judgment that one endeavors to protect, emotion is born in what is understood and known as a water center. And that is where all judgments are given birth in the emotions. They're given birth there, and they're given birth to protect what we believe, at the time, that we are.

*Thank you. Would you please share with us the spiritual significance of the sunset and the sunrise?*

The setting of the sun [is] the waning of the energy (our receptivity to it) in a world of conception, and the rising of the sun [is] the influx and increase of our receptivity to the continuous flow of energy in the universe. The rising and the setting of our sun. That is the power that we permit our self to be receptive to. Now in a mental world a person can, at their own choice, set or rise the sun of their own endeavor. What I mean to say by that, they can permit themselves, through conscious choice, to be receptive to this divine flow of Energy that is constantly available to all the forms that it sustains. But it is a matter of effort.

Ofttimes you hear that a person has no incentive. They're not inspired. They don't feel like doing anything. They don't even feel like thinking. Well, the truth of the matter is that they have made a choice, a choice of accepting a judgment of failure, based upon past experiences, which are the effects of other judgments before them. And so in time, one makes little or no effort for they are convinced, by believing in their own mental substance, in their own mind, and in their own past experiences, that whatever the endeavor may be, for them, it too shall fail. And so failure for them has become their successful way of living, unfortunately.

*Thank you. When I permit myself to entertain in consciousness discordant experiences of the past, I find my errors increase dramatically. What is in truth occurring at those moments and would it be more beneficial to redirect my attention or to work with those forms?*

Well, first of all, if a person is experiencing a continuity in their life of past experiences that they find are not beneficial, it reveals to a person, having those experiences, that they continue to believe they are the judgments that have entered their mind in days and years long passed. Therefore, it is not in a person's best interest—a student on the path who is yet to make a little more effort not to identify with the self and [not] to identify with shadows of the past—to battle with them or try to educate them at those times. Redirection, [which is] placing one's attention upon a positive avenue of expression, placing one's attention on the eternal moment and using it wisely and constructively is, in truth, the wisest path to follow until the student is able to disassociate themselves from the past experiences in their life by declaring the truth. And the next step [is] applying that truth: that they are responsible for what they have created; however, they are not that which they have created, for they are only the creator of them.

*Thank you. Does the soul faculty duty mean duty to your own soul and its expression?*

Indeed, it does. Duty is the duty, the responsibility for that which you are, by making greater effort from refraining from what you are not.

*Thank you. Does tolerance refer to tolerance of your own creations as they evolve?*

Tolerance is—tolerance through understanding that you have created these forms. You are responsible for them, as you are responsible for creating anything in your life. And therefore, [tolerance is attained] through a greater understanding and an acceptance of personal responsibility, which is placing and disciplining and guiding the forms you have created. Yes.

*Thank you. Does talking in your sleep have anything to do with not expressing yourself or saying what you need to say while awake?*

Well, as far as need, which is the denial of truth, and the denial of truth is, of course, illusion and delusion, ofttimes a person does not say what they feel that they would like to say for other judgments that they believe that they are tell their minds that they had best not say that, for they may need something or want something from that person. And so the expression is suppressed. Ofttimes it does express itself during what you know as the sleep state when the conscious mind is set aside and the judgments from the water center express through the emotions.

*Thank you. What is the cause of things coming to a standstill and how can it be resolved?*

We are the cause of anything in our life that comes to a so-called standstill. And we, of course, therefore being the cause of anything in our life coming to a standstill, we also are therefore in a position to bring those things into movement. It's a matter of educating the uneducated ego. It is a matter of applying the demonstrable truth which you are.

*Thank you. When one speaks to one's forms, is it wise to use friendly acceptance of them or a firmer, harder approach?*

Well, first of all, you don't get very far with a child that you do not use some kind of understanding and consideration with. And so, first of all, understanding that you have created these children, these forms, these judgments, to serve a purpose based upon fear in a time in your life, one should use kind, firm, intelligent communication.

*Thank you. In working with a longtime habit pattern, what affirmation is the most helpful?*

The declaration of truth which is: "I am responsible for this thought pattern, this expression of judgment, that I alone have created. I have created it. I am responsible for it. I know it is not me. Therefore, because it is what I have created, because I know that it is not me, I therefore have the power flowing through me to guide it to constructive good in my life."

*Thank you. Is the heart the door to one's soul?*

The heart is the expression. It is the avenue through which the soul expresses itself in the form in which you presently find yourself.

*Thank you. Please discuss confidence. Is it a function or a soul faculty?*

Confidence is so often used as a sense function that one should more wisely be interested in consideration. So often we find a person so confident that, through certain expression, they are irresistible. It is a trap that one would best refrain from entering.

*Thank you. Why does man mistake kindness for weakness?*

Man mistakes his own kindness for weakness; therefore, that is what he offers to the world. One mistakes kindness for weakness for one does not value total consideration when one is over-identified with themselves.

*Thank you. Why is it that some people are very good at making money so that everything they touch turns to gold and others are not good at making money?*

Judgments. You see, we always get what we really want in life. It is a matter of being honest with our self. Ofttimes we think we are not getting what we really want, but we really do get what we really do want.

Now you've brought up the question of money. So often a person says that they want money. That some people can touch anything and it will turn to gold. They are not special incarnations. If that's what you really want, then you have to be honest with yourself and find out what it is that you've got to give up in order to have that, if that's what you want. But to say that you want the gold of earth and the money of earth—when the law clearly reveals by making certain changes in the judgments that you believe that you are, you can have all of the money that you could possibly want. And therefore, we really do get what we really do want.

So often a person says they want money and when it comes to the demonstration and the application, what they really mean is they want glory for the judgments they believe that they are, and they will readily push the money aside. However, there's a balance in all things in life sooner or later. We all hit the bottom of our judgments, and when we do, we find that we are now getting what we want for we have made a change in what we want. I do hope that's helped with your question.

*Thank you. What is the corresponding soul faculty for guilt?*

Guilt, as I have stated so many times, guilt is a very destructive and detrimental function of the human mind. It is truly a device, if one could understand what devices really are. Now, acceptance is the will of goodness, the Principle of Goodness, which is God. And so when a person says they feel and they believe they're guilty of this and they're guilty of that, if they will take a few moments and speak to their mind and say, "I accept. I accept the possibility of good in my life. What has been, has been. And I accept that it has been. And because it has been, it is not now, only by the devices of my mind, which, once again, call the shadow into my conscious awareness."

And so if a person wants to glorify themselves, all they have to do is to take a few minutes a day and sit down and think about their guilt, about what they should have done that they didn't do, about how things have gone in their life, about what a great failure they are and nothing ever really works out. All they have to do is take a few moments and think about how little money that they have and they'll soon find they'll have less. For they are transgressing the Law of Gratitude, you see. And so anyone who wants to use those devices in order to feel a greater stimulation of their senses, for which the house of the uneducated ego is responsible, certainly is going to have a field day.

*Thank you. What is meant by the statement in the Bible that, "Whenever two or more of you are gathered together, there will I be also"?*

Two or more. Yes. Now two or more is not speaking about something you're not responsible for. You are a physical body and you are a mental body. Now that's two of you, and there's possibility of more. Indeed, there is! There's a spiritual body. So when two of you or more are gathered, there I shall be! So when you have the mental body and the physical body in harmony together and you've got those two and more (the spiritual body), why, certainly, there is the Truth, the Power, and the Light. So where two or more of you are gathered, there shall I be. I do hope that's helped you.

*Thank you. Are the persons who have merited very cold climates apt to be more secure in the water center due to an adaptation of their physical surroundings?*

Well, I find people—and it's not dependent on being in 20 below zero or a 126 below zero, if you'd like to go to Antarctica—I find that people who choose, through the light of reason, to maintain a cool temperature are people that are very secure. And so let's have more cool heads in our class and less of the hotheads.

*Thank you. What is the difference between casting your pearls before the swine and helping another soul?*

Well, there's quite a difference between casting one's pearls before the swine and helping another soul. You can readily tell if you have cast your pearls before the swine or you have shared with another soul, for if you have cast your pearls before the swine, you will feel quite a stimulation of self-importance and glory. And if you have shared the light that you have received with another soul [and you are] not feeling any stimulation or any charge or sensation or thrill, then you will know that you're doing the job you have to do.

*Thank you. Experiences repeat themselves until we no longer believe we are the judgments. Does this mean we adjust—correction. We just—one more time. Does this mean we are just perceiving these experiences from a different level of conscious awareness?*

Experiences no longer repeat themselves when we no longer express the judgments which are the causes of the experiences. So therefore, experiences no longer repeat themselves when the cause of those experiences we no longer believe that we are, which, of course, are the judgments. And so what that means and what we're saying here is that when a person disassociates themselves from falsehood and turns to the Light of truth (that which they are), they do not service their judgments; and therefore, those experiences, which were the effects of the judgments that they believed that they were, no longer continue.

*Thank you.*

Yes. Go right ahead, please.

*When we pass out of form, is it just a continuation of our growing and learning processes as it is here?*

When we shed this form, this physical form, of which I accept that you are speaking, we continue on in the mental body. The mental body is not composed of physical substance. Therefore, we have a mental body in which to continue to express. In that mental body, of course, are a multitude of judgments. Many of them we believe we are. Some of them we no longer believe we are, and they're not as active in the mental body. Then, of course, we have an astral body; we have a spiritual body.

Now if over 51 percent of your judgments have control of your mind, then you believe 51 percent that you are a mental body. Therefore, when you leave the physical body, being convinced that you are a mental body, by 51 percent of the judgments in the mental body, then you cannot move on to the higher consciousness until you disassociate, which means no longer believe that you are the judgments, which are composed of mental substance.

*Thank you. Are our surroundings what we have been identified with over 51 percent of our lives?*

If you are speaking of the surroundings after leaving the physical body, those are effects of the judgments, if they are 51 percent of a mental body. Now many people come over to our side with 75, 85, 92 percent judgments in charge. They're taken into schools, and there they are helped. Many people are fortunate before leaving the earth, flesh body and through pain and suffering they, slowly but surely, begin to disassociate and do not continue to believe that they are the judgments they once believed that they were. That, in truth, is one of the best things that could possibly happen. For when there is less than 51 percent mental substance in control, they express, then, through a higher state of consciousness in one of the finer bodies of expression, and the surroundings are effects of that.

*Thank you. Are thought forms less active when we sleep in colder temperatures, as was recommended?*

Yes, they are less active when we have cooler temperatures. And this is why I look forward to all cool heads as my students on earth.

*Thank you.*

Try to understand, my good students, that a cool head is an effect of the light of reason and a hothead is an effect of the water center of childish emotionalism.

*Thank you. If one lost a fetus forty years ago, considering the ratio of earth time to truth, would that baby now be adult or still expressing as a baby or small child?*

No. No. In reference to that, in reference to—you see, you're in a world of limit, a world of form, which is governed by what you understand as time. And so in that respect they would be at that age of whatever the time had passed in your consciousness. For example, if forty years had passed, then it's forty years. However, when you leave your physical world, for identification purposes, those souls who are in the higher bodies of consciousness and spiritual bodies, they are able, of course, as you go into a closet and you put on a different suit, they are able to put on different forms in order to identify with you. You see, my friends, your form is an effect of your judgments, of your own limits. Your form is an effect. It's a suit of clothes that you've taken out of your own closet of your consciousness. And so your body, whatever body that is, is an effect of the 51 percent or more of your own identification.

*Thank you. We generally feel much better after showering. Is the water an electrical vibration removing things that have been attracted magnetically?*

The water is a magnetic vibration that is soothing the judgments that you believe that you are. And so we find many people just as calm, seemingly calm as little babies as long as they can have all of that water to soothe the judgments they believe they are. And so it's a very magnetic expression.

*Thank you. It was once said that we do not receive our names here on the earth realm. How does that work?*

Your identification, your calling card, or your name is, in the realms of higher consciousness, is an effect, an identification of the work that you have done to get where you are. And so names in your world are not very honest or let alone expressing [of] the true being. And so you do not have names in your world that express your efforts in your evolution. However, you are identified with a name. When you reach the higher realms, everyone will know you for your name reveals all.

*Thank you. I understand that dogs in spiritual realms do rescue work. What does that mean and what other work do they do?*

Well, certain animals are very, very loyal. And they are used for benefiting those souls who are struggling to rise to higher realms of consciousness. And a person who, on the path through evolution, is trying to evolve always feels good that there's someone they can rely upon, someone they can depend upon for they're trying to struggle through those realms of dependence. And so if they have a friend, such as a loyal dog, that comes every day, doesn't fail to appear, is always there when they need them, then, of course, you would understand that those forms are used by the spiritual guides and teachers in order to help you in your struggle evolving through the realms of limit, the effects of dependence and over-identification. Yes.

*Thank you. Is it likely that all the dogs one has lived with will live with us on the other side?*

Oh, no. No. So many of them are so happy they won't have to. And, of course, then there are those who look forward and meet us when we go over, you see, speaking of your realm, over to ours. They, they stand at the borderline and they wait patiently and they're very loyal. And then there are those who, kind of, sigh with relief. They are so grateful that they don't have to go through that phase, hopefully, again. So they all don't wait for us. No, no, no. It depends on what we did to them while we were in charge of them.

*Thank you. What is the best way to be in a relationship [and] not become attached or control the other person?*

Well, first of all, you would have to be willing to give up what you feel is necessary. And from what I understand, you're speaking of relationship. Relationship is a dependence. And as long as you have a dependence, you're going to have attachment. As long as you have attachment, you're going to have need for you have denied what you are. And therefore, you're going to be tempted constantly to control what you think you need. And so if you want to be freed from what you understand as attachment and you want a relationship, don't try wanting your cake and eating [it] too, because it won't work. You're going to have to give up relationship. And if you want freedom from that trap, [then] be grateful for the friendship of the sunlight of your day.

*Thank you. May I use my dreams to get in touch with my higher states? And if so, how?*

I would not be tempted to use my dreams to get into my higher states. It's enough to just try to use your conscious awareness to get into your higher states. Most dreams are expressions of unfulfilled desires. And certainly, [it] is not in our best interests to tempt our self to deceive our self.

*Thank you. Why does anxiety well up so quickly in me?*

Anxiety? Well, of course, anxiety is an expression of one's frustrations, which, of course, is an expression of their own suppressed desires, which, of course, is an expression of the lack of honesty with oneself. And a lack of honesty with oneself guarantees anxiety and frustration and a very turbulent life.

*Thank you. What is the source of the energy boost I feel when changing states?*

Well, the source of energy boost that you may be feeling when changing—I accept that you are saying changing thoughts of your mind, changing states of consciousness—the energy boost could be the feeling and the charge that a person gets when they're just about ready to fulfill a, a desire that may have been waiting for some time. And so people get boosted and charged with energy not only from the faculties, they certainly get, usually, charged and boosted from the functions. Now as far as a boost from the spiritual faculties, I think you're going to find it more like a feather instead of a rocket ship.

*Thank you. When I catch a limiting thought in mid-thought and there is some lingering doubt, how may I blast it all out of me?*

By declaring that you alone have created the form, the thought, that is, as you say, midstream in your consciousness.

And because you have created it, you can form it into any form you so choose. Positive, negative, constructive, or destructive. You alone are responsible. You alone are in charge. Declare the truth, and you'll have no problem.

*Thank you. Is there a faculty we should cultivate that is consistently most important or do they change in importance as we evolve?*

Reason. Keep your faith with reason, she will transfigure thee. Reason. Use reason and balance in all things.

*Thank you. You have said that in forty years there will be a change in people's attitudes about nature and conservation, and we will begin to care better for our natural Earth. You have also said that inside growth is reflected outwardly. Does this mean there will be a spiritual shift at that time? And will people begin to care for themselves and others because of that at the same time?*

Necessity, of course, we all understand, is the mother of invention and survival is a great stimulator. And so as man continues along the path and he begins to realize that if he doesn't care for himself, then he doesn't care for others. If he doesn't care for what he truly is, then he doesn't care for the air he breathes. And so as the pollution, the effects of the lack of care and consideration, begin to reveal to mankind, as they are, detrimental effects that he does not like, man is broadening his horizon, considering what he is and, in so doing, considering the world around him. And so that, in truth, is what is taking place. It is a matter of self-survival.

*Thank you. Do animals choose to come into people's lives to help in the people's evolution and do they also evolve in their service to the people?*

Animals enter a person's life in keeping with the laws of evolution. They have merited the lives of the people and the experiences that are offered. And, also, the person who receives the animal is meriting that experience and what the animal has to offer. And this is why many animals, so grateful for the evolution and experience they've had on earth and so loyal to their masters, wait for them to come over, and sometimes have to wait for many, many, many, many years. While other animals are so grateful that they have learned the lesson they've had to learn from the master that they had, and because they have learned their lessons and have accepted them, they move over to other experiences with other people in other worlds and are extremely grateful.

*Thank you. Do nature spirits exist in other realms? If so, are they similar or different? Is the nature they are controlling similar or different? And is it of the lower realms or does some form of nature exist also in higher realms?*

Wherever there is nature, there is nature spirits. And so, for example, on the planet Uranus there is form, there is nature. It is different than the planet Earth, as it is on the planet Venus, as it is on the planet Saturn. And so wherever the planet is, there is nature and the nature spirits, composed of the elements of nature of that particular planet.

*Thank you. Edgar Cayce predicted great physical earth shifts and changes and also some safe areas left. Are his predictions of those safe areas correct?*

They are indicative. Now as far as safe, think of this: you could move from your present location to where you judged you would be safe. Come back for an afternoon visit, though it be thousands of miles away, and while you're on your visit, the entire city went into the ocean. So, you see, there are no guarantees. The only thing that you can rely upon is an understanding of the laws of evolution and the lessons that you have to learn. And so when a person is honest with themselves, they begin to understand their evolution and, in understanding their evolution, understanding and accepting the lessons that they have earned, they have no problem and, therefore, are not worried or concerned that they're going to disappear in an earthquake or a volcano when they could just as readily disappear from your world in a highway experience or in a fire or some other catastrophe, you call it.

*Thank you. When I set a goal, expectations in me arise. Can you tell us the usefulness of expectations in acquiring our goals? What can I do to remain in a peaceful vibration when my expectations lead to anxiety?*

Expectations cannot lead to anxiety until you accept in your consciousness that you are the judgment that you have made. Now one expects wisely by expecting the possibility of change in their expression and effort in any endeavor. And so when you expect something to happen, accept it is happening with the possibility of change. Then you will keep yourself freed from that trap known as attachment. Do not permit yourself to be tempted to have a relationship with your expectations.

*Thank you. I would like to heal myself of attitudes and response patterns that are a result of past conditioning. Can you please explain what I can do to make a break from the old and renew my spirit each day?*

To do so each day, to renew one's spirit each day, one declares, "This is the moment that I can do everything with. This moment is the moment through which power flows through my being." And to make great effort, moment by moment, to remain in the eternal moment known as the present, for we are constantly hounded with shadows of that which has passed. A person truly wastes precious moments by permitting their minds to identify with judgments which only offer a drain of one's vital energy to shadows, to forms that have been, that can do nothing that is constructive to the good of the moment. And so anyone who makes that effort to declare, "This is the moment. This is the moment I can think as I choose. I don't have a temptation in me now to think of what has gone. I can do nothing with that. But here, in this moment, I can do everything, for in this moment the power flows." Choose wisely what you do with the power you are receptive to. Use it constructively. Creating forms is the nature of the human mind and mental substance; then create forms that are constructive, that can do something in the eternal moment of now.

*Thank you. Does the astral body leave the physical body when sleeping? If so, what is the spiritual purpose for this?*

Well, there is a rejuvenation of the vital body which is covered by the astral body and the mental body; and these bodies, of course, are rejuvenated by the vital body. And so as the body leaves, the astral body leaves the physical body, there is a rejuvenation of those bodies, depending, of course, on what a person is doing in those bodies.

*Thank you. Was the entire surface of the Earth completely covered by water at any time in its evolution?*

No. No, the fireball known as the Earth planet [is] covered by land, mostly by water. And so that is shifting again. It has shifted many, many times over the ages. It will continue to shift for it is the very nature of planets. They are created from gases, and they're created from great heat. And they are children of other planets and suns. And so they're born and they grow and they pass on.

*Thank you. Is the clearer a person['s] image [of] their reflection in a mirror revealing their attachment to creation or their judgments?*

Why, yes, indeed, a person—many people like to look at their reflection, and sometimes a person looks at their reflection to try to change it in keeping with the judgments of what has been. They like to—the judgments of years ago want to express themselves again. So they color their hair and change their skin and do whatever the judgments dictate that help to feed the judgments that they were in love with so long ago.

*Thank you. Is a physical marriage in principle the same as what God gave to Lucifer?*

Well now, I think we should reconsider this question here. A physical marriage. Well now, first of all, a person makes a judgment that they're half there, and the other half must be someplace. In other words, they do not feel complete. And some people only feel a quarter there. And they're ever looking for that other half in order to make them feel, sometimes they say, full or complete or whole. Well, I would like to once again assure all of my students in the class that you are whole and complete. That which you are *is* whole and complete. There's not another half somewhere that's going to fill you up and make you complete.

Now if you insist on believing that there's a half somewhere, then you're in for many experiences, not very tasteful, not very pleasing. Sometimes when you feel tempted and your judgments get stronger that, "Yes, this one fits very well. This is my other half. It does exactly what I tell it to do. It thinks the way that I do. It's as emotional as I am. And when I tell it how I want anything, it does it." While the other half is thinking, "Well, now if I do just exactly what he tells me he wants me to do, then he'll become dependent upon me or vice versa. And once he's become dependent upon me (or she has become dependent upon me), then I can do whatever I want with them because their dependence upon me reveals to me their attachment. And their attachment to me reveals that they are weak, have a weakness in the moral fiber of their character. And therefore, I will be in full control. So, first, I will do exactly what they want that I may please them and weaken them as much as possible through a dependence and attachment to me."

Now if that's what you understand about marriage, then I certainly would consider matrimony a contract with what you understand as Lucifer. And I'm sure you will all agree, if that's what you consider marriage is.

*Thank you. When we no longer have emotions concerning attachments, are we freeing ourselves from those attachments?*

How appropriate the question. Must be from a person that is, ah, not in that blissful state of matrimony. Well, whatever now. I don't want you to understand that I'm just an old bachelor that doesn't have any consideration for that institution. I just would like to share with you that with so much good in the world, and so much to experience, and so much joy and happiness, and so much to see, that I am not tempted to place myself behind the bars of institutions. I do hope that's helped with your question.

*Thank you. What is our responsibility to those who we come in contact and are in rapport with during our lives?*

Well, those who you come in contact with and are in rapport with, of course, are reflections of states of consciousness that you are in. Now ofttimes a person enters a state of consciousness and gets into a beautiful rapport with another person. And then they change their state of consciousness and the rapport that they had no longer exists and they have all kinds of problems, especially if they continue to see each other. And so one must understand that we permit ourselves to come into rapport and out of rapport with many people in our lives.

And it is a revelation, when a person moves in and out of rapport with another person, to continue to see them. It is very important to see a person that you've moved in and out of rapport [with]. It is important to see if the other person is still in rapport, living in the past or if they're moving in and out of rapport. It's a very important experience in a person's evolution. Yes.

*Thank you. Please expand on the Law of Gratitude and how to free oneself from concern about supply.*

Well, first of all, if one is applying the Law of Gratitude, then one has no concern about supply. Now when one says that they are concerned about supply and interested in the Law of Gratitude, then we must be honest with our self: How concerned are we about the Law of Supply? Do we feel that we are short in supply? I can assure you that in some areas of expression in everyone's life, they do not experience a shortage of supply. They have a supply of thoughts that flood their consciousness.

A person gets into self-concern, they certainly are not short on supply. There is a limitless supply to feed the concern.

Now if a person truly wants to move into the supply of material, increased material wealth, then the first thing they do is move from this constant flood of supply that's going to these judgment forms, which are expressing as concern, and make the change necessary to move the supply that is going into concern into another area of consciousness so that they may enjoy the supply in an avenue of their conscious choice.

We have time for one more question, please.

*Thank you. Life is ever as we make it and just the way we take it. How can we remember this and incorporate it fully in our lives?*

I'm so happy to hear that question as our last one in concluding our seminar this evening, as time passes so quickly. Life is ever as we make it and it is just the way we take it. Declare that a hundred thousand times a day. Declare it when the forms of your mind rise up and judge that someone did you in. Declare it when a judgment tells you you're concerned about your bread and butter. Declare it when you're concerned about your supply. Declare the truth: "Life is ever as I make it and it's always as I take it." Therefore, as every dog has his day in court, make your life better that you may take the full joy of living. For that is what you truly are. Only you can do it. For life is ever as you make it and she's always as you take it. So let us make life beautiful by remembering to declare that great truth.

Thank you and good evening.

JANUARY 9, 1986

## A/V Seminar 10

*[The recording of this class begins a few moments after the teacher has begun to speak.]*

—which is the effect of denial. Therefore, in our evolution through limit, we experience the gravitational pull of force. To overcome what one is in service to one must first accept its right of existence. And in so accepting, the meek, those who demonstrate acceptance of the effect of the law they have established, return to the kingdom of God, Power, or good.

We think; therefore, we limit. We limit and experience division. And so it is the destiny of force to divide and conquer. It is the expression of goodness to accept and free. In our many experiences in service to the Law of Gravity, we find ourselves resisting, resisting the experiences in our life which are the effect or return of the law established in our errors of ignorance. Whoever accepts the experience they encounter is freed from the payment thereof by a return to that which they are, rather than insisting on being what they are not.

I'm going to pause for a few moments, now, to speak to your questions that you have prepared.

*Thank you. What is the cause of swelling feet?*

There can be many causes to the question that you have asked. One of the basic causes is the retention or over-identification with the water center. There is an obstruction to the flow of the fluids. And through a greater acceptance of the law which has established or is the true cause, one frees themselves from the obstruction. Let us understand in these questions that whatever we resist, by the Law of Resistance, we create friction; by the Law of Friction, we create adhesion. And so the things I fear the most—that is, one in service to a mental world—befalls us. Yes.

*Thank you. Are we always the ones obstructing ourselves or are there sometimes higher beings doing this for our own good?*

In keeping with the magnetic laws of like attracts like and becomes the Law of Attachment, all things that affect us we are responsible for. That is the path of reason. That is the expression of freedom.

*Thank you. When we are striving to create different surroundings, what can one do to help themselves from being pulled back to the old, especially when it is all around?*

What is all around us is ever in keeping with the Law of Attraction. And so it is that one attracts many things in their life, and the freedom in attraction is what you consciously choose to identify with. For example, to be with a thing and never a part of the thing is to free oneself from force. By accepting what is, one cannot experience what is not.

*Thank you. The Living Light text states when part of ourselves is expanding—correction—when part of our universe is expanding another part is contracting. How does this work and what is the relation to the faculties and functions?* [In this seminar, questions were written in advance, submitted to a director, and then read aloud by the vice president, who also acted as cameraman.]

Functions are an expression of force. Force is the governing principle of limit, form, or creation. As we expand in that which we are (power), we contract in that which we are not (force). When—for example, as I stated a few moments earlier, force is power that has recognized its own potential. When we recognize anything, we establish the Law of Identification. When we identify, we individualize or separate. Force is dependent upon separation for its own expression. Therefore, when you experience these many difficulties in life, which are in the domain of mental force, creation, by accepting its right of expression, you free yourself from identification with it. Man is freed through his own acceptance. Man is bound through his own denials.

*Thank you. What is the reason for somebody taking everything so literally?*

Anyone who over-identifies with themselves is a person who will take things ever in keeping with service to their over-identification with themselves. Now when we understand that we, as children growing up, find many different ways to gain attention or energy—ofttimes in life effort is not made to bring about the changes, consciously, that must be brought about for a more peaceful and harmonious life. And when those changes are not brought about, we still act as little children in order to receive the energy and vitality that is needed for our own good. Now, because we have dissipated the energy that we are receptive to by an impractical use thereof, one has a responsibility to oneself to use wisely that which they are receptive to and not fall into the pit of allowing compassion to leave the guiding hand of reason.

*Thank you. In an earlier class reference was made to parallel laws, the Law of Creation and the Law of Light. Are there other parallel laws? Are there triune laws? Would you please speak on the nature of laws?*

Well, in speaking on the nature of law, let us understand that as a function is an undeveloped faculty, as force is a separation of power, that which is darkness is lesser light for it has separated itself. Now that which separates itself loses its own totality, and in so doing it resists in order to survive. For example, whoever resists survives; whoever accepts lives. So living is acceptance, and surviving is resistance or denial. Now when we have a thought in our mind and other thoughts in our mind rise to resist the thought, that which we resist, in truth, begins to grow and to prosper. It begins to grow and prosper in a mental world that is subject to the Law of Force. So whatever we resist, we, in truth, increase by the Law of Friction and are, therefore, bound and controlled by it. To accept is not only to free, it is to use what you are consciously rather than to resist what you have created in a time of error and ignorance.

*Thank you. Why does man give mental process an identifying power over him? What does he gain by scattering his true power of concentration?*

Man gains what you know as a feeling, which is a sensation of importance. You see, as force is merely power that has seen its potential, that which sees its potential sees its potential at the expense of what it truly is. And seeing its potential at the expense of what it truly is, it experiences the lack thereof and moves into the realm of force, where need or denial reigns supreme. We are tempted as an effect of denial. We are not tempted as an effect of acceptance. Man is only tempted or weakened as an effect of denying what he is. For only by denying what you are can you possibly experience what you are not.

*Thank you. Awareness is the first step in evolution. To move through awareness to objectivity is the second step. How do we move through awareness and what is objectivity?*

Objectivity is an awakening that what you view, what you sense, and what you experience is an effect. It is something that, by law, you have created. It is not what you are. Now when you have a thought that is disturbing your mind, if you accept it for what it truly is—an effect of what you have created—by your acceptance of it, you refrain from resisting it. By refraining from resisting it, you refrain from the friction, which in truth is an adhesion which binds you through identification to it.

*Thank you. How do we know when our duty is done?*

We know when our duty is done when we are no longer tempted by it. Now you may ask the question, Can duty tempt? Duty tempts ever in keeping with the Law of Limit.

*Thank you. Alcoholics typically deny their problem when confronted with it. Is this a denial of the judgment in control, fearing that any admission of the condition would result in a loss of control?*

That's why one is bound by it. One is bound by what they deny. One is not bound by what they accept.

*Thank you. Why is it that the darker the night, the brighter the light?*

For identification with the darker the night guarantees the desire in consciousness to be freed from it. And it is through that process that man finally grows from denial to acceptance and is freed. As I stated in some of our classes long ago, man is freed in hell and saved in heaven. And so if you enjoy the struggle that you may have made at any time in your life, all you have to do is to continue to deny that you are responsible for it and from that denial you will continue to experience it. Now when a person permits the mind to declare that it is doing everything possible to improve their life and due to circumstances beyond their control, for some unknown reason, their life is not improving, that person is denying what is and must pay the price, temporarily, of being what they are not, for they have denied the law that they, in truth, are continuing with.

*Thank you. When our physical body is in a spiritual class, are our other bodies also in the class or do they go to their own class?*

Hope's eternal and truth's inevitable. I like to have all my students spiritually present in a spiritual class. However, there are times when that experience is not what I experience. It is nice and practical for a person in attendance with any class to bring all their bodies with them and to keep them there through the class. However, there is no guarantee. Now if you go to a class to learn, for example, to be a computer programmer, which is so popular in your world today, and you permit your mind to make the judgment that the teacher that's teaching you about the computer, that you in truth know more about that than they do, you establish a law to escape from the class, for you are bored. And so one of your bodies leaves and you don't know what's going on. I do hope that's helped with the question in reference to bringing all of your bodies when you come to class and to keep all of your bodies in class while class is in session. Thank you.

*Thank you. We are taught that through the soul faculty of acceptance, something good is happening. Something good does happen. How does this work?*

Well, it works for you have refrained from denying what you are. And by accepting what you are, you are the goodness, you are that experience thereof in that respect. So when you declare and truly accept the possibility, you experience its effect for you have moved from denial (the obstruction) to acceptance (the way). Now if you will understand that it is only through denial that you experience obstruction—obstruction is form or limit. You have to identify and to express denial in order to experience obstructions. And when you accept, the obstructions move from your universe, and you experience the way, which is the life, the light, and the love of being.

*Thank you. Why is it that discipline exercised by people, educational institutions, and businesses in America has deteriorated during the twentieth century?*

Self-motivation, over-identification, and service to force, which is limit.

*Thank you. Why does power corrupt?*

Power corrupts only when you are aware of the power. What you are not aware of, you cannot corrupt. The corruption—force is power when it recognizes or sees its potential. That is the corruption of power. And that is what is known as corruption of power; it's known as force. Force is the limit of power. It offers to you a temporal, false sense of glory or superiority or self-importance. You see, a person who insists that they are different than anything that has ever been, that is, or will ever be is a person who is in total service to the Law of Force.

*Thank you. If my mind is empty during normal activity, should I try to keep it actively involved?*

Well, I would be most interested, personally, in meeting an empty mind. I have yet to meet one. Now to meet a person who is making the effort to empty it, I have met many. But I have yet to meet an empty mind because an empty mind, to me, would be a person who has left the realm of force, limit, creation and returned to the source of their true being.

*Thank you. Is it helpful to create a mentally stressful situation during relatively calm periods in order to progress more quickly?*

Well, it's not necessary that I have found on your Earth planet to make that effort. For in keeping with the laws of ignorance and in keeping with the laws of temptation, you have no problem in experiencing stressful situations. They are guaranteed ever in keeping with the Law of Ignorance.

*Thank you. Is physical exercise, to strengthen my body, helpful in furthering my spiritual progress?*

Only if there is mental exercise and spiritual expression.

*Thank you. Can you please explain the water center, its meaning and effect from emotions, its location?*

Well, first of all, I have discussed that, of course, in my private classes. And the water center is the center where all judgments are created. And it is a service to force or mental substance, that which force is, an expression. And when you bring about a balance between the fire center and the water center, then you're going to be on the path to express through higher centers of consciousness. Now for every action there must be a reaction. And so when the action of the fire center is reacted by the water center, and the water center is reacted by the fire center, you begin to bring into balance the expression of those two centers. And therefore, that which is brought into balance one is freed from.

*Thank you. What causes tension and how can we best minimize its occurrence?*

Tension is an over-identification, through error, to the mental world. All beings who are in limit or form have that temptation ever before them. And for a person who is suffering from tension, then a person should take more time to themselves and make greater effort to identify with what they are and not take the weight of the universe on their shoulders. For the weight of the universe, which is the Law of Gravity, is not limited to any one person.

*Thank you. We have been taught—correction. You have taught us that as the soul is impulsed into being, it splits. A part of it enters the physical world and its other part enters the ethereal world.*

Correct.

*And that part is our guardian angel.*

That is correct.

*Does our guardian angel have form and could we see it, if we could see the spirit world?*

Well, first of all, that part of you, known as your guardian angel expressing in realms of Light, is not subject to the Law of Force, through which the other part of you is expressing. Now when you truly accept, then you return to that which you are. And when that takes place, there is no longer the temptation to, to limit. And no longer that temptation to limit existing, you are freed from the gravitational pull of force, and you are what he is: whole, complete, and perfect.

Now I realize that it is difficult for you to accept in a world of limit and identification, known as creation, that form, as you know form, is not necessary for awareness. You understand awareness of something as something that you identify with by what you believe that you are. Therefore, when you look to a guardian angel, to the higher self or higher being, you look from eyes of limit and form and, therefore, do not recognize the limitless, unless you make the effort to rise above the limit, to rise from that which you are not to that which you are.

*Thank you. I've been doing my best to free myself from a terrible trap. And it seems that each day there is progress followed with what seems like hell. Can you help me to understand more clearly?*

Well, of course, hell is an identification with the, the fruits of our effort. And the fruits of everyone's efforts, of course, are hell to the one who is viewing them.

Now I spoke to some of my students here just the other day and explained to them that a person who over-identifies with their efforts in life, with the fruits of their action, of course, is known as a fruit. Well, no one truly wants to be a fruit, for we all know that fruit rots and none of us want to rot. So if we don't want to be a fruit, then we should make greater effort not to identify with the fruits of our action. And when that happens, you see, we do have these difficult experiences because we've looked at what we have done because we believe that we are the doer. We are the creator; we are not the sustainer, not as long as we believe that we are the thought of I, the limit, and that special something.

It is indeed tempting for man to believe that he's unique, special, that [he's] one of a kind in the universes, never before and never again. Of course, that does feed that realm of consciousness known as glory. And one does, just like a vampire, thrive on that type of energy being received. Though others may well consider it a negative type of energy, energy is energy. And so, my friends, let us make effort and encourage our self not to be so attached to the fruits of our action that we may be freed from being fruity and rotten in that respect. Yes.

*Thank you. When I am at peace with myself, my mental processes seem to slow down. Accordingly, most times, while in this state, I do not have an abundance of spiritual questions. Is this a reflection of slowed spiritual growth or that I may not be putting forth enough effort spiritually?*

Well, whereas we are not always in the slow down process, we should prepare our questions when we're in a more speeded up process. And therefore, they could be more wisely applied in our life. I know that we will find, as students, that most of our days and evenings are a rather speeded up process. And that is only a slowing process, usually, while we are in spiritual classes. Therefore, I have asked my channel, in times past in your world, to have the students prepare their questions as an effect, of course, of the many things that rise in the course of their speeded activities during a day and evening. Especially when they wonder why they are experiencing an obstruction to their desires, for then the sharing of these spiritual laws benefit all of us. I do not expect you to have a mountain of questions while class is in session, and this is why I have recommended that you prepare your questions during the course of a week and not wait to the last minute, just as you're ready to sit down to class to start thinking of questions, when I find your mind so filled with questions of, "Why has this happened to me?" during the course of your many activities. Yes.

*Thank you. How can I be sharper, more clear mentally?*

Well, the question has several questions contained within it. How to be sharper and more clearer mentally? For what purpose? The question must be asked. Does one wish a greater identification with the mental realm, which is governed by force? So first we must ask our self the question, "What is this that is motivating me to desire to be sharper?" I accept by that word, *sharper*, you mean many different things depending on the experience and more alert, well more alert—gaining control that you don't fall asleep during class, be that in Divine order. Yes.

*Thank you. When one is establishing a new law and endeavor, does there have to be an equal amount of spiritual, mental, and physical energy directed to it for it to manifest in the physical?*

If you wish something to manifest in the physical world and it is your sincere desire that you be not attached to it and, therefore, controlled by it, then a balance between the mental and physical realm is absolutely necessary under the guidance of the spiritual light, yes.

*Thank you. What is the process by which we use one law and it diversifies into many laws?*

The diversification of the Law of Life, which is the Light, the Love, and the Law, the diversification thereof is when power becomes force. And so when we identify, that's when we leave power and enter force. It is only when we dent the I of eternity. That's known as identification, individualization, that's when we enter the realm of force and are controlled by the Law of Denial and experience need. You cannot experience need without denial. You cannot experience denial until you dent the I that you are by the Law of Limit. This is why I teach you to be in the world and not a part of the world, to be with a person, place, or thing, not a part of a person, place, or thing. This all takes place within your own consciousness. You alone have the power to remain free while yet in a world of limit.

*Thank you. Guardian angels are the inseparable better half of our soul and someday in eternity we will meet our better half. Is this because of the Law of Duality and are they a part of our spiritual body?*

In order to enter—yes, they, of course, they are what we are. You see, here we are in physical form. Believing we are physical form, we have accepted what we are not. That which we are is not in this realm of limit. And therefore, it is ever available to you, that which you are. So when you permit yourself to believe that you are the fruits of your action, when you permit yourself that luxury, then you must pay, and the payment is very great. For creation extracts 10 to 1.

*Thank you. Is the weather always an effect of our collective thoughts, attitudes, and vibrations?*

The weather is an effect of the expression of the nature spirits. There's times of peace. There are times of truce. There are times of war. And there are times of preparation for war. And so it is with human beings and with all forms and with all limit. And the seasons are ever in keeping, and the weather, with those laws established. For weather is an expression of creation. Seasons are an expression of creation, as man is an expression of creation, until he rises in consciousness to what he is, for a moment refraining from what he is not.

*Thank you. If we have made the effort to separate truth from creation before transition and have succeeded over 51 percent, what kind of environment will we be in after transition?*

The lack of concern. For, you see, environment is limit. And you have stated 51 percent effort has been made and you have succeeded to free yourself from limit. Whoever frees themselves from limit enters what they are, and what they are is not limit. Environment is limit. Therefore, there's no thought, there's no concern. Now to the human mind, to which we often over-identify, frequently over-identify to limit—now to limit—where there's no environment, there's no limit and there's no form, then the human mind says, "That's annihilation. Then there's nothing." And the human mind in a sense is correct. There is no thing, for things are limits or forms. There are no forms, there are no limits; there is the Light, the Life, the Law, and the Love and living. Yes.

*Thank you. The Earth has much water on it. Are we here to learn about the water center and how to be in control of it?*

We are here, in speaking to your question, on the planet Earth to accept that which *is*, through what is known as the power of faith. Now water is a part of the planet. It's one of the elements of the planet. And it is a great magnetic pull. And so you find that whenever you permit yourself to be emotional, then you find yourself magnetically pulled into what you are not. Ofttimes to such an extent that you believe for years what you are not, ever at the expense, of course, of being what you are.

Earth is the planet five. Faith. To once again free yourself from creation while in creation. You can only do that on the planet Earth through what is known as the path of faith. Not belief, for that binds you to the water center that you're working your way to be freed from. Faith, not belief.

*Thank you. What are positive aspects of the water center?*

Positive aspects of the water center?

*Yes.*

I think there is no question of the positive aspects of the water center. Without the water center, you would not be in form and experiencing what you are not. And because so often people believe they are what they are not and the experiences thereof, without the water center, that would not be possible. Without the water center, you could not experience the glory of self-importance. And without that, I don't think many people on your planet would feel very good.

*Thank you. Is it beneficial to have plants in one's home? If so, are there certain types more preferable?*

Well, plants, of course, are important. You are an inseparable part of them. And they are important to a person: to have living, what you understand as living things, although all *things* are living in that sense in your world. Plants are important. They serve a good purpose, and they're little manufacturers and they help to bring about a balance with the oxygen. Yes.

*Thank you. If one has become imbalanced in the area of health, how can one restore the balance?*

One restores the balance by a readjustment in conservation of their vitality and the wise use thereof, and through their continued effort along the path of faith.

*Thank you. Do flowers have the ability to communicate through vibration to other of their species?*

Well, they are not limited to their species in reference to communication. In that respect, they certainly do. Some flowers are very selfless, and some are rather selfish. Just like other forms of limit upon the planet Earth.

*Thank you. Do angels and teachers of the Light have someone they answer to?*

All teachers of the Light, all angels in service to the Light must answer to that which they serve. Yes, indeed.

*Thank you. In personal relationships I have noticed that husbands seem to become so critical of their mate's flaws and vice versa of wives to their husband's. Why is this?*

Over-identification. You see, when you permit yourself attachment, the effect of over-identification, after a period of time of the attachment or over-identification, the self rises up to express in a little different way. And in order to continue to feel its self-importance after the conquest has been made, it must see the weakness, the frailties, and the flaws of the one that it has judged that it has conquered, through, of course, attachment. And so it is a natural process of the human mind, in order to maintain and to sustain its glory of self-importance after the conquest is complete, to find the weaknesses and the flaws of that which is attached to them in order that they may continue to experience the glory of self-importance and superiority.

*Thank you. Is there a recording of time in other places in the universe or is it a function of only the human mind?*

Well, time, the great illusion, is an effect of limit. And so wherever you have form or limit, then you have that illusion, the effect of limit or denial. Without the principle of denial, you cannot and do not experience form. Form being the effect, of course, of resistance, and friction, adhesion. The Law of Duality.

*Thank you. What thoughts cause skin conditions, as rashes and itching? And how do these thoughts affect the skin chemically?*

Well, of course, in reference to the skin, the sensitivity of the image, if one is over-identified with the image that they believe, at any time, is them, then, of course, that sensitivity expresses itself through various ways in the skin or the covering of the image.

*Thank you. What are the best methods for working with the mind at such times of skin suffering?*

Well, in reference to skin suffering, the greatest benefit one could experience is to make great effort to identify with something besides the image. You see, not to be concerned and not to be worried about what other people think. If a person has a pattern of mind of wanting to be liked and very concerned about what other people think, then it does create various problems with the skin or the covering of the image. And so the best thing that one could do is to begin to work on the pattern of not being concerned what other people think and to be busy with what one has to do and not be so subject to the whims of other people. And proper breathing and a proper cleansing breath, which has been given to you, is indeed most helpful because it helps to calm the nerves, which are irritants to the image, which are expressed in the skin. Yes.

*Thank you. What sources of nutrition are best for helping to remedy skin problems in animals and people?*

Well, a balance in nutrition, of course, is going to have some effect upon the physical skin. There, however, must be effort made and balance of the mental world where the problems must be corrected. Now the skin condition improves as a chemical balance is brought about. And a chemical balance is brought about by caring for the physiological needs, as well as the psychological needs of the being.

*Thank you. If it is proven that an individual has given threats of violence to other members in a community, but denies responsibility for such actions, should the individual be allowed to remain in the community with a warning to conduct himself properly? Or should he be expelled at the risk of his retaliation? How should this be handled?*

Well, in reference to a person threatening a community, one should grant unto another what one desires to be granted unto oneself. And I think we will all agree that we would want granted unto us at least two warnings to prepare us before action is taken. And so if a person is given a forewarning and they understand that the second forewarning is the final one, the third is no warning at all, it's simply an action, I think you'll all agree we would desire that for our self. And we should grant to others what we desire for our self because that's all we can grant in truth; everything else would be a lie. For we can, in truth, only grant unto another what we first grant unto our self. And to do opposite is a house divided and, therefore, cannot succeed.

*Thank you. Are persons right-handed or left-handed in keeping with the lessons they have to learn about giving and receiving?*

Well, people are right-handed or left-handed in keeping with many lessons, including with [those] lessons is giving and receiving and understanding the laws. But it is not limited to that. For left-handed people and right-handed people are also left-elbowed, left-armed, and right-elbowed and right-armed people. So it isn't limited just to the hands of action. Yes.

*Thank you. Please speak on what it is that is happening when a person is having a relationship with their expectations.*

Well, I think that my good students will all agree: whoever has a relationship with their expectations is one who is thrilling with their fascinations. And that's so beautifully put: having a relationship with your expectations. And I think you should all record how nicely my student has put that. A new expression of the word *fascination*. And it's wonderful that some of my students, and I'm truly encouraged, would find the true definition there of the word *fascination*: having a relationship with my expectations. And I think if you would talk to people and they would be honest with you, they would tell you, yes, they began having relationships with their expectations when they were just young boys or girls. And that's the word they use in your world as fascination. But of what benefit is it to have relationships with your expectations at the expense of not experiencing your expectations outside of a mental world that's absolutely void? You put a lot in, but what do you get back?

You see, you know—excuse me, I'll straighten this out here. *[The teacher makes an adjustment to an item just off camera. It may have been the flowers.]* You know, when you have relationships with your expectations or fantasize, what do you think is receiving your energy? Well, I'd like to spend a few moments with that wonderful question or statement: having relationships with your expectations.

You see, as you are in the process, asleep or awake, however you want to call it, as you are in the process of having this relationship with your expectations, you're putting in a lot of energy. Because it takes your energy and your vital life body, taken from your vital life body and your vitality, it takes energy for your mind to first create these expectations and then to relate to them to such a point and such a degree as an actual relationship. So it's all give and no take, and the giving is going to something that you can't physically grab ahold of and you really can't order them to do anything because they only exist like a cloud. And they go on and do what they have to do after they've drained you like a dried prune. And they don't bring you anything back. And some people would say having a relationship with their expectations is daydreaming, but you have nothing in the physical world that has been accomplished, but you do have a great deal of drainage of your vitality. And it is true that it does take you out into that dream world for quite a while. And it is also true that you do come back empty-handed, only to be tempted again to have another relationship with another expectation that you may see passing down the street.

So having relationships with one's expectations is certainly not practical or reasonable for anyone to spend any time with. Much more wisely should the time be spent to make a conscious decision to have a relationship with constructive physical, mental work and to experience the benefit of work, which is God's love made manifest.

Thank you very much. And I do hope that you will have a very nice evening. And I hope you've liked my new attire. It was by special grant, although my channel didn't personally care for it. *[Mr. Goodwin was properly dressed for all his classes. But in this class, perhaps, in part, because he was in the east wing upstairs and the students were downstairs, he wore more casual attire.]* Thank you and have a nice evening and enjoy your refreshments.

FEBRUARY 13, 1986

## A/V Seminar 11

Now I know the class seems [to have] a little, perhaps, different arrangement for you this evening. This is the arrangement that will be for our seminars at this time. And so this evening we're going to discuss, in keeping with your understanding and growth, we're going to discuss experience, the movement of limit, and time, the viewing thereof, for that's what time is. It is the viewing of the movement of limit, which you know as experience.

And so your time in any realm of consciousness, whether it is on Earth or whether it is on another planet in your solar system or other solar systems, in dimensions that you are aware of and not aware of, is, of course, dependent upon your belief that you are the experience that you have created. That is the law that governs the so-called time that you spend in any experience. Now the time that you spend on Earth and your planet is established by the law of your belief that you were experiences that you had created at other times and other places.

And so you go to the planet, in this case we're talking about Earth. You enter the planet in keeping with those tendencies to be attached to that which you create, which you understand as experience and believe that they are you. Therefore, while you're on Earth, your time is known by you (how long you will be on Earth, how many experiences you will encounter), because that is the laws that you set into motion.

Now one might want to compare that with predestination. So many people like to believe in predestiny, and then it's easily used for a justification to make no effort to change or to evolve. One likes to tell themselves, "Well, I'll probably live so many years in that particular planet, and therefore when my time is up, I will just go. It doesn't matter what I do or I don't do." It does matter. In fact, I know that some of you, at least, have had experiences or had at least heard of people who no longer have the will to live. Why, even animals demonstrate that on your planet. They've lost the will to continue on. What they are really saying is they no longer have the desire to believe that they are the experience that they have created. And so when you free yourself from the desire of the experience that you have, which, of course, is what we create, when you free yourself from that belief, you have freed yourself from the attachment: you have shortened your time in that particular realm of consciousness.

Now we're going to give you some moments here to ask questions. Specifically, in reference to what has been discussed, which, as you know, is the movement of limit, known to you as experience, the effect of what you create. And when so viewed, you understand it as time. When a person creates many experiences and they have difficulty in supporting and sustaining the many experiences that they are creating, then you understand that as the bombardment of conflicting desires, and you understand that, in your world, as time-pressure. Now many people register time-pressure. It only exists because of a lack of effort of taking control over your vehicle known as your mind that is just running off by itself, creating many types of things; and you have what you understand as time-pressure.

So if you'll be so kind as to raise your hands, I'll be happy to speak to your questions in reference to what we have been discussing or anything pertinent to the classes that have already been given. So now is your time.

*[After a pause, the teacher continues.]* If you are fearful that by asking a question you are creating an experience, well, you create the experience by the very thought of even asking the question. So we'll go to the ladies first. Yes, here.

*Yes. Why does form have to have a movement?*

Because without movement, it does not exist. Form only exists—you see, experience is the movement of limit. Form is limit. It is that which is created, separated from what it truly is.

*Thank you.*

So without limit, there is no form. Without form, there is no expression, as you know expression. Does that help with your question?

*Yes.*

Continue on with your next one.

*The infinite, intelligent Energy, which we are, there is no movement to that.*

There is no movement to that which is, for that which is, is everywhere, everyplace at all time. So that which is does not move to express. It *is*.

*Thank you.*

For example, you do not see that which you are, for it is formless and free. That that is formless is free. That that is not formless, that which is form, is not free for it is controlled by its own separation from that which it truly is.

*Thank you.*

You're welcome. Yes, please.

*Following what you said then, is vibration the movement of light or the interference with it?*

What you understand as vibration [is] an effect, which is created by attitude of mind. Now attitude of mind is the movement of mental substance. Mental substance does not exist without movement because mental substance is sustained by that which is. That which is does not move. It *is*. That which is the effect of that which is, that is what moves. The vehicle moves.

For example, a person understands that they are [at] one place at one time because they believe that they are the limit. They have identified with separation. By identifying with separation, they are not therefore the fullness of the whole. By not being the fullness of the whole, they cannot be everywhere and still be where they are. For what you are, what you truly are is everywhere and everything, for it is the sustenance, the Power itself that sustains all things.

Now it is difficult—the mind—the belief that we are mental and [that] that is what we are—that belief that that is what we are, that is where the difficulty and the problem is. As long as we separate our self from what we are and we believe what we are not, then we will continue to have difficulty in being everywhere and everything for we believe we are the effect. And believing we are the effect, we become the victim of what you understand as circumstances. For vibrations have a direct control over that which is limited.

That which sustains anything is always greater than that which is sustained. So as long as you insist on believing that you are that which is sustained, instead of accepting that you are the sustenance, then you will have those experiences.

Yes. Did someone else have a question?

*Yes. In the last seminar you were speaking about power becoming force when it recognizes its potential.*

That is correct.

*And I'd like to know how this relates with the teaching now, about experience being the movement of limit.*

Well, experience, which is the movement of limit—experience, that is force; that's what it is. The movement of limit is force. And it is affected by force. So what is your question in that respect?

*That, that answered it. I just wanted to know if that was force.*

That is force. Yes.

*Thank you.*

That does not affect what you are. It can and does affect what you believe that you are. Man believes for man denies. If man did not deny, then man would not believe. Man only believes because man only denies. You see, the sparrow does not believe that the bush will not have enough berries on it for the coming year. The sparrow does not believe that the bush will have enough berries for them because the sparrow does not deny. So whoever denies, limits. Whoever limits, believes they are that which they have denied. Therefore, they are limit.

Yes, please.

*Yes. Could you clarify the difference between the preknowledge upon coming to earth of the circumstances of the life to be and predestiny?*

Yes, well, for example, the knowledge—knowledge, of course, is a function. It is a function of the mental world. Wisdom is a faculty of what you truly are, an expression of what you truly are. So when a person is aware, they are knowledgeable. They are knowledgeable of the experiences and the lessons that they have set into motion. And when they enter the limit, that awareness is prior to entering the limit. It's prior to the indentation or identification. And when they enter the limit, at the moment of entering the limit, that recedes into the consciousness as they identify with the limit to express through the limit. Does that help with your question?

*Yes.*

That, that awareness exists within the consciousness.

*Yes.*

That does not leave the consciousness. The over-identification with the limit, [instead of] that which a person is, in entering the limit, the over-identification with the limit is the density of that awareness. You see, the intensity of density is measured by acceptance. And so when you accept a limited form, then you increase, by the acceptance of the limited form, you increase the density; that is, your awareness of your consciousness of what [you believe] you are. So a person who overly identifies with any experience they've created or with any form, they do so at the cost of the density of their consciousness. Yes, I think we discussed that some time ago. Didn't we?

*Yes, sir.*

About the intensity of density is directly measured by acceptance. And so the less acceptance that you have or permit in your life, the greater density that you have. Yes. The greater density that you have, the greater are your needs in life. For the greater density that a person has in their life is, of course, in keeping with a great denial. Yes.

*Is acceptance, then, stopping the resistance to the experiences that we encounter?*

Well, you only resist an experience that you encounter by first denying that you have created the experience. You see, you see, when you refrain from denying that you and you alone have created the experience, when you refrain from doing that, you gain control over that which you have created. You see, as long as you deny that you have created the experience—and you deny that you have created an experience by resisting the circumstances and conditions that you are living in, which, of course, are an effect or an experience of what you have created. So if you want to move through that experience, [and] you would like that experience to come to an end in your life, then all you have to do is to accept truth: accept it is an experience, an effect of what you have created. And when you accept that, you gain control over it.

You cannot gain control over experience as long as you resist experience. Because by resisting experience you are expressing your denial that you have created it. You see, you can't control what you don't create. And as long as you insist on believing the deception of the human mind (that you had nothing to do with it; it was just circumstances and conditions that did it to you), then you, you don't control it, and it continues to control you. You see? That which disturbs us, controls us, you see. We are bothered by the things that we deny. We are not bothered by the things that we accept. I'm sure we'll all agree to that. If we don't, let's speak up. Does that help with your question?

*Yes, sir. Thank you.*

Well, certainly. Yes.

*What would be an effective method to move from belief into faith, in acceptance?*

In acceptance. Yes. Well, of course, the moment that a person moves from the function of belief, which, of course, is an effect of over-identification with limit, then they move into the faculties, where they—you see, by accepting—yes, I see your question. In reference to the best possible method. Well, there's only one method that really works that I am aware of. When a person makes the effort, sincerely, to accept the things in their life which are distasteful, they soon gain control over those distasteful things. And in gaining control, they wisely, then, choose what they wish to create. You see, so the first step and the best method to free oneself from that type of bondage is to say, "Now let's see. I don't feel very good at this moment. That didn't work out. That didn't work out. This person was a terrible person and etc." And one says, "Hmm, most interesting. Wonderful experience. I didn't like a bit of it. I don't like being controlled by it. I am controlled by it for I am disturbed by it. And the only reason that I am controlled by it and disturbed by it is because I deny that I created it." Because a person must think well of themselves. It is the law, the Law of Goodness.

So one person, having experiences that are distasteful to them—they don't stop thinking well of themselves. They say, "Gee, just think how, how easily it was for me to create such a distasteful experience. I wasn't even consciously, consciously aware of doing that. So if I'm able to create such a powerful experience in my life by not being consciously aware of it, I'll have no problem at all of consciously choosing what I wish to create." You see? So [in] working with that type of thinking, what you do is you gain control by the acceptance of the truth that you are.

An experience in a person's life is tasteful or distasteful in keeping with the forms they have created that say, "This is the best way. That's the worst way." This is all based upon the experiences that one has encountered, which are in truth, of course, effects of what they have created. So one must look at these things in a neutral way, intelligently, and say, "That's a terrible experience, but isn't it wonderful that I was able to create that so quickly. Now if I'm able to create such a terrible experience so quickly, I can create, just as quickly, surely a bit quicker, consciously, another experience." It brings about, of course, a readjustment in a person's thinking, in their attitude, changes vibration, like attracts like, and so we have those wonderful growth steps.

Now, as I have stated to most of you students, that the mental substance, the movement of limit is directly controlled by the breath that you take. And so when effort is made to do your proper exercises, then you'll begin to gain control over the movement of the mental substance. And by gaining control of it, you direct it in the way you wish and choose to direct it. Yes.

*Thank you.*

Does that help with your question?

*Indeed. Thank you, sir.*

But, you see, unless the effort is made, consistently, to control the breath, which, in truth, is controlling mental substance, then one cannot move intelligently and constructively in creating those things which would be in their best interest.

Now try to understand this: to one level of consciousness, bad experiences (so-called) don't exist as bad or good. They only exist as experiences. They only exist as effects of what one has created. Good and bad is ever in keeping with what one believes that they are. Now if a person believes that they feel good, and in that belief, they create that experience from their limited view and belief, then, of course, if they do not have those experiences, which, of course, they create themselves anyway, if they do not have those experiences, then they say the experience that they have is bad. But good or bad is ever dependent on what we are attached to.

Good and bad do not exist. What exists is the law. The law is not good. The law is not bad. The law just *is*. So what you are just *is*. That just is. Man calls many things good and bad. Try to understand that good and bad are limit. For, you see, we have all this reference for good and bad. Good and bad does not exist to truth. That which is truth *is*. There's no defense of it. So you can't call truth good and you can't call truth bad. It's neither.

However, the moment you identify and believe that you are limit, then, of course, you are controlled by that denial of what you are. You are controlled by so-called good and so-called bad. And so certain things make you feel good and other things make you feel bad. Well, some people, just flying in a machine, you know, that makes them feel good. To them, that's good; therefore, they experience God. And in your world, I see many things, you know. Lying down, that makes most people feel good. Hmm? But what they do there—some feel bad; some feel good. Most feel good. Yes. I think they call that sleeping. Yes.

So, you see, there's good and bad. All this, [what is it] all about, you see? A person says, "Well, I have this much money; therefore, I'm experiencing God." Well, they say they're feeling good, and when one says they're feeling good, then they're experiencing that good, that which they have created, you see. But that does not exist. That has nothing to do with truth. Truth is. Good and bad applies to the Law of Duality. The Law of Duality, of course, applies to what you call is creation. As long as you believe you are creation, then you have good and bad, you have black and white, you have night and day. You only have that ever in keeping with that division from what you are.

You see, the moment you divide, you conquer. And so when you divide yourself, you see, when you tempt to divide yourself—by entering limit and believing you are limit, then you have divided. And when you divided, you have conquered. And so here you have a part of you that says you're good; another part of you that says you're bad. Well, you're neither good or bad. You just are, you see. But as long as you divide, then you conquer; and you have this conflict within yourself. You have the limit, which you believe you are; then you have the limitless, which you know you are. And so you have a problem in that respect. Would you not agree, you see?

Now, you see that in many experiences. Many people say, "Well, if I don't have this and I don't have that, then I feel bad and something is wrong." But that is what one is creating.

Are there any other questions here tonight? Yes.

*I'm wondering if I understood you correctly. If we—did you say that when we have learned the lessons that we came here to learn . . .*

Yes?

*If we learn them sooner than the projected way of viewing them, we can cross back home again?*

Well, if you consider your lessons as a, part of your lessons, if you consider that you freed yourself from attachment and the belief that you are limit, then you have no problem in that respect, you see? But each time that a person says, "Ah, I'm free. I'm free!" in the very statement they have reattached themselves. Hmm? So, you see, it's more than just saying it. And it's certainly more than believing it.

*Certainly.*

True? Don't you see people moving from one experience they've created right on to another, to another, to another, ever denying what they are and working like a little beaver to be what they shall never be? Hmm? Yes.

*Thank you.*

Certainly. Well, it's just like religions. They certainly do serve a good purpose. And let's take a good look at them while we're having our little class this evening. You have a certain set of rules. You follow the rules and you have no problem. In that respect, in most people's thinking, you're very religious and you're very good. And they try to have as many rules as possible to govern your entire life. And, of course, they're usually only aware of the ones that you make public. And so therefore, that constitutes a good person or a bad person. So, you see, that's the type of thinking. That's duality. Hmm? What does that have to do with what you are? It only has to do with what you believe you are. Hmm?

I'm trying to help you to move, slowly but surely, kicking and crawling and screaming up the mountain, to free you from that kind of foolishness. And when you pause for a few moments each day and you awaken to what you are, I'm sure you would consider it foolishness, too. Hmm? Considering how very greedy and selfish those things are that they gobble up so much of your energy and time. Hmm? In a world of time. Yes. Yes, please.

*So you're saying that it's foolish to feel bad about the experiences one creates.*

One should always feel good about the experiences they create in keeping with the law. "This is a terrible experience. I'm having a terrible time. Thank you, God, I have created it." Hmm? You see, you see, in a world of identification you've got to have something that is greater than your mental world. Well, what is greater than your mental world is what you truly are. But, you see, the mental world likes to take ahold of that and say, "Well, this is me." Well, it's still mental, you see. So let us, as you say—Yes, you should feel good about all experiences that you have in your life for they are returning to you what you have created. Then you can make an intelligent choice and say, "Now I don't like that experience at all. That was not—I do not consider that beneficial to me." Well, the level that you believe you are, of course, it doesn't consider it beneficial because it's not the way—you see, here's the division—it's not the way that you think that you have created it. See, that's the great awakening, children.

You see, this is why we insist on resisting the experiences in our life because we say to our self, "I never created anything like that. I never wanted anything like that experience. I couldn't possibly have created that." Well, the problem is, you can't remember from moment to moment what your desires are, you see, most of the time. And so when the effect of that creation returns unto you, you're in another level of consciousness. "This is absolutely not—I certainly did not create that experience! I don't know how that got into my life." Well, you only make the experience compound itself by resisting it, you see. You create a friction and it adheres to you just like, what do you call that, that sticky glue, yes. Oh, Krazy Glue! I think they call it Krazy Glue. Does that help with your question?

*Yes. Thank you.*

You see? Now we are speaking, of course, in reference to one's own individual universe in respect to belief that they are individuals. When you create and establish laws that affect others, of course, they are affected in keeping with laws they have established which affect you. You see, we are affected and react to people that we have any emotional tie to. Hmm? Well, now a person might say, "Well, that person at the store, I have no emotional tie to them whatsoever." But if you will search deeply in your consciousness, though you never met the person before, you see, in keeping with the laws of association, you are relating within the depths of your consciousness to someone who is similar. Therefore, you have established that law and you are affected by that individual. Does that help with your question?

Because many times a different individual could say, another perfect stranger, say something and it doesn't bother you at all. Correct? Well, now there are many things at stake there. You see, for example, you are receptive to that level inside of yourself at the time. The Law of Association is working or the Law of Association is not working, and you have not made the effort, through proper breathing and daily spiritually exercises, to gain control over those realms which you are supporting. Yes. Did that help with your question there?

*Yes. Thank you.*

Yes. Yes, please.

*Thank you. Sometimes we have a repetitive experience, the same thing, like . . .*

It's wonderful. Wonderful! Isn't it? Yes, it is just wonderful. I've had many of them over these eons. Yes.

*For example, could we say losing one's temper.*

Oh, that's wonderful. Intensity of density is measured by acceptance. Now I want you to speak, because, you see, the moment we accept that we are not making sufficient effort, yet, to gain control over that within our consciousness—go ahead—but it takes a lot of temper and a lot of repetition to accept that, doesn't it? Go ahead.

*Yes.*

Yes, I wouldn't want to interrupt you. Go right ahead. *[The teacher laughs joyfully.]*

*Well, one can say, well, one can say at the time and each time, "Well, I created that."*

But one should be joyous and say, "Thank you, God, for the awareness from those realms of stupidity that I can honestly accept: isn't this beautiful? I created that." Yes.

*So after so many years, does this ever end?*

Well, it doesn't end suddenly because it didn't begin suddenly. And, you see, the law fulfills itself ever in keeping with its birth. You see, the birth of anything is in keeping with its so-called death, for death and birth is one and the same thing. So if you have a temper that, you know, you've supported for a long time and you would like to see it come to an end, try to understand that it wasn't born all of a sudden. It was a slow process, and you will find there's a decrease in the frequency. There may not be a decrease in the intensity of the expression of energy through the form known as temper, but you will find that there is a gradual decrease in the frequency. Would you not agree? Pardon?

*Yes.*

Yes. Well, you see, you don't explode as often as you used to. Would you not agree?

*No, but I still do.*

I didn't say that you still didn't. I just said it wasn't as frequent.

*Yes.*

Hmm? Well, now why do you, why do you think it's not as frequent? What's happened? There has to be a reason, you know.

*Well, at times, you can steer away and, and . . .*

How is that made possible? What was the one thing that you did over a period of time that decreased the frequency of your expressing all of that energy through that particular form?

*I think I had greater faith.*

Yes. So, you see, you are benefiting. You see, you made a little more effort. Hmm? Would you not agree?

*Yes.*

You made a little more effort. And I'll tell you, you'll make even greater effort if you will take a look each time and say, "There. Well, I did it. It's done. I gave my soul so cheaply to that form." Hmm?

*Yes. Very cheaply.*

Very cheaply. Because, you see, they didn't pay you anything. It was a one-way street. You felt terrible after. And the energy that you expressed, well, when you add that up, you see, probably about ten thousand, maybe twenty. When you add it up, you see, because so-called money is the effect of directed energy. And it's like one of my students said, you know, he'd rather have the cash. Don't you see? And I think that applies to the world of cash, you know. "I'd rather have the cash." See? Wouldn't you rather have the cash? Wouldn't you rather have $20,000 cash than a few explosions of your energy with no return that you could see any good in?

*Sure.*

Hmm? Well, first of all, then, it's important that you encourage yourself because the frequency is decreasing. Hmm?

*OK.*

And slowly but surely, as the frequency decreases, the intensity increases, you see. You don't release quite as much energy. As you find better avenues through which to direct your energy, you will find less energy going into those truly self-destructive areas of consciousness. Hmm?

*Yes. Thank you.*

However, you may use that form for constructive good at any time, when you consciously choose, intelligently, "Now I will express what most people will judge is my temper, and when I've finished and have accomplished my job, it is over." You see? And when you intelligently choose a judgment to serve you in order to bring some good for the greater good of the whole, because, you see, temper is a form that's created from a judgment—you understand that—when you choose to use it intelligently, you send it out to do its work. You tell it how long it has to get that job completed. You understand it's using your mouth and your mind, but you have separated, you've made a conscious choice for it to do so for a certain length of time. You decide what the time is, right to the second. And when you're finished, you say, "All right. Go back there and go lay down." Do you understand that?

*Yes, sir.*

Now when you make the effort through your exercises daily, then you can tell those forms that you create—for, you see, you are the father of them, and therefore they are responsible to you. They must do what you tell them. And they *will* do what you tell them, once you gain control and respect. You see, once they respect you, by your guidance, then they will do what you tell them to do.

*And when do you tell them that?*

You tell them that when you decide consciously, "This is the job you have to do. This is how long you have to do it. Now you get back here at that time. I am watching you. I am monitoring you." And when you send them out to do that job and you decide their time is up, you tell them to get back. And if they don't get back, you see, then you don't let them have any more sustenance. That means you don't let them have any more of your energy. And they won't be very happy about that.

You see, it's like having a child and you feed them their meal. And if they don't do what you tell them to do, as long as you are responsible to guide them—you understand that?—then you don't feed them the meal. They learn very quickly. Did you know that? You see, your emotions, they're all created in the water center. And they will learn very quickly if you don't give them any more energy. You see, if they don't respond and do what you tell them to do when you tell them to do it, then you just tell them the truth: you're not going to let them have any more food. And that food is your energy which you direct to them by your attention of them. Hmm?

How long does a child misbehave once you put them under control and ignore them? How long do they misbehave?

*If you ignore them?*

Yes. Well, of course, you first restrain them.

*Could be a long time.*

Could be a long time they'll misbehave after you ignore them?

*If you ignore them—well, oh, if you ignore them, no, they won't get the energy.*

They won't get any energy. You have children, don't you?

*Oh, yes.*

Well, when you have consciously chosen to ignore them because they have been misbehaving, then just how long do they continue to misbehave?

*Not long.*

They know where their sustenance comes from. And don't forget, the forms you created (all your feelings and emotions), they all know [the source of] their sustenance. You are their sustenance for they have no soul. They are created in mental substance, and they will do what you tell them to do as long as they are convinced that you will remove their sustenance. Does that help with your question?

So when you—you know, you want to encourage yourself in gaining control over what you understand as a temper child. And just work with them each day, you know. Encourage him if he's doing better, and if he's tempted to misbehave, let him have it. That means, you put him back there in the box, you know, like a little coffin there. See? Create one there, you see, for a little coffin. And just have a three-quarter lid [to] let the thing breathe a little bit. And put it there and say, "All right now, you're not getting out of there and you're not having anything to eat," which means it gets no attention after you created that, you see, consciously created that. You'll see. You'll see how quickly those things will straighten out. Because you are their sustenance. Without your attention, don't you understand, they don't move. They only live at your grace, for they have no soul. Hmm? Yes, are there any other questions? Yes.

*Yes. The higher realms, do they exist in a higher rate of vibration and is that an increased movement?*

Yes. Of course. Form which is increased in its rate of vibration (accelerated)—for example, why don't you visualize yourself standing on a turntable where the speed is gradually, but surely, increased. Now tell me, first of all, as you are moving slowly, what do you see? You see everything around, right? Rather detailed, if you are moving slow enough. Well, if you increase the speed, tell me what you see.

*Just a blur.*

Well, you haven't increased it sufficiently then.

*You won't see anything.*

Pardon?

*I don't see anything.*

No, when it is sufficiently increased, you go beyond the blur, you go beyond the void, and then you are home; you are what you are. So, you see, first of all, you have to remove fear. Now most people in acceleration and the increased rate of vibration, they start to move and they say, to their eyes, things are blurred. And as you accelerate the speed there, the next thing you know, they feel that they're getting dizzy, they're passing out. And what grabs ahold of them is what? What is the one function that takes control of their mind?

*Fear?*

Fear. Certainly. And so fear takes control of them because, you see—who, who grants unto the form fear?

*Lucifer.*

Of course. And so that is granted to the form so that the form won't move at any higher rate of speed, move on through the void—you understand—to the domains that Lucifer cannot control, for he is sustained by those higher realms. And that which sustains anything and anyone—that which is sustained cannot control that which sustains it. That's why your mind cannot control you until you permit yourself to be convinced you are your mind. So when you permit yourself to be convinced by the forms you have created that you are them, then, of course, you lose control over them. Yes. And whoever loses control over anything believes they are the victim thereof; and, of course, in truth they are. Yes. Yes.

*Could you please discuss that in relation to the principle of being at peace and being perfectly still to get beyond creation?*

Yes. Well, now tell me something, what do you think happens in your mind when you begin to make the effort to be perfectly still? Do things begin to move a little faster? Close your eyes and tell me. You should know as students of mine as long as you've been. What happens when you close your eyes?

*It seems that, at first, they do move faster.*

They do! The mind speeds up when you first make the effort to enter a state of peace. And as you continue with your effort, the mind begins to slow down, fear begins to take control, and all other things start to happen. Then you have experiences of various forms, suppressed desires, and you name it for you know who has control of your meditation now. Hmm? You see?

Yes.

*How can we free our self from these controls during our meditative state?*

Continue on with the effort of acceleration.

*How do we do that, sir?*

Well, for example, I'll sit here for a moment, perfectly at peace, and everything starts to increase in speed. And when that happens there, you see, that is at the point where you do not allow fear to enter. Hmm? You see, you see, fear enters and it convinces the mind that you're losing control, for that which you believe that you are *is* losing control as you enter the realm of conscious awakening of what you are. So what you believe you are does indeed lose control. Hmm? So if you want to, then you simply in your meditation—you've done your proper breathing [then]—you permit this speed, this acceleration to continue to increase, and that's known as letting go. You see? But what happens is that you reach a certain point and you almost, like stepping over, you see, and then you get scared. And after you get scared, different forms start rising up in the mind; you call them thoughts. Well, of course, they're forms that have been created. And they pull you back down again. Hmm?

*How can you overcome that?*

Well, how one overcomes it is from a continued daily effort, every day, minimum of twenty minutes a day, to work towards acceleration, that increase of speed and letting go. Now sometimes, I know, in your meditation, you let go and you have a fine meditation, but it's not as often as you would like it to be.

*Indeed.*

But it has and does happen, you see. Well, those are the kind—that's, that's a meditation. That's a real meditation, you see? You see, you come back and you say, "Well, what happened? I feel real good. I don't know what happened, but I feel real good." Is that not true?

*Yes, sir.*

Well, see, that's the only meditation that you want to have all of the time. Certainly. Now, as you continue with that effort, of course, that which is real meditation, is truly meditation, that will increase. And as that increases—now each time that you have that type of meditation, which is a true meditation, you encourage yourself. Be sure and encourage yourself. And when you have attempted meditation, have all those forms and distractions, you see, "Well, that wasn't so good. Next time will be better because I will just keep working on it." Then, during the course of a day and all the time that you're out of meditation, you say your affirmations. You see, if you do not make the effort to flood your consciousness with what you consciously choose, that which you have created in the past will rise up and flood your consciousness for your mind is constantly moving, because that is the principle and the law of the mind. It's moving, you see. So if you want to gain—[if] you want to free yourself from anything, you see, you must learn to increase the speed of the mental substance. And when you increase the speed of the mental substance, then that which you are is freed.

*Thank you.*

And so one has to have more effort directed frequently to gaining control over the mental substance. So one gains control over the mental substance in the course of a day or night by flooding their consciousness, their mind, with what they choose to flood it with, you see? You see, by you making the conscious effort to flood your conscious, because, you understand, now, that these forms, these thoughts that you believe that are in the mind—you try to visualize that the mind and mental substance is a movement, all right? It's constantly moving. And, well, more like, you say, like a merry-go-round, you see. And there's all these, what are forms and judgments, you see, that a person has created. And when you create them, they step on the merry-go-round. Well, now you believe you are the merry-go-round. Why, you even believe better than that: you believe that you created the merry-go-round, and in that sense, you really did, you see. That's how the mind works. So now you place all of these little forms on this merry-go-round. That's what you do. And so they have a ride. You see, they have a great time. They're riding in your consciousness round and round and round.

Now the more of those that get on to your merry-go-round—and I'm not saying you personally, but all minds, you see, they believe they are this merry-go-round—and the more thoughts and the more forms, the more judgments you put on there, the slower the merry-go-round spins. Do you understand? After all, you know, we have to consider the Law of Gravity. And so the more weight you put on, the heavier [the] cross you have to bear, the more load you're carrying. See, you're carrying all those freeloaders.

So if you will understand that by not making the effort to flood your consciousness with what you choose to flood it with, then you're, you're spinning; your energy is being utilized for all of those forms to have a free ride. Well, you know, I don't think you like free riders, do you? No, I don't think you like free riders. Well, if you'll understand they're free riders, you'll have no problem booting them off and keeping them off. But you boot them off and you keep them off by making a conscious choice of who will ride your merry-go-round. Do you understand that?

*Yes, sir.*

You see? And if a person will be honest with themselves, and they say, "Yes, that's true. Yes, because sometimes there's something in my mind and it just keeps right on a-spinning. I can't seem to let go of it." No, it's not true. It won't let go of you, you see. Oh no, no, no. It's not about to let go of you. It's having a wonderful free ride. Hmm? Yes. And then after that free rider is finished and he's taken up the whole spin of the mind, then you've got all those other forms that rise and say, "Well, hey, what have you been doing? You haven't made a penny today. What's a matter with you anyway?" Then you have to see all those other ones. Yes. And they go on for a ride. *[The teacher laughs joyfully.]*

Yes. Does someone else have a question? How quickly time passes. Yes, please.

*Yes. Years ago you taught us that if we think of a word, like, say* peace, *for, for a meditation.*

Yes.

*Repeat it three times in the mind and then you speak it out.*

That's true.

*Will that help accelerate these* . . .

Well, it'll help that particular form that you've created to boot off the other forms that are used to riding the merry-go-round. Yes, certainly. Certainly. It's at least a conscious choice. You've made that conscious choice, you see. You see, sometimes I see some of my students, they think of the word *peace,* you see—of course, you not only have to think it, you have to work to believe it because all those forms are there in that realm of consciousness. And you've got to convince yourself. And they think of peace and the next thing I look at, I look at a merry-go-round.

Here's the liberty bell. Here's a flowing river; somebody's sitting fishing. Here's someone else riding a roller-coaster. There's all those forms on that merry-go-round. And I take a look and I say, "Isn't that interesting. Now that's what they call peace." Yes. *[Some of the students laugh.]*

So let's try to be honest with our self and let's say, "Now what's peace to me?" You see. [For some, it's] a waterfall. It's walking inside of a bank vault, to some people, is peaceful. And I mean, you have all these different things, you see. Fifty pair of shoes, you know. Two hundred dresses, perhaps. No, even better yet, most of it's loaded with diamond rings and gold bricks. That's true. Yes. But, you see, a person says *peace,* and what happens in the mind? So the mind relates, "Well, I felt real good and peaceful, yes, when I first got married to my first husband." And so all of those forms—and they're not even consciously aware—all of those [forms say], "Oh! Here! We got a ride!" And they all land on your merry-go-round and they go spinning around, you see. So try to understand that the Law of Association in the human mind, you're not exempt—no one is exempt from that as long as they insist on believing they are the limit, you see.

Why, it might be, a mother, for example, when she had her first baby and she felt so relieved she considers that a state of peace. And so she thinks of peace and then she, maybe she's had eight children, and the next thing you know you have eight grown children sitting down there—you see what I mean?—with all those experiences. You see? So that's what you want to consider. You want to consider all of those things.

If you don't make the effort to control it, then it controls you. So that's the simple choice to have. This is the simple choice in creation: if you're not doing it, then you are just allowing them (those freeloaders) to ride your merry-go-round. And sometimes you're even aware. You say, "Gosh, I've been in a real spin. I feel like I've been on a merry-go-round." You know. There's no time. No this—well, what happened is, all of those freeloaders got on there and it did not include time. The time ones weren't having a ride. And the money ones weren't having a ride. But [for] all [of] those other ones, it was just a real heyday, you see. And when they finally—the merry-go-round exhausted itself for a while, all those other ones were standing waiting in line. And they didn't get on and you didn't have any energy left to spin again.

So let's, let's try to understand that's what they call the human mind. It's really something for a person to believe they're that, but that's what happens. Yes. Hmm? Any other questions? Yes, please.

*I'd like to know a little more about the friction and adhesion.*

Well, don't you find, in your experiences in what you believe that you are, the more adhesion you have, the more attachment you have because the more energy you direct to it? Now tell me something. Do you fight with anyone that you're not attached to?

*No.*

Do you have friction with people you don't have attachment to?

*No.*

So we clearly see that we have friction with those we are attached to, ever in keeping with the law—hmm?—of friction and adhesion. Why, certainly. Our adversities become our attachments, don't they? And our attachments, indeed, become our adversities, and there we experience what we understand as friction. Right?

*Yes.*

Yes. So if you like to have a lot of friction, prepare yourself for a great deal of attachment. Hmm. Yes. Hmm.

*May I ask another?*

Certainly.

*Friction on the earth is, you know, they rub two sticks together and it creates a fire.*

Well, yes, that's how you enter the fire center. Yes. Hmm. People talk about temper, well, they're going to have to understand friction and adhesion. Why, certainly. Do you enjoy being in the fire center?

No.

Why, I wouldn't think so, especially when sometimes it's so warm. Hmm? Yes.

*Thank you.*

Did you have any other questions?

No.

That's fine. Well, now there's my students over there. *[The teacher addresses a number of students by name.]* And who else do I see? Yes. Were you conserving your energy this evening? Oh, I have plenty. Yes, [Jane] has a question, please. *[Although the teacher frequently called students by name, public copies of the classes have deleted any personal names. However, for clarity in this exchange, a name will be used; however, the name has been changed.]*

*I would like to know if there's an affirmation that we can say to ourselves to get over the attachment of another.*

Oh, yes, yes, of course. First of all, the attachment—what we want to accept, first, is that we created the attachment as an effect of denying what we are. Do you understand that, [Jane]?

*Yes.*

You see, for example, by judging that we are half a person, by that judgment we deny what we are. Now, you see, here's a glass. *[The teacher picks up the glass of water that is by his left side.]* If you accept what you are, the glass is full. *[He takes a drink from the glass.]* And it runneth over. Now if you accept what you are not, then the glass is half full or less. Do you understand that?

*Yes.*

So a person who denies what they are, believes what they are not, seeks to be fulfilled. For they have already established the law that they are only half there. So when a person establishes the law that they are half there or half a person, then they experience a need for someone to fill that half. Do you understand that, [Jane]?

*Yes.*

And so the mind goes out searching to find their other half. Now when the mind searches for its other half, having first believed that it's only half there and it wants the other half, we must understand that we are then in a realm of consciousness that's searching for our other half. So whoever is attracted unto us must realize that they are not a person, whole and complete; they are [Jane's] other half. Do you understand that?

*Yes.*

And so they must first believe that they are [Jane's] other half; so they must be willing to do exactly what [Jane's] other half believes [Jane] is. And if they don't do exactly what [Jane's] other half believes she is, then they can't possibly, they cannot possibly stay with [Jane]. Do you understand that, [Jane]? And, of course, vice versa, you see. Do you understand that, [Tom]? Pardon? *[Again, the name of the student has been changed.]*

*Yes.*

Now that works for both [Tom] and [Jane]. It works for all these other people. It works for all of us when we believe we are mental substance. So if a person wants to free themselves from attachment, they must first make the necessary daily steps in their proper spiritual exercises and meditation to declare the truth of what they are. When you declare the truth of what you are and you accept what you truly are, there is no attachment for there is no denial. And need is the effect of denial. And, of course, following that, from need cometh attachment. Would you not agree?

*Yes.*

Yes.

*Thank you.*

So to be—first of all, do your spiritual exercises and declare the truth unto yourself: "I am whole, complete, and perfect." That which you are *is* whole, complete, and perfect. You see? That's what you truly are. Temporarily or at times, we deny what we are, you see, by believing what we are not. And in those moments, we experience being half a person, for in those moments we are only half a person, you see.

*Yes.*

But anyone who believes that they are half a person, then they ever search for their other half. But there's no one in creation—it does not exist—[who] is the other half. How can you have another half of you when in truth you're whole and complete? Hmm?

*You can't.*

The only part you can tempt to fill is that part that has denied what you are. And that part that *is* what you are shall rise up, and therefore you stop [and] have a moment [and] say, "Attached?! I'm not attached to that person!" How could you be attached to that person? You're whole complete and perfect. Kind to the person, you can be, for then you shall be kind unto yourself. Do you understand?

*Yes.*

But need the person? How could you possibly need a person and accept what you are? Hmm?

*You're—yes.*

Is that not true?

*Yes.*

But a person allows their mind to say, "Now let me see, well, I don't like to have dinner alone. Ah, I have denied what I am. I now believe that I am separate and I am alone." You see? So you've entered that realm of deception in that type of thinking, you see? Because you would have to have denied what you are, and being an inseparable part of the whole, you could not possibly have an experience of being alone. Hmm?

*Thank you.*

Did that help you, [Jane]?

*It does.*

Yes. And a person in their growing processes through those realms of bondage and attachment, the effect of denying in ignorance what they truly are—it serves a good purpose, for then a person, growing through that, becomes an instrument of the Light that they truly are and is able to help another. Now one should not tempt to step over the cliff in growth. One should make little steps. Slow steps, but sure steps. Take a look at the attachments; your little mind says, "Well, I can do without that." Try those little, small ones [first], you see. See, when you can live with it or without it, you are free. Would you not agree?

*Yes, I agree.*

You see? And so when a person awakens, they can say, "Well, I can eat whether I have a table or I don't have a table." Is that not true?

*Yes.*

You see?

*Yes.*

And so work in those areas, and experience: you do with it or you do without it. It really doesn't matter, for you alone create it, you see. You see, when, especially like, you know, when a person has attachments to another person, you see, it'd be better to be attached to the glass. *[The teacher picks up the glass of water.]* You can do something with the glass, you see. You can live with it or without it, right?

*Yes.*

Is it not true? So if you must have attachments, choose something in the domain of your personal responsibility, and you know you can do with it or without it.

*Yes.*

You see? And say, for example, you prefer wine. Well, you take a look there. *[The teacher looks at the glass of water that he is holding.]* [And] say, "There's a beautiful wine there. I'm thirsty. I'll have a bit." *[The teacher takes a drink of water.]* And you have created that. You see, that's what man has permitted himself: through the intensity of density, he has lost what he really is. Only temporarily, you see. You see, you can drink a glass of water and it will taste like wine, if that experience has been recorded in your consciousness. So everything is dependent on your own conviction. But your conviction you have made dependent upon certain things happening in your life. You see—but you alone are the creator of that. Awaken to that truth once again. You create that. If you want to have a good moment, you create a good moment, you see? You no longer permit yourself to be subject to what (something) is done out there that you cannot control. For, you see, you originally in creation created all of that in your mind.

*Yes.*

Hmm? Yes, [Jane].

*I would like to know if experience ever ceases to exist and if we carry experience over, if experience continues over to the other side.*

Only as long as you have denial of what you are.

*So—*

You see, experience is the movement of limit. As long as you insist on believing and identifying with limit, then, of course, you continue to experience; you continue to create, you see. See, God is the infinite, divine, neutral, sustaining, intelligent Energy. Man is the creator. So man stops creating when he accepts what he is. Hmm?

*So then, it is possible to continue experience when we're out of physical form?*

Physical form? Oh, experience continues right on. Oh, yes. Yes, yes. If you should leave your physical form this moment, this very instant, the thought in your mind would be the same: freeing yourself from attachment.

*Yes.*

Do you understand? You see, there is no change in that respect.

*Yes.*

Now, you will also experience, you see, your greatest desires and beliefs, for those are in keeping with what you have created. Hmm?

*Yes.*

Yes.

*Thank you very much.*

Certainly. Now, [Tom] has a question, please.

*Thank you. The thoughts that snap into my consciousness and capture my awareness...*

Yes?

*Seem to come instantaneously. Isn't there an opportunity to inject awareness to see them coming and, thereby, control our reaction—my reaction to those thoughts?*

Yes.

*Do I always have to react—*

No.

*—to the thoughts that are...*

No. No. You don't have to react because the thought is there. The moment that you accept you put it there—and it's got so cunning. You understand that, now? Because the mind is very cunning. It's got so cunning; it just pops in, you see. It doesn't even give you a chance to say, "No, I don't like this thought." Right? It pops in. But that's good, because when it pops in, that's when you tell yourself, "Now this is not me. Somehow or other it snuck in here. I'm going to wake up to how that's getting in there. But this is not me." And so you won't react. Correct?

The moment you separate truth from creation, you gain control over creation. Hmm? But as long as you believe that the thought in your mind is you, as long as you believe that—when you make the change in consciousness, "This is a thought that's in my mind. This is not me. I have created this. I have created this, and I shall find out how I created it. For the moment, however, I shall tell it what to do. It's in here. I don't like it. I don't want it. And now, I send it out." You see? You exercise the lord of your universe, that what you are, that will. Hmm?

*Thank you.*

Certainly. Yes. Yes, you see, that's known as an open door. See, there's a wide-open door there. Unfortunately, it's the backdoor and you're sitting at the front. You understand? You see, they're sneaking in the back, you see. You never know what's coming from—you see, you don't have to be concerned [about] what's in front of you. That's clear. Be interested in what's sneaking up behind you. You see? You see, for, you see, your awareness you have limited to that which is in front of you, you see. I mean, that's what people do. Yes. They take a look and say, "What's there?" you see? Very interested [in] there. They should be a bit interested in what's coming from behind, you see. For in creation your eyes are designed not in the back of your head; they're in the front, you see. Be more interested in what's sneaking up from behind. And then you won't have to be so worried about the shadows that keep slipping in, you see. You'd be amazed what slips in when you're not looking. Oh, yes!

Now, of course, you don't want to get, what they call it, paranoid, you know, and have your head moving everywhere. No, no, no. It's your consciousness. You don't have to move your physical head. No, no. Be aware. Be aware of what's trying to get in from yesterday and yesteryear, you understand?

*Yes. Thank you.*

And if you're aware of that, you won't have any problem about what's right there in front. Oh, no, no, no, no, no. Because it won't be able to cast its shadow there and distort it. Hmm?

What is an obstruction? Who of my students knows what an obstruction is? Hmm? Yes.

*A solidified judgment.*

Thank you.

*A shadow of the past.*

Indeed, it is. Indeed, it is a solidified judgment, a shadow of the past, a distortion of the true purpose of design.

And I best say good night. [I] do hope you've enjoyed our new classes here. And I see that we—time passes so quickly. Haven't heard any complaints about anyone [who] can't see. Now I can see you all very clearly and I hope you didn't strain your necks. If you did, don't forget to take care of them. Thank you and good night.

MARCH 13, 1986

## A/V Seminar 12

Good evening, class. Please be seated.

This evening we will discuss the purpose of design. As the physical body is designed as an instrument to serve the mind and does so until such time as the mind believes that it is the physical body, at which time the physical body acts upon the mental body. And so it is, as the astral body and other bodies of consciousness are designed to act upon the bodies that are designed to be servant to them, the process continues: action and reaction, through the belief that we are that which we have created.

Some time ago in your Living Light textbook [*The Living Light*], I spoke to you in reference to the soul, that it can and does all things create. For example, we've had much discussion on self, the love of self, and what it has to offer to the human being. So we must first ask our self, What is self? Self is the belief that we are the images, forms that we have created. And so when we believe that we are that which we have created, we become at that time the created and the victims of that which exists only as a form that we have created for a purpose, a purpose that is no longer being served.

Now I know that all of you, most of you, anyway, receive the tape, and it's good for you, who wish to, to take notes. And we're going to take a moment to speak on what has just been discussed. I'll come to you as you raise your hands. *[After a short pause, the teacher continues.]* Almost happy to see that I have such illumined students after all these years. Yes.

*OK. At what stage of our evolution will we be able to see or view the forms we create or are creating?*

Yes. At what state of our evolution?

*Yes, sir.*

At the state of evolution known as reason. For when we permit our self to be receptive to the soul, to that which we are, in so doing we awaken to the true purpose of design. At that moment in so-called time we will evolve and clearly see that we have created that which we know as our experiences, and that we alone, having created them, can change them. Yes, go ahead with your other question.

*Well, what I want to ask—OK. We will, we will be able to see them as you all have described them to us? I mean, in—because some of them, some of them we're told are very gory or horrible looking.*

Well, of course, in that respect we all view from a different perspective in our evolution and [it's] ever dependent upon our own perspective. In other words, I think they say, in your world, one man's love is another man's poison. Or is it better said, different strokes for different folks? Isn't that what's rather common in your world? And so, you see, your stroke may be different because you're a different folk in respect to your evolution at any given time. However, in keeping with the level of consciousness to which you will awaken, in that respect, of course, the forms will be the same to all viewers. Yes.

*Yes, sir.*

Does that make you happy?

*Yes.*

Good! Yes.

*Thank you.*

You're welcome.

*Is it possible to see forms prior to arriving at that particular level of evolution?*

Well, it is, of course, possible to see forms at any level of evolution in that respect. For example, we spend much of our time in creation seeing the forms that we have created. We do that and we call that in your world—you call that love. For example, love is the reflection of the images we have created, the reflection in another of the images that we have created and believe that we are. So a person says, "Well, I'm in love with this. I'm in love with that." They are seeing the form reflecting to them the image they have created. In other words, one says that they are convinced. That is the judgment they have made. That's what makes them feel good for that's what they have created in order to feel good. Does that help with your question?

*Well, it, then—I take it from your answer that, that no one is able to see any forms created by mind or in other dimensions until they arrive at a certain level of evolution.*

That is correct. They see them in keeping with the level of evolution that they are on. For example, a person, as I stated in opening the class this evening, a person who—the mind acts upon the physical body. A person in the mind who believes they are the physical body becomes, then, a reactor to the physical body. Now let's take it a step farther. All things created, all things created become demons when we believe we are that which we have created. Do you understand that?

*Yes.*

For when we believe we are that which we have created, we go contrary to the law and become the servant of that which we have created when that which we have created, by the Law of Design of Purpose, is to serve us. Go ahead with the rest of your question there.

*That was all the question.*

That was all there was to it. I see. Fine. Yes. Yes, please.

*Thank you. Since—is it so that we originally were the true purpose of our design and is it coming into form that starts the process of believing that one is what they are not?*

We are and shall always be the true purpose of our design. We can only be deluded by that which we have created for a time. Only for a time. For time is, of course, the illusion. So we, at times in the very course of one day, we believe we are the thought that we have created. Time, in a short day, passes, and we no longer believe that we are the thought, the form, the feeling, the image that we have created. And so that process is taking place in truth moment by moment. Yes. Does that help with your question? You have another one?

*Yes, I do.*

Go right ahead.

*That did help. I'm interested in what starts the, what starts that—if we were originally the true purpose of—*

Yes, yes. Thank you. I will be happy to answer that question. What starts the process is attachment to the fruits of action known as the love of self. For self is the images that we have created; that's what self is. Does that help with your question?

*Yes.*

Yes. You see, attachment to the fruits of action or attachment or belief that we are what we have created is ever in keeping in degree and extent with the love of self. So as we love the thoughts that we form and create—and that's known as the love of self—then, of course, we are controlled by those things that we have created, which is contrary to the true purpose of design.

Yes, and the gentleman has a question.

*Then a person that is expressing the love of self deeply, are they, then, unable to show faculties, such as gratitude?*

They cannot show gratitude. Gratitude is ever subject to and dependent upon total consideration. Now total consideration is not being considered by anyone who is over-identified with the images that they have created. Do you understand? Therefore, they are not, at that time, able to express the soul faculty known as gratitude, for the soul faculties have become the victims of the sense functions. And they are temporarily, what is known as, out of balance. Did that help with your question?

*And to [help us] get back into balance?*

Yes, to come back into balance then, one, of course, must make the effort to gain control over the vehicle of their mind. And to do that, one first accepts that they are responsible for what their mind is creating; however, they are not that which they have created. They are responsible for what they have created. That's the separation of truth from creation. The love of creation is ever at the expense and sacrifice of the loss of the Principle of Goodness, known as God. Yes.

*Thank you.*

You're welcome. And—yes, please.

*How does the soul create all things?*

Well, first of all, the soul is a covering or an individualization of the divine, infinite Spirit, which is known as the Principle of Goodness or God. Now this individualized soul is an instrument through which the Divine Spirit expresses itself in form or world of creation. Now many people do not seem to understand, let alone to accept, that the soul, being a covering, is form; being form, it is individualized; being individualized in that respect, it is limited. Do you understand? So the Living Light Philosophy teaches you the broadening of horizons, the expansion of consciousness in order that you may have the awakening of all being, for that's what you truly are.

Now the soul, in its individualization, which is, of course, sustained and maintained by the Divine Spirit, in that expression of individualizing or separating from the whole, that which is form, that which is created, is separated from that which is the whole. It is separate in consciousness. And so the more we separate ourselves in consciousness by what is known as the love of self or the pride of being, in that respect, then the more we limit our lives and the fullness and enjoyment thereof.

Now in reference to your question of the individualizing of anything, the moment something is individualized, it is separated from its source and through the process of the separation of its source is a moment of crisis, for that is the moment at which a person is tempted; tempted to believe that they are the covering and not that which is sustaining the covering. Did that help with your question?

*Yes. Thank you.*

Yes. Yes. Yes, please.

*Yes. Right here, the physical body is designed to serve the mind.*

Correct. As the mind is designed to serve the astral body, on and on and on to the soul and the Divine Spirit. Yes.

*Yes. It was also stated in the last class, as we cease to believe in our judgments and believe—cease to believe and have more acceptance of what we truly are ...*

Yes?

*These experiences that we had once believed we were ...*

Yes?

*Where that realm—I won't say the word* stops, *but there is a—the word doesn't come to me that was used. But there no longer is that attachment and that energy directed to that particular realm that we believed we were. Now with the physical body—is my understanding correct?—it seems like the less we are attached to our forms and our body, it would appear the less we're attached to earth and our body and we move on into other realms out of the body.*

That is your question?

*Yes.*

Or your statement?

*That is—*

Or both.

*That's my question and—both.*

All right.

*Thank you.*

All right, thank you. Now the more we love what we create, the more we believe we are that which we have created. The more that we believe we are that which we have created, the more bondage we have in our life, known as experiences or limits. When you begin to further expand your consciousness, you permit your vehicles, your beings, your mind, which, in truth, is a servant of your higher bodies, which in the final analysis is a servant of the Divine Spirit, when you expand your consciousness through understanding, which grants tolerance—for without understanding, there is no tolerance—when you expand your consciousness, the soul faculties begin to express in your life. As the soul faculties begin to express, the soul—for the faculties are faculties of the soul—the soul, once again, gains its just and proper control over the vehicles that have been designed to serve it.

Now when the vehicles, designed by the soul to serve the Divine Spirit, that which we truly are, the Light, when the vehicles gain such control that the soul, that is, the expression of the Light through the form known as soul, can no longer express any of the faculties, then the soul is driven from its house and waits in what many of your philosophies understand as limbo. Does that help with your question?

*Yes.*

Fine.

*Yes. Thank you.*

Yes, yes.

*We're taught that we have nine bodies.*

Correct.

*Which of those nine bodies is expressing in this broadened horizon of tolerance and expanded consideration?*

Which of the nine bodies?

*Yes.*

You have the soul body. You have the cosmic consciousness, the universal consciousness, the terrestrial consciousness. Yes.

*Well, let me rephrase the question, then. It is not the mind that is having these broadened horizons and tolerance—*

Ah! Thank you.

*And consideration, is it?*

Thank you. The mind is a vehicle which is a servant of the higher bodies. As the mind is expanded and broadened in its understanding—you see, see, understanding is a faculty of the soul; it's an expression of the soul. To the mind—it is an awakening to the mind. For example, the soul faculties express through the vehicles which are the servants of the soul for its expression. Therefore, as the mind is broadened in its horizon, the soul and its faculties are more fully expressed. Does that help with your question?

*So the mind or the mental body is able to view all the other bodies, the soul body and all the rest?*

No, no, no, no. No, it's not able to view them because it is subservant to the soul and the spirit body. It is able as a vehicle, it permits the expression of the faculties of the soul through the body known as the mind. It will be all right there, Mr. Red, yes. *[The teacher addresses the church's dog.]* Go ahead with your question for . . .

*It permits the higher bodies to express through it.*

Correct.

*But it does not express itself to the higher bodies.*

No. No. The lower, the lower is not designed to control the higher in that respect. Absolutely, positively not! Although the lower bodies are tempted constantly to control the higher bodies. Yes.

*Thank you.*

Yes. It is not possible. You see, creation was not designed to control God. Creation was designed and is sustained by the Divine Spirit and the Light to serve the Light. The Light is not designed to serve creation. Yes. You see, there is no way—and it is contrary to the very law, demonstrable law—for the limited to control the limitless. Does that help with your question? Yes. And that which sustains anything is greater than the thing which it sustains. Yes. Yes, you had a question, please.

*Yes. Other than form being a tangible item for the mind to view, is there more to the purpose of form?*

Well, the purpose of form is to be a servant or vehicle through which the Light may express in a world of limit or creation. Yes.

*[After a pause, the teacher continues.]* Do you know why you don't fly? It's not because you don't have wings. Why don't you fly?

*I don't identify with flying.*

Therefore, you can't fly.

*Right.*

Why don't you fly? *[The teacher addresses another student.]* Yes, why don't you fly?

*I've never accepted the possibility.*

Correct! Because to accept the possibility that you can fly without the restrictions created by a mental body, you understand, is to go against the authority and supremacy of the mental body that you believe that you are from having a love affair with it. Does that help with your question? That's why you don't fly. That's why you don't levitate. Yes.

*What you said at first helped more. You said—*

I'm happy to hear that some things help less. Thank you.

*OK...*

Some things I'd like to help more and some things I'd like to help less. Yes. Confusion, I like to help less.

*OK...*

Judgment, I like to help less. Yes.

*Well, the only, the only way that I'll be able to ask the other part of the question is to hear what you said again about the purpose of, the purpose of the de—more what I, what you said about the purpose of the design of form is more for the expression of the soul. You...*

Well, I'm not going to say it the same way.

*OK.*

So I do—perhaps it'll be helpful; perhaps it won't. Hmm? Because I won't say it the same way. No, no, no. It'll be something a little bit different, you see. Because there's something a little different in you that's taking place. I said that the true and only purpose of form or limit is for the service to the Divine

Light, that which you are, to express in a world of limit known as creation. Do you understand that?

*Yes.*

Now, for example, as the soul or the Light sustaining form and limit expresses more fully through it, you understand that?

*Yes, sir.*

You see, then the vehicle, known as limit or form, the body, the mind, its rate of vibration is raised; as its horizon is broadened, its consciousness is evolved! You see?

*Yes, sir.*

You see, if you take water and you pass it through a pipe, the pipe is benefited by the water which passes through it, be it dirty or clean. So your vehicles, which are designed to serve the Light, the very River of Life, as that purity passes through those vehicles, as there is an acceptance of more of the life flowing through it, then those vehicles of limit are broadened in their horizon, expanded in their consciousness, and evolved in their rates of vibration. Do you understand that? That's the purpose of creation. Yes. Does that help you?

*Yes, sir. That helps a lot.*

Good!

*Thank you.*

Now, yes.

*Are all the vehicles, vehicles of limit, and are the only vehicles that we have any control over just the mind and the body? Those two vehicles?*

Oh, no, there are nine bodies. So you have your mental body. You have your astral body. You have your desire body. You see, there are nine bodies. There are—for the physical body, there are nine. You are aware of one. For the mental body, there are nine. You are aware of one. For the astral world and the astral consciousness, the astral body, there are nine. You are aware of one. Yes.

*We only have control over the mental—one body of the mental and—*

No, no, no. You, perhaps—yes, you are aware of one body. But, you see, there are times when you're aware of another body of the mental body. You're aware of the desire body, at times. Hmm? Would you not agree?

*Yes.*

Yes. And so there are several bodies. Remember that there are eighty-one levels of consciousness, and a level of consciousness, in keeping with the law, must have a vehicle through which it can express itself. Hmm? Yes.

Does someone else have a question?

*The soul is a covering for the spirit, for our—*

Yes, yes. It is individualized. The individualized soul is, of course, form.

*Is our—and then our spirit, is it a covering for, no. It is—*

The Spirit is. The Spirit, the Divine Spirit is the Light. Yes.

*Thank you.*

That is what we are. Yes. That's all that we are, for there's nothing beyond that. Everything else, of course, would be an illusion. Yes, please.

*Is it possible to have an imbalance among the bodies in which one body is at a higher level than the others, thereby causing the imbalance? If so, how do we—*

Yes, yes. Are you speaking now in reference to one particular body and the other eight bodies that are not in harmony with it in keeping with the attention and the energy which has been fed to them? For example, some people with a mental body, the desire body has received so much attention and identification that it is not in harmony and out of balance with the mental body through which the function of logic is expressing itself. Would you not agree?

*Yes.*

You see. And so when the desire body, when a person identifies with the desire body, then all logic seems to go completely out the window at that moment that it is in control. Yes, that does reveal an imbalance between the bodies of the mental world. Absolutely and positively. Yes.

*Does that mean that the forms that are attached to the individual bodies are, are not being—are taking control?*

It means that they take control whenever we identify with them for we, in the error of ignorance in our evolution, through over-identification and a love of the self, believe that we are that body. That is correct. Does that help with your question?

*Thank you.*

Yes. Yes, please.

*I was wondering how we can lessen self-love. And is self-love a product of, a manifestation of the ego? If so, how can we direct the ego positively, in a positive way?*

Definitely. You see, the faculty of reason is what will bring about a change in respect to the illusion created by an over-identification with what we create. And through the faculty of reason we will awaken that that which we have created we are not. You see, for example, a person says, "Oh, well, I just had a thought, but I know that that isn't me." However, when it is the thought that they have attached themselves to, to such an extent through their love of that which they have created, then it is indeed most difficult for them to pause and say, "Now that thought and that desire is not me, but I have created it." Would you understand that?

*So it's just a constant affirmation of that?*

Yes. And so, therefore, because our consciousness is in a constant process of being flooded with forms, forms that we have, in our error of ignorance over-identified with, [and] believe that we are that which we have created, which in turn strengthens the love of the forms, which is known as self-love, then, of course, it is advisable for anyone in their efforts to awaken to the Light that they are to choose consciously in their faculty of reason what they wish to flood their consciousness with. Yes. Remember, whatever we create—and we are in a constant process of creating. We are aware of our mind creating. Then we become aware, at some times, of the desire body of the mind creating. All right. Whenever we permit our self to be so satisfied with what we have created, we, at those times, convince our self and believe that those created forms we have created are us. Understand? Now the created forms are the very instruments who build what is known as pride which offers to us the love of self.

*Yes.*

You see. There is no light of reason in it at all. They do that in order that they may continue to exist. Remember, that which we create lives only by energy directed from our attention to it; it is a soulless creature. Do you understand that?

*Yes.*

All right. And because it is a soulless creature, because it is created by the intelligence of the human mind, it has, as a soulless creature, access to all information that is in our mind at any time. Do you understand?

*Why, why is that? Why—*

Because it is created by our mind. You see, that which is created by anything, by the very Law of Creation contains within it all of the constituents of the original. Hmm?

*Yes.*

For example, a drop from a body of water contains within it all the constituents of all the body of the water, you see?

*Yes.*

And so that which we create in a mental world has access to the source, and we, being the source, for we have created it—do you understand?—it has access to every thought, every feeling that we have in our mind and those nine bodies of the mental world. So we must understand that it, being created by our mind, knows that it is a soulless creature, for we know we have created it. And we are not God in that respect and, therefore, [have not] granted it an eternal soul. Do you understand that?

*Yes.*

So the forms that we create with our mind know they are soulless, know that their existence is completely dependent upon energy, vital life force, that we direct to it. When it does not receive what it judges is sufficient for its life, its continuity, then it will come and control, possess, and obsess our mind. Do you understand that?

*Yes.*

This is why sometimes a person says, "Oh, it is so difficult for me to get rid of that thought," you see. "It's so difficult for me to let go of that great love that I know that I have." Do you understand that? You see, you see, because they have created a form. And ever in keeping with the love of the form they have created, it must have that vital life force for its continuity.

*So I—*

And because we believe that we are that which we have created, because we are in love with our self—the self being all that we have created. That is what self-love is, is the love of all the forms we have created, you see. Hmm?

Now why is it and how is it that some forms that we have created that we have such great difficulty to let go of? We must pause and think and look deeply at these things. When we permit our self to create a form and make a judgment, have a thought and create it, form it, solidify it—it becomes a judgment, you see. And if we permit other forms in the consciousness to rise up, who take a look and see that this new form, oh, yes, that would be a good friend of theirs because they, in turn, would get a little feeding whenever this one got fed. And so you get this false charge of satisfaction, which you misinterpret as a feeling good, you know, like, like when you go on a honeymoon or something, you see, and you have all these so-called good feelings.

You're very, very pleased inside. You feel very satisfied. Well, if you would pause for a moment and look with the light of reason, you would see that this form has a whole army that is now following it, you see. And so if anything goes contrary to these forms receiving the energy and vital life force from your being, by your attention to them, then you have a terrible experience if you believe you are the forms that you have created. Does that help with your question?

*Yes.*

Yes, you're welcome. Yes, please.

*We're supposed to—we're not supposed to be in love with our creations.*

Well, then, you know, that is true because, you see, the love of self is contrary to the design of what self is: these forms that are designed to serve us. Yes, yes.

*Then what's—*

That's very true.

*What's the responsibility to the forms?*

The forms that we have created? An awakening that they were created by your mind to serve you for a certain time and to do what you tell them to do. And when they stop doing that, then you're going to annihilate them. You annihilate them by not giving any attention to them, you see.

*OK.*

It's human to forgive; ah, it's divine to forget. It takes the Divinity in order to free oneself from that which they have created because of the great love of those things. Yes.

*So once you annihilate your forms then, is there a void that, that you have to protect yourself against other things entering?*

Well, you see, for example, I see, you know, I haven't yet met anyone who has annihilated all of the forms. The mind is constantly creating them, you see.

*I meant in one area, for instance.*

Oh, in one particular area? Well, you know, pages of the past reveal quite a bit to all of us, I would say. They'll always be—like the shadows, of course, they sometimes get very thin. Sometimes they look like little skeletons with their last breath. But with their last breath, they will breathe forth their desire, and therefore tempt us, you see.

You see, this is why I have given to all of my students affirmations designed to free them from these soulless creatures which are created by the mind, you see. Because they tempt and rob us of the joy of life. See? You see, energy which can be constructively used—now any time you direct attention, through which energy follows (the vital life force), any time you direct it to the creating of anything, if you will put, what I used to say to my students so many times, put God in it or forget it. That means to put the Light in it, you see. The Light, the Light, the faculty of reason. Knowing that you have created it to serve a purpose and, you see, it's like a child. When you have a child and the child is dependent upon you for its food and for its care, and when you permit yourself to believe that through an attachment to what you have created, you see, you'll believe that that is you. And when that happens, then that which you have been an instrument for the creation of will take control of you.

And so the same thing happens, of course, with the soulless creatures that are created. When we love them—we love them through an attachment to them—they take control of us and no longer serve the purpose of their true design, you see. That's, as I said earlier, that's when creation becomes the demons, you see: when it goes against the very law of the purpose of its design. And that happens when we believe we are that which we have created because we love what we have created so much.

*Yes.*

Hmm? Does that help with your question there? Yes. Anyone else have a question? Time passes in your world so quickly. Yes.

*When these forms no longer serve their purpose and they're not abiding by the rules of our house . . .*

Yes, then they usually cause a phenomenal amount of frustration. You experience it as a frustration; it's a war within. Yes.

*How do we—is it my understanding, then, since they don't go by our rules, to order them out? How do we do that and is that correct?*

Light cast upon the shadow, you see, dissipates it. It's the light of reason. You don't have to order anything. All you have to do is permit the light that you are to flood the consciousness. And when that happens, then, you see, they cannot, they cannot remain in the light. You see, they are created in the depths and the darkness of what is known as the human mind. And whenever the human mind is flooded with the truth, then in the human mind there is an increase of the light. It's known as the light of reason. This is why I have stated for years keep faith with reason. I never have taught to believe in reason. God forbid! Keep faith with reason; she will transfigure thee. Don't ask me why reason is magnetic. You advanced students in my private classes certainly know that. Yes. Yes, go ahead.

*So the teaching of love thy neighbor as thyself, is that because of the . . .*

Well, that is an effort—thank you—on the part of the prophets of centuries, centuries ago, an effort to, to try to get people to, to think of something besides their own soulless creatures they have created. However, what happens, you see, usually when a person thinks of someone else and feeds their soulless creatures, they only feed the ones that in themselves are demanding their own feeding. Do you understand that? Yes. But it was, it was and is an effort to help a person to think of some other soulless creatures outside of their own. You see, "He who loves himself," as the Divine Light speaks, "He who loves himself more than he loves me shall lose himself to find me." Perhaps now some of my students can understand what that means. Yes. Does that help with your question?

*Yes, I was wondering if it meant, also, maybe it was an enlightened, an enlightened statement; knowing how much people loved themselves, they could love their neighbor as much, so they'd be . . .*

Yes, it is a step. It is a step in a positive direction, but I think in your world they would say it is a slow boat to China. However, it is a positive step. If you can get a person to think of someone else's soulless creatures outside of the ones that they have created, then you do have a step in the right direction. Yes.

Yes, they couldn't get them to love God; so they tried to get them to love something else they're attached to. Their neighbor, of course, would have to be someone they liked; otherwise, they couldn't possibly love them. Do you understand that?

So in that sense, it did serve and does serve a good purpose. For example, say that, you know, you want to be freed from frustration, strife and struggle, and all of this heartache and experiences in creation. And so someone teaches you, well, love your neighbor as well as you love yourself. And you look around to see, "Well, which neighbor? I have that one and that one." If you're fortunate you've got a choice, of course, and a high fence. But there's that neighbor, that neighbor, that neighbor, that neighbor, and that neighbor. And then your mind will say, "Oh, no! Not that one! No, not that one. This one over here. Yes, I don't mind helping them." So who are we helping? Hmm? We are helping the very neighbor that our forms tell us that would be receptive to our help. Would you not say? Hmm? And so here we have the forms known as prejudgment (prejudice), you see; so we start off by loving who? We love the neighbor as long as the neighbor is in keeping with the soulless forms, known as judgments, that we cherish so dearly because of our love of our self. Do you understand that?

*I do.*

However, I did say it's a step in the right direction. It's a positive step, because it does broaden our horizon because it opens up our little house to untold multiplication of the soulless creatures. And, you know, when we've had enough, we're bound to make a change. So it is a step there, a step, a positive step, yes. It's a long way. I did say it was a slow boat to Asia or something, but definitely.

*Thank you.*

Yes. Well, if you can't get a person to love God—if you could get them to love someone besides themselves—of course, they can only love someone besides themselves who is in keeping with the increased love of themselves, you understand, for someone else is only the mirror of reflection that reflects best the forms that we have created in our mind, known as judgments. Do you understand that? That's why I say I've yet to find anyone rise in love, but I've seen millions fall in love. Yes.

Someone else have a question? Yes.

*So this is happening so constantly, this love of self, moment by moment . . .*

Well, it doesn't have to. The flooding of consciousness can be to our choice. It's designed to serve our choice, yes.

*So one should then—I, I—what I want to know is: it is a constant process that is occurring.*

Yes.

*Moment by moment.*

Correct.

*So the flooding of one's consciousness with the goodness of what one chooses . . .*

It is a constant process to students who having received control of the mind through control of the breath and are not practicing it, then, of course, it is a constant process; yes, in that respect. Because I have taught and demonstrated that no new thought form can enter the consciousness while the breath is held in keeping with the proper exercises. Yes. Does that help with your question?

*Thank you.*

Yes, please.

*The feeling of, of self-importance is continuous . . .*

The feeling of self-importance is continuous ever in keeping with the destiny of our own denial. When we deny what we are, we experience what we are not and, therefore, have an insatiable need of feeling important. Yes, go ahead with your question. Thank you.

*And in dealing with individual situations, others arise immediately following, in addressing a form . . .*

Yes?

*And accepting the, the form and the fact that I created that form, another immediately takes its place.*

That is correct. Because, you see, if you have, if you have a few thousand children that haven't eaten for some time, they're very hungry. And you have a table all set of food, and you have them all looking at it, and you say, "All right, you can come over here." And you bring one over—you understand now? And he takes a look at it and you say, "You do such and such, and such and such, and you may have that to eat." He doesn't do what you tell him to do and you send him out. Well, you have a whole line of them waiting to get in. They rush right in.

*And . . .*

Yes?

*You mentioned just previously that in order to, to deal with that, we should flood our consciousness with the Light.*

Yes, with the declaration of truth of that what you are, instead of the belief in what you are not, you see. You see, a person says that, "This is me." Well, what, what is saying that "This is me," is that which they have created; [it] is using their mouth. Yes.

*So the affirmation, the affirmation of, that affirmation will effectively...*

Absolutely! Definitely, because it declares what you are. And when the declaration of what you are floods the consciousness, what you are not cannot exist in the consciousness. You see? It'll go looking for some other house to get inside.

*Thank you.*

It usually has no problem. Yes, you're welcome. Yes.

*We've been taught how important it is to be united in consciousness in any endeavor.*

Yes.

*And I'd like to know with these eighty-one vehicles that you've mentioned...*

Yes.

*They seem to be scattered at times. How do we get them all back, united at once?*

Put your house in order before confusion sets in. Through your daily spiritual exercises, you put your house in order before you do any service to creation.

*Thank you.*

Yes. And if you put your house in order before you go to serve the soulless creatures, you won't have to be concerned about soulless creatures for within your house they will not exist.

*Thank you.*

You're welcome.

*[The teacher continues after a pause.]* Well, everyone is telling me that class is over. Hmm? My, oh, my. Do we have a few questions before we conclude this little seminar here this evening? Yes.

*I'd like to ask, we've been told that we're in creation to evolve the form and these forms.*

Yes.

*I'd like to know at the point at which that happens, do they recognize the source? And if so, how do they act?*

Do the forms created recognize the source? Is that the question?

*I think my real question is, we've been told that our purpose in creation is to evolve the form.*

That is the purpose. How do you evolve a form if you don't keep control over it?

*Right.*

So one must control the forms they create. And one cannot control the forms that they create when one believes they are the forms that they have created.

*Right.*

You cannot control what you believe that you are. You can only control what you know you are responsible for by not being attached to it. Yes.

*I'd like to know how those forms are going to be once they are evolved.*

How they're going to be?

*Yes.*

They're going to be a little bit more obedient to the purpose and design of their own creation than they were before they came. You see?

*OK.*

They will not be so easily tempted to get something for nothing. Yes. Yes.

*Thank you.*

You see, try to understand that forms created—whatever that which is created and is not obedient to its creator is a form that is tempting to get something for nothing. Yes. Yes.

*Could you recommend a way to put the house in order...*

Yes. The first thing upon arising in the morning is a minimum of twenty minutes should be set aside for spiritual affirmations and controlled breathing. Consistently, preferably, of course, at the same time every morning, seven days a week, year in and year out. Yes. Now if one is not able to do that for certain beliefs at this particular time of their evolution, then, of course, it is extremely beneficial that they flood their consciousness with the spiritual affirmations that they have been given, which are designed to keep them free from those soulless creatures that have been created, you see. And if we do our part, we will experience an increasing freedom from their control. Hmm?

*Could you, could you recommend an affirmation?*

I have already given those affirmations, and I will have the secretary and my vice president here, my directors, check with you after class, before you leave. Yes.

*Thank you.*

Because they are in our other seminars. They have been given, yes. All right? Yes, were there any other questions? Yes.

*It has been said that irritation awakens the soul.*

Yes.

*Is that the process by which the first step is we—with that irritation there is an awareness of the forms and, therefore, the beginning of the separation?*

That which is irritated is that which is affected, would you not say?

*Yes.*

And therefore, we believe what we're affected by, usually, don't we?

*Yes.*

And we do not believe that which doesn't affect us.

*Yes.*

And therefore, we find our self constantly crying for affection, something to affect us. Well, there's many ways to be affected, of course. And so when the forms are affected and it is not in keeping with their selfish desire, they register that as an irritation. And in that irritation the soul arises. Yes.

*Thank you.*

That help you with your question? The soul rises because no one wants to remain in love with that which is irritable. So you begin to pull back from the attachment of the things you have created. You don't love it quite as much. And when you don't love what you have created as much, your soul awakens. So irritation wakes the soul.

*Thank you.*

You see? As you're freed from the bondage of belief that you are what you have created. Hmm?

*Yes.*

You see, and in that respect, you don't have to be concerned about self-love because in time none exists. Irritation wakes the soul. So pray for irritation. Yes.

*Is all this irritation directed by the soul through the mind?*

Well, let us examine the demonstrable law: all experiences in our life are effects, effects of laws we alone have established. So we establish laws through which we may be irritated, when irritation awakens our little soul. Hmm? So we really should be grateful for irritation whenever it comes our way for we have called it forth and are freeing our self from the sleep of satisfaction. Hmm?

*For sure.*

You see?

*Yes, sir.*

You see, people have such great difficulty with change. They have difficulty for change. I can assure you, my good students, whoever is fully in love with themselves has great difficulties in making changes. Hmm? They hold tenaciously, for that which holds them is that which they have created and believe that they are through their love of that which they have created. Self-love is the love of that which you create. Yes, please.

*Yes, I was wondering, I know that we've been taught that the soul knows all before it enters the earth plane; it sees all. And therefore, it would know when its time is to depart from the earth realm. Is it through the light of reason that we can see that? Or how do we, how do we reach the ability—*

Well . . .

—*to see when our time is over?*

Well, you already have the ability. That already exists. That's part of the whole purpose of design. Because you do not see and are not aware is simply dependent upon believing that you are that which you have created. And so a person believing that they are that which they have created has limited their perspective, and they can only see a portion of the whole that they are. Yes.

*So there's—*

You already have the ability; that's a part of your evolution, a part of everyone's evolution.

*By—*

Because you don't express it is, is simply because there's an imbalance. And the faculties, that serve, are in service to the soul and to the Light, are not in balance. That's all. Yes.

Yes, *[The teacher calls the name of a student.]* has a question for us all here, and time has certainly passed. Go ahead. *[The teacher continues after a short pause.]* I would think quickly if I [were] you, considering that you're—you have a question on serving something that closes your eyes. Isn't that the question that you had?

*Yes.*

What do you know about it? Hmm?

*Very little.*

Well, express the little that you know. Express the little that you know. *[After a pause, the teacher continues.]* Did you choose to close your eyes? Did you make a conscious choice?

*No.*

Then something else did, didn't it?

*Yes.*

How else—I didn't close your eyes.

*True.*

No one else here closed your eyes. So something closed your eyes. Now I want you to tell us what closed your eyes. You said that you did not make a conscious choice to close your eyes. Something had to close your eyes. What closed them?

*Well, it would be a form.*

Which one?

*Ah...*

For you, because, you see, there's different forms for different people that close their eyes. There are forms that open the mouth; there are forms that close the mouth. There're forms that open the eyes; there are forms that close the eyes. Now which form closes your eyes? In your life experiences, which is the form that you service to close your eyes? Yes?

*I'm not sure.*

Well, time is passing. Try to be sure quickly, would you, please? You have ninety seconds.

Anyone else have a question while [he] is investigating the forms that come in and close his eyes when he doesn't make a conscious choice? I can assure you, my good students, when you do not make a conscious choice of what you're going to do and what happens in your life, then, in keeping with the Law of the Error of Ignorance, the things you have created and fallen in love with are controlling not only your body, your mind, but all of your experiences. Yes. The soulless creatures known as the demons. Yes. Yes.

*Being that this is the planet Earth and there are nine planets in the universe...*

Yes, in the solar system.

*The solar system.*

In that solar system, yes. The universes are filled with them.

*Yes.*

Yes.

*This being the fifth planet and being in the middle is pretty, ah, is, it would be pretty import—*

Oh, it's in the middle, is it?

*I'm, well, I'm—*

Oh, yes, that's all right. I just wanted to, perhaps—I don't think all of my students will agree with you.

*OK. Not being—*

Here's one that won't, either. But that's all right. That's only a matter of where it's located. Go ahead.

*OK. It's the fifth planet in the solar system.*

That is, that—yes.

*Yes.*

That is correct. It is the fifth planet.

*And we were—I—*

The number of faith, the purpose that you're here on this planet is to wake up to faith and free yourself from the bondage of belief. Yes, go ahead.

*Right.*

But, you know, in order to express faith, you know, you must have an awakened faculty of reason. The soul faculty of reason must be expressing itself in order to express faith. Yes.

*Yes.*

Yes. Faith in what you are. Yes. Because faith in what you are not is known as belief. Because that's what it is, you see. That's the difference, you see. You see, many people say, "Oh, I have faith in this and that." Many of the things they're in love with that they've created. That's not faith. That's belief. Yes, go ahead.

*I—I'll wait on this question.*

You want to wait 'til next month?

*No, sir. I just, it's, it's, it's a cre—*

Months pass very quickly in your world. But it's all right. We'll wait 'til next month.

*Yes, sir.*

You should write it down. Yes, now, [you] and then your ninety seconds are up. *[The teacher calls upon another student, and then addresses the student who is trying to identify the form that closed his eyes.]* Yes.

*Is there, then, an order in which the faculties should be developed in order to bring about—*

Oh, yes. Absolutely. Yes, I gave that many years ago. Many, many years ago. Just begin with duty, gratitude, and tolerance. And move to faith, poise, and humility. And if you'll work on those six, you won't have to worry about love; you'll be filled with divine Love. Hmm?

*Thank you.*

I can assure you of that. Duty, gratitude, and tolerance. Faith, poise, and humility. For you cannot have faith without poise and humility. Now, thank you.

And we'll conclude here our nice seminar this evening. As [he] wants to express to us what comes in and closes his eyes when he does not make a conscious, intelligent decision, "I wish my eyes now closed." Go ahead, please.

*A form of judgment.*

A form, a judgment. Thank you. That's so interesting. Which one? There's so many.

*Well, it is one particular one about the length of the class.*

Oh, how encouraging! Perhaps we could stay—how long is that tape? I do have extra tape downstairs. No, no problem at all. You might just have to go get it now. I always like to have forms order me around. I don't seem to act too well in that respect. Do you have a watch?

*Yes.*

Take it off and set it there where you can watch the dial move. Take it off, please. Now what time does this little thing say here—put it across the light there, so you can have an obstruction. See, it creates a shadow for you.

*It says eighteen after.*

Eighteen after.

*Yes.*

Eighteen minutes after. Do you notice, you see—what, of course—what is a shadow? That's all it is: an obstruction to what you are. That's all it is. That's all it ever can be. Hmm?

Now if I were to permit myself, after these, so many, many centuries, to come to a class and be controlled by anyone's forms, I would first have to allow myself to be controlled by my own. So I would first have to call up all of the shadows that I had created out of the eons of time in order to service [his] shadow, known as a judgment that the class is taking too long. So I will not sell out to that which I have spent eons to free myself from, because I would first have to do that in keeping with the law that we first grant unto ourselves whatever we grant unto another. So prepare yourself. Is your chair soft enough?

*Oh, yes.*

Do you have enough cushion on that chair? Perhaps we should have benches put at the table. Yes. Now if you don't have questions, I'll just sit here and talk to my little student right here. *[The teacher refers to the church's dog, Reddy.]* Yes.

*Since—*

That's enough. *[The teacher addresses Reddy.]*

*Duty, gratitude, and tolerance are the first three things that we should—*

Well—excuse me, but I certainly wouldn't call a soul faculty a "thing." I would call a function a thing, because it is designed for things. But faculties, no, I would not call them things. Yes, go right ahead.

*Since those—*

Functions are designed for things, and faculties are designed for principles. Hmm. There is a difference. See, things are personalities, you see. Go ahead.

*Since those are the first three faculties, could you, would you give a definition of what duty is and what it encompasses?*

Well, I gave that explanation years and years ago on your planet. Duty: duty to what you are. And grateful for the ability to serve it. And tolerance for all the forms you create that insist on standing in the way and tempt you. Yes. [Does] that help you?

*Yes. Thank you.*

You're welcome.

*Yes. OK. We—the purpose of our design—OK. We are evolving forms. I mean, we are—*

Well, you are the Light.

*Right.*

Responsible for the evolution of what you create. Yes, yes.

*OK. Of what we create.*

You are not an evolving form unless you appreciate slavery and bondage.

*Yes, sir.*

Now if you like slavery and bondage, then you can be an evolving form, yes.

*OK. All right. Other forms, other than the ones that we create, attach to us sometimes.*

Yes, like attracts like.

*Right.*

Yes.

*OK. As we, as we evolve our forms, do those forms become evolved or do they leave us? Are we only here to evolve the forms that we create?*

It's just like a child. They either do what you tell them in your house or they soon find a new one. Correct?

*Right.*

They're a form, too, you see.

*Right.*

Now do you understand? Either they do what they're designed to do . . .

*Yes.*

You understand that?

*Right.*

Or they go. Like attracts like and becomes the Law of Attachment. If you are truly making the effort, that which you have created shall, once again, serve in keeping with the purpose of its design. Do you understand? And it will take orders from you for you are the father of it, or it will leave your universe. Do you understand that?

*Yes.*

You see? You see, you see, it's just like sitting here at the table. Here I have this real sleepy thing descending down over me. I'm very well aware of it. And I'm so well aware of it, I could go on for another three and a half hours for this special seminar and have to go down and get a new tape there, another two-hour tape in there [in the videotape recorder]. But, you see, you must take control of your mind. Because when you refrain from doing so, something else controls it. Hmm?

*Yes, sir.*

Now, you see, here, here is *[The teacher names a student.]* tonight there. You see, through a declaration of the truth, the affirmations, and the spiritual exercises, you understand?

*Yes, sir.*

Then he would not have come to the table in such a love affair with himself. Because you cannot be controlled by these forms until you direct your energy and your attention to the love of yourself, which is, in truth, that which you have created. The love of self is the love of those things that you create, you see. Hmm?

*Yes, sir.*

So it is encouraging when a person stands up and separates truth from creation, you see, and experiences the goodness that it has to offer.

Now I'm going to leave you in a few moments here now, and I'm going to give you, as my students, the opportunity for a democratic vote that if you would like to have your future seminars without chairs or benches (that means you would stand), and if you would rather continue to sit at your seminars and your classes, then you will do your part in helping the soul of one of your co-students. And should you not care to do your part in helping his soul, then I can assure you—I don't want to take this off yet; promised myself to stop doing that *[The teacher refers to his microphone.]*—I can assure you that we will have stand-up classes. And won't that be nice. We won't have to worry about getting sleepy, then, I don't think.

Thank you very much and good evening.

APRIL 10, 1986

## A/V Seminar 13

Good evening, students.

This evening and this moment marks the end of what you've known as public seminars. However, in keeping with demonstrable law of our teachings, the ending of anything is, in truth, the beginning of something. And so this evening is also a beginning: It is the beginning of our monthly private seminars.

What does that mean? That means that all students shall be required to have notebook and pens. Is there any student who doesn't have [those]? Fine. It also means that private students in private seminars not only are required to have note[book] and pen, they are also required to do their homework. It also means [a] regular monthly attendance commitment. It also means if, for honest work, one is unable to attend their spiritual commitment, their material commitment applies, their spiritual commitment applies in the sense that their thoughts are in consideration on the class that is given at that particular time. It also means that all private students are required to have either an audio or videotape of the private class. It also means that no one but the student in class shall hear or view the tapes available.

*[At a membership meeting that was held at the temple on January 19, 1983, Mr. Goodwin provided guidance on the publication of these teachings. He said, "It is my responsibility to now share with you the sincere wish, desire of the founders of your temple of Light, Serenity, that upon my demise from your physical world that it be disbanded, that all assets be converted to cash, that all teachings revealed unto you, including after my departure [from Earth], the higher teachings of the initiates be printed and distributed throughout the land of flesh, throughout the Earth planet."]*

If there are any questions on that, please raise your hand, so we can go on with our class, our private class, this evening. No questions? Fine.

I will give you an example of what is required by your homework by asking a simple question. The question is, How did the angel Lucifer fall from grace and become the king of the shadowland? The answer is one word. Kindly mark it down on your notes. Raise your hand as soon as you have done so, and I will call upon you. Remember, it is one word.

*[After a short pause, the teacher begins to call on students.]*

[Yes], please. *[When the teacher calls upon a student by name, the name will often be replaced with "[Yes]".]*

*Self.*

Thank you. [Yes], please.

*Denial.*

Thank you. [Yes], please.

*Self.*

Thank you. Yes, please.

*Separation.*

Thank you.

*Judgment.*

Thank you.

*Judgment.*

Thank you. *[After a short pause, the teacher continues.]* I have no other answers from my students? Yes.

*Denial.*

Thank you.

*Pride.*

Thank you.

*Judgment.*

Thank you.

*I put down "belief."*

Thank you.

*Limit.*

Thank you.

*I put down "denial."*

Thank you. Some of my students are still waiting. [Yes], please.

*Need.*

Thank you. Some of my students are waiting to answer.

*Denial.*

Thank you.

*Identification.*

Thank you.

The question is based upon the teachings that you have already received. And the answer, the one word that was the cause of the fall of the angel Lucifer into the realm in which he became the king of the shadowland is *belief*. One word: belief. From belief, all of the answers that you have given mushroom.

So Lucifer, the angel, viewing the many forms of so-called creation, first had to believe that he, too, was form and, in that belief, bound himself to the shadowland.

Are there any questions? Is there anyone who feels they do not understand? Many answers were given: pride, judgment, self, denial, and they all are the children of belief. And that is why belief is bondage. For belief is based upon, what? What is the one word that belief is dependent upon?

*Limit.*

Thank you.

*Experience.*

Thank you. How does one get experience?

*Limit.*

Thank you. Now what was the question? Yes.

*Judgment.*

Thank you. What was the question that I asked you?

*What is belief based upon?*

What is belief based upon?

*And I was thinking judgment.*

But how do you get to judgment? Can one judge anything without what?

*Over-identification.*

Thank you.

*Thought.*

Thank you.

*Denial.*

Thank you. Comparison! How can you have judgment without comparison? You cannot judge anything until you believe in limit. And believing in limit or form, there is no way possible to judge unless you have something to compare it with. Therefore, without comparison, there cannot be judgment. Without judgment, you cannot establish the Law of Denial, which, of course, becomes your destiny. Therefore, everyone's experiences in form, limit, or creation is dependent upon what? One word.

*Belief.*

Well, now that's the trunk of the tree. And we've been talking for a few moments about the limbs. Thank you. Yes.

*Experience.*

What was the question that I asked?

*You asked . . .*

What was the question that I just asked? Sixty seconds have yet to pass. Yes.

*Everyone's experiences in form are . . . no. Therefore, everyone's experiences in form, limit, or creation is dependent upon what?*

And what is it dependent upon? What are all of your experiences dependent upon? That's the question. All of your experiences in what you believe is life, creation, form, and limit, all of your experiences are dependent upon judgment. The judgment that you make and, therefore, are the servant of.

Truth is simple and unconcealed. It does not take many words. Many words are necessary until one awakens that they express through eighty-one levels of consciousness and must concentrate to maintain on one of light and reason.

So now we've stepped through from belief, through comparison, through judgment to experience.

Who controls the mental world?

*Lucifer.*

Is everyone in agreement?

*Yes.* [Two different students respond.]

Who sustains the mental world?

*God.*

Indeed!

*Could you repeat that, please?*

Who sustains the mental world? We all know who expresses and manipulates the mental world. The question, however, is, Who sustains it? The answer is God, Truth, Light.

When you are—when you believe what you create, you do so at the expense of placing what you truly are into what?

*When you believe what you create, you . . .*

When you believe you are what you create, you place what you are where? Under who's control?

*Into the realm of belief or into the lower realm, under the control of Lucifer.*

Into bondage.

*Bondage, yes. Limit.*

Then the question is, How do you live without belief? [Yes.]

*Faith.*

Faith. [Yes.]

*Well, if one does not have belief, then one does not live in this realm, in this physical form.*

So what is the answer? How do you live, as you know life, without belief? *[After a short pause, the teacher continues.]* Where are my students? Yes.

*By separating truth from creation.*

Which is which?

*Truth is God and creation is belief. Truth is faith in God. Creation is belief.*

So how do you know the difference? How does one know the difference between belief and faith, truth and creation? How does one know the difference? Does one know the difference? Is it possible to know the difference between truth and creation?

*Yes.*

It is? Thank you. Yes.

*You have to get to the light of reason to differentiate.*

My students have not been doing their homework. To those of you who are interested in continuing with monthly private seminars, this is only a sampling of your requirement, of one of your many requirements. Do your homework.

Is knowledge a function or a faculty?

*It's a function.*

It is a function. Thank you. Is wisdom a function or a faculty?

*It's a faculty.*

Indeed! So now, we all agree—or do we all agree?—that knowledge knows much; wisdom knows better. There is a difference between knowledge and wisdom. What is the difference between knowledge and wisdom?

*With knowledge, you have experience, and with wisdom, it comes from a higher source.*

That is truth. Wisdom is what you are. Knowledge is what you believe that you are. For knowledge is based upon experience. And what is indispensable to experience?

*Judgment.*

And how, and how do you get judgment?

*Comparison.*

From comparison. And how can you have comparison?

*Belief.*

From belief.

You see, I know that all of you students, even my monthly seminar students, have had the teachings. I am not asking you any questions that you do not know beyond a shadow of any doubt, beyond a shadow of any doubt the answer. For you have received the answer in so many different ways, yes. Now I'm not going to hand out diplomas nor certificates, nor any type of that foolishness. That's Lucifer's department. I'm not interested in that. Because then you will be tempted: tempted to believe something and, in so doing, at the sacrifice of what you are. Hmm?

One takes pride in what they believe they have accomplished and, in so doing, must pay the price. The price is far beyond the mental world of which most people upon the earth realm are quite familiar. Hmm? Yes. Yes, you had something to say.

*No.*

You have forgot it already. You had an answer to my question and you let it go by.

*I'm sorry, I just . . .*

Whatever is important, is important. And try to understand, ofttimes when we have a question and we judge that we did not have the opportunity to answer [ask] it when the question was in our mind, is how we censor our self. So the next time you have a question, hold your hand up or put a little, a little brace there. Keep it up there until your turn comes. Hmm?

*Yes, sir.*

All right. Now, a little homework. Just a little homework.

Well, we'll go on to another step here now. I expect you to have these answers and because I don't expect to keep giving them to you when they don't seem to somehow register. Oh, I know they've registered. So therefore, you make the effort to get into the realm of consciousness on which you receive them in order that you can answer, for you've already received all of the teachings, yes. Yes, now you have your question.

*Yes. I would—*

Glad you got it back.

*I am interested in the answer to the question you asked of, Can you live in the world without belief?*

I'd be interested, too. There's the question: Can you live in the world as you know it without belief? Can you?

*I don't think so.*

Can you? *[The teacher addresses another student.]*

*I don't think so. I think without belief, there is no form.*

Ah, there is no form for you to manipulate. Correct! Can you live in your world without belief? Only for a short time. Short times. In your meditation whenever you go beyond what you have created as a self, in those moments you're not aware. You're not aware of the world of bondage and belief. Depending on your efforts and abilities—and you all have the ability; therefore, it's dependent upon your effort: how long you can live in a world of form without belief.

Now, can you move the form when you're free from belief that you are it?

*When you're free from the belief that you're it, yes.*

And, for how long?

*For the times that you're free from belief.*

Correct. But if you remain free from belief, free from identification with limit, for [an] extended period of time, you will find you do so until limit and form does not exist for you. So often—some time ago I spoke to many of you on this so-called death. Go beyond the bondage of believing that there's some type of a book somewhere in the universe on which the date has been set for you to remain in limit and in form. For many souls leave your physical world and they're still in limit and still in form. Sometimes it's eons. Sometimes it's centuries. And sometimes it's a very short time indeed. That, of course, is dependent on what they've done with the lessons they've entered form or limit to learn.

So when you find yourself thinking of what has been, wanting to change what you have created, as you've moved in your evolution beyond that, remember, you just bind yourself deeper, of course, in consciousness and make it more difficult for you.

You see, when we refuse to learn the lessons that we have to learn ever in keeping with the ones that we have, well, as you would say, flunked before, failed, refused to learn before, when we do that, then we repeat them. Again. And again. And again.

Now if you want to know what lessons you have to learn while you are in limit and form, become aware, make a little effort—it doesn't take very much—make a little effort of the things, the forms, limits, experiences you call them, that you refuse to let go of. That will tell you the lessons that you have flunked in your evolution. And if you find it extremely difficult to let go of the things you have created, what you call experiences, then you can be rest assured that you flunked that lesson in evolution many, many, many, many, many, many times. And so each time you flunk it, each time you refuse to let go of what you have created—remembering, in a mental world, that you create ever in keeping with your denials of what you are. That, of course, is how denial establishes the Law of Destiny.

And so you create something with your mental world. You create various limits to serve a purpose for you. And when that purpose has been served for the lesson that you had to learn in evolution and you refuse to let that which you have created to go, you refuse to let it go, you transgress the law of the true purpose of the design for which you have created the experience and, in so doing, bind yourself on what some of your philosophies in your world tell you as the karmic wheel. I've never ever heard the karmic wheel [called] a wheel of evolution. A wheel spins round and round and round and round.

So, my friends, you know the way. There's no problem there. It's like saying, "Well, perhaps this one and this experience that I'm creating will be different." Well, you always get to learn how different it really is. Time passes and you see; you start to compare with all the ones you've created before. [You] say, "There's quite a similarity here. Oh, my! History, my history, is once again repeating itself!" Why, of course, it is repeating itself because you never let it go. You did not use wisdom to see clearly that you have created it for a purpose.

Now let us move on here in our evolution and let us go in your world back to the late '60s. You received your textbook [*The Living Light*]. Because some of you, my newer students here, have a tendency to think and believe that everything is created by the mind. Well, of course we know better than that. "The soul can and does all things create." The soul! For the soul, you understand, is the covering. The individualized soul is the covering of the formless, free Spirit. "The soul can and does all things create." It's stated very clearly in your textbook. It can and does all things create in keeping with the Law of Evolution, in keeping with the repetition of the lesson until you serve the purpose of its design.

Let us ne'er forget, the angel who fell from the right hand of God, Lucifer, took form. God is not form. God expresses through all form for God is the sustaining, intelligent, infinite Energy. Gods of form are those of belief. God is not a form. God cannot be a form. God sustains all form. God is formless, free Spirit. Lucifer is form. Lucifer is limit. Lucifer gives and takes—and takes much more than he ever gives. God does not give. God does not take. God is a sustaining, intelligent Energy. God is not a sex, for God is not a form. Lucifer is a sex. Lucifer is a form.

Choose wisely what you identify with for you establish the law to become it. Choose wisely what you are adverse to for you guarantee it. You have directed intelligent energy flowing through you to create the very form that, by the law governing the functions of limit, known as fear, it shall befall you.

Fear is a great magnet. From what center of consciousness does it express? Earth, fire, water, air, electric, magnetic, odic, ethereal. Hmm? Celestial. From which center of consciousness does it express? You had the answer, did you?

*I guess water.*

You don't have to think about demonstrable truth. It is demonstrable. Why is it the water center? Other students, other hands.

*That's where form is created.*

And how is it created in the water center? *[The teacher calls upon a different student.]*

*Emotions and thoughts together.*

Emotions and thoughts. Thank you. [Yes.]

*Through solidified judgments.*

Through solidified judgments. Anyone else?

*They're created through belief.*

Do you believe when you are in the air center?

*No.*

Do you believe reason?

*No, I have faith with reason.*

Why can't you believe reason?

*Because reason is limitless. It is. It just is.*

Thank you. Do you have some answers? *[The teacher addresses another student.]*

*Why, I agree with what he just said.*

I see.

*And . . .*

Yes? You've been a student for many, many years.

*Well, reason is a faculty and faculties aren't ruled by belief.*

How right you are! Reason is a faculty of the soul. By keeping faith with reason, what happens?

*She will transfigure thee.*

That's right. In what center of consciousness are emotionally immature humans expressing? In what center of consciousness?

*The water center.*

The water center. Why is it the water center? It is the center in which all what are created?

*Judgments.*

All judgments are created. A god of form appeals to what center of consciousness? *[The teacher speaks the name of a student.]* A god of form appeals to what center of consciousness?
*Form—more than likely the fire center.*
Thank you. Anyone else?
*The water center.*
Thank you. Why is it the water center?
*Well, all forms are created in the water center.*
All forms are created in the water center. A god of form demands what from you? *[After a pause, the teacher continues.]* Students, this is not a new class. [Yes.]
*Payment.*
Payment. What precedes payment? Yes.
*Temptation.*
Temptation! What did Eve do to Adam?
*Tempted.*
How did Eve tempt Adam?
*Symbolically, you mean?*
*[The teacher laughs.]* [Another student] has an answer.
*By appealing to his desires?*
Thank you. [Yes.]
*By offering to him what she had first offered to herself.*
Thank you. Eve tempted Adam by promising to return unto Adam what she had stolen from him. And what had she stolen, like a thief in the night, from Adam? Hmm? What did Eve steal from Adam?
*Knowledge?*
Thank you. What did Eve steal from Adam? Surely, you've all read the Bible. Yes.
*A rib.*
She stole his rib and tempted him by returning what she had stolen. Did Adam believe that he was incomplete?
*Yes.*
Why did he believe he was incomplete?

*As a part of himself was taken to create Eve.*

That's right. He knew beyond a shadow of any doubt that he had a missing rib. Now tell me something, what happens to a ship that has a missing rib?

*It's greatly weakened.*

That is correct. It is greatly weakened. What purpose does the rib serve to a sail ship?

*Stability and strength.*

Stability and strength. My, students. My! In what center of consciousness must Adam have identified with in order to be aware that he was missing a rib?

*The water center.*

Correct! The water center. The rib, the symbol of stability, strength. And what is stability and strength? What is stability and strength? What is the one word that expresses best stability and strength? Yes.

*Character.*

No. *[The teacher addresses another student.]* Yes.

*Security.*

Security. Security. And so the Adams of your world chase the universes seeking security, the rib that they believe they are missing. Unfortunately, yet spiritually, so beautiful, the rib they find doesn't fit for long. The rib tries to adjust, and the little ship tries to adjust to the rib. It just doesn't work. For Adam had to believe he had to enter the water center of consciousness. Earth, fire, water. The center, the triune function controlling limit. He had to believe. And when he believed, he lost what he is. He lost the Light for the lesser light.

And when one sees in the lesser light, one does not see as clearly, for one sees forms where forms do not exist, for one sees obstructions to the Light. That is what the lesser light offers, for it is an obstruction to the true Light that you are. So whoever sees in the lesser light shall ever be incomplete, ever seeking fulfillment and yet not fulfilled for their cup overfloweth.

You cannot be what you are not. Therefore, denial of what you are is a thirst that cannot be quenched.

Whoever denies what they are shall experience what they are not, and your world calls that frustration.

And, my good students, let us not forget a titanic ego is ever in need. For a titanic ego, in that respect, is one greatly lacking education. Attachment to the fruits of action reveal a titanic, uneducated ego. Lucifer has great pride: he believes he is perfect. He still believes that he was able to con the very Power that sustains him.

Time passes so quickly, my friends—are there any questions?—time in your world. Yes.

*Why is Lucifer expressed in the masculine?*

Lucifer is expressed in the masculine or positive vibration for it is the water center, the magnet, that ever seeks the electric. And therefore, it is only when one is in the water center, in the magnetic vibratory wave of expression, that one is the victim of the forms they create. Does that help with your question?

*Yes, sir.*

Yes. Yes.

*Why did Eve steal the rib?*

Eve stole the rib—now try to understand your, your teachings of Adam and Eve, allegorical as they are, and so totally changed from the falsifying hands of the copyists, is an ancient story, long before your Bible was ever brought into being. Try to understand that Eve was the effect or the creation of Adam's denial. And if you will work on that for these coming weeks in preparation for your homework for your next private seminar here, next month, then you'll have your answers or certainly have questions very clearly stated. Hmm?

And I did want to try to get a few things else in this [class, but], you know, you're in a world of form. I've entered your world of form so I must abide by the laws that govern it. Those laws are known as the laws of limit. You have a little thing that keeps tick, tick, ticking. That, you call time. That's the name you give of that illusion that you create.

But I want to leave you with one parting thing; time has passed on us here in your world. Remember this: he who lives to hurt another shall live to see the day when all his selfish motives pain shall take away. So when you experience what you judge as pain, remember, it is an effect of laws you have set into motion. You are not without hope, for that is eternal. You are truth. You are freedom. You are the fullness of life for you are the goodness of life. And therefore, when you permit your mind to tell you that you need this, [that] you need that, you permit your mind to offer to you the opposite of the Law of Peace and Goodness, which is harmony, you permit your mind to grant unto you discord and all of those disturbing things and leave you frustrated, remember, it is what is offered to all of us. When we deny what we are, we must pay (and we do pay dearly) for what we are not.

Thank you very much, my good students. And please remember your homework. Good night.

MAY 8, 1986

## A/V Seminar 14

Good evening, class.

Let us begin this evening's class with the questions and understanding of the homework that you have received. So let us raise our hands in that respect.

*Thank you. In following last semester's class, in which you were discussing the steps from belief to, to experience, my question is, For one to change one's belief, would one have to go back that same way, right to the initial belief?*

No, that is not necessary. It is not necessary in order to change one's belief in anything to return to the experiences, which are the effects, of course, of the judgments made, to move from the bondage of that particular belief. For example, a person believes that their life is happy; it is joyous in keeping with certain experiences that they have. And when they don't have those experiences, they then believe that they are unhappy, that they are miserable. And remember that a person can only believe that they are unhappy and miserable and not getting what they want in life by a dependence on something that is beyond their own control. For example, if you will examine all beliefs, you will find that they are dependent upon what someone else does or does not do. A person may decide that they want to become a professional in some particular interest that they have; and with that belief, they accept and make the judgment that they shall become such and such in keeping with what someone else does. And they call that opportunity.

Now opportunity is something that we create. It's something that *we* create. We create our opportunities. And unfortunately, we ofttimes—and many of us still—believe that opportunity is something that happens by chance. They had a lucky day or an unlucky day. Someone crossed their path, and they experience what they understand as an opportunity. Now opportunity is something that we alone create. When we understand that we create opportunity, then we will begin to free our self from the dependence on what something or someone, that by divine law we cannot control, does or doesn't do. That help with your question?

*Thank you.*

Yes, you had a question, please.

*How do we create our opportunities?*

We create our opportunities as effects of our judgments. For example, we make a judgment of this is what we'd like and that is what we'd like. And we're speaking now, of course, of a mental world. So our mind goes to work to establish the necessary experiences so that we may create what we understand as an opportunity to fulfill the judgment that we have made. Do you understand that?

*Yes, sir.*

So, you see, a person says, "Well, I would like to have more money." Well, what happens when they make that statement, they come up against the judgments that are stronger in their inner mind that have already told them that they will never have enough, you see. And so they have created that opportunity, yes.

Do you have a question?

*No, sir.*

As long as it's not a personal, domestic one. *[The teacher laughs joyfully.]* All right. Fine. Very fine class this evening. Nice and short. No other questions? Yes.

*Then, to clarify, an opportunity is an experience which we have created for ourselves, which is a positive and therefore desirable experience, as opposed to an undesirable experience.*

Well, no, it can be either positive or negative. Of course, it depends on how you look at it. For example, say that a man has created the opportunity to experience the lack of sufficient funds in his life, all right? Now he's created that opportunity. So then he tries to create another opportunity to have sufficient funds. So dependent upon how much he believes that he is this process that does the creating, he has that much difficulty in creating an opposite experience. Does that help you?

So, you see, when a person, ofttimes when they're young and they have, they have this desire that they'd like to have more and more and more, and there's never enough, and they have created that. They have formed that judgment. Do you, do you follow that? All right, now, they get a little older and they have varying experiences. And then their mind tells them, "Well, this one has that, and that one has that," because they begin to look outside. And when they do, of course, they become more dependent outside, you see. And they take a look and say, "Well, now I have a right to have more." And so they start talking to themselves about *their* right to have more. And when they do that, they come up against the judgment they have created, early in their life, that says that's all they [have] got and that's all they're going to get. Do you understand that? And so, dependent upon how much they believe they are—you understand?—the forms they have created, of course, is dependent on their struggle in creating new forms that are different, you see.

Try to understand that when you create a thought, an attitude of mind, you do it with the breath of life. This is why I teach you that no new thought, no thought may enter your consciousness when your breath is held, for the breath of life is absolutely indispensable to the creating processes of the human mind. In other words, the created form in a mental world requires oxygen—do you understand that?—in order for the form to be created. So when the breath is properly held, no new form can enter the consciousness; no other form can enter. This is why, in proper meditation, you've created a form, you see. A person, they think of "peace." Well, while they're in a mental world, then peace is a certain form they have created in their mind. Do you understand that? And so when they hold their breath in this form they have created, which you understand in a mental world is peace, no other form enters, you see. The form that they are holding cannot leave and no form can enter. Hmm?

So when you have a thought, remember, it is absolutely dependent upon the breath of life for its survival and, of course, for its movement. Now when man understands and demonstrates the control of the forms is subject to the control of the breath of life, then he will be well on the way to using creation instead of abusing it. Hmm? Does that help with understanding there a bit? Yes.

*Yes, with the meditation, when we breathe in, are we creating the forms at that time because we're taking oxygen in?*

You are feeding either forms that you are holding in consciousness or you, also—because so few people do control their mind, they are feeding new, created forms that they're bringing in. Yes.

*And then at the pause, there's no form. It stops them in their tracks?*

Well, when you inhale the breath, you should be very awake, aware, and alert to what form you are directing this life force to, you see? You see, with the several centers of consciousness, there are forms you've already created in those centers of consciousness. So the first thing is to be aware of what center of consciousness you are in, on what level, for in that center of consciousness are various forms that have already been created. Hmm?

*And then, when we breathe out—now they're not getting oxygen when we breathe out, so what happens to them—*

Oh, they're not?

Well . . .

They're receiving the oxygen as you are inhaling. And when you exhale, what do they move out with? The oxygen that you took in.

*Well, they move out on the exhale.*

Yes. Yes, they go out to do their job on the exhale. Oh, yes, yes, yes, indeed.

*Thank you.*

Yes. You send them out. As you bring them in, and then, you send them out, you see. Hmm? So this is happening all the time, although people are not consciously aware of it. It goes on all of the time. All of the time. Each and every moment of your [life], it's happening. It's happening while you think you're asleep. It happens when you think you're awake. And this is why I've taught over these years, "Dreamer, dream a life of beauty before your dream starts dreaming you." So if you send out beautiful forms, they, of course, in keeping with the law, do beautiful work, and they return that unto you. And you call that experience. Hmm?

*Thank you.*

Yes. Yes.

*Yes, when we have inspiration . . .*

Inspiration, yes. Do we know the difference in a mental world? But go ahead, please, with your question.

*That's what I was going to ask. When you were speaking of opportunity created by the forms in a mental realm, and from the soul we have inspiration.*

Yes?

*I would like to know how the inspiration, if it's—*

May I say this? I think, perhaps, we might be able to answer your question. Inspiration, to that which you are, is perspiration to that which you are not. Does that help with the question?

*Yes.*

Yes.

*Thank you.*

Do what you don't want to do so you may awaken to who you are. And by doing what your mind tells you it doesn't want to do, your mind understands that as perspiration. "I don't want to do that, but I have a responsibility. And I know the law: personal responsibility." You see, you have an opportunity, and in the opportunity—which I have stated is something that you have created. Now because you have created it, you have a responsibility to it inside of yourself. So, for example, take a lady, she gets married. She created the opportunity to get married. Now she has a responsibility to that which she has created in her own consciousness. You see?

*Yes.*

Now if she takes and hands her responsibility or tempts to hand her responsibility or, more properly, to dump her responsibility on to someone else, then she is denying the very thing that she has created; and in so doing she is destined to the experience. See, our destiny is the effect of our own denials.

*Thanks.*

Our adversities indeed become our attachments. Yes.

*Thank you.*

See, each person creates their own experiences. Hmm?

*Yes.*

And when we awaken to that responsibility, to what we really are doing, you see—we are creating all experiences. Every experience we encounter we have created. We do not often appreciate the experience. The reason we don't appreciate it [is] because we know deep inside of our self we have created it. And we are upset and ofttimes angry that we have created such a foolish experience, you see. We don't appreciate that; yet we created it. And because we did create it and because the law does not fail and we know inside of our self that we have created it, but we created it on a level of consciousness that we are not presently on when the experience returns unto us, you see.

*Yes.*

See, see, we always get what we really want. The question must be asked: What do we really want? Because, you see, when the experience returns, when these forms we have created return unto us, in keeping with the law, oh, we don't like it ofttimes. We don't like it at all. Yet we are getting what we wanted in that moment of weakness, temptation, and ignorance. Oh, yes, we're getting what we wanted. But we did not make the effort to go through the various centers of consciousness to bring about some agreement and accord with all the other forms that we have created. You see?

*Yes.*

So when we say, "Oh, I've had such a miserable day. That person's just been terrible," we can say, "Now just a moment. Now I want to go to that center of consciousness and to that level on which I have created this. For this is only an experience, an effect of what I've created. This is returning unto me. This is my opportunity." Hmm?

This is why a person, you see, has all this indecision. You see, they move from one level to another level of consciousness. And one level says, "Yes, go ahead." Another level comes up immediately and says, "No, don't do that. You'll be very foolish. Oh, my! Don't get into such a mess." That shows an absolute lack of control of the forms we alone have created. Hmm? Yes. And we call that indecision, which, of course, its inevitable path is confusion. And then we're even tempted to believe that we're that. Hmm?

Beautiful, beautiful. Yes. Yes.

*In order to, to bring about the opportunity that we would like to have, but our forms that are always preventing us have told us that it's not the way it is, that that's not possible . . .*

Yes? Yes?

*Constant repetition of an affirmation including what you want, is that . . .*

No, that's effect. Anything that you can find that will help you to stop thinking of yourself will free you.

*Oh!*

For the bondage is in the over-identification with the belief that you are the form. And by believing you are the form—and it is form that creates form. God is not a creator. God is formless and free. You, that which you are, is not the creator; that which you believe you are is the creator. You see? So whatever you have found or can find—and you have plenty to use, you're not without tools—that will assist you in keeping with the laws you have established to help you refrain from thinking about yourself, then you will experience a life—the way life is. Not the way we believe it is, the way it truly is.

*Thank you.*

You're welcome. Yes.

*When we're doing our affirmations during the course of the day . . .*

Yes?

*And we find ourselves not in a positive level . . .*

Yes?

*And we really don't feel like doing the affirmations, yet we force our self to do it anyway. We find our self saying that affirmation by rote, just trying to remember to keep it in sequence in one level. But yet wallowing in that lower level of consciousness—*

Yes?

*About 90 percent, roughly.*

Yes.

*Is that—A: Is that beneficial? And B: What can we do to, to, to place the 90 percent on the affirmation and 10 percent on the level?*

Fine. I—yes. First of all, you're dealing with the law, of course, of—repetition is the law through which change is made possible. Even though it is rote—that means it's coming from the mental or the air center and the problem lies in the water center, for it is the water center forms that are working so diligently for you to feed them and make them stronger—even though, from the, from the water—from the air center, which is the mental consciousness, 90 percent of it is coming from it—it's not coming from the heart, for the water center is flooding the consciousness, is what it is—continue on with the repetition and accept [and] declare the truth: "Thank you. This is not what I am. And I am not going to waste my energy in this upset for this is not what I am. And I have no intention to continue to feed what I am not. I spent enough years doing that. I have more important things to take care of." Then distract the consciousness. You see, that's the time to put on something, some beautiful music or something you like because, you see, that will help and assist you, though you continue on with the affirmations. It is important to have some beautiful music, something that you really like, because what will happen: those forms will rise up, which will be more beneficial and in keeping with your effort to free yourself from those other forms that are demanding that they have energy. Does that help you?

*Yes, sir.*

You see, you see, put on something that you like. That's important. This is why it is very important in affirmations to have the proper music, you see. That's very, very important. Affirmations are most beneficial when they are, what do you call in your world, subliminal with music that you truly like. Hmm? That's when they have their greatest effect, you see. That's when they're able to slip through and bypass so much of that censorship, you know, in the water center. Yes.

*While we're in this 10 percent affirmation and 90 percent water center . . .*

Yes.

*And we're verbalizing that affirmation even though it's by rote . . .*

Yes.

*Are we still creating a positive form?*

Oh, yes. Absolutely. But they are created in the air center, you see. You, you must realize that. They are definitely being created in the air center for the water center is blocked with the battle that's going on for they want energy. And what they are, they're furious that you are sending forth the life-giving energy of the spoken word to the air center when they're down there starving, or at least they believe they're starving. Hmm? Do you understand that? That's very important.

*Yes, sir.*

Yes, yes, definitely.

*So one should verbalize as, whenever possible.*

One should verbalize whenever possible. As I say, in time it will get through. It's like a drop of water on a, on a, a concrete slab. Sooner or later it's going to get through, you see. Sooner or later it will get through.

And the thing is, if you battle with those forms, what you are doing is you're battling with yourself. Because, you see, they can only have expression in your consciousness by belief that you are form. You see? And so when you battle them, you're battling yourself in keeping with how much you believe you are the form, you see. You see, you take a person, for example, if they, if they make the effort, through the years of meditation, concentration, meditation, contemplation, then it doesn't matter what happens to their physical body for they do not experience any effect upon their physical body for they have made the effort to free themselves in consciousness from their physical body. It's like taking off your shoe. Now if someone, after you've taken your shoe off, hits it with a sledge hammer, you do not feel anything, for the shoe has been removed. Now if you witness that happening, you may not appreciate it and you will immediately get back into the shoe. Do you understand that?

So, you see, when you take off your, your suit of clay—you see, most people believe they take off their suit of clay at the time of, of so-called death. No, no, no, no. You take off your suit of clay many times because you leave many times your suit of clay. But what realm do you enter? Does it bind you when you return more to your little suit? Or does it free you more from your little suit, you see?

The classes are designed to help to free you from the little suit and, yet, remain in keeping with the law of responsibility to that which you have earned in evolution, you see. You're evolving. Your lessons in evolution are the very thing that—your passing them or not passing them are the very thing indispensable to the creating of your form, you see. You see, this foolishness that some God somewhere has created your form is, is, is ridiculous. It's absolutely ridiculous. Your form is an effect of the various nature spirits brought together in keeping with divine laws, in keeping with the lessons that you have passed or have not passed. So therefore, you have so much height. You, you, you're a certain complexion and etc. For your house, your vehicle tells you, like a book, your entire evolution, you see. Your entire evolution. Yes. As it does everyone. All you must do is learn to read it. But, you see, you cannot read a book as long as you believe you are the book. So as long as you believe you are the suit, you cannot analyze and examine it, you see. You can't. You cannot be objective with that which you believe that you are. It's not possible. Because you lack the demonstration of the Law of Disassociation.

So the place to really work is on this belief that you are this limited form. For it is only belief. It is an illusion that has been created. Hmm? The more you believe you are the form, the more you'll suffer in all eternity, for flesh and bones is only the form of your planet. And when you leave flesh and bones, of course, you have your other forms inside the flesh and bones. So the more you believe that you are form, the more you're destined to suffer. For it is through the process of suffering that the soul is freed, you see. The shell must, must crack in order for the, the angel to fly. Hmm? Yes.

*It's the tendency of a, for people to identify. Would it be in our best interest to identify with one of our, say, the celestial body or . . .*

Oh, absolutely. Definitely. You see, feeling good is a necessity; it certainly is not a luxury, for feeling good is an expression of the Divinity, which everyone is. And so it is a person's, not only their responsibility but it is [an] absolute necessity while visiting creation or form. However, the great trap they have created, the mind, the mental world, is the judgments, the forms they have created: "I feel good when I have this. I feel bad when I do not have that." That makes them dependent upon the forms, you see. That's the terrible trap.

One feels good when one chooses to free themselves from the illusion that they are limit and form. Now say that a person has a desire. They have a desire to go here or to go there. The moment they free themselves from their form, they are unrestricted—fly anywhere and have all the experiences without all of the suffering and the cost and expense, you see? But as long as they insist on believing that they are form, then they must carry this heavy—which it really is; the form is a very heavy weight—they must carry that to whatever they want to experience, ever in keeping with their belief, you see. That's because they insist on being in creation and being a part of creation. And that is the payment that they must make.

You don't need to move the form anywhere to experience everything. Hmm? But if you believe you are the form, you believe it, then you are bound by it. It is only the belief that binds you. Nothing else binds you. There are no laws that bind you; only that one law that man alone establishes for he has absolutely convinced himself. Hmm?

Now when you say you go to sleep at night and sometimes you have a dream. It's a beautiful dream; you wake up [and] you feel wonderful. There are those rare occasions. I say rare because with many people they are rare. Well, what happened? Then, the mind, controlled by belief, says, "Well, that was only a dream!" I tell you, you are dreaming in order to be bound by the forms in which you believe that you are. That is—that's not just a dream; to me, it's a nightmare. *[A few students laugh.]* It is a nightmare. It is a nightmare for by believing in one's own form, then one is controlled by all forms. You cannot be controlled by forms until you establish the law of believing you are form. And the moment that you believe you are form, then you are controlled by all forms. And so you react to whatever form does or does not do.

That's not truth, and that's why it's not freedom. There is no freedom without truth. Truth and freedom are inseparable. They are one and the same. And truth does not and cannot be contained [and], therefore, does not exist in limit or form. As we stated some time ago, "When of thy mind thou seekest to know the truth, / On the wheel of delusion thou shalt traverse." *[This saying can be found in Discourse 1.]* For the mind can only offer the letter of the law. It cannot offer the spirit of the law, for the spirit of the law is formless and free. Only the letter of the law. And the letter of the law killeth. Whoever believeth in the letter of the law is one who is killing the forms that they inhabit. Slowly, but surely.

Try to understand: you create form; you give it birth. And you alone give it death. Did that help with that?

*Thank you, sir.*

Yes. You had a question, did you?

*No, not that I'm consciously aware of.*

Oh.

*Thank you.*

Fine. *[The teacher addresses another student.]* Yes.

*Since that which we believe we are is the creator, could you please explain—*

No, no. That which you create and believe that you are, yes, I think that's, perhaps, what we're discussing.

*That which you create and believe that you are—*

Believe that you are.

*Is the creator.*

Well, you are the creator by believing that you are form.

*OK.*

You see, that's, see, God, the Divine, does not create. God, the Divine, sustains. All right?

*OK. Yes.*

Belief is the bondage, and the bondage is creation. All right? Go ahead now with your question.

*Then, could you please explain in the last seminar ...*

Yes?

*If I understood it correctly, you said that you could move form for a short time without belief.*

Why, of course.

*Could you ...*

Why, of course. Well, you can move form for a short time without belief, certainly, because you are that which sustains form. But for how long a time can you move form without belief and return unto form? We have the Isle of Hist to consider. It can only—you can only—once that is separated, then you are no longer in form. So, you see, there is, of course, in keeping with the Law of Limit, then there is a limit on the time. That is time, which is a created thing of the mind. It is not that which is. It is something that the mental world has created. And so you can, in keeping with that Law of Limit, you are therefore restricted in order to return into limit. In other words, if you hold your breath for a sufficient time, you will find that if it's, if it's long enough, in keeping with the laws of limit, that you will not be able to return unto form, the form that you believe that you were prior to that. Now does that help with that?

*Yes.*

[Do you] understand? And in speaking of the creator, it is the soul that can and does all thing create, all things create. For the soul, individualized, that's when the Divine Spirit enters form.

*Thank you.*

Hmm? See, God is not form. Individualization, separation, that's what form is.

*Thank you.*

Hmm? That which separates, divides; that which divides, conquers. Conquering is the sole domain of limit or creation. It has nothing to do with that which is; [it] has everything to do with that which is not. Yes.

*I need some more understanding, please, on, on sleep.*

Sleep? Yes.

*And, and in so far as, I mean, am I [to] understand that forms come in and inhabit our body, our, our being while we're asleep, supposedly, so-called asleep.*

Well, if you don't make the effort to stay guardian at the portal of your consciousness, why, certainly, they do.

*OK. Also, OK, they are celestial forms.*

Yes, there certainly are.

*OK. And they can come in and also, I mean, they would take our soul and we would go to the celestial realms, rather—*

They cannot transgress the law of which doors you closed or left open. For example, if you go to sleep at night, what you call sleep, and you're all upset and you make no effort to rise your consciousness to higher realms, then those [higher levels] in your consciousness are closed off, and the only forms that can enter, while you think you are sleeping, are the forms in keeping with the doors of your house that you have left open. Be they the earth center, fire center—usually they're the water center. Hmm? They don't have to be, for you alone make that choice. You see, when you—say you go to sleep at night; you make the effort to, to program your mental world until you rise up into a realm of consciousness where you feel good. Because when you feel good, you are aware to what you are. And then, when you awaken in the morning, your first feeling is a good feeling, a real good feeling inside because that's where you went when you went to sleep. Hmm? See?

*Thank you.*

And you can feel good at any moment that you choose to feel good. All you have to do is stop believing that you are that limited form which you are moving around your world. That's all you have to do. Hmm?

*Yes, sir.*

And when you do that, you feel fine. Whenever you think of something besides [yourself], you feel very good, don't you?

*I do.*

Everyone does. Hmm? And try to understand, when someone doesn't do what you want them to do, try to remember that that is a form you've created in your mind and, having created that, it expects more than the person, in their stage of evolution, is willing to give at the time. Hmm? So if you're not dependent upon [yourself], you will not be dependent upon them.

*Right. Thank you.*

Hmm? In this philosophy it's known as grow or go. One never has to establish in their consciousness that, "Well, I can no longer tolerate that person; therefore, get out of my universe." No, no, no. The person is inside of their own consciousness. That's where they are. They have created the person, don't you see? And when they look out to see the person and that person is not in keeping with the way they have created them and believe that they are in their mind, then that person, looking out at that other person, has problems. Do you understand that?

*Yes.*

You see, and it reveals they have no faith in the Divine, you know. It's like so many years ago when my channel and, and his mother were counseling a party; and the wife came for a counseling. And she said that her husband had a very severe problem. A very severe problem. Something had to be done with him. And Isa said to her, she said, "Well, we see absolutely no problem with your husband at all. We do see a great problem with you." Well, she got very upset, needless to say. And Isa said to her, she said, "Well, you're the one that's disturbed, and you're the one that's upset. Therefore, that which disturbs anyone is that which controls them. So you're the one that has the problem. He's just doing fine." *[Isa Goodwin is Mr. Goodwin's mother. She would regularly instruct, guide, and correct the students and those requesting help through Mr. Goodwin's mediumship.]* Yes, I hope that's helped with your question. Yes. Yes.

*If we're divided and then we conquer, is that how we use creation or—*

Well, that's how we abuse creation, yes. You see, first of all, in order to divide, we have to—that which we, we truly are is fluctuating from that which we are to that which we are not. And that which we are not is gaining, what you would say, headway or control. So therefore, one experiences all types of needs. Needs are fulfilled by divide and conquer. Hmm?

*So then what we want to do is just have the desire, give it to God . . .*

Return it to the Source from whence it came. That is correct. Return it to the Divine. You see, desire is divine expression; the divine expression is desire, the principle itself. So when you are aware of desire, accept the demonstration: you have received this desire, right? The principle, desire. Now you have a responsibility. You have experienced it within your consciousness: return it to the Source which sent it to you. Don't steal it from the, from the Divine Source. Hmm? Yes. You know, it's like reading a book. And each page you turn, you believe that you are. You have difficulty in turning the pages. Hmm? Yes.

*It's true.*

Someone else have a question? Yes.

*How do we get out of belief when our beliefs are all stored in our computer?*

Well, there's no problem at all. You see, if you believe you are the computer, then, of course, you have difficulty in getting out of what you believe that you are. So the first step is to say, "I'm using this. I call it a hand. It is not me. I am using it." It's like, it's like picking up a shovel. You look at the shovel, say, "This is a shovel. I have given this an identification, known as a shovel. It is not me. I can set it aside any time I want to." Now you can—and it is the divine law that you use the vehicle that you have, but never enter that realm where you believe that you are it.

You put your shoes on; you take your shoes off. Some shoes you like, and some shoes you don't. Well, so it is with the form that you have earned in evolution. You like it at times, and at times you don't like it. Well, at the times that you don't like it, those [are the] lessons, you understand, that you haven't passed in [your] evolution. And so [you] say, "All right. This is what I'm stuck with and I best do the best I can with it. Because I'm stuck with it because I didn't accept that in my evolution before. I don't want to have to go through that all over again. I wanted brown eyes; I got stuck with blue ones. I wanted to be six feet tall, and I got stuck with five feet, six and a quarter," like my poor channel. Anyway, so you go on down the list. This is what you have earned in keeping with those laws of evolution. And so when you find yourself upset over a part of the vehicle that you have earned in evolution, pause for a moment and take a very good look. Because those are the lessons that are being revealed to you that you didn't pass before. Now you know the body, the vehicle, has all of these different parts (the thumb, the finger, the nose, and etc.) which reveal to us, just like a book, what they represent spiritually in our own evolution.

Now, I want to excuse [you]; you can take care of your little boy. That's all right. Careful you don't trip there, though, won't you? *[The teacher excuses the father of a child to attend to the child, who was also in class.]* Now someone else had a question? Yes, please.

*Why is it oxygen is essential to the forms? Why did they choose oxygen of all the elements?*

Well, now that's fine. Now I tell you what you do. Now you sit there and don't breathe. I don't want you taking in any oxygen.

And during that time, see if you can awaken to why form requires oxygen of all the elements. Go ahead. Now take control of your mind and return to me with the answer. And please don't try breathing through your nostrils because I have my eye on you.

Yes, did you have a question? *[The teacher addresses another student.]*

*I don't think so.*

Yes.

*I'm wondering if we will evolve enough while we're in these classes to be able to be taught what the different things that, that our parts of our body represent. I'm talking about the color of the skin and all that.*

Well, now, to the mind, which, of course, is controlled by belief, there is never enough. So to answer your question would be very foolish on my part.

*Yes.*

And I do not feel tempted.

*Thank you.*

To be so foolish. I have a boy over here answering the question about oxygen. Ah! You breathed! Just a moment. *[The teacher addresses the student who asked about oxygen.]* Did you come up with your answer?

*No.*

Why did you breathe? Why did you breathe?

*Belief.*

Belief in what?

*That I was the form.*

Why, certainly! If you didn't believe that you were the form, then, therefore, you wouldn't require any oxygen, now would you? So what is the answer to your question? Do you want to breathe again and hold your breath?

*No.*

Well, now I gave you that opportunity to answer your question. You asked a question, Why, of all of the elements, form has chosen oxygen? Is oxygen an element of the fire center? What center is oxygen an element of?

*The air center.*

Why, of course! And so where is belief?

*Belief, then, is in the air center.*

Well, of course, it's in the air center. And it creates the forms in the water center. I've taught you that before. Without the air center, how can you form it? That's where you form it. And the water center is where you create it. And then it goes down through the fire center and into the earth center. Hmm? Now you should have perceived that in holding your breath. You know that if you don't have a mind, you cannot believe anything, can you?

*That's true.*

You must, you must enter the air center. Why, certainly, certainly. Would you like [to] breathe again and stop believing? You see, you see, you must learn to take control of your mind. It's your mind, you see. It's your mind is where it is. Because before you enter the water center and form those forms, you must realize it starts in your mind. Take control of your mind, you see. You see?

*Yes, sir.*

And experience the joy of life! But if you're not willing to take control of your mind, then you cannot experience the joy of life. So do not deceive yourself. Yes.

*Well, concerning desire, I am not aware of desire until it's already been formed into, I guess, need and want. How—*

It has many names.

*How do you—*

Some call it flowers for father's memorial. Yes, go right ahead, please.

*How do you become aware of it before your mind has had a chance to channel it into what it wants?*

One first makes the effort, through daily meditation, their affirmations, to know their self. When you know yourself, you will know, you will know that it is arriving, you understand, that you are beginning to create it in a mental world before it enters the water center, where you are totally controlled by the form you have created. Hmm? And so that's why it's so important to—one of the many reasons to do your meditations daily, and your concentrations, because without that, then there is no stability of the mind. There's no stability, you see.

You see, you cannot awaken to the Light of truth and not make the effort to do something with it, because, you see, in awakening, what you are—the law you are establishing is a threat to that which you have created, which you insist on believing that you are. You see? However, if you do your daily meditations, your daily affirmations, then you have nothing whatsoever to, to be concerned about in that respect because you will stay in control. But if you don't make that effort, then you'll be controlled by that which you've always been controlled by, through belief, and creating the forms, and the experience that you have to look forward to is a great deal of disturbance and frustration because you are threatening that which you still believe that you are. Does that help you?

*Yes. Thank you.*

You see? And say that you believe that you are a certain way. You believe that, you see; you've convinced yourself. And then you begin to establish the laws to awaken to that which you believe that you are is only what you have created; it is not you at all. Then that is a threat to what you believe that you are. You have a house divided. You have a great deal of frustration. You have a great deal of upset because you still believe you are that which you have created, although you have awakened in the air center—you understand that, in a mental world—that that is not what you are. That is what you have created. So you see that—and as long as you insist on believing what you have created is you, as you are awakening to the demonstrable truth that it is not you (it is only what you have created), then you have a house divided, a great deal of struggle, and a great deal of difficulty. And many, many of those forms rise up out of the water center, a great deal of emotional upset and upheaval because you are divided in consciousness: you know the truth and are not applying it. Do you understand that?

*Yes.*

You cannot know the truth, you understand, and then turn right around in the same breath and believe you are that which you have created.

*Thank you. I don't know what you mean when you say "spirit of the law."*

The spirit of the law. You don't know what that means.

*No.*

Well, no, because you see, that which is formless, that which is free, that which is truth is not perceived by the human mind. The human mind conceives; it does not perceive. Yes. The letter of the law is very clear. You say, "This is the way that you do this and you do that and you do that. Now you go ahead and you follow those instructions." I'm putting it the best way I can put it. But your heart isn't in it. Do you understand that? You see? The heart, you see. The mind is in it, but the heart isn't. You see?

Now, for example, I have shared with you over these years, the heart is the vehicle through which the soul expresses the faculties of being. The heart. All right? Now I've also shared with you that a function is an undeveloped faculty. Understand? All right. Now when you enter the water center, you experience what you understand as feelings. When you believe that you are that which you have created, which lives in the water center, when you believe that you are those things, then that which is your heart, the vehicle of your soul, and that which you are, is now a function. Do you understand that? And you experience the emotions and you say, "Oh, this was the greatest love I've ever experienced." That is a function of the heart, not the faculty.

So until you separate yourself from what you believe that you are, you cannot experience that which you truly are: the goodness, the joy, and the happiness: life itself. You see, that's what you are. Now when the heart, the faculty is flowing, which flows through the heart—remember, the function of the water center also flows through there. You understand? So, you see, every faculty and every function—every function is an undeveloped faculty, for it lacks, as a function, it lacks the light of reason, you see. The light of reason is necessary for a function to awaken and express its true being, which is a faculty. Hmm?

So, so often a person *feels*, you see, they say they feel this great love. Well, all they have to do—it isn't that one doesn't *feel* this great love; it's that this love that they're feeling is the love of what they are flowing through them. They've mistaken it, you understand, as something outside that they must have. For love, that which is love, does not contain within it want, need, and desire. Want, need, and desire is a function, you see. It is a function of a form created in the water center. See. Love is like a river; it flows, you see. And it will quench the thirst of the shore, regardless what is on the shore. That's what love is.

Now what people believe is love is filled with dependence and need, for it is denial. It's the function; it's not the faculty. Yes. Hmm? You see, one more, more rightly may call that love, freed from want, need, and desire, and lust, filled with want, need, and desire. There's all the difference in the world, you see. You see, when it's a faculty, it's love. When it's a function, it's lust. And it's that simple. So a person, you see, they say that they love, yes, you see. You rise in love, you see. When you fall in love, you have made an error: you have fallen into lust. That's the difference. Only lust contains want, need, and desire. Love does not contain that. Only lust contains that. Yes. Yes.

*I was wondering how doing things that we don't like to do— we've created something; we don't like it, but we go ahead and do it anyway. How does that get us closer to who we are?*

Well, that depends on how graciously you do it. I mean, if you do it by the letter of the law, then you've got [a] problem: the experience will repeat itself. Yes, I know. Thank you. *[The teacher is addressing the recording technician.]* If you do it by the spirit of the law, then the lesson will not, will not repeat itself. Hmm? You see, how does it help you? Well, take a look. You see, you do something that you don't want to do: that's instrumental in separating you from the bondage that you believe that you are the form, the judgment that you have created, that doesn't want to do it. For it's not *you* that doesn't want to do it. It is that which you believe that you are that doesn't want to do it.

*Oh.*

Hmm? It's not what you are. See, what you are is not subject to these laws of limit. Not what you are, no, no, no, no. What you believe you are has all the limits and all the restrictions, you see. If you believe that your form is the, the sustaining power and that which carries on, then you [have] got a, you [have] got a very serious problem, very serious problem, like anyone has, you see.

Because the greatest benefit to birth is the death of the form that one has become addicted to. You see, death is birth, and birth is death. So they're one and the same thing. And so all of the fear and all of the suffering is instrumental in freeing oneself from that terrible bondage. Hmm? See, one always wants to receive freely, but they don't want to let go freely.

And I do see that our time is up. How quickly time passes in your world. And it's been very nice speaking with you again. I shouldn't take this off before I'm finished talking, however. *[The teacher refers to his microphone.]* I have a tendency to do that, you know. It's like one of my students said, "Well, after all, they're not perfect." Well, after all, I never expected them to be because I wouldn't expect that out of myself, you understand. It would be so foolhardy on my part. Thank you.

JUNE 12, 1986

## A/V Seminar 15

Good evening, class.

This evening we'll begin our class with the questions that have been troubling some of you, especially on the subject of retaliation. So we'll begin our class this evening as you raise your hand on the question and the struggles you have with needs to retaliate. Yes, please.

*It seems that when I'm at a higher vibration that others around me that are in a less high vibration want to, are attracted in a negative way to me.*

Their expression is in a negative way? Yes, that's most understandable. Yes.

*And I was wondering if, if it is appropriate to enter the level that they are operating in, in order to deal with them effectively.*

It is not advisable at this stage of growth. In fact, it is most unadvisable.

*Yes.*

Yes. Now, for example, as a moth is attracted to the light, for a moth expresses a great need, and so it is that humans who are in great need, the effect of the over-identification with their self-image that they have created with the uneducated ego, so it is that they are attracted to the Light, which is energy, a high vibration of energy. And for their own survival—for feeling good is not a luxury; it is a necessity of survival—for their own survival where they have depleted the energies available to them from an over-identification with thinking of themselves so often in the course of a day and evening, they require energy. And so as the moth is attracted to the light, so are the sponges attracted to the water. Do you understand?

*Yes.*

Now, so as you walk upon the spiritual path, you will find that there is, of course, an increase attraction of those who seek to feel good, for they lack the necessity, when it is a necessity to feel good, they lack the frequency of feeling good from a dissipation of the energy to create forms in service to their uneducated egos. Does that help with your question?

*Yes. Thank you.*

Yes, now we'll continue on with retaliation. Yes.

*Does retaliation first begin in the mind and then does it travel to the water center where . . .*

Well, first of all, the, the judgment is made in the water center. The judgment is made that, by a person who is over-identified with themselves, which is an expression of the uneducated ego, the judgment is made that they are being rejected. You see, when you permit yourself the most disastrous force you can experience, and that is the thought of self, over-identification with the images you have created, when you permit yourself that type of a luxury, then you must realize that that is created by believing that you are everything that you have created, believing that you are that which you have created. It's known in many philosophies as an attachment to the fruits of action.

Now you find in your work, many people, of course, that whatever work or job that they do, they are so attached to the fruits of their action, if they are instructed and corrected, then you find an expression of the water center without control of the light of reason from the air center, you see. Does that help with your question? Yes, you go ahead, please.

*So is that what is called retaliation?*

Yes. A retaliation is an expression of a person who believes they are being rejected for they are attached to their fruits of action and truly believe at those times that they are being rejected, as you would understand it perhaps better, that when a child does not get what a child's judgment tells a child that he wants or needs and the person, the parent does not give what the child wants, the child immediately registers rejection. And without effort and consideration of those in control and guidance of the child, the child immediately retaliates.

Now that is an error, of course, in the thinking that, with adults, was not corrected when they were children in their formable age, yes.

*Thank you.*

Yes. Some other—any other questions? Yes.

*Does a person retaliate in, and, in retaliation—excuse me. When a person retaliates, do they express that retaliation through a particular function?*

Well, yes, of course, they do. They express it through the function—you see, you have the human ego. The service to the human ego, in this philosophy and in your understanding here, is you have money on the left and sex on the right. So those are the two functions that are available to an uneducated ego to express, to tell the world and to tell anyone who is awakened that they feel rejected and that it is the person's fault—it's not their fault—that they feel the way they do; it is the other person's fault. You see, it is a denial. An uneducated ego is a blatant denial of the Law of Personal Responsibility. So bondage to creation and the suffering that the human mind goes through is ever in keeping with a person's refusal to accept responsibility for all their thoughts, acts, and deeds. Yes.

And so you will find that retaliation has the principle of two functions through which to express itself. And you will also find that if it isn't using the function on the right and it's only using the function on the left, then it's going to cost you money. You do understand that, don't you? Have you not had experience with people feeling that, retaliating against you, they did not cost you financially in some way? Pardon?

*Yes.*

Yes. See, see, it only expresses through those two functions. Did that help with your question?

*Could I continue?*

Certainly.

*In order to, our response to the retaliation, when it expresses through that function...*

Yes.

*Is it, is it helpful, then, to express the corresponding faculty?*

Oh, indeed! For the individual that is experiencing the effect of the retaliation?

*Yes.*

Why, yes, that's the only saving grace, if you can call it a saving grace, is the demonstration by what you might consider the victim in that respect. Although we our self have constant choice, moment by moment, to be the victim or to rise through that. You see, if we permit our self to sell out to the child who is retaliating, we must understand and realize that we are selling out to that level inside of our self. Now if we permit ourselves to do that, justifying conditions and circumstances or whatever excuses one might care to use, if you permit yourself that luxury, then you indeed are the victim and you have indeed lost control of your ship of destiny. Yes. And so a person has that choice, that free will choice, moment by moment, to, to stand firm on the principle of right because it's right to do right or to sell out and the sellout, of course, takes place within our own mind, and we alone, then, make ourselves the victim.

You see, when you look at retaliation, if you will free yourself from the thought of I, then you will be able to see clearly and to demonstrate the principle which will free you from being the victim, and by so doing, you will experience in life being the victor. Yes, did you have any other questions on that?

*Thank you.*

You're welcome. Yes.

*So let's say that you are in, you have, you're experiencing a rejection. Let's say you've been corrected by somebody; you've been—*

Yes?

*—caught at something.*

Yes?

*And you don't like it. Your mind rises up.*

Yes?

*So that would be the point to nip it, to take the personal responsibility right at that—*

That is the moment at which you have choice. You have choice at that moment to be the victim and experience the effects of the retaliation that someone didn't have their own way—because there are many children, of course, in the universe—that a child didn't have his own way. Or at that moment you may choose the Law of Personal Responsibility and stand firm in what you know in your heart is right and do what is right. And then you will be free. Yes, that is the moment at which you have choice. Yes.

*So what would one say to oneself at that moment when you are in that full feeling of rejection of—*

Well, you don't permit yourself to enter the fullness of the feeling of rejection. You're speaking as a victim of someone's retaliating?

*Yes. No. Let's say that you, like a boss corrects you, like you've made an error and—*

All right. Now you may stop at that point. You are working for an employer, which you call a boss—

*Right.*

—who is responsible to see that your work is done ever in keeping with the corporation from which he is employed. We follow that, don't we?

*Yes.*

Fine. You accept the demonstrable law you have established: that you are working for that employer. And in working for that employer, you are having these various experiences. And you don't like it. So you have a choice. You have a choice at that moment—and any moment thereafter because this is a continuing thing, I accept from your discussion—you have a choice at that moment to declare inside of your mind the Law of Personal Responsibility. You have, by the law established, exposed yourself to that rate of vibration of a child who doesn't have their own way, in your understanding, who retaliates, correct? Now you have a choice to make the effort to find another boss or employer or to separate yourself inside your own consciousness from those experiences that take place when someone retaliates against you.

Don't permit your mind to justify and deny personal responsibility. If you permit your mind to justify and come up with excuses to defend your uneducated ego, then you will find yourself the victim of those forces inside your own consciousness and be bound by them. That is not the path to follow. Does that help you with your question?

*Yes.*

Go ahead.

*Thank you.*

Yes.

*So the personal responsibility is the fact that you have attracted this to you.*

Yes. You're not left without, without choice, however. For example, if you find that that is a job not only that you like but you have found it your responsibility in life, then you stand firm in your own consciousness and accept it as part of the whole process. Do you understand? Because, you see, your denial of its right of expression is your bondage, for denials are our destinies. So you do not deny the level its expression. You take firm action in your own consciousness if you are in a position of responsibility and you are the boss and the tables are turned. Do you understand that?

*Yes.*

So, you see, this is part of the whole process. You know, you don't start at the top. If you try starting at the top, you'll find yourself always on the bottom. You start on the bottom of anything worthwhile in life, and you learn all of the things that the bottom has to offer as you climb up the ladder. Now when you get up to the top of the ladder, you understand, you have your responsibilities. They are broadened and expanded from being down at the bottom of the ladder. You have, however, paid your dues, as some of my students say, and therefore you are now the boss. So, being the boss, you have already been at the bottom, and you have understanding, you have compassion, and you realize the childishness of those levels of consciousness for you have learned them as you've climbed up the ladder. Do you understand that? And then that qualifies you to handle them in a more intelligent manner. Hmm? Yes.

You see, you always have the choice. Now here in your little school, there's not a day goes by that there isn't an expression of rejection from the minds of our own students—there's not a day that passes—as the students make effort to grow through the uneducated ego, the attachment to the fruits of action, you see. However, just because our school is filled, like a hailstorm, with retaliations, devious and blatant, you see, the school could not exist if the retaliations were permitted to pass on by, you see.

So what one is always faced with, as they climb up the ladder, so to speak, in your world of creation, a boss is always faced, constantly, with the temptation to sell out or to stand firm and to have the child find other ways to increase their retaliations until they grow up and be men and women. Does that help with your question?

*Yes, it does. Thank you.*

Yes.

*OK. It's similar to this question. I just wondered what if it's turned around. What if the employer is the one who is constantly retaliating, while we're trying to stay in a higher vibration?*

Yes. Well, then you want to accept the demonstrable truth: like attracts like and becomes the Law of Attachment. You, however, are never left without the moment of free will or choice.

*Yes.*

One can easily change their employer. If one finds in their experiences that their employer is a child, constantly retaliating, they have a choice: change employers, you see.

*Yes.*

However, in any change there's always an adjustment for a human being to make within their own consciousness, within their own mind.

*Yes.*

And so we find that people do not make changes so readily with those areas in which they permit themselves to become dependent. You know, a person becoming, allowing themselves to be dependent on a certain person or persons for their security in life (emotional or financial) goes through a great trauma when they are tempted to make a change with those people. Hmm? Yes. However, the—without change there is no evolution, and change is extremely beneficial for it reveals to all minds how attached they are to the fruits of action of what they have created with their minds in days gone past. Does that help?

*Yes, it does.*

Yes.

*When we have certain thought patterns rise up . . .*

Yes.

*And we reject them by either moving on or changing the tape or moving up or down our levels . . .*

It is not advisable to reject our thought patterns. They are forms. Go ahead.

*That's what I meant. Do they retaliate? They seem to retaliate.*

Oh, yes. Yes, well, you see, first of all, the rejection of their right of existence, you see—you, you give birth to a child in your mind. You see, if you reject that which you have given birth to, you deny the Law of Personal Responsibility. You understand that? So when you deny this demonstrable Law of Personal Responsibility, you move from freedom into bondage. Because, you see, the denial, the denial establishes the law and the destiny of the very experience. So acceptance is the will of good. Acceptance is the divine law of God's expression, and denial in the consciousness is an absolute destiny to bondage. So one does not reject the divine right of expression. The divine right of expression is very varied. One does not allow themselves the luxury of rejecting its right in consciousness. That does not mean that one must demonstrate the expression of everything. However, one, in order to be free, must accept the right of its existence. Do you see that?

*Yes.*

So if you permit yourself to reject a thought pattern which you have created, then you are denying the very expression of that which you have created. You are denying personal responsibility for it. Yes.

*But certain thought patterns put you into a water center or—*

That is correct.

*So—*

So one recognizes what they do, and it is not a rejection to tell your child to go to sleep, is it? For, you see, it is, it is your child you have created. You are responsible for your child. Thought patterns are thought forms are children we create. They remain children. They do not grow up. They only grow old, old in the sense of becoming stronger and stronger because we permit our self to think of the thought of I and that opens the door for them to come in and demand energy. For without energy, they cannot activate, you see, cannot express themselves. Does that help?

*Yes. Thank you.*

Yes.

*Then when we talk to them firmly and tell them what they may or may not do, that's an acceptance in itself that, that you, you have created them, isn't it?*

Why, certainly. First of all, if you have demonstrated self-discipline, your child—as a mother—does what you tell them to do while you are responsible. That is your personal responsibility for having been the instrument through which that child is created. If you have, through the demonstration of self-discipline, [then] your child does what you tell them to do ever in keeping with the Law of Responsibility. Then, when you tell your children, which are thought forms, "This is what you, this is what you have been created for. I am the one who has created you. You are created for this purpose and this purpose only. I do not require at this time an expression of the purpose for which I have created you. Therefore, you go back to sleep," [they obey].

*Thank you.*

And so if you have demonstrated the Law of Personal Responsibility—without self-discipline, personal responsibility does not exist. And so if you have demonstrated self-discipline, then your children will be disciplined, and they will obey ever in keeping with the law that you alone demonstrate. Yes.

*Thank you.*

Thank you.

*Is asking them to go to sleep (the forms), the same as the law of, of ignoring them or . . .*

Well, when they go to sleep in your consciousness, they no longer exist because they don't bother you. You put them to sleep. You tell them to go to sleep. That's right.

*When would, oh, so it's—when would ignoring them come . . .*

Well, for example, if you have demonstrated the lack of self-discipline and you tell them to take a nap, they won't take a nap. Then you have got to redirect your energy—and energy follows your attention—then you must ignore them. And I find in your world that many mothers are very capable of ignoring their children they, they have been responsible for creating and have no problem whatsoever, especially ignoring them when it comes to discipline. Yes, I don't find that my students—some of them have no problem at all. It is as though they don't even exist, their children they have created. Yes, does that help with your question. Yes.

*If you ignore them, does that strengthen you so they will obey you in the future?*

Why, certainly. It strengthens you. You, you have demonstrated your conscious choice. And to demonstrate one's conscious choice requires personal responsibility and self-discipline, you see. You see, say that, for example, a person makes a conscious choice and they say to themselves, "Well, now I make a conscious choice to make a $1,000 this week." And they demonstrate that they did that. Do you understand that?

*Yes.*

And so that required self-discipline and personal responsibility. Wouldn't you say?

*Yes, it does.*

Yes, why, certainly. Then your created forms act accordingly. Yes, oh, yes, because they know you mean business, you see. You see, the terrible trap is the denial of personal responsibility. To permit one to tell oneself that, "Well, I didn't know any better." Or "I didn't ask." You see, if you don't ask, you don't have to worry about personal responsibility, do you? You can do whatever you want because you didn't ask. You see, that's how presumption's the Law of Descent. Descent—we all know where.

You see, uneducated egos don't ask. By not asking, they don't have to face personal responsibility, see? Uneducated egos don't investigate; they presume, you see. Contrary to the beautiful truth that is demonstrable: investigate everything, *everything*; presume no thing. For the moment you presume one thing, you are presumed upon. It is the law, yes, of old creation. Yes. Did that help you?

*Yes.*

Yes.

*Can I ask another?*

Certainly, certainly.

*I find that my response in retaliation has been, not as outwardly blatant as breaking things, but it's a stubbornness and a not doing. That's been my response.*

Have you not found it most destructive, self-destructive?

*Yes, it is. Definitely.*

Does it bring you goodness in life?

*No, not at all.*

You see, the forms, the children created, they're not interested in you. They're only interested in their own survival and their own continuity, for they are soulless creatures. We're speaking of the thought forms, you understand, at this stage of evolution. And so they're not a bit interested in you. They're only interested in doing what they have been created for. And we created them in days of ignorance. That [our goodness] doesn't mean anything to them when they want to express. If we don't demonstrate refraining from thinking about our self all the time and we don't demonstrate that Law of Personal Responsibility and self-discipline, then we must pay the price. We are the ones who have created them. Yes.

*May I have one more—*

Certainly.

*You spoke something about the purpose for which they were created. Is there a—*

You know the purpose. Why, certainly, the purpose of design. All things created have a purpose of design. You, being the creator of your thought forms in your life, you have created them to serve a particular purpose in your life, you see. And so through honesty, you awaken within your own consciousness [by asking yourself], "For what purpose did I design that form that I have been servicing all these many years?" See, you created it at a time in your evolution to serve a purpose for you. Do you understand that?

*Well, would it basically—*

So when you think of you, they all rise up. Of course, they do. You see, this is, this is how self-thought is the most destructive force that you will ever know in, in all of the universes. For, you see, the moment you enter that realm, you have all of these forms you have created waiting for you, for the energy that you have. They all wait for you because they have been created by self. So when you enter the realm of self-thought, you enter the realm of all of the forms you have created to serve as yourself. Do you understand that? That's why it's so destructive for so many forms have been created that are no longer in any way useful or beneficial. Hmm?

But you don't have to go to that path. All you have to do is to demonstrate personal responsibility and to do your proper breathing exercises and to demonstrate self-discipline without which there is no personal responsibility. Hmm?

*[Thank you.]*

You're welcome. Yes.

*Once you've caught yourself already in the retaliation, the form, what's the best way to deal with the forms or discipline them so you won't do it again?*

Well, it's quite simple: first, you discipline what you, you understand is your self. You see, you see, we all create an image, and that image is what must be disciplined. And you see what it has to offer. And so you make greater effort to refrain from entering self-thought, for as you enter self-thought—try to understand, the forms that you, that you have created, that retaliate when they don't have their way, they're not going to change. Your only chance is to put them to sleep. And your only chance of doing that is to demonstrate personal responsibility and self-discipline.

And so as you demonstrate personal responsibility and self-discipline, you will find yourself refraining from entering that realm of self-thought because you are not going to change the forms you have created for they are created forms that do not grow with you. You see, a person grows and expands their consciousness. That which they create does not grow and does not expand its consciousness, you see. You see, just take a look at your beliefs that bind you, you know, [the ones] that you believe that you are. This is the great difficulty in experiencing the will of God. Because, you see, when you go to tell your mind, "Acceptance, the will of God. I accept the divine right of all expression," instantaneously the forms all rush in and tell you, "Oh, no. You're not that way. You're not that way. You're not that way. You would never think of doing that!" And so you instantly enter denial and are destined to bondage, you see? Yes, does that help with your question?

*Thank you.*

Yes. Yes.

*Yes. Thank you. When we go against our mind and—*

You go against what you've created, yes.

*We're going against these forms . . .*

Yes?

*It was said, then, we would get to know who we really are.*

Well, certainly. As long as you believe you are that which you create, then you cannot possibly experience being the very intelligent Energy which sustains your forms that you create. You see, for example, God cannot be a creator. We know that God is not a creator. The divine laws of nature create. The mental realms create. God is not limit; therefore, God cannot and does not create limit. God is limitless. So you cannot understand a God that is limitless, divine, intelligent, pure Energy, formless and free, without limit or obstruction, [and] then turn around and say that this very same God, this formless, free, divine Spirit that you truly are, created, limited, that which He is. It's just ridiculous thinking. Yes, yes, go ahead.

*And by going against our mind and these forms—*
Well, may I help you with one thing?
*Yes.*
You see, that's a form that's speaking. You are consid—you are stating that the things you have created is your mind. Your mind is what creates.
*Yes.*
You see, so there's a fine line of distinction between the forms you create and the mind that creates them. Yes, go ahead.
*Hmm. I'll have to think about that for a moment.*
Yes, well, I'll give you opportunity to think about it. Yes. *[The teacher addresses another student.]*
*Thank you.*
Yes.
*What is the mind trying to accomplish through deviousness?*
Well, the mind is ever work—you see, the mind is, is an empty vacuum that can never be filled, if you want to know what the mind is. It's like—it's a vacuum. You cannot fill it. Yet it ever strives to be filled. It ever experiences need. However, it is designed as a vehicle through which the formless, free Spirit, which you are, may express itself in a world of limit and obstruction. You see, limit is obstruction. You see, without the mind, without the mental realm, then, the created forms do not grow, expand, and evolve. For example, in the sense you have a form that is created. The created form has many experiences, you understand that? So the next ones that are created are a little bit more expanded, a little more broadened. You see, you know, as I've said to you many times: broaden your horizon. Well, you don't change a form that you have created. You create another form, you see. It's a little bit, a little bit more expanded. Do you understand that? And then you create another form and another form, and it keeps expanding and expanding. That's the broadening of your horizon. Then, what happens in the soul

faculties? Which faculty is awakened as you broaden your horizon, as you create forms that, that are ever more encompassing? What faculty is awakened?

*Reason.*

Pardon?

*Reason.*

Well, we finally get to reason. But what faculty is awakened in that process? Do you know? *[The teacher addresses another student.]*

*Understanding?*

What triune faculty?

*Duty, gratitude, and tolerance.*

Duty, gratitude, and tolerance is awakened, you see? You see, what happens as you broaden your horizon, you awaken your soul faculty, the first triune soul faculty of duty, gratitude, and tolerance, you see, as you work to expand your consciousness, you see? Yes. You see, if you want to, to awaken yourself to how much tolerance, how expanded you have become through your efforts, if you want to take a look at your tolerance, how awakened it is, the first soul faculty, the triune faculty, pause for a few moments and declare the truth, "I accept the divine right of all expression." And be patient. You won't have to wait long to find out how tolerant you really are. Did that help you?

*Yes.*

Yes. Now [you] back there have a question on retaliation. Yes, this evening's class on retaliation. I'm so grateful that I had some of my students demonstrate it so blatantly just before our class this evening. We're still on time, though. Yes.

*Would it ever be or when would it ever be necessary to trace why a certain form was created that you're trying to—*

Why, certainly. It takes honesty. You see, all one needs to do is to be honest and go inside. That's all available, waiting for them. They're always waiting for they're always hungry. They're always waiting to be fed. Yes. But you go slowly, you see. You see, you see, it's a terrible trap if you're not very, very careful and do your breathing properly. Because if you don't, then you start fascinating with the forms you've created, and it could affect the mind in a most detrimental way. Yes. Because of one's own over-identification with their uneducated ego, yes, the self-thought process. It's a very slow process. Yes.

*Thank you.*

You're welcome. Yes.

*I perceive a correlation between—at the moment that you realize that you're rejected and would be moving into retaliation—*

We must pause at this point. At the moment we realize we've been rejected—no! We reject our self. It's an error of ignorance. Because we deny the divine right of expression; that's how we reject our self and, and as an uneducated child we retaliate, you see, in hopes to bring about a change. You see, a child does that very early in their life. If they don't get what they judge they want, they immediately retaliate, you see. And then the parents responsible usually sell out to the child. And this is why—they, they [the parents] sold out to themselves—a child grows up to be an adult and acts like a little two-year-old girl or boy. Yes, go ahead.

*Well, I was perceiving a correlation between the first triune faculties . . .*

Yes?

*Duty, like personal responsibility—*

That's right. Duty to the true self.

*And then if we follow that with gratitude for the exposure . . .*

Yes?

*And then tolerance for our forms and ourselves—*

Absolutely.

*At the level that we're at, then we're using those faculties.*

Absolutely. You certainly are. That was given to you many, many years ago in one of our seminars. And that is the process through which one evolves and brings about a balance in their life, you see.

And so remember that all things ever seek, as water reaches its own level by its own weight, all created things ever seek a balance and a counterbalance. So, you see, in order to express and experience the joy of living, then one must bring about a balance in their life in the forms that they have created and make a conscious effort, through the broadening of one's horizons, to create forms which will serve them well in their present state of growth and evolution, you see. You see, you can't tell a person to just stop thinking of themselves because they spent so much time doing it. It's indeed most, most difficult to just make a change like that. That is not how we evolve. But, however, you can make the conscious effort to create intelligent forms that will serve you in your present state of evolution. Hmm?

*Are those faculties—if we—are those faculties part of those forms?*

No. Those forms are not faculties. However, those forms will be instruments to serve the human mind for a greater expression of the soul faculties in a world of creation. Do you understand that? Yes. In other words, it's known as, "Keep faith with reason; she will transfigure you." However, you must have the forms of the mind that have a broader horizon in order that there may be greater duty served, and gratitude, and therefore the tolerance must be expanded. And it is expanded as we evolve. Yes.

*What forms are you speaking of that are the ones that—*

Forms that would be in service to more of the light of reason. Hmm? In service to the light of reason. You see, if you don't use reason in your thoughts and activities, then, of course, you are in service to the emotional center, through the water center, and you act and react, you see. And you reject and retaliate. When there's a much, a much finer way, a much more intelligent way: you use the vehicles that you have earned in an intelligent way to serve the purpose of your soul. That is the *only* purpose, by the very laws of creation, they have been designed [for]. They have been designed in the divine design of creation to serve as vehicles for the Light that you are. Hmm? You see? And when we permit our self to believe we are the things we have created, we become the victims of that which we have created, and that's absolutely contrary to the divine design. Yes.

*Thank you.*

You're welcome. Yes.

*Let's say a person has found that he is retaliating. He's, he's in a pattern in his life of retaliation.*

May I say one thing at this moment? I have not in my experiences throughout these eons of time been aware of any human being that is not aware when they retaliate. Now I have been aware of many human beings who believe they are not aware, you understand? But try to realize, you are, in truth, as everyone is, responsible for every thought that enters the mind. We alone permit the thought to enter. We alone permit the thought to express, for we alone can demonstrate personal responsibility. We alone.

Now if a person says, "Well, I don't know why I did that. I guess I must have just retaliated." You see, that's a device of the mind. Try to understand that's only a device of the uneducated ego. That's all that it is.

We all know, for retaliation is a premeditated thought process. And it is our responsibility to lift the lamp of honesty that we may shine it over these forms we have created. It is a premeditated thought process. Therefore, all philosophers of all times have spoken the truth: O Man, know thyself and ye shall know the truth. And so therefore, the effort and responsibility is for man to make the conscious, daily effort to know himself, to know what it really is, all these created forms that he's responsible for. Yes, go ahead now with your question.

*Thank you very much.*

You're welcome.

*My question originally was that—*

We're still original. Thank you.

*Yes. Would it be helpful to put your attention not on the obstruction, but on what it is you want to become? And if so, would that be when you'd be creating these more intelligent forms?*

Yes, of course. We've always stated: take your attention off of what you want to overcome; place your attention or energy on what you want to become. For by so doing, you create forms with broader horizons, more acceptance, which is more of the will of God, and can serve in a more intelligent way. You see, people who are tempted to constantly see the obstruction are people who are dissipated of intelligent energy by the constant self-thought process. And they just feed off themselves and whoever else they can find to feed off of. For misery doesn't love company, it's indispensable for its existence, expression, and continuity. So I have always found, for myself, that people who are miserable demand to express their misery. They demand it. Their uneducated egos demand it. They demand to constantly see the obstruction.

Now in your world you call those people negative. Everything is negative. Everyone and everything is against them, you see. That's how they get the feeding, like a sponge, soaking up the water, you see. That's how they get more energy to feed more of their forms, you see. It's a device that the uneducated ego uses. You will find few, if anyone—anyone with any intelligence doesn't want to be around negative people because something inside of them knows that they are negative only as a sponge that is constantly draining whatever it can drain to feed its own glory, you see. This is why people don't, in truth, don't want to be around people that are negative. People that are negative are people who are constantly seeing obstructions in order to feed off of someone else. I think they're best known in your world as freeloaders. Yes. Does that help with your question?

*Yes. Thank you.*

Yes.

*So how do you, if you're in a higher vibration and you're attracting people that are complaining and like that, how do you deal with them, if you don't go to their level?*

Discipline. Self-discipline. Self-discipline.

*You ignore them or you, or you . . .*

Well, is that what my channel does? *[The teacher refers to Mr. Goodwin.]*

*You don't want to go—*

Is that what my channel does?

*No.*

What does my channel do?

*He—*

Because I'm not monitoring him, you know, every minute of every hour to see if he follows orders.

*He—*

I have others for that responsibility. Yes, what does he do?

*A lot of times he redirects the, the energy or, or he just continues to be positive.*

Well, I certainly should hope so. He knows better if he isn't. He knows what'll happen. Because, you see, those levels of consciousness are sponges. That's all they are. They're freeloading levels; they want something for nothing. Don't you understand that?

*Yes.*

They just want something for nothing. And they, of course, deceive themselves in the final analysis. It is contrary to the law. There is nothing for nothing. Everything has its own price tag. Creation is a price tag. Choose wisely what you purchase, you see. So if you want that great, seeming luxury and tempt yourself to constantly think of yourself, then you must realize that it is a very expensive process. Yes. Yes.

*Thank you.*

Yes. Time's passing quickly in your world, you know.

*If one perceives a lack of tolerance within oneself...*

A lack of tolerance within oneself, yes. One has just perceived a titanic uneducated ego. Yes, go ahead.

*So that's where you begin. You—one must begin with tolerance of oneself.*

Yes, indeed. That's, that's personal responsibility. Certainly. Duty, gratitude, and tolerance, that's personal responsibility. One must be honest with themselves and tolerant with their own prejudices and with their own needs of glory. One must be tolerant with those levels of consciousness, with those forms they have created. Yes. You see, people who have need are people who are denying the goodness that they are, are people who are feeding off of the temporary stimulation of self-glory, you see. Yes. Go ahead.

*OK.*

*[After a pause, the teacher continues.]* Your question was on perceiving having a shortage of tolerance.

*Yes.*

There is no shortage of tolerance. Well, let me put it this way. Perhaps you'll understand better. A person who experiences a shortage of tolerance is a person who has a fullness of self-glory. Does that help it? Because, you see, now we can understand as we educate our ego, we have less self-glory; we have more tolerance. However, with more tolerance, we have more goodness, we have more freedom, we have more joy, we have more happiness. Yes.

*So that—*

We have certainly less need.

*OK. So that would deter—that is that, that old thing of wanting to—the illusion of perfection of, is that—would be, would that be the root of intolerance?*

Well, this illusion, this need of perfection you will find is restricted to oneself. One wants themselves perfected for greater glory, yes. You know, the only king that exists is like the only queen that exists: creation. There are no kings and queens in the realm that is, the truth that is. Doesn't have kings and queens. It doesn't even have princesses and princes. No. You see, you see, we, we work—everyone is a father, everyone is a mother for we're fathering these forms we create and we're mothering them. Take your pick. And so what we create, you see—you know, we create these little babies and these forms. And we feed them and we look at them and, of course, they have to be princes. How could our uneducated ego create anything but a princess or a prince? So here we go to work and make great effort with this little thing we've created, either a prince or a princess. Well, then we grow old and wake up and find out they all became queens. You see? And we're not happy at all. Oh, yes. So, you see, that's all to feed the self-glory. Yes.

What is the uneducated ego? Let us look at the good, you see. Let us look at the good. Let us look at the good in retaliation. There is good, there is God in all things. This evening my channel, [at] the very last minute, he only got about—well, it was actually eighty seconds for his meditation. And all the demands came to him in his earth realm. He got just over a minute, eighty-seconds worth of meditation to do his part, you see. And his mind was very upset about that, but the retaliations were like hailstorms here, you see, prior to class.

Well, now he had a choice. He could have had himself terribly upset and not been receptive, so that I could be with you and give you a class tonight or to demonstrate the very things that he has been studying as a channel of mine. Do you understand? And so, you know what he did? He took that eighty seconds and gave all of that retaliation to God. He did what he was told to do by my assistants in reference to how this retaliation would be handled by my students, for you are my students. And then, in the short time he had for his meditation, he gave it from his heart, all this retaliation, to God. And when class is over, he still has to work to instruct those responsible in this little school in reference to the refreshments. Because the retaliation will not be served in this school because he knows the law: that's a sell-out to those realms inside of himself, you see.

So *you* have a choice in all this retaliation foolish—all this little childish, you know, these uneducated little children, you see. That is not the soul. That is, that is what we're trying to free our self from. That is what we make effort to free our self from. So we must make effort, first, inside of our self to understand that is not what we are, the uneducated ego, you see. And in doing that, in applying the laws that you have received over these many years in your earthly realm here, in applying those laws, you free yourself. Do you understand that? You see? And then, you become the living demonstration of being in the world, of being with a person, place, or thing and never—Yes, I know—and never—thank you—never a part of them. *[The teacher interjects comments to the technician recording the class.]* You see? But you cannot do that if you do not apply the laws that you have received and continue to receive in these classes that you receive every single week here. You see? Then, you make a little more effort to apply those laws, to do your proper breathing exercises, which is critical to being freed from those realms, and you will live in your forms to experience the objectivity which is absolutely necessary and indispensable to the freedom and the experiencing of what you truly are, and not what you have permitted, through errors of ignorance, to believe that you are.

Time passes so quickly. And I know it's time to go. So I will say good evening to all of you. And do have nice refreshments. My channel will be instructed by my assistants in reference to what refreshments will be allowed to be served. Because there's one thing—someday we'll have a class on [it]. Whenever you consume anything, whenever you expose yourself to anything that is filled with the forms of retaliation, you must work diligently not to come in rapport with them. So the more evolved you become, you know, your fingers will tell you things, although you're not awakened to that, and you consume things or you drink things, you must understand what it's really like. And so over these years you've had experiences when, when good wholesome food was thrown in the garbage. Well, it wasn't so good and wholesome, if you could look in other realms of consciousness, yes.

And so I know if you stop thinking of yourself, those little boys and girls who entered this evening in their childish retaliation, if you stop thinking about yourself, you'll feel real good and have a wonderful evening. Thank you.

JULY 10, 1986

## A/V Seminar 16

Good evening, class. Be seated.

Love all life and know the Light for the Law of Light, the Law of Life is Light. The Law of Life is Light, and love, the manifestation or expression thereof. And so we find that an obstruction to the Light that we are is a transgression of the Law of Life. It is known as an error of ignorance for Light is intelligent, pure Energy. That is what we are. Therefore, in your daily spiritual endeavors, declare the truth that you may fulfill the law and experience, from that fulfillment of the law, the abundant good that is your birthright and your responsibility. For example, "I accept the possibility of experiencing the goodness that I am." If you understand that you are Light, that identification is a focusing, a directing of the Light that you are. One does not express the fullness of their life until they awaken to what they are, for in that awakening, there is no obstruction to the expression of what they are. We experience the fulfillment of our errors of ignorance for those errors of ignorance are transgressions of the law.

Truth, as I have said so long ago and so often, is individually perceived. Truth is not individual. Your teachings that are given to you are given in many different ways. Same truth, for there's only one truth. Truth cannot be divided; it is indivisible. Therefore, truth requires no defense, for that which is cannot be defended. We defend errors of ignorance. We defend our conception of truth, as our conception of truth is ever dependent upon the intensity of our density of our own identification with the passing panorama of mental substance.

Over these years with you, I have had many students request, at various times, affirmations, guidance, and instruction in reference to their spiritual meditations. Breathing, I have given to you. Affirmations, I have given to you. But an affirmation does not do it for you. It is an avenue through which you pass to free yourself from the errors of ignorance. The use of an affirmation permits you to gain control over that which is obstructing the fullness of the goodness that you are. Each time that you declare, "I accept the possibility of experiencing the goodness that I am," you are speaking to the human mind, you are speaking to the obstruction that you have identified with and, through over-identification, temporarily believe that you are.

Now when you do your proper cleansing breath and you do it daily and you do it consistently and you declare that truth, that which you have spent so much time believing that you are begins to weaken. It begins to weaken because you direct less energy to that which you have created as an obstruction to what you are. Through that daily effort, through that flooding of your consciousness, you awaken to what you are; you no longer transgress the Law of Life, and you begin to live. To live is to demonstrate personal responsibility of the goodness that you are.

Move from making things in life to guiding things in life. Do not battle what you believe that you are, for to battle what you believe that you are is to be disturbed by what you believe that you are and, therefore, controlled by it. One does not battle what they believe that they are. One, through proper, daily spiritual exercises and awakening, begins the slow and sure path of disassociation. Whoever does not use that which is designed by the law of the creator—and the creator being each and every person who has entered what is known as identification, for we create our thoughts and we create our experience—whoever does not use them for the purpose of the design they have created them is destined to be used by them. Through the Law of Disassociation, you will know who you are, and you will know beyond a shadow of all doubt your responsibility for using all that you have created wisely.

And when in your evolution, it no longer serves the purpose for which you have created it, you remove it from your house. That's putting your house, daily, in order.

Your world has entered over this past twenty, thirty years now of your earth time, your world has entered—and I spoke to you some time ago on the advancing technologies. Understand what you are: Light. Study this great energy that your scientists have brought into your world, your so-called laser beams. Nothing more and nothing less than directing light, energy for constructive good or destructive.

You are, by conscious choice, you are the laser beam. You construct for the good or you destroy from errors of ignorance. It takes energy; you, being energy, it takes you to create. And it also takes you to destroy.

So when you create obstructions to what you are by permitting your mind to drift into what used to be—I spoke so many times to so many students: if what used to be was so very good, why have you ever left it? So that which has passed has served its purpose. But what does it have to do—except through disassociation and proper observation, of what benefit is it to where you are this moment? It has come by your law into your life. It has left by your law your life. You cannot grow if you do not permit yourself to awaken. You brought it into your life by laws you established. Though you may be ignorant in mental substance of those laws you have established, that does not exempt us from that law. Therefore, man is the world's, the universe's greatest borrower. He borrows things and never knows the moment that the law shall take back what has been loaned to him. So to permit oneself to over-identify with what they have borrowed—borrowed in the sense of not awakening to the law established. And not awakened to the law established, you do not know how long what you think you possess will be in your personal world.

Now, it's time for your questions. Yes, please.

*Yes. Would you, would you speak a little more on one battling what they believe that they are?* [In the background can be heard the chiming of a grandfather clock.]

Would you be so kind as to repeat your question?

*Would you speak up on, well, I guess, ways in which one is battling what they believe that they are?*

Yes. I think you could understand best when you experience what you know in your world as frustration. See, frustration is an expression of a war and a battle going on within oneself. A person experiences what they understand as frustration. You see, when one faces what they believe is an obstruction to what they believe is their right to have, they become what you know as frustrated. Would you understand that?

*Yes, sir.*

So when a person permits themselves to experience emotional turmoil, what you understand as, in your world, as frustration, that is an awakening within them that they are trying to force something in their world, and they feel the victim of circumstances or conditions. And it reveals, also, frustration does, an effort on the part of the human mind to control that which is not within the divine right of the personal responsibility of the individual. Frustration is not experienced without dependence.

Now when we permit our self to depend upon limit, there is guaranteed, by the very Law of Limit, that we will find where that limit is. And so when we find the limit in our life's experiences, we become frustrated. Does that help you with your question?

*Yes, sir. Thank you.*

Yes, certainly. You're welcome. [Yes.]

*Yes, please. It was said [to] move from making these things into guiding, and making—*

Why, certainly. One cannot guide what they do not accept they're responsible for. One may tempt to, in foolhardiness, but one cannot guide. You guide through education. You see, first of all, a person creates a thought, you understand, and they create it to serve a certain purpose in their life. And when it doesn't serve that purpose for which they have created it, they must guide it and remind it [of] its purpose of design. And if it no longer is serving its purpose of design and it refuses to obey its creator, then it's put to sleep. It's put to sleep by not permitting any more energy, through attention, to be directed to it.

*Thank you.*

Yes. You're welcome. Yes, please.

*Could, could it be said that being in creation is, is like—is it like a snare by, like being in a snare by choice? Caught in limit?*

Well, only as long—you see, you can't be caught in what you do not over-identify with. For example, when you identify with limit, then, of course, through that identification you establish the law through directing of attention, energy, you establish the Law of Attachment. And anyone who's attached to anything believes that that is theirs. Pardon? And so when one attaches themselves to what, by the very law, they have no right to attach themselves to, then they meet their limit and have their experiences. Now in that respect, one might say that's a snare, why, certainly, in the respect that one tempts themselves to believe that they are what they have created. Yes. Yes.

*Thank you.*

Certainly.

*And I have one more question on that. Would that be the purpose for being here to—*

The purpose of being here on this planet—as I've stated many times, there's a responsibility of the souls that enter the planet Earth: it is their work and their duty and their responsibility to refine and evolve limit, forms, and creation. You see, when you educate limit, you expand its consciousness. You see, you expand the consciousness of anything by directing consciousness to it intelligently. For example, the little glass of water here is controlled by the laws, in your world, of gravity. And so when you put it down, it stays down. Do you understand that? It does so for you and everyone who believes they are limit. Now, you see, because this is created—the law that has created it is greater than the created glass. Do you understand that? All right. So when you move in consciousness and are no longer controlled by limit, then you use limit to serve the purpose for your evolution through limit.

Now a person cannot levitate that which is under the control of gravity until they first do it to themselves. Do you understand that? You see? Because, you see, the law—like attracts like—the law does not fail. One must demonstrate for themselves before they can be an instrument of fulfilling the Law of Demonstration for anyone else. Does that help with your question?

*Yes. Thank you.*

And so, you see, when you do your daily activities, and especially before going to sleep and upon awakening—you see, that's when your bodies return, you see. You see, you are whole, complete, and perfect, that which you are. Perfect, for there is no obstruction to what you are, only your belief that you are what you are not. That's the obstruction, you see. And so when you go off to your sleep, you see, the body that you are convinced that you are, that's the one that you go out and have your experiences in, in these other worlds, you see. There's your nine bodies, and there's your nine planes of consciousness, your nine spheres, and the nine planets. There's your eighty-one and your totality. That is what—when you leave—you leave your body when you lose conscious awareness. That's when you leave your body. So at that time before actually leaving your physical body, your affirmations, your flooding of your consciousness must be done. Upon a return, when you awaken to your physical world, your affirmations, you understand, flooding the consciousness must be done, you see.

And so as we've discussed before, a twenty-minute rest is certainly more valuable and more reasonable than eight hours of sleep. For so many, so many people work so hard and use so much energy when they think they're sleeping, you see. And they go out into these other worlds, and there they work and believe that they are that particular body that's out there working. And they come back with that. And they awaken to their physical world and they're exhausted. Certainly, they experience exhaustion, because so much energy has been utilized while they thought they were sleeping.

And so it is certainly, certainly in one's best interest to rest. Rest—being perfectly still. Perfectly still, you see. No movement of the physical body is the first step of rest. Absolutely no movement of any part of the physical body. Eyelashes or anything. Now through a practice of that, you see, you begin—that little small step—gaining control of a physical body. A physical body is [the] effect of a mental body. So when you have absolute stillness, a total absence of movement, then you have made that first little step in controlling the mind or the mental body. Hmm? So that's what one should be working on: working on that absolute stillness, you see. No movement, you see. Because that reveals to you a slowing down of the activity and the energy utilization of the mental body.

Now you demonstrate that each day, and then, we'll move on to the next body. But first gain control of the mental body. And you will know when you have really gained control of the mental body for the physical body will do exactly what you tell it to do when you tell it to do it, and it won't try to do what it wants to do when you don't want it to do. Do you understand?

*Yes.*

You see? And so we have that whole area of chemistry to understand, and we have this entire area of laser and light to understand, you see.

*Thank you.*

You're welcome. Yes, please.

*What would be a good amount of time for someone to start practicing that rest period?*

A good amount of time is twenty minutes. Not to exceed twenty minutes. Yes. Twenty minutes. You see, when you gain control of your physical body, as a step in gaining control of the mental body, which is a step in gaining control of what you are— this fluid, this *prana*, this, this white light that's manifest in your physical world as, what is understood as, as *prana*. It's just pure, white energy. That's all that it is, of a sufficient low frequency that it can be measured by your scientists and their equipment, you see. Remember, the higher the frequency, the lesser the density, you see. Hmm? Yes.

*Two brief questions, sir. Are you referring to the twenty minutes in our, regarding meditation?*

No. A twenty-minute meditation is something entirely different. [A] twenty-minute rest may be at any time during the course of a day. Meditation—effort should be made to demonstrate the Law of Value and have your meditation in the morning. A twenty-minute rest is advisable, usually, for people around, after the noon hour in your world. A twenty-minute rest or rejuvenation, you see, and you'll be amazed if you make your effort and do your part now. I don't see any problem with any of my students having a lunch break, I think they call it. So I don't think there's any shortage of twenty minutes for a spiritual break. Yes.

*Could that be done in a sitting position?*

In a 45-degree angle position is preferable. A reclining position for rest is preferable. Yes, definitely.

*My second question, sir, is, How can we become soldiers of the Light on a daily basis?*

Through the demonstration of what you are. An absolute demonstration of what you are. Not permitting the mind, not permitting your mind to convince you of any obstruction. You see? For whoever, whoever permits their mind to see the way is never controlled by the obstruction, for there is no obstruction. Whoever makes that effort is a soldier of the Light.

So, you see, in one of your many affirmations that have been given: "I accept the possibility of experiencing the goodness that I am." You see, by so doing, you're speaking to mental substance, by so doing, by accepting the possibility—you see, if you say, "I am experiencing the goodness I am," you have all of these created things that come in immediately. And unfortunately, through errors of ignorance, they have no problem convincing the human mind that that is you, you see. No, no, no. "[I] accept the possibility of experiencing the goodness that I am," then they start to go through all this question: "What's he up to?" The true you. You understand? *[Many students laugh.]* I know how they work. I spent eons with them. So always accept the possibility.

Now remember, in accepting the possibility, you have no dependence on anything that is not within your divine realm of right. You accept the possibility of good health. You accept the possibility of happiness. All of that comes to you as accepting the possibility of experiencing the goodness that you are, for the goodness that you are is not dependent. Do you understand that? So, you see, it's not dependent on what someone does or doesn't do.

You see, that really puts those created forms, who are used to having their way and using that mental energy there from our divine being, that really puts them in a terrible state of question. You see, they cannot relate to anyone declaring accepting the possibility of experiencing the goodness that they are, for they have convinced mental substance, who [my] students, in errors of ignorance, believe that they are temporarily. So, you see, that's without their realm of possibility. That doesn't exist in their realm. You're speaking to them, but they cannot offer that to you. Because, you see, they come to you in to your mind and say, "Well, to experience the goodness that I am, I have to have so much money in the bank; I've got to have so many wives or girlfriends; I got to have this; I got to have that; and I got to have that." That's their realm. So when you speak to them and say, "I accept the possibility of experiencing the goodness that I am," don't you understand, they can't relate to that. You're not asking for them to bring you a tidbit. Do you understand that? You see. So always remember, accept the possibility of experiencing the goodness that you are. And no matter how many times you tell those things, they just cannot relate, because, you see, they have no control over that law, you understand. None whatsoever.

Now when they try to come into your mind to tell you, "You can't experience the goodness that you are; the goodness that you are is dependent on me!" You see, that's what they do, you know. I'm sure you realize that. You've had the experience, you see, like if your tire goes out on your car and they say, "Ah, you see," and you lose the goodness that you are because they tell you what you have to do. Do you understand that? Oh, yes, yes, my. Does that help you?

*Yes, sir. Much thanks.*

Oh, yes. Definitely. Yes, please.

*I'd like to—*

I'll be with you in a moment. *[The teacher addresses another student.]* Yes, please.

*I'd like to know if when your expanding and you're creating more expanded forms are . . .*

Yes?

*Are the . . .*

Accepting the possibility of experiencing the goodness that you are does not create limit or forms on which you must depend. That's what I just spoke to [your co-student] about in reference to those forms. They can't relate to that, you see.

*Are the forms that, the ones that you want to put to sleep, are they—would they relate to being the hissing hounds of hell before the victory?*

Oh, they, they won't relate to that because, you see, they've already convinced the uneducated ego, they've already convinced [uneducated egos] that they are, through them, that they are the ones that give you the goodness of life. See, they tell you in your mind you have to have this and you have to have that and you've got to do this and you've got to do that in order to get that goodness that you already are. So to tell them, you see, that you're accepting the possibility of experiencing the goodness that you are without their control of you, you must separate in consciousness. That's the purpose of the affirmation, is to free what you are from all of their dictates, to free you from being their slave. Does that help you?

*Thank you.*

Yes. Yes.

*Yes, you spoke that man is the universe's greatest borrower.*

Yes.

*He never knows when the law will make it time to give it back.*

Man is the world's greatest borrower for man *believes* he is the forms he has created, and they don't do something for nothing. Show me a person who believes they are limit, and I'll show you a person who does not, in any sense of the word, do something without the thought of return or profit. Yes. Yes, go ahead with your question.

*Is that law established at the time of the borrowing to have it removed from the universe of the individual?*

That law is the Law of Self. It's the Law of Selfishness, the effect of self, the denial of what we are. This is why all forms created by the mind are self-forms. They are self-forms; their expression is selfish. They do not do anything that they don't first judge there's a sufficient return. So if they give you one penny, they take back a dollar. Yes. Did that help you with your question?

*Yes. Thank you.*

So, you see, that's the—that is the transgression of the law. You see, it's the transgression of the law to believe that we are the limit, you see. That's a very, very selfish type of thinking. It is an effect of an over-identification, you see. And its expression is selfishness. So this is why this, this affirmation—which I've now given you the other half of it, right? You've had for some time, "I accept the possibility." Now you know what you should be accepting the possibility of. I thought it would be in your best interest to give you "I accept the possibility" in hopes that someone would perceive "The possibility of what?" Well, of course. The possibility of experiencing the goodness that you are. Yes. Anything else on your question?

*No. Thank you.*

Why, certainly. Yes, yes. Yes, please.

*When through our efforts what we believe we are—*

Thank you. Stop right there. You know, we're going to make a change here. Here we have a husband and wife, and I want you sitting close together, because if you sit close together, then you won't be obstructing my other students. Move your chair there. You know, oh, so long, long ago, even—there, you see! Now I can see everyone, like I should be seeing everyone. Yes, I can see right through there. I don't think it's necessary to ask her to move her hair to the other side of her shoulder. *[The teacher laughs joyfully.]* No. I'll be right with you. Because it's just brought to my—see, the laws of association, even the time there when I was married for so long, I never sat that far away from my wife: she wouldn't allow it. *[All the students laugh.]*

Now where's that—at that time—where's [the student who was asking the question], please. You can get just a little bit closer there. *[The students laugh again.]* That's fine, fine. Oh, isn't that lovely! Now, you have to move just a tiny bit to the left. She's the only one that has to move. Thank you. Sit right there. Now, you see, there we have an unobstructed view. Unobstructed. Isn't that lovely. Now let's see that these chairs are properly set. Isn't that nice. Very nice. Well, you have no problem with the camera. Very nice.

Yes, now we'll get to your question.

*Thank you.*

Yes.

*When through our spiritual exercises what we believe we are begins to weaken . . .*

Yes?

*How is, what is that experience of that belief weakening? How do we experience that weakening?*

Well, you experience it very well in the uneducated ego: you think you're losing your identity. You have an identity crisis. I've had students who have gone, in many of my classes, who entered what you call the identity crisis. Which only reveals to, to anyone who has eyes to see and ears to hear that man's uneducated ego is what has the identity crisis for he has all these forms that he has created. I think in your world you call it judgment. Yes. Now do you know how you experience it?

*Yes.*

You see, just have someone face their adversity, which is inevitable, you know. And anytime a person—you see, our adversities become our attachments by the very Law of Denial. And so when a person begins to experience their adversities—hmm?—why, certainly, they scream out, those forms; they're losing their identity. Because, you see, they're facing their adversity which only guarantees their attachment to the very thing that we're adverse to. If you want to be attached to anything, just be adverse to it. So do you see anything in your world you would like to be attached to? Oh, yes. Just establish that law and direct that energy, you see. You live in a world of duality; that's known as creation. So spend your life adverse to anything, I can assure you, in fact, I'll guarantee it—the law doesn't fail—you will live to see the day, here or hereafter, that you are absolutely attached to it. Yes. For you have directed energy to it, don't you see?

You see, say you direct energy to a, to a prejudgment and you become adverse to it from that constant thinking about it and sending it energy. And so here it is; it is an adversity expressing itself—you understand?—expressing your great uneducated ego. You see? "Oh, I wouldn't do that. I'd never do that. I would never do that, you see." And pride rises up. And so here's this little form you've created out there in the world working like a beaver, don't you see. And he finally—because he's created by selfishness; he's created by self, an expression [of] selfishness—well, he decides he's going to come home and take a break. A long break. That's called attachment. Does that help with your question?

*Yes, sir. Thank you.*

Yes. Yes, please.

*May I ask a question that is actually not related to what we were talking about?*

As long as it's related to life, it's related to me.

*OK.*

And should be related to you. Thank you.

*I would like to know the—a question on kissing.*

Yes.

*I would like to know if that urge is the forms attempting to consummate something.*

Well, try to understand in reference to this word *kissing*, even though it isn't Valentine's Day. *[The teacher and many students laugh.]* You know, I said long ago, you know, let's all have round hearts. You know, for pointed hearts, you know, they pee on what they can't control. So let's all move to round hearts. I gave that to you years ago. I think three or four years ago, whatever.

Now let's see, kissing. Oh, yes, of course, well, it's understandable, certainly. You know, here, you enter into physical form, and you receive your nourishment, your survival, you understand, by the use of your mouth, don't you? I don't know of any other way that you [or] little babies are fed. *[Again, the teacher and many students laugh.]* But anyway—oh, technology, your advancing technology will soon take care of that. And so if you permit yourself, you understand, to become over attached—now think about this—overly identified, overly identified to feeding, you see, then you become dependent. And so you grow up, a little child there, very dependent. And so if you don't get, through the Law of Association, this nourishment, which you believe your survival is dependent upon—and, of course, it is in a physical world, in your world in your present state of evolution (though all the chemicals you require are in fresh air, you understand, if you can find fresh air left on your planet). *[And once again, the teacher and many students laugh.]*

But anyway, so, you see, you believe that that's you, you understand? And so you reexperience in principle that very early stage in your life, you understand, of comfort, you see. You feel comfortable and secure. It's an emotional-security thing. And so you grow up and you got to walk around kissing all the time. You want to kiss the dog, but not usually. You want to kiss another of your own kind. It only really shows an uneducated ego, you know. You could kiss the flower and still have the same experience—but your uneducated ego won't allow it—if you understand the law, you see.

And so here we find in your world so much of this, "Well, I don't get enough kissing; therefore, I don't have enough affection." Well, I can affect you. I have, no, my boots here—he *[The teacher refers to Mr. Goodwin.]* doesn't have his boots on, does he? But anyway, I can affect you. Affection's affection. I have all kinds of ways of affecting you.

So, you see, what it is, is an over-identification with the un-educated ego; through the Law of Association that little baby rises up. You understand that, you see? And so it says, "Oh, well, nobody's kissed me lately." Well, I find it interesting: if you kiss them on the forehead, they say, "Well, what is that supposed to be?" Oh, no, no, no, no. It's got to be a kiss where they're used to nursing. Do you understand as intelligent people? That's what it's all about. It was never about anything else. You see?

So you make it what it is, you see. You, you make it what it is in your mind by believing you are what you have created and not understanding how the form was created when you were just a little, bitty baby and not even walking yet, let alone crawling, you see? And so had you been educated at that time to kiss the flower, well, when you kiss the flower, you would have that same good, so-called comfortable feeling and affection and all of that foolishness they talk about, you see? You see, you could have been educated that way. But you were not educated that way, you see? Do you understand that?

*Yes. Thank you.*

Yes, yes. Well, you could kiss a stone; you have the same effect. It's just as beautiful. All of those—you see, they're all created by your mind. You see, that is not what you are, but it certainly is what you're using. Hopefully, the world will start using it more wisely. Yes.

Were there any other questions? I am not—you know, some students that have come and gone here in the public classes that we used to have here in your, your little association—you know, my channel, I remember so long ago there in your world that so much—[some students would say,] "Well, we have a teaching of no emotion." That is not what we teach.

It's an understanding of what causes these forms that you experience as emotion, you see, when they don't have their own way, you see. Now if you cannot kiss the flower—which the Intelligence expressing through that flower is identical Intelligence; it is the same Intelligence that's expressing through your form. There is no difference. Now if you can't touch the flower and be affected by touching the flower, then you have a ways to go in educating your uneducated ego. If you cannot experience through a conscious choice of your mind, by creating the forms necessary, if you cannot experience the same experience that you have if some man comes by and touches you, well, then it's a long ways to go, you see. For all of that is created. That's all been created by your mind. That's all it is.

You know, I'm so happy to see that in your world, coming closer each moment—it's just wonderful—that this birth process, you see, it'll take place entirely, entirely in the laboratories, you see. And it is so beneficial to your world. It is so beneficial. It is beneficial in the sense that the forms, the human forms that come out of the test tube, when there is understanding (the proper colors, the proper music, the proper vibration is established in your laboratories), you'll have human beings without all of these problems, you see. You see, because those forms won't be created by their mental substance. Do you understand that? And it isn't a matter of what some of your people are so afraid of that there'll be a super race. That's all of the justification that, "Then what's the purpose of me being around?" Well, your purpose never was to be a rabbit, you see. *[A few students laugh.]* No, no. That's the rabbit's purpose to be a rabbit. That's the guinea pig's purpose to be a guinea pig. Your purpose—you've entered the world to be something more than—in, in the what you have earned as a form to be able to accomplish—certainly, something more than being a rabbit. Yes. That help with your question?

*Yes. Thank you.*

Oh, yes, I do hope so. Thank you. And [yes], please.

*When these more advanced form, human forms, work on refining creation and forms, which is what our purpose of being here, will eventually that refining process cause the physical Earth, which is limit, to cease to exist?*

No. The law is established by the Law of Birth. Birth and death is the Law of Creation. Whoever in ignorance permits themselves to believe, through over-identification with limit, must experience birth and death. Birth and death do not exist.

They do not exist. Change exists. Evolution exists. Birth and death do not exist, only to the ignorant.

Now, in reference to your planet, from the sun of your solar system was it born; to the sun, it is already returning. Very slowly, of course, for you see, these things, like you would say in your world, they don't happen overnight. Hopefully not. They happen in a day. *[The teacher and many students laugh.]* But anyway—by that I mean light. Yes. A brighter light, you see. Night is lesser light, and day is brighter light, all right? And why is that so?

*Night has obstruction, and light is without obstruction.*

Yes. Night—what is it that is obstructing that which is? How do you have night on your planet?

*Form.*

Well, what form?

*Earth.*

*The moon.* [Different students offer different answers.]

Anyone have anything to say about that? Does anyone have anything to say about how do you experience day and night—yes—in your—do you know?

*We turn our backs to the light.*

That's true! And you cast a shadow and you call that night. That's lesser light because there's an obstruction to what is. Now, what, what turns its back to the light?

*Earth.*

Yes. Now do you understand that? Is there anyone who doesn't understand that? So as it moves, it turns its back, it casts its shadow, and you understand you have night. Do you understand that? Pardon?

*Yes.*

So, you see, all creation has its spin. Hmm? So whether it's a planet or an asteroid, a human or a rabbit, it all has its cycles. If you understand its cycles, you say, "Oh, yes. I see. I'm going through this cycle where I'm turning my back to the Light.

However, I have memory par excellence and recorded within that are all of my experiences when I was facing the Light." So, you see, one in making their effort, through their affirmations and spiritual exercises, as they move through their cycle—as all things do, they all spin. All right?

Now remember, when you spin and counterspin simultaneously and equal, then you are what you are. And when you don't, you are what you are not. All right? Yes.

*How, how can we know that we're following our inner light for what's true for us, what's right?*

There is no question: when you are following that which you are, then there is a peace that one experiences within their being. And one does not battle anything or anyone to do it their way. Do you understand that? You see, there is an inner awakening, you see. One must do what one must do. You understand that? That is their evolution, you see. Now let us look at it this way: if that is what one has set into motion (to go that way in order to go home), then surely there is good in it. Would you—you understand that, don't you? Pardon?

*Yes.*

Now it may not agree with everyone else. Well, how could it? Not everyone else has that exact same law at that exact same moment expressed in that exact same way. Do you understand that? All things, you understand, their survival and their expression are temporary, for that which we are is passing through it, you see.

*Yes.*

The planet Earth and everything upon it, you see. And [in] all of these things that are taking place, declare the truth. Declare that truth. Flood your consciousness with what I have given you this evening on the affirmation—given you the other half of it; now you understand. Experience the goodness that you are, you see?

*Yes.*

By accepting that possibility, you enter that which you are, regardless. Regardless of what others think or don't think. You see, when one finds themselves becoming freer from concern of what others think or don't think, then one is following the inner Light.

You see, so many people, you know—you see, it shows our dependence on our mental substance by being dependent on what someone else thinks or doesn't think.

We are all returning to the Source from whence we came. No one can stop us from that. No, no, no, no. All of the scientists of the universe cannot stop your planet from going home to where it came from, you see. Certainly, the planet has demonstrated by its birth its own death. It's demonstrated how it shall die, for it has demonstrated how it was born. It was born in fire and gases, and it shall die the same way. Certainly, it is going home. And it is returning, slowly, very surely to the sun from which—you see, the sun is the father of all of the planets in the solar system. Each solar system has its own sun, you see? And it has its own children, you see? And so here's the, the father; there's the, the mother, and there's her nine children. And there's your solar system. Do you understand that?

*Yes.*

You see. Now it is true there are sometimes that the children grow up and then you have a few grandchildren around, in the planets. You understand? You see? And it is also true that sometimes, the little family you see, some of them went and died off. Do you understand that? So, you see, the, the life as you understand—you're the microcosm of the macrocosm. What is happening inside of you is happening in the universes. Everyone is going home. So let's be of good cheer on the way home and not sad about it.

Thank you and good night.

AUGUST 14, 1986

## A/V Seminar 17

It is indeed good to see that all of my students this past month of vacation have been doing so well in adjusting their perspective.

I realize that it is difficult, in times of error, to see the good in all things. The reason that it is difficult at those times to see the good in all things: for it is at those times we are seeking things, and that is the error that, at times, we fall into. We can easily tell at any time whether or not we are seeking things or whether we are seeking that which sustains things. For things lie on the thirsty banks of old creation, and it is the river of life that sustains and moves them. So when in our seeking for things, we realize that things are loaned to us and when we demonstrate they are but a loan, we care for them and never know the moment in which things, creation, shall go along its way.

The difficulty we often find is that we seek things as victims upon which we may express our emotional upheavals or frustrations. It is known as the lack of care. It is also known as a person, in time of error, who truly believes at that time that they possess things. For when so doing, one becomes the worker of the true possessor of things: the king of creation. That is where most all struggles and difficulties truly exist. We believe that we are the possessor of form, limit, and things. That makes us king of creation, and the battle begins with that king of creation.

Now this evening, for our seminar, I know that all of you have been making adjustments in your perspective, and I also realize that you judge those things to be experiences. To some, they have been seemingly difficult. Certainly not something that they believe they have consciously chosen. But let us not forget, whatever experience we encounter in life, eternity, we have established the law through which it comes to us. And it comes to us so we can make certain adjustments in our perspective.

Therefore, all experiences, all things in truth are good, for that which sustains them is the Light and is good.

Now we go along in our life and we see these certain cyclic patterns that reappear and reappear. We find our self on the mountaintop, only to blink our eyes and find ourselves in the depths of the valley. Well, of course, we make adjustments in our perspective never on the mountaintop, [but] always in the depths of the valley. So let us look with the spirit of joy where the lessons that we learn truly are.

When a person believes they're doing great, you usually find them, in a short time, telling you they're doing just the opposite. But they only do that for a time. That is the Law of Creation. That reveals a necessary adjustment in perspective.

Now we're going to take a few moments here at this seminar for the questions that you have. You will kindly raise your hand. Remember, to those who see the Light, there is no difference between the valley and the mountaintop, for they are not controlled by the fluctuating laws of duality. Yes.

*So you're not controlled by duality when you're down in the valley and you're learning the lessons that you need to learn to change your perspective . . .*

Yes? You, you are controlled by duality only in the sense that you *believe* that you are. You believe that you have need. Whoever believes they need destines themselves to the heights and to the depths. For need, as we have discussed so many times, is a denial of what one is. To permit oneself to believe that they need things, that they need limit is denying oneself of what they are. Yes. Yes.

*But just to, to use limit, to use it for your purpose . . .*

Yes. It is loaned to us for a purpose to be used. Yes.

*To grow through our, our—to learn.*

Well, we learn when we believe that we possess things. That's when we have our experiences. For example, if you accept the demonstrable truth that something has been loaned to you, you are not its master; and therefore, you cannot dictate how long the loan shall be, when it shall come and when it shall go. If you keep that perspective, then you will not have the bondage of the heights and the depths. Yes. Did that help you with your question? Yes.

*So to change—that's there to help us to change our perspectives.*

Yes, indeed, it is. And one experience only guarantees the continuity of the experience until such time as one makes necessary adjustments in their perspective.

*In that particular level of consciousness, or . . .*

In the one in which the experience is coming back to one as a lesson, yes.

*Thank you.*

Yes.

*Yes, in making this necessary adjustment, this perspective change . . .*

Yes, that's what all of my students have been doing—I'm so happy to see—this past thirty days. Yes. Without exception. Yes.

*The separation from that particular level or form—is it the steps that we have been taught, you know, in getting, in gaining a different perspective on this particular experience that's repeating itself, is to accept the particular form, that we created it, separate ourselves that we are not it, and our breathing and our affirmations, change the perspective on this particular form so that it does not keep repeating itself?*

Yes. Well, a very fine exercise that can be easily done by anyone is to choose—and you'll have no problem doing that, I'm sure—something that you, you truly believe that you possess, something that you believe you cannot live without because that reveals the degree of possession, an extreme possession, you see, in the mind. So choose something that you absolutely have convinced yourself that you cannot live without. Then convince yourself that it's leaving you. Then experience emotionally, mentally, with objectivity all that it has to offer you. You see?

*Yes.*

Now if you will do that as an exercise, you see, you will gradually, slowly, but surely, grow through the control of those forms that have been created by the mind. Now all of my students have many things to choose from. So I don't see any difficulty in making a choice. The thing is, you know, you don't want to overdo all at once; so choose something that, perhaps, there's the slightest possibility in your mind you could do without first, you see. And convince yourself—because we have—we will find that there is no difficulty whatsoever in convincing our self of what we need and convincing our self of what we must have. So because there is no difficulty in convincing ourselves of what we must have, the law is established of conviction: we have no problem of convincing our self of what is going to leave us because we have no problem in convincing our self of what we must have and what we need. Does that help you?

*Yes. Thank you very much.*

Yes. You're welcome. Yes. You see, to do something like that, an exercise of that type, consciously, then you have the light of reason to help you to maintain and to sustain reason, the very, very faculty, the soul faculty that will make the transformation and help you to evolve. If you do not do it consciously, then you do not have that support and that guidance from the faculty of reason. And you have it as experiences, for those are lessons that are coming into your life to help you to make the adjustment in your perspective. So a person, surely, would want to consciously choose to make the exercise rather than to have it come as some seeming disastrous experience that they have no control over, you see. So what I'm saying to you is that the same thing is happening, but you call those experiences distasteful experiences, but the same thing is happening, you see.

*Yes. Thank you.*

Yes. Yes.

*Am I to understand that you still have the experience, but it won't disturb you as much because you've already learned how to work with it?*

Well, certainly, when you learn how to work with it, then, of course, it will not have control over your mind and your emotions, you see. You know, as I've discussed before, that judgments, of course, [which are] solidified thought forms, their birth is in the water center, and we all know that the water center controls our emotions. Yes. So if we consciously make those efforts, you see, with a little exercise, there's some of the things [that] there's a possibility that we can do without, then we'll have no problem, you see.

In other words, what you'll be doing is consciously choosing, consciously choosing your direction in your evolution, rather than to have the evolution take place in errors of ignorance, that it's someone else's fault, you couldn't help yourself, and all of these defense mechanisms that the water center has to offer, you see; number one being discouragement. And when we learn how cunning and how clever the human mind is—to discourage us it likes to say, "Well, I have been studying for so many years. I don't see any change at all. There's no improvement whatsoever." That's when a person's in the valley, you see. However, when they get up on to the mountaintop, everything is beautiful, you see?

*Yes.*

So that's—we must understand how those things work in our minds, and work with them consciously. Yes.

*Thank you.*

You're welcome. Yes.

*Is there a relationship between jealousy and guilt?*

Jealousy, of course, is indeed a most destructive function of the mind. And, of course, rejected desire is guilt, as we all know.

And so a person rejects a desire and from that rejection of desire feels guilty. And in feeling guilty, one who feels guilty doesn't feel that way without a defense mechanism in order to continue to feel guilty or reject a desire. Therefore, they must look out to find someone to be the victim. Because our egos will not permit us to accept, until they're educated, to accept that we've done it to our self and we're getting just exactly what we really wanted. You see, our egos won't permit us to do that. Not, not uneducated ones, they will not permit that. So in that respect rejected desire, feelings of guilt, are related to what one understands as the function of jealousy.

And I think I spoke some time ago, you know, that a person always looks out and sees, "Oh, well, that person was so lucky," because that's their only way of justifying that they haven't made the effort. I think you'll find that we discussed that a long, long time ago. Yes.

*Thank you.*

You're welcome. Yes.

*Earlier in the class you mentioned in order to care, we have to accept that things of creation are truly loaned to us.*

Why, absolutely! You see, you can tell whether a person has accepted that things are a loan, you understand: you see, it's wisdom [that] reveals clearly a person who accepts a demonstrable truth that things are loaned to them cares for them and guarantees the continuity of the flow of things. Because they do not believe and possess. So, you see, they are not in competition with the king of creation. When you accept they're a loan, who knows how long they're going to be in your care? Now a person who does not care for the things that have been loaned to them is a person who believes that they possess them and is in competition with the king of creation and has a great many problems, you see.

You see, you cannot win in a battle with the king of creation when you believe that *you* are the king of creation, you see. You can't win that way, you see. There's no, there's no possible win. It's, it's, it's an absolute guaranteed lose situation. So to believe that you own anything, that you possess anything and to demonstrate that belief by not caring for it, you're, you're battling with the actual king of creation himself.

*Thank you.*

Yes. You're welcome. Yes.

*You said when, when we're seeking things, this is the error.*

The error is in seeking things, yes, rather than in seeking that which sustains things.

*OK.*

The seeking of things puts one in competition with the king of things, yes.

*So I was wondering, how does this fit in with our seeking our goals type of thing? Does that make sense to you?*

Yes, indeed, it does. Now, for example, a person has a goal. If you will examine the goal, you will find that the goal is subject to—that is, 99 percent of the time, so we're speaking about the world of creation now—we will find that the goal is subject to many things or conditions, what one would call conditions. Now, for example, say that a person wants to be a baseball player. Well, that's fine. That's what they want to be. However, that is not all that they want. For when they are offered a job to play baseball, for example, there are certain conditions that come along with that desire. And they will not just accept a job playing baseball. There's all these other conditions; that's where the failing is, you see. It's like a person who wants to be a singer. They want to be a singer; that's fine. It is the conditions that their mind, in errors of ignorance, put upon the desire.

Now, some time ago I spoke about the stealing of desire. Desire is the divine expression. The principle of desire is not the problem. It is the personality of desire or the conditions that the mind puts upon the divine expression which is known as desire. Did that help you?

*Right.*

See, it's the conditions. The conditions are mental substance; the desire is spiritual essence. Desire is the divine expression for it is spiritual essence. All conditions—but the mind puts conditions upon it, and when the mind does that, it is under the control of the king of creation. And that is where the problem lies.

*OK.*

Yes.

*Thank you.*

You're welcome. Yes.

*Is the—so the seeking is the condition.*

No. The seeking is not the condition. It's the, it is the—condition is—the, the problem is the conditions that the mind puts upon it. For example, a person seeking to be a singer or a person seeking to be a writer, that is not the problem. The problem is the mind's requirements. That is the problem. That's when the desire, the divine expression, it is stolen. It is no longer the principle. It is taken from a spiritual essence and covered with mental substance. Yes, yes.

*So the desire is pure within itself.*

The desire itself—all desire is pure. All desire is divine expression. It is the stealing of desire that contaminates it, and the stealing of desire is the conditions, which are mental substance, that are placed over the spiritual essence and the principle known as desire. Did that help you?

*Yes.*

Yes.

*Thank you.*

You're welcome. It's what we put over it. Yes.

*If the desire is also your livelihood, how do you—*

That's a condition that one places upon desire. It is now in a mental world, controlled by the king of creation. You see, you see, our livelihood, when we say that, "I'm a writer. My livelihood is dependent upon it." Your livelihood is dependent upon the truth and your demonstration of the truth, you see. So when you awaken to that truth—do you understand that?

*Yes.*

Then you will remove the conditions or the contaminations put over the spiritual essence of the principle known as desire.

*And the rest will take care of itself.*

The rest will take care of itself in keeping with the demonstration of whether or not the person truly has returned the desire to the Source from whence they have stolen it, you see, in errors of ignorance, you see. You see, if a person wants to write, then they write. Their livelihood is from the Divine Light. You see, it's all these conditions that we put over everything. It's all these conditions.

And this is—you know, a person says, "Well, if I don't do such and such, then I won't eat." Well, that's a condition that they have placed over eating. Do you understand that? And then another person says, "Well, if I don't do such and such, I won't have a roof over my head." That's the condition that they have placed over having a roof over their head. Someone else says, "Well, if I don't do such and such, then I won't have transportation." Those are the conditions that they have placed over transportation. Yes. When transportation, a house, eating, and all of these *things*, you understand, will fall into place.

Seek ye first the kingdom of heaven, and all things shall be harmoniously arranged around you. You see? So seek first the Light, for the Light sustains all things. And that which sustains anything has the power of controlling it—do you understand?—has the power of moving it into your life and taking it from your life, for it is sustained by that power. Now, for example, your automobile doesn't move until that which sustains your automobile takes charge. Isn't that true?

*It's true.*

So if you seek the automobile and you do not seek that which sustains the automobile, then you are under the control of the king of creation, you see. Do not seek things, for the seeking of things shall destroy you. It shall rob you of your peace, your harmony, and all of the abundant good which is your divine right. It is the seek—it is not the care and use of things; it is the possession and abuse of things that destroy us. For the possession and abuse of things takes place within our mind, and they are demonstrated out in the world, in the physical world. Hmm? Did that help you?

Yes.

Yes, please.

*Is there a particular direction to desire?*

No. Direction is condition of mental substance. The Light shines on everything. Nothing is excluded. Acceptance is the divine will of the Principle of Good, you see. So nothing is rejected and nothing is denied. So in that sense, you see, you cannot—to think that desire has direction is a condition which the mind places upon the divine expression. Hmm? Yes.

See, it's like a person saying, "Well, when I go sailing I feel good. And when I don't go sailing, I feel terrible." That's the condition they have placed upon that divine expression known as sailing. You see? That's what they have done. And that's where—I'm so pleased to see such wonderful adjustments that have been taking place these past days with the class and with all my students. I would like, of course, to see a conscious choice of those adjustments in perspective rather than an unconscious choice, so to speak, and having them disturb some of my students by what is known as experiences. Hmm? Yes. Why do it unconscious and blame the world, when you can do it conscious and know exactly what's going on? *[The teacher laughs joyously.]* Wouldn't you say? Yes! I think in your world they like to say the Russians are doing it. Isn't that what's popular? *[The teacher and many students laugh.]* Or your president has done it. Or someone else has done it, you know. Yes. If we're going to do it, let's do it consciously, and then we know who's doing it. Yes.

*Could you please speak on the laws governing the properties that matter can be used to generate a beam of light, known as a laser?*

Oh, certainly: crystal. Yes. When your world, you're coming to that, I mean between your gamma rays and your laser beams and all these other beams, you see. You see, the problem that you have in your world at this time is because the crystal is not fully understood, the beam of light only goes straight, you see, and your Earth has a curvature. But once they reach the point, your scientists, to [understand] how that can be bent—I think you call it bent—to follow the curvature of the Earth, and then . . . we'll see. It's always been crystal. It is the natural crystal and it's always been. I know you have many manufactured ones, but that which is manufactured does not contain what is necessary [for it] to contain. Hmm? For that purpose. Yes.

*Thank you.*

Did that help with your question?

*Not specifically, but it points out—*

Well, then you just clarify a little bit more—And Mr. Red, you can come over here right now—Yes. *[The teacher addresses Mr. Red, who was also known as Reddy, the church's dog, and continues to speak to him as the student asks his question.]*

*I—*

Right now.

*I was specifically interested—*

I know what you're doing. *[The teacher again addresses Mr. Red.]* Yes.

*In the—earth's scientists perceive that matter can be used to generate discreet units of energy* [Mr. Red begins to bark.] *of an identical wavelength.*

Well—Yes?

*And to create this beam of light called laser.*

*[Mr. Red approaches the teacher.]* You're late. Yes?

*I was wondering—*

Well, because, you see, all matter *is* light. And because it *is* light, of course, it emanates energy or light in varying degrees, you see? You see, the glass, you know, an object or the little vase here of flowers, that's all energy that's emanating its light. Everything emanates energy, and energy is light, you see. Yes, yes.

*That would follow from the law that all form is an electromagnetic energy field.*

That's all that it is. That's all that it ever was. It isn't anything else. Some more magnetic than electric; some more electric than magnetic and etc. It is nothing else. That's all that it is.

And, you know, when you say that you pass things through an object, well, you have to change the electromagnetic field. You make it similar and, of course, it'll pass through. Pardon?

*Yes. Thank you.*

Does that help you with your question?

*It does. Thank you very much.*

Well, all right. Certainly. You see, we seek the complexities in life when the simplicity is the joy. Hmm? Yes. Why do we seek such complexities? Because we take pride in our knowledge, you see, even though we really do know that knowledge knows much, yet wisdom knows better. Hmm? Yes.

Yes. We'll come to your question now.

*When we're working with letting go and letting God, in other words, when we recognize that our mind has taken hold of a particular job or situation . . .*

Yes?

*We feel that we can go as far as we can go . . .*

That is, our mind feels we can go as far as we can go, yes.

*Right.*

Because only our mind makes such error. Certainly not what we are.

*Doesn't the faculty of tolerance come in and help us expand our horizons?*

Yes, you want to be successful in going farther than your mind has allowed you.

*Yes.*

Is that correct?

*Correct.*

Well, without tolerance, there's no success. Yes, yes, yes.

*But then there—*

But what a wonderful lesson. One gains in tolerance and then, you see, it guarantees success.

*Without the mind's limit or the mind's judgment of how things should be.*

Well, now, let us, let us not forget the mind is something that we have come to use. It's not something we've come to have it use us. I mean, when we get to the point that—if we believe we are the mind, then the mind's in control, and we are limited by it, you see. And we have all these conditions and requirements. And if they're not fulfilled, then the mind won't let us go any farther. But you're not the mind. You know you're not the mind. You are the one that's using the mind. You are the one that programs the mind, changes the program, adjusts perspective, and moves on. There is no limit. You see, you cannot limit the limitless, you see, and we are limitless until we fall into the error of ignorance and believe we are king or queen. Then we become limited and can't go any farther.

*That's when we feel we possess it, right?*

That's when we feel we possess anything.

*Right.*

You see, possession isn't limited to an automobile. It could be limited to one's foot or one's toe. If one really believes that they possess their toe, when their toe is removed they have a real problem, wouldn't you say?

*Definitely.*

You know, if someone came along and chopped off your toe.

*Yes, well . . .*

Yes, well, I—*[The teacher laughs joyfully.]* You see, certainly, yes, yes. You know, and then there's so much difficulty with people in this so-called aging process and all that because, you see, they believe they are their body. How dare their body change, when they didn't tell it to change. Do you understand, you see?

*Yes, I do.*

You see, that's with all these so-called problems with so-called death, you see. They possess that body. Who dares to take it away from them? Where are they going to be because they are their body? Do you understand that?

*Yes, I do.*

Why, certainly. I know that you do. So you don't have any problem at all, do you?

*Yes.*

Hmm? Whoever sees the obstruction cannot find the way. So we all know that all we have to do is stop looking at the obstruction and the way appears. Doesn't it?

*But we have to find that within ourselves first, before we can apply to something outside of ourselves.*

Well, what's outside of our self is a reflection of what's inside our self. You see, outward manifestations are revelations of inner attitudes of mind, aren't they?

*Yes, sir.*

Yes, indeed. Yes.

*So if we feel that someone—no—we're having a problem with someone that's involved in our lives, we feel that they're not acting or responding the way we feel they should, in their own best interest—*

Well, what does the Light that is inside of you say? Hmm? That's the question, you see. That's the question one must ask themselves. Now, for example, I could sit here and say, "Well, now, [this student is] not acting the way I want her. And [she's] not acting the way I want her. And [that student] over there. [He] has not been acting, this last week, the way I want him to. And [she] is not acting—[he] is not acting the way I want him to." *[The names of students spoken by the teacher have been replaced with pronouns.]* Where do you think I would be? I think you call that place a booby hatch. *[Many students laugh.]* No. No. I'm not interested in those places. You see? Because it's a booby hatch of the mind. Hmm? So, you see, the thing is that when you have something to do, you turn to the Light within you, and you give what you have to give and you care less what they do with it. However, if, in error of ignorance, you permit yourself to believe that such and such a person does such and such and that's going to control *you*—

*Yes.*

—then you have made them your god. You see, you do what you know is right to do.

*All right.*

You see?

*OK, but then the mind comes in with fear and says well—*

Fear? For what? Where's God? Where's the goodness inside of you? You wouldn't call the goodness inside of you fear, would you?

*Definitely not.*

Well, there you are, you see. You see, it's a wonderful, wonderful lesson in adjusting perspective, you see. You can lead a horse to water, but you cannot make them drink. Only the Power that sustains them can make them drink. Do you understand that?

*So then you can only demonstrate what you have faith in and hope—*

Why, cer—No, you don't hope at all. No, no, no, no, no. You, you demonstrate what you know inside of you is right.

*Yes.*

For you.

*Right.*

Hmm?

*Right.*

And that that is around you, by the law that like attracts like, shall grow or it shall go. Do you understand that?

*Yes.*

You don't have to do anything about that. It'll grow or it'll go. One or the other. Do you understand?

*Yes. Thank you.*

And that's a wonderful opportunity for you to experience the great power of faith and the Light that you are. Hmm?

*Then that's where you bring in all your tolerance, too, for your own . . .*

Well, first of all, you see, we cannot grant to another what we have not first granted unto our self. And so wouldn't it be nice to grow in tolerance for our self? Hmm?

*Right.*

That we may have it to grant to another. Hmm?

*Because that's the thing that keeps coming to me, is tolerant.*

Well, wouldn't you like to be tolerant with yourself?

*Yes.*

But one cannot gain in tolerance until one learns the wisdom of patience.

*That's right.*

Hmm?

*Yes.*

Is everything to be done in one night?

*No.*

Then what will be left for tomorrow?

*That's right.*

Hmm? No, no, no, no. No, let the years roll by. Yes. What's two and a half, three years? It's a short time in eternity. I think that'll help you.

*Thank you.*

With patience and the wisdom thereof, don't you think? My! When a person fears what another does or does not do, then, you see, they've lost their God and they've got a new one. And so they're subject—they've, they've made themselves a victim.

*Yes.*

Do you understand that?

*Exactly. Yes.*

And even the most uneducated egos don't want to be victims. *[The teacher laughs joyously.]* I haven't found one yet that says, "Oh, I'd like to be a victim." Hmm? Now, you see, you see my student here, Mr. Red? He knows what he was doing over there. He took his sweet time to get over here, but he did get over here, didn't he? *[Once again, the teacher refers to the church's dog.]*

*He did.*

And behaved himself. He was over there digging. I know what he was doing. And he knows what he was doing. So, you see, you have your choice, you see. You have your choice to say, "I've called him; he didn't come," and get all upset.

*Yes.*

Right?

*Right.*

So what good do you do yourself? From a lack of tolerance and lack of understanding, one moves a little slower than another, you see. You see, this student here is very intelligent—known him a long, long time. And he has to go through all of this censorship. He has a great deal of censorship, like most people, you see.

*Yes.*

Hmm. And finally, the message gets through, and then he saunters on over. But, you see, when you want someone to do something just because you've told them, and you don't have the wisdom of patience, then you have a real problem. Because while they're moving, like a snail, to do what you've asked them to do, you lose the whole thing because you convince yourself that they're not going to. Try convincing yourself that God is greater than all of that and that there's no problem with God getting through by your own demonstration. Hmm?

Aren't you happy for all these wonderful adjustments? It's been such a wonderful month. You know, don't think I've been on vacation. I haven't. I've been watching all of you. Not all day. No, no, no, no, no. Well, I—it's my responsibility, and I have found it not only most beneficial, I have found it enjoyable, you see. Yes. It's always enjoyable when one is working up the stairs to the Light that they are. Hmm. Nothing else could bring about the adjustment in perspective than what you have as experiences. Hmm?

*Yes. Thank you.*

It's worth it.

*Definitely.*

Don't ever forget it. It's truly—it's wonderful. Hmm. And you know, the law doesn't fail us. If it doesn't come one way, it'll come another. Yes, someone else have a question? *[After a short pause, the teacher continues.]* So quiet this evening. I know very well none of you are afraid of me. He's not; look how long he took to respond! *[The teacher again refers to Mr. Red.]* That certainly isn't the demonstration of fear. Yes.

*You said that there was no difference between the mountaintop and the valley.*

No, there's no difference.

*Is it belief that makes us think that there is a difference?*

Yes, it is our belief that we are on top of the world when we're up on the mountaintop, you see. That's where we're totally deluded. That's where we are not facing the lessons, you see. They're not up there; there down in the bottom, you see. And we don't like the depths. That is true; our minds don't. But our minds delude us when we believe we're on the top, you see. So therefore, it is certainly more beneficial. We turn to the Light when we're in the depths of the valleys. We do not turn toward the Light when we believe we're on top of the world, do we?

No, that's not when we turn. So, you see, the benefit is when we're in the depths, you see. That's where we are willing to face the possibility of making some adjustments in our perspective. Hmm? Did that help with your question?

*I've got one more.*

Yes, certainly.

*So what is belief exactly? Is it electrical or magnetic or—what is belief?*

Well, belief, as far as electrical-magnetic, is absolute magnetic, you see? You see, a person in belief is controlled by the water center. And people believe many things. And in the believing of many things, they possess many things. The truth of the matter is, they're not the possessor. The things are possessing them. That's the sadness, you see. Yes.

*Yes. Where is gratitude experienced in that gradation of the valley and the mountaintop?*

Well, for example, when a person is in the depths of the valley, and they are demonstrating gratitude—they're really grateful. They're grateful for the experience that they are having—they start moving up into the light of reason, you see. They gain objectivity. You see, for example, you have a person with an experience, and they blame something beyond their control, someone else or something else, for the experience that they are having. Then at those times, they are not demonstrating gratitude. Hmm? For they are denying the law that brought it to them. Do you understand that? And in denying the law that brought it to them, they are not grateful for the living demonstration. Do you understand?

*Yes, sir.*

So, you see, a person looking at the world through the censorship—of course, we all have this censorship, you understand; we're in the mental world; we're censored—a person looking at the world and seeing things that they don't like [and] things that they do like, is equally grateful for all things. Do you understand that?

*Yes, sir.*

You see? When we are as grateful for the things that we like, as, as the things that we don't like, then we demonstrate gratitude. Hmm?

*Yes, sir.*

See? You see, when you have—say that you'd like to have steak and eggs for breakfast and your wife brings you cornmeal mush. And when you feel just as grateful [for either], because breakfast is breakfast—do you understand that?—now then you're demonstrating gratitude. But if you say "Where's the steak and where's the eggs?" then you have a problem: there's no gratitude. Who knows? It may come tomorrow, the steak and the eggs. You don't know. So if you're grateful for the cornmeal mush, because it is something—do you understand that?

*Yes, sir.*

That's gratitude. And if you feel just as good about the cornmeal mush as you feel about the steak and eggs, then you know that you're, you're moving along the path of Light. Hmm?

*Thank you.*

You see, everything is a loan. How long will the flower be loaned? Hmm? You must ask yourself the question. Everything is loaned. Everything. Man possesses no thing. And to permit oneself the luxury of believing that we possess anything is a terrible error of ignorance and a terrible struggle in life, for it's competition with the true king of creation. Hmm? Yes, please.

*When we are doing the exercise of, of controlling our experience of giving up something that we think we possess . . .*

Yes? And can't do without.

*And can't do without.*

Oh, yes, yes, because we possess many things. We can do without the glass if we want. That's no problem. There's another one in the kitchen, you see. Yes, go ahead.

*And . . .*

Yes.

*By association we start to think about all these experiences that we are attached to, that we're, that we possess and are possessed by. How do we deal with that in that exercise?*

Well, now remember this: we are not possessed by anyone or anything without first believing we possess person or thing. You know, you know, there're sometimes you'll see in life, we'll say, "Now that person is really possessing me and changing my whole life." Correct? Well, now we want to be very, very, very patient with our self. We want to be very honest. And we will find the seed of possession is within our self. That there is a part of our self that believes that we possess them. Do you understand that?

*Yes.*

See, the law doesn't fail there. So we go to work on that with the light of reason, objectively. And it'll take, sometimes it'll take a little while to accept the demonstrable truth: that we believe we possess them. We have no problem in our mind of believing that someone else is trying to possess us. No, no, no, no, no. That's not a problem for any of us. We have no problem with that at all. We see that everywhere. "That person's not doing what, what I want them to do; therefore, they're possessing me." Do you understand? You see? It is guaranteed. "They're trying to make me into something that I'm not." But, you see, that reveals, in truth that reveals that that person is trying to possess the other person. Do you understand?

So, you see, we want to be honest with our self and say, "Now just a minute, where in my mind here—I'm, I'm truly convinced that this person's trying to possess me. Now where in my mind am I trying to possess this person?" You see? Be honest about it inside yourself. Then, looking at that, and looking at what it offers you (your thought of possessing the other person)—do you understand?—who you believe is possessing you, looking at that, objective[ly], you say, "It's ridiculous. I don't need that anymore." You see? "That's, that's something I created long ago. It's not serving me well because I'm not happy." Do you understand that? You have no problem, do you?

*No. Thank you.*

Hmm? But you must be honest with yourself and see what they are offering to your mind. Hmm? Deeply seated. You find it in the emotional realm. Always. Always. Possession springs like a fountain from the realms of judgment. Just like a fountain. Yes.

*I'd like to know more about under—writing, writing and, and understanding what you're writing about so that you can paint the picture, sort of.*

What would you like to understand about what you're writing?

*Well, I guess the question is, Do you need to, when you're inspired to write about something, do you need to understand?*

Why, certainly not. If you are inspired, you simply write. If you are inspired to write, you write. Is that correct?

*Yes.*

Why, certainly. What does it matter? Ask my channel, if you see him later. Ask him how he felt, oh, ten years ago, oh, certainly longer than that, fifteen years ago, perhaps, '68, '69—that is quite a few years ago—when he was given an entire written discourse on the laws of entropy. He didn't even know what the word meant. Was most difficult for him. It happened to be a scientific discourse that was given to him many, many years ago. And there wasn't two or three words in the entire thing—and it, it bothered his mind, but it helped him also. Yes.

*There wasn't two or three words in the . . .*

That he could understand.

*Oh.*

Well, no, he couldn't understand it at all. You see, first of all, it was brought through with what you understand as automatic writing. It was several pages on the laws of entropy. And then, of course, when we left, we left. And he was left with the papers.

*[Many students laugh.]* Yes. Don't be attached to the fruits of action. Write what you have to write. Give what you have to give. Care less what the world does with it. Hmm? Because if you're inspired to write, if you're inspired, then you cannot be attached to what's happening. Isn't that true?

*Yes.*

Yes. Why, do you think that I would come here and work with you people if I had my channel bugging me every two minutes, [saying], "Say, what's going on? What did you say?" I know it takes time. But he doesn't. Anymore. That's many years ago. *[Many students laugh again.]* Didn't last too long.

Now time's passing quickly. Are there any other questions here this evening? *[The teacher addresses a student.]* You're always so interested in all these scientific things. Hmm?

*Well, the only question that was, I was interested in this evening was the, you mentioned belief was related to possessions.*

Why, certainly. Why, certainly.

*Belief in many things is possession in many things.*

And certainly not the care of them. We care for, you see, we care for that which is loaned to us. Do you understand that? See, when you care for something, you have accepted it's on loan. Now if you don't, for example, if you have a car that's loaned to you and when it's called (the loan time is up) and you take it back—do you understand?—if you haven't cared for it, well, you have a penalty to pay, don't you? So, you see, we know every moment of every day and every night whether or not we have accepted the path of freedom and [that] that has been loaned to us, you see. Now if we scratch it and destroy it, we have demonstrated we haven't accepted it as a loan. No, no, no, we own it; we possess it! And that's where the problem is, you see. The faculty of care. It's practical to let it express. Indeed, indeed it is. Otherwise, you pay the price of competition, and you're in competition with a king that you cannot control. Hmm?

*Yes, sir.*

You cannot win that battle. Yes. You cannot win that battle. You cannot believe that you are creation and win the battle with the king of creation. That's very foolish to try. Yes, we have a few moments left.

*OK.*

And *[The teacher calls the name of a student.]* has no question this evening. Shame on you. He has loads of—Well, you'll be feeling fine. I tell you, things will change very quickly. Seventy-two hours or less. Yes.

*Is that where, then, the destruction comes in, because the mind gets frustrated? We cannot control this king of creation when we're in competition, so this destruction—*

One enters competition when one believes that they own or possess anything or anyone. And it's a no-win situation because you cannot win in a battle against the king of creation and demonstrate that you believe that you are creation by not caring. You see, caring for anything that is in your universe, that has come in according to the law that you have set into motion, to care for it is a living demonstration that you have accepted that it is a loan. Do you understand that?

*Yes.*

It has come to you; it shall go from you. You do not know when. Maybe years, months, days, hours, or weeks. To believe that you own it and possess it, you are in competition with the king who truly owns it: the king of creation. And that's where all of the problems are.

*Thank you.*

Hmm? Well, how quickly, I would say, you think the time passes in your world. One hour is of naught, isn't it?

*Yes, sir.*

Well, I'll tell you, look up because the light's very small, sometimes, but it's still there. It's like when, in one of our meetings a long, long time ago, I stated that the soul, you know, it is so small, kind of like a pinhead. Bothers my channel terrible. And I said, "The only thing it bothers is that you're so small." You think that you know the size of a pinhead, but that's only mental substance.

Well, I'll say good night to everyone. Good to see you again in class here, though I've seen you in many other classes adjusting your perspectives. Thank you and good night.

OCTOBER 9, 1986

## A/V Seminar 18

Good evening, class.

This evening for our class seminar we will discuss what is known as the function of rejection and what we experience from it as a so-called feeling of being left out. Now when we understand and apply the laws that have been revealed to us, when we pause and think, we quickly view the law we have established. For man is a law unto himself; therefore, we must ask our self the question, What are we doing with the law that we are?

If we permit our self to believe that we are that which we have created, known as judgment, and, in that error of ignorance, we demand the fulfillment or expression of what we have created, known as judgment, to infringe upon the rights of another, we come up against what is known as the wall of reason. When so doing, we begin to experience feelings of rejection and [of being] left out, for our judgment has not the ingredient of the domain in which the very Law of Expansion and Contraction reveals is logical, for logic is a function of mental substance.

Now change is the Law of Evolution. Without total acceptance, change does not come easily. We do not evolve harmoniously. And when anyone does not evolve harmoniously, through what is known as the Law of Personal Responsibility, one evolves discordantly in discord and disease. For one is tempting to resist the infallible Law of Life.

All things come. And by the Law of Coming, all things go. Things are forms or limits. And in speaking on the feelings of being left out, we leave our self out of many things in life for we believe we are things.

The principle of a law is impartial, for it is formless and it is free. When we tempt to define the law, we put it into limit. We put it into restriction and in service to the use of self. The oxygen, the law through which it flows, supplies the tree as well as the human being. The law is clearly revealed: those who expose themselves to the oxygen become receptive to it. Those who place obstructions between themselves and the oxygen experience and receive less of it. The only obstructions in our path are the temporary beliefs of the judgments that we have created.

Let us not forget that method is legal for it contains the motive of purity; it is a principle. Deception is well contaminated for it is a function of the human mind in service to the judgments we have created and for a time believe that we are. Deception is dependent upon mental substance for the faculty of method has now been stolen by the human mind for self-limited interest.

Some time ago I spoke to you on the foreseeable move of my channel. I spoke to all of you in principle, impartially, all of you present in class. Therefore, you all have been aware for some time that my servant, my channel, is leaving your present location. All of you, as my students, were informed. All of you regular students. Therefore, to be informed, a wise person prepares themselves. If one is not wise, one does not prepare oneself and experiences the frustrations created by their own mind of what shall be or shall not be for another. That is indeed a most difficult and distasteful experience. We, as a class, as a school, in principle are evolving. You, as my present students, are welcome and well aware. You, however, do not dictate with mental substance the teachings of the school you attend, for in so doing, when the light of the student exceeds the light of any teacher, the student grows or goes in pride.

Now this evening the tapes that you have been receiving shall be withheld and will be available to you students, who remain my students, after the change of the school in your world. Should you at that time still remain students of mine, your tape of this lovely class will be waiting. Should you decide not to be, after the change is completed, then you will have no interest in what has been for you have already learned that what has been is not where you are in the moment that you are. Now if that does not make intelligent understanding to you, I will be more than happy to answer your questions at the question-and-answer time.

For many years in your world, in your physical world, my channel, being guided on the various changes that are to be made, for many, many years few minds have been aware until the change has been made. The reason for that is not a matter of the function of deception, as some in moments of ignorance like to think, no. It has proven beyond a shadow of all doubt, of all shadows, it has proven to be the wisest path at that time of our evolution of our school in your world. Only those absolutely essential to bringing about the physical change have ever been informed. And for my channel this is indeed a great change in the methods that we have always used in the evolution of this school in your world. However, you and his mind should be well encouraged that after forty-six years of his efforts in serving the Light that the school has evolved that you, your minds, may be informed in more detail while the process is taking place.

This school is moving to the northern coast of California. You are welcome to attend our monthly classes. You will have a long drive. You will have the opportunity of demonstrating how much you say that you value what you receive. You will have that opportunity. You will not have your way of dictating where the school shall be, how long it will be, how short it will be, when class will be in session, when class will not be in session, and whether or not the teachings that you receive can be used by your mind to justify and to defend the functions that some students temporarily believe, in moments of error and ignorance, that they are.

Yes, we are moving. I have informed you for months. You have been informed. There is nothing compulsory for anyone; you are never left without the golden opportunity of choice.

It is not necessary for you to hire a helicopter to reach where we're moving the school. It's not the Tibetan mountains, though it could well have been. However, it would greatly reduce the size of our class. Principle is not dependent upon quantity, for principle is not what is dependent: it is the form or limit of principle by the uneducated ego that is the problem, not principle. When we take the divine, impartial laws and we put them into form of mental substance and we use the Light to serve the vehicle which sustains the Light, then we indeed have problems. Yes, indeed, we do. However, each problem contains its own solution. Each attachment contains the indispensable ingredient of adversity. If an attachment did not contain an adversity, divorce in your world would be unheard of. It could not possibly exist. For example, Honey Dew, California, could not possibly have evolved to Divorce Flats, California.

And if you do not wish to accept what I tell you, then check with my channel and drive to Honey Dew and see: it is Divorce Flats. It has two names. It has evolved. The next name will be the principle of nothingness. Thank you.

Now it's time to raise your hands for your questions on this evening's class. Yes, please.

*Could you please explain to us the, what you mean by the next name being the principle of nothingness?*

Why, certainly! Principle is not dependent on form. Personality is dependent on form. Nothingness is no thing. Certainly. So when you have no thing, you do not have Honey Dew or Divorce Flat. You have principle; you are in principle. Does that help you with your question? Yes, remember that all dependence—all attachment is dependence. And so whatever you attach yourself to, you become dependent upon and are the victim thereof. You can create anything in consciousness and believe that is what you are, then you are in service to it, dependent upon it. And when you get weary of serving it, then you divorce it. And that's known as placing your attention or your energy and identification upon the ingredient that the attachment contains. So, you see, all attachment is adversity; all adversity is attachment.

Yes. Nothing's good or bad but thinking makes it so, for it is mental substance that limits principle. Does that help with your question?

*Yes. Thank you.*

Certainly. Yes. For example, in one moment someone says what a nice and intelligent person that you are, as long as you are in service to what they believe that they are. When you are no longer in service to what they believe that you are, then you have a different answer to your question. Did that help with your question?

*Yes.*

Pardon?

*Thank you.*

So that only reveals the, the interactive dependence. For example, even in your world today, you have what is known as—what do you call them?—crises lines. You have telephone numbers, you see, that you can call for your stresses and etc. Well, now you have in your world people who, who listen to you and who sympathize with you, and in time you become dependent on that telephone number. Well, in your world, in your technology right now it is human minds that are answering you, but with your new computers and your interactive systems, all of that will be programs and interactive systems. And so electronics will take care of you.

You see, all magnets who, who believe they—all who believe they are mental substance are magnetic. In the moment of believing that you are that which you have created, you certainly understand that in that moment and in that error of ignorance you are magnetic. Whether you're a male form or a female form, we're talking about a law. And so the minute you create something and believe that you are what you have created, you are at that time magnetic. Magnets are dependent. What are they dependent upon? They're dependent upon the electrical. You've had the teachings. And so when you choose to be, to be dependent and when you seek outside for what you consider [to be] that which is your right, then you place yourself into a magnetic sphere of consciousness, and you are dependent upon the electrical.

And when one has their own powerhouse, I don't know why they would want to choose someone else's. I mean, after all, the utilities cost enough without trying to build another one. Yes, any other questions? Does that help with yours?

*Yes.*

Yes. Yes, please.

*Could you explain the meaning of the word* principle?

To define principle is like defining truth. It is individually perceived. Because principle is an expression of truth, to define it is to limit it. It is individually perceived. A person evolves and becomes receptive within their own consciousness to that which is, to that which they are. Now, for example, there are many thoughts and feelings, emotional, that you have expressed in your life. You have had the experience. And time has passed and you've looked back in hindsight and said, "Well, that was never me. I can't imagine why I, I had that nightmare." Correct?

*Yes.*

Sometimes you awaken in the morning and say, "Ugh! Well, I'm glad that was only a dream!" Well, you see, life is a dream for the mental world; so "Dreamer, dream a life of beauty before your dream starts dreaming you." You see, a person's mind is a dreamer; it dreams, you see. You have the choice of what you want to dream. Choose wisely what you dream, for the tendency of one who creates with their mind is to believe that they are their mind. And when they do so, that which they have created becomes their master. Does that help you? Pardon?

*Thank you.*

Yes. And so, you see, if you accept, "I am the dreamer. My life's experiences are what I have dreamed. I can change my dream at any moment that I choose to do so." Hmm? However, when you make the choice to change your dream, you must face, and shall face, all of the dreams that you have dreamed and believe that you are. For they will rise up and they will disturb the tranquility of your mind. Do you understand that?

*Yes. Thank you.*

Yes. And so one pays their own price for moving from personality, the limiting of principle, to the freedom of what it truly is. Hmm?

*Thank you.*

Yes. It's like a person [who] says, "Well, I want an ice cream." But an ice cream must contain a holder, and I think you call that a cone. And if it doesn't have a holder for your hand, then some people don't want it. Many children don't. They want what they call a cone. Now other people want an ice cream, but they want it coated. And therefore, if it doesn't come and look like a bar, you understand, though the ice cream is ice cream, then they, they have a problem with it. Do you understand that?

And so another person says, "Well, I want some fresh air." Well, fresh air to them is restricted by what they have created with their mind and believe they are. Fresh air for them may mean that they want the breath of the, the scent of the pine tree as they inhale the fresh air. Do you understand? And so each one creates, you understand, an obstruction to the principle which they are. And so as you move along life and you meet up against these walls of reason, they are only in keeping with the laws that we have established. We find that here is an obstruction for we are tempting to move into the zone of another's rights. Do you understand that? And so this takes place within our consciousness.

If the goodness of life is dependent upon a golf club, then if you don't have a golf club, you do not have the goodness of life. Would you understand that as moving principle into personality? Pardon?

*Yes.*

And so one experiences principle in keeping with the censorship of believing the forms that they have created that will permit it to flow through their consciousness. Does that help with your question?

*Yes, it does.*

Yes.

*Thank you.*

Yes.

*Why is it considered the wall of reason? And are all obstructions and judgments considered, all our judgments and obstructions come against the wall of reason and when—*

Keep faith with reason; she will transfigure thee. For the wall of reason, we meet when that which we have created and believe that we are face the mirror, their own reflection. Does that help with your question on the wall of reason?

*Yes. Thank you.*

You see, you see, if you tempt to permit yourself to believe that you are a judgment you have created, and that which you have created and believe that you are demands to transgress the Law of Personal Responsibility and require another to service that which you have created, then you're going to meet the wall of reason.

*Thank you.*

Does that help with your question?

*Yes.*

Yes.

*Thank you.*

Who's wall of reason? Your own wall of reason. Yes, please.

*Is dreaming the same as the imagination?*

No! No, it is not. It does not contain conscious choice. If you're speaking of dreaming and you're speaking of imagining, imagining is a conscious choice of using mental substance to create that which will serve you and, in so doing, be constantly monitored, then you have made a conscious choice [of] creating. Now dreaming is the fulfillment of desires that you believe that you are.

For example, say that you have a desire to sing. And so you permit yourself to create a form that in order to do so someone else must do something. Then, because you have allowed yourself that luxury of ignorance, then that which you have created and believe that you are ever prompts you—you understand?—in desire to work to manipulate that which is outside of you and that reveals a path of frustration. Does that help with your question on the difference between dreaming and imagining? Pardon?

*Yes.*

Good. Do you have another question?

*If—so if you imagine and you consciously create . . .*

And release to the Source from whence you have temporarily borrowed it. You see, put God in it or forget it. Putting God in anything or forgetting it is not only the path of wisdom and reason, it's a path of personal responsibility. You see, when you create something from this—you see, desire is a divine expression. Now you steal the desire and you put it into a container. And you want that which you have formed to serve you, all right? Well, the only way that that's going to take place intelligently and reasonably is to take that little form that you have borrowed, that you have stolen from the Divine, and return it to its Source. Now when you permit your mind to tell the Source what day it shall be and you permit your mind to tell you that some other individualized soul must be a servant to what you have created, then you have serious problems. Do you understand that? Pardon?

*When I have, when you have somebody and you create another form . . .*

Yes?

*And service what you've created?*

Yes. And that form that you have created in ignorance is dependent upon another person.

*Thank you.*

[Do] you need another person in order to, for example, to paint?

*No.*

[Do] you need another person to express that which is your right of expression?

*I understand. Thank you.*

Pardon?

*No, no.*

For when you do, you are in slavery and bondage. And you are the victim of mental substance: first your own, then everyone else's that you create in your mind [that] can possibly service what you desire. Is that freedom?

*No.*

Is that principle? It is indeed the bondage of personality, for when they do or don't do what you demand with your mind for them to do or not to do, then you experience the law. When your judgment meets the wall of reason, you have what you call rejection and being left out! And to further justify your demand of what someone else should do in service to your judgment, which you believe you are, you're even tempted to believe that's deception because they won't do it. Does that help with your question?

*Yes.*

Well, certainly.

*Thank you.*

If you want to know the two paths there are: there is the left path, my way; there is the right path, God's way. Well, who is God? That's what you truly are. You are the God; you are the goodness; you are the Principle of Good. That is within you. You cannot control it with mental substance for mental substance is designed to service it. And when you tempt and try to manipulate the goodness that you truly are to service what you are not, you experience what you call frustration and discord. Yes.

That which you are is whole, complete, [and] perfect, for it is impartial. That's it. That is what you are. Now when you want to believe that you're something else, you start depending on form. You take the goodness that you are (principle) and you put it in a container. The problem with putting it in the container is you hold on to it tenaciously and you won't return it to the Source that owns it. You see?

When you borrow, you incur an indebtedness. So when you borrow from mental substance, by believing you are what you have created by mental substance, you must pay for it. The payment is your service to it. And if you do not wisely create it and you do not wisely consciously monitor it, and when it refuses to do what you have created it for, then you've got a serious problem. You remove yourself from it, and by so doing in consciousness, it has no more energy and it starts to disintegrate, you understand, to the shadow, you see, that it truly is.

Any other questions? Class this evening—yes, please.

*Could you explain more fully the faculty of method? And is the counterbalance the function of deception?*

Yes. Yes, indeed, it is. Absolutely. You see, all right, fine. Method is legal for its motive is pure. It is a servant of principle, the law impartial.

*Yes.*

Now when that is taken by mental substance, put into a container—do you understand?

*Yes.*

It now becomes partial, a servant of personality. You see?

*Yes.*

It is the same law, you see. However, when it enters mental substance, when it enters restriction and limit, it services the functions, the senses of the self, of the limited being. You see, functions are servants of self; faculties are servants of soul. Did that help you?

*Yes.*

Faculties are independent; they are not dependent, you see, for they are not limit. Functions are dependent. Indeed, they are dependent. Now tell me a person—we can list all of the functions. And the functions say, "Well, I need a partner. I need this. I need that." Functions reveal their dependence. Faculties reveal their independence. Faculties, you see, are freedom. They serve faith. Functions are bondage; they serve limit. Hmm?

*OK.*

So there's nothing wrong with a function, as long as you remain in charge with it, as long as you say, "All right, function, I know what you are. I know who you are. This is how long you have. No longer. And don't give me any problem by disturbing my mind when your five minutes are up." You see?

*Yes.*

Then they serve the purpose for which you have designed them.

*Yes.*

They have no problem taking orders. They don't try to deceive you that you are them. For when they do that, your little soul is bound.

*Yes.*

You see?

*Yes. OK.*

Does that help?

*It does. Thank you.*

Why, certainly. Yes. Any other questions this evening? [Did] you have a question?

*Not at—*

We're moving on, you know.

*Good!*

The upward way. Yes. *[The teacher laughs joyously.]* Yes, indeed. Yes, indeed. Those who intelligently choose faith will not experience fear. How can you experience fear when you have chosen faith? How can you possibly experience fear without believing you are the judgments you have created, and they plague you and demand that you do this and do that.

You see, my friends, the classes are evolving. Shall we survive when the glass is gone? When the paper no longer is, shall we still breathe? What shall happen? That's the question. You alone have the choice of evolving. You alone make the choice for you. My channel, forty-some years ago, made his choice. He made a choice to serve the Light. He has been taken to many, many places over many, many years. And so is he without bread or butter? Is he without survival? No.

However, one only grows for oneself. Hmm? You see? And you see, whenever we face the possibility of making a change, we must face all of our judgments who sit so satisfied and give us the false sensing that we are secure. Hmm? Show me what is secure that is not in the Light of eternal truth within itself. Show me what is lasting, everlasting. What is it? Only that which has no beginning has no ending. Everything else begins and ends. And so that which sustains it moves into another form, you see, ever in keeping—for that which sustains it is the same in everything. There is no difference.

They say communicate with a flower and the other creatures. Communicate with what you are; you'll have no problem with the language of the flower. Communicate first with what *you* are, not with what you believe that you are, you see. Do you think that the dog who looks at you does not think just because it doesn't speak English or French or German or something else? No. The dog, the cat, they speak very clearly. They understand very well, you see.

Man has the problem. He's over civilized himself and attached to the fruits of his action. Hmm? Yes. Only man has risen so great in creation for only man is the greatest servant of limit, obstruction, and form. For whoever believes they are form is the greatest servant of all the forms that they create. Yes.

*Can I have more information on the change that the school—*

Well, I'll be more than happy to give you all the information. In fact, my channel will awaken after I'm gone, and he'll have as much as a surprise and probably more than even [you] or all you students present. Yes. We are in process and are moving to the Northern California coast in the area of Fort Bragg. Hmm? Now there, there in that area in the country, we will place our channel. And those students who care to survive in that type of an atmosphere—you know, that means many adjustments for them. But many will choose to commute. And, you see, we will be approximately 3 hours and 36 minutes from this present location, depending of course on your safe driving records. And are there any other questions?

Yes, we will, of course, continue to have a monthly class for our students. That will be open to all present. No, the student group will not be living under the same rooftop as my channel. No, that will not be. *[The teacher and a few students laugh.]* He has one philosophy and a good philosophy does he have. He learned it when he was a child: high fences make good neighbors. These don't happen to be quite high enough. *[The teacher refers to the "fences" of plants that surround the temple.]* They're living fences and he did everything he could to get them to grow thicker and higher, but, of course, you see, things don't grow overnight and it's ten years later, you see.

No, it is time to move on. There is a great change taking place in the general area of this particular community. There, across, as you look across at the hill, right now you might see perhaps a dozen of what you call houses. You won't recognize it in times ahead. It'll look more like the Riviera, you understand? I'm talking about congestion, you see.

*Yes.*

You have a yacht harbor that is pending. You have an Air Force base over here that's being built within the next three years, not as an air base, but the whole thing is changing.

And so we informed our channel and all of our students at the time that we built this temple here, that it was built as an asset for our church, for our school, that it would serve its purpose, and when its purpose was served, the purpose of its original design, it would be used as an asset to move on to continue to serve the Light in a material world. And so that time has come, you see. And so that asset will be used in order to move the school to the country. And, indeed, country it is! However, the atmosphere is clean.

But, you know, like anything, when you leave any place it's always difficult. It was difficult for the mind to get wherever you are. And once getting where the mind is, it has all its created forms. And then to face making another step, all of those forms that we believe that we are give us a lot of problems. However, it's a wonderful awakening because, you see, that shows us how much we are in service to that which we have created. Hmm?

And one certainly could not consider that freedom. One might consider it security, but surely not freedom. Yes. And so no one is left out, you see. Those who wish to go are welcome to the area. We have put up no restrictions that our people couldn't move to that lovely area.

In fact, you know, so many times, over the years, my students have said to my channel, "Well, just exactly what this and what that? And what hour and what time? And how much?" You see, when he himself doesn't ask those questions, because he does know better, you see. Knowledge knows much, but wisdom does know better. And so he's learned to know better long ago. He doesn't plague us with that foolishness of, of trying to find someone to lean on, you see. The mind is tempted, and the judgments, to lean on someone else, you see. So that in case something doesn't work out, it has something else to blame, you know, kind of like a husband and a wife, you see. "Well, it was your thought," was really a thought. If it causes a problem, it was a thought. If it was an idea, there's no discussion about it; it just is. But it—so, "It was your thought. And this is the mess that I'm in, and it was all your thought." You see, that reveals ignorance of a human being truly identifying and believing they are the forms and the judgments they have created. They're always looking for a fall guy, don't you see.

So my channel was taken on, one day, 200 hundred miles, driving along the Southern California coast. All right? And so when our driver said, "Well, have we touched it yet?" And he's on his way back home, and he was informed, "It's more north." And so my channel was directed to go in the general area of Eureka. And so he did. And so there he rode for 12 straight hours, 720 miles and on the way home, we said, "This little area here."

Well, now if you understand the human mind, then you can understand he's sent—he goes all the way up to a little town—it's not so little anymore—called Willits, where we happen to have started our Camp Serenity many years ago, you see, in the woods and have released that property, sold that some time ago with a little income. And you go from here all the way into the town of Willits, and then you're told to go there, north. And you go all the way up north and you pass through all the mountain ranges and you go all the way up to Eureka, and then you come all the way back down the coast. You see, you kind of made a horseshoe. It's so ridiculous, the human mind, isn't it? But it gives the opportunity. Where is your fai—Is it faith that you have or is it fear? Is God, goodness at your convenience? [If so,] then it's censored by the forms you have created.

So, you see, everyone has their opportunity. "How will I survive?" Well, you turn to God. You turn to the God that is inside of you for that's the only God there is. But never forget that very same God sustains the flower.

*Yes.*

Hmm?

*Yes.*

See? And so, you see, what is concern? Concern is not good business. Ask my student. We have a little statement on concern. It's not good business, you see.

You see, there's one principle that the pioneers of your country demonstrated. They demonstrated in the wilderness, not even the grizzly bears could they freeload off of, because the grizzly bears had to go out and search and work for their own. So, you see, the country offers not only fresh air, the fresh air also of reason. Whatever you have, however you live is dependent on your efforts, when you live in the country. Now in the city, you can go through all of these manipulations. [There's] too much city moving around us, you understand? The time has come, you see. And so [we're moving] out into the country.

Of course, my channel will have no problem because, you see, that area is also an area that was originally brought into being by generations of the very state that he's from: the coast of Maine. You know, that's who came and settled that whole area, you see. And so although I wouldn't want you to think that in our classes we're partial to the state of Maine, but they do have a reputation of surviving, you see. Twenty below zero has a great temptation to personal responsibility, you know. And when you take a look at your stove and it's getting chilly, you know very well that your wood bin is filled, that the barn has plenty of wood that's been cut. And it's already brought in because 20 below at midnight, you see, or one in the morning, well, you've prepared yourself, you see. You have forewarned yourself. You never know. Who wants to go outside in their night shirt in 20 below blizzards of snow? Pardon? Did that help with your question?

*I see.*

Yes. And so isn't it so wonderful that we have in our ways demonstrated the Law of Personal Responsibility, not depending on anything outside for our survival, you see.

You see, the classes are not something you depend upon. The classes are simply a sharing of understanding that is, in truth, inside of yourself. Do you understand that, students? And so our purpose is simply to reveal, to expose the obstruction. Exposure frees the soul for it casts the light of reason on what you have mentally created and what [is] now, thrilling your senses, [and] you believe that you are. That is not what you are. That is only what you have created. Do you understand? You see?

And so it can only bother or disturb you when you think you are your senses. So when you think you are your senses, everything that you have created to serve your senses demands that you do certain things. And if you don't do certain things, you have a real problem. Hmm? You see, you see, well, as one of my students said so long ago—a little something right there. Oh, well I thought so. Yes. It's not, it's just a little bit of dirt there. From tape I, yes, that could be tape. Yes. *[The teacher finds some dirt on the table he is sitting at.]* You see, you want to open your eyes and see everything. I see you, but I also see that little speck of dirt there. It's from a piece of tape. We'll take care of that later. Do you understand that, you see?

*Yes.*

You see, you have two eyes. They encompass many things if you permit them to do so. It depends upon your mind. You can see the clock. You can see the chair, the library. You can see the window. You can see what is in front of you, you see. You see, man has restricted himself to believe that when he looks straight ahead, he only sees the object that's in front of him. That is not true. When your eye looks singly, you encompass everything, you see. You see, you see, the eyes are restricted; as vehicles for the soul, you see, we have restricted them by the mist of that which we have created and believe that we are. Hmm?

And this is why there are times when people feel, "Well, I can't see a thing, you know. I have to have the glasses." Well, you see, that's when the mental substance begins to get in the way. That's what's disturbed my channel so much. You know he's very practical and after he bought some new glasses and he sets them down and he sees better than he does with the glasses on, it bothers him terrible because they were rather expensive, you see. Then there are times that he can't see a thing unless he does pick up the glasses. So now what does that prove for everyone, you see?

*Yes.*

You see? And so when he goes to the doctor and the doctor says, "Well, I'm really impressed at your age you don't have glaucoma." He doesn't even know what glaucoma is. "And you don't have cataracts." And he says, "Well, what's that?" And then the fellow explains that to him. And he says, the doctor, you know, "Well," he says, "I really don't see anything wrong with your eyes, except you, you are farsighted." He didn't know whether that meant he could see things at a distance or close-up. But anyway, he sees very well at a distance, and when he is calm and peaceful, he sees things very clear close-up.

So, you see, what it is and what we want to understand is that our beliefs—you see, we call that ofttimes, we, you know, you know, our judgments like to make—what is the name, you know, they like to use that, you know, "Well, I'm just being natural. Well, can't I be just human?" Well, you know, our judgments use all kinds of things, you see. You know one, one calls it being natural. Another one says, "Well, can't I be normal?" or "Can't I be human?" Well, how can you be human unless you understand that human means animal, human means senses, human means limit, you see. You can expect the dog to say, "Well, can't

I be human for a while?" because the dog is usually human. But a being with two legs, an individualized soul, and supposedly an intelligent mind of logic, you wouldn't expect them to say, "Well, can't I be a dog for a while or a grizzly bear for a while?" You see? *[The teacher laughs.]* Isn't life beautiful?

Well, this is what we want to face, you see; it's known as growing up. Growing up is personal responsibility, the ability to respond—as I did to the five minutes, they tell me, you know, he tries to tell me *[The teacher refers to the cameraman who is recording the class.]*—personally respond, your ability which you have. It's, it's, it's a part of your very being. Your ability to personally, *personally* act to everything you have created.

Yes.

And so your survival is what you create, you see? You want to believe you are your mind? Well, then your mind tells you, you must have this, that, that, that, and that or you won't survive. What it's telling you is the forms you have created, if you don't do what they say, they'll make sure you starve to death. Do you understand that?

Yes.

Well, I'll tell you, with the freeloading system of society in your country today, I don't think anyone's going to starve to death, for they have no problem joining the victims on the line of welfare. And when welfare becomes workfare, we'll all be free and happy.

Thank you and good evening.

NOVEMBER 13, 1986

# APPENDIX

## The Divine Healing Prayer

I accept that the Divine Healing Power
Is removing all obstructions
From my mind and body
And is restoring me
To perfect health, wealth, and happiness.
My heart is filled with gratitude
For the Divine Law of Acceptance
That is healing both present and absent ones
Who are in need of help.
Peace, the power that healeth,
Is guiding my thoughts, acts, and deeds
As God and I go hand in hand
Living a life of joyful abundance.

## The Total Consideration Affirmation

I am the manifestation of Divine Intelligence. Formless and free. Whole and complete. Peace, Poise, and Power are my birthright.

The Law of Harmony is my thought and guarantees Unity in all my acts and activities, expressing perfect Rhythm and limitless flow throughout my entire being.

Without beginning or ending, eternity is my true awareness and sees the tides of creation, as a captain sees his ship.

As the Light of Truth is sustained by the faculty of Reason, I pause to think and claim my Divine right.

    Right Thought. Right Action. Total Consideration.

              Amen. Amen. Amen.

## Divine Abundance

Thank
*(Gratitude)*

You
*(Principle)*

God
*(Divine Intelligence)*

I'm
*(Individualizing)*

Moving
*(Rhythm)*

In
*(Unity)*

Your
*(Realization)*

Divine
*(Total)*

Flow
*(Consideration)*

## The Controlled Spiritual Environment Affirmation

You are in a controlled spiritual environment of truth
   and freedom
Where peace and harmony reign supreme.
Be awake, be aware, be alert.
Your purpose of being is freedom from what has been.
Thoughts of self are foreign to this environment.
Take control of your mind and experience the joy of living.